# Lecture Notes of the Institute for Computer Sciences, Social Informatics and Telecommunications Engineering 264

Jiann-Liang Chen · Ai-Chun Pang
Der-Jiunn Deng · Chun-Cheng Lin (Eds.)

# Wireless Internet

11th EAI International Conference, WiCON 2018
Taipei, Taiwan, October 15–16, 2018
Proceedings

 Springer

*Editors*
Jiann-Liang Chen
National Taiwan University of Science
and Technology (NTUST)
Taipei, Taiwan

Ai-Chun Pang
National Taiwan Normal University
Taipei, Taiwan

Der-Jiunn Deng
Department of Industrial Engineering
and Management
National Changhua University of Education
Changhua, Taiwan

Chun-Cheng Lin
Department of Industrial Engineering
and Management
National Chiao Tung University
Hsinchu, Taiwan

ISSN 1867-8211        ISSN 1867-822X   (electronic)
Lecture Notes of the Institute for Computer Sciences, Social Informatics
and Telecommunications Engineering
ISBN 978-3-030-06157-9        ISBN 978-3-030-06158-6   (eBook)
https://doi.org/10.1007/978-3-030-06158-6

Library of Congress Control Number: 2018964698

This Springer imprint is published by the registered company Springer Nature Switzerland AG
The registered company address is: Gewerbestrasse 11, 6330 Cham, Switzerland

# Preface

We are delighted to introduce the proceedings of the 11th edition of the 2018 European Alliance for Innovation (EAI) International Conference on Wireless Internets (WiCON). This year, it took place at Howard International House Hotel, Taipei, Taiwan, during October 15–16, 2018. This conference provides an opportunity to connect with researchers, developers, and practitioners from around the world so as to discuss recent findings in the area of the emerging wireless Internet and networks.

The technical program of WiCON 2018 consisted of 36 full papers in oral presentation sessions at the main conference tracks. These technical papers cover a broad range of topics in wireless sensor, vehicular ad hoc networks, security, blockchain, and deep learning. Aside from the high-quality technical paper presentations, the technical program also featured three keynote speeches. The first keynote speech was entitled "IoT Applications on Campus: The IoT talk Approach," by Dr. Yi-Bing Lin from National Chiao Tung. The second keynote speech was entitled "IP-Based Data Communications with Space: Protocols and Mobility Management," by Dr. Mohammed Atiquzzaman from the University of Oklahoma. The third keynote speech was entitled "Towards Connectivity and Intelligence for Future IoT," by Dr. Tony Q. S. Quek from Singapore University of Technology and Design. We were excited to invite these three outstanding international researchers to share their vision on future research and development of wireless Internet technologies.

Coordination with the steering chair, Imrich Chlamtac, and general co-chairs, Prof. Jiann-Liang Chen and Prof. Ai-Chun Pang, was essential for the success of the conference. We sincerely appreciate their constant support and guidance. It was also a great pleasure to work with such an excellent Organizing Committee team and we thank them for their hard work in organizing and supporting the conference. In particular, we thank the Technical Program Committee, led by our TPC co-chairs, Prof. Der-Jiunn Deng and Prof. Chun-Cheng Lin, who completed the peer-review process of the technical papers and compiled a high-quality technical program. We are also grateful to the conference manager, Dominika Belisova, for her support and to all the authors who submitted their papers to the WiCON 2018 conference.

We strongly believe that the WiCON conference provides a good forum for all researchers, developers, and practitioners to discuss all science and technology aspects that are relevant to wireless Internet. We also expect that future WiCON conferences will be as successful and stimulating as indicated by the contributions presented in this volume.

November 2018

Jiann-Liang Chen
Ai-Chun Pang
Der-Jiunn Deng
Chun-Cheng Lin

# Organization

## Steering Committee

### Steering Committee Chair

Imrich Chlamtac          Create-Net, Bruno Kessler Professor, University of Trento, Italy

## Organizing Committee

### General Co-chairs

Jiann-Liang Chen         National Taiwan University of Science and Technology, Taiwan
Ai-Chun Pang             National Taiwan University, Taiwan

### Technical Program Committee Co-chairs

Der-Jiunn Deng           National Changhua University of Education, Taiwan
Chun-Cheng Lin           National Chiao Tung University, Taiwan

### Web Chair

Chien-Liang Chen         Aletheia University, Taiwan

### Publicity and Social Media Chair

Yong-Li Hu               CITI, Academia Sinica, Taiwan

### Workshops Chair

Chih-Heng Ke             National Quemoy University, China

### Publications Chair

Tseng-Yi Chen            Yuan Ze University, Taiwan

### Local Chair

Shin-Ming Cheng          National Taiwan University of Science and Technology, Taiwan

### Conference Manager

Dominika Belisova        EAI - European Alliance for Innovation

# Contents

## Security

## Internet of Things

**Services and Applications**

# Wireless Network

# Improving Uplink Resource Batch Utilization in LTE Licensed-Assisted Access

Chih-Cheng Tseng$^{(\boxtimes)}$, Hwang-Cheng Wang, and Ling-Han Wang

National Ilan University, No. 1, Sec. 1, Shennong Rd.,
Yilan 26047, Taiwan R.O.C.
{tsengcc, hcwang}@niu.edu.tw, a561975400@gmail.com

**Abstract.** Due to network congestion, access to unlicensed spectrum gives new hope for extending the available bandwidth. Licensed-Assisted Access (LAA) is the technology that can be applied to deliver services in the 5 GHz unlicensed spectrum. In general, there are two schemes to access the unlicensed spectrum, namely, random access and scheduled access. Two types of UEs, basic and premium, with two different preferences are considered. Without violating the size of a coalition, UEs with the same preference are put into disjoint coalitions. Likewise, the resource batches are partitioned into two parts and are allocated to the coalitions. The resource batch utilization (RBU) is used to measure the uplink utilization of the resource batches. Compared to the case when all resource batches are under random or scheduled access by all UEs, the numerical results show that the proposed approach is a viable solution in the design of LAA under different degrees of interference from Wi-Fi.

**Keywords:** LAA · Coalition · Resource batch utilization · Uplink

## 1 Introduction

Due to the growing mobile traffic, the demands for radio resources are increasing exponentially. Hence, new technologies have to be developed to meet this forthcoming demand. LTE-A was finalized as a solution that met the full system requirements of the 4G mobile communications with several added features and modifications. Carrier Aggregation (CA), one of the important features of the LTE-A, is used to add secondary component carrier in the unlicensed spectrum to deliver data to the users with best effort QoS requirement. Further, LTE-A Pro, a name for the 3GPP releases 13 and 14, was announced by 3GPP with one of the enhanced features [1], Licensed-Assisted Access (LAA), to extend the LTE technology into 5 GHz unlicensed spectrum. However, this 5 GHz unlicensed spectrum, which is also called U-NII (Unlicensed National Information Infrastructure), is currently used by Wi-Fi and radar systems. Hence, it is a challenging issue for the LTE technology to harmonize with the legacy systems in the 5 GHz unlicensed spectrum. In particular, unlike the traditional LTE systems which is operated in the licensed spectrum, transmission collisions and interference between systems are possible and unpredictable when operated in the 5 GHz unlicensed spectrum. Hence, increasing the radio resource in the 5 GHz unlicensed spectrum to be successfully utilized is one of the key challenges in the design of

J.-L. Chen et al. (Eds.): WiCON 2018, LNICST 264, pp. 3–13, 2019.
https://doi.org/10.1007/978-3-030-06158-6_1

LAA. Conceptually, coalition is regarded as an alliance or union between groups, factions, or parties, especially for some temporary and specific reason. The coalition can be formed based on different criteria and approaches. In this paper, UEs form coalitions based on preferences and radio resources are partitioned into resource batches to improve the uplink utilization of the resource batches in the LAA and Wi-Fi coexistence environment.

The rest of this paper is organized as follows. All the preliminaries are provided in Sect. 2. Section 3 describes the ideas of coalition formation and the allocation of resource batches. The performance metric used in this paper, i.e., the resource batch utilization (RBU), is also defined and derived in this section. In Sect. 4, the numerical results are presented. Finally, Sect. 5 concludes this paper.

## 2 Preliminaries

Game theory deals with scenarios where two or more individuals, called players, make decisions that determine the final outcome [2]. It is a study about the processes of how and why people make decisions. There are different types of games. Cooperative game [3] is a type in which players are convinced to adopt a particular strategy through negotiations and agreements between players while the non-cooperative games refer to the games in which each player simply decides a strategy that maximizes its own profit. Coalition game is a type of cooperative game.

LTE-U (unlicensed) and LAA are two application modes which originated from the supplemental downlink (SDL) and CA techniques. SDL, the first major technique enables LTE technology in the unlicensed spectrum, significantly enhances the network downlink capacity and user experience by employing the unpaired spectrum. The second major technique enables LTE technology in the unlicensed spectrum is the CA, which allows network operators to logically obtain a single large spectrum by combining a number of separate carriers or component carriers. With the CA, the peak user data rate and overall network capacity are greatly improved. The third major technique enables LTE technology in the unlicensed spectrum is the dynamic frequency selection (DFS) [4], which allows the UE to switch from one channel to another frequently in order to mitigate the interference from Wi-Fi stations. In addition, the selected channel can be updated with the changing traffic based on the occupancy of Wi-Fi. Specifically, to expand the system spectrum, LTE-U and LAA allow UEs to use the LTE radio communications in the unlicensed spectrum by aggregating the licensed spectrum and the 5 GHz unlicensed spectrum. Figure 1 shows one of the application scenarios of the coexistence of the Wi-Fi and LTE-U/LAA in the unlicensed spectrum. This figure shows the uplink/downlink transmissions of the UE can be performed in the licensed primary carrier and unlicensed secondary carrier. Besides, in the SDL application scenario, the whole secondary carrier in the unlicensed spectrum can only be used for downlink transmissions. In such application scenario, all the uplink communications are performed through the primary carrier in the licensed spectrum to the LTE-eNB.

One of the main challenges of utilizing the 5 GHz unlicensed spectrum is to share the spectrum with the existing systems, e.g. Wi-Fi and radar systems. For example, as indicated in Fig. 1, the downlink transmissions of the unlicensed Wi-Fi AP#1 may interfere with the UE in receiving the downlink transmissions from the LAA-eNB. In addition, the uplink transmission of the UE to the LAA-eNB may also be interfered by the downlink transmissions of the unlicensed Wi-Fi AP#2. In fact, as pointed out in [5], the above-mentioned interference is caused by the well-known hidden terminal problem. To minimize the interference between systems operated in the 5 GHz unlicensed spectrum, DFS technique has been adopted by the Wi-Fi systems and is also mandatory for radar systems. However, since the DFS has been recognized by 3GPP as an implementation issue, it is not part of the LTE specifications [6].

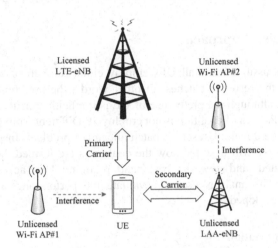

**Fig. 1.** Application scenario of LAA.

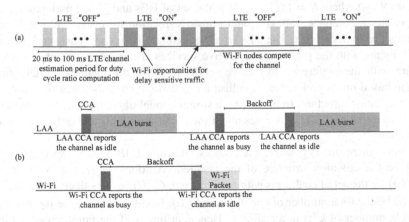

**Fig. 2.** (a) LTE "ON" and LTE "OFF" periods in the CSAT. (b) The CCA used for the coexistence of LAA and Wi-Fi.

The main difference between LTE-U and LAA is the mechanism used to determine the availability of a channel in the unlicensed spectrum. In LTE-U, carrier sense adaptation transmission (CSAT) proposed by Qualcomm is used to sense the activity of the shared medium. Based on the long-term carrier sensing of the Wi-Fi activities on the shared medium, the LTE "ON" and LTE "OFF" periods of the TDM transmission of the LTE-U eNBs are adaptively adjusted as illustrated in Fig. 2a. Jointly proposed by 3GPP and IEEE, listen before talk (LBT) or clear channel assessment (CCA) [7] is adopted in LAA to comply with the global regulations. In LAA, as shown in Fig. 2b, a channel can be utilized only when CCA reports its state as idle. Otherwise, a backoff procedure is activated. The CCA can be done by two major functions called carrier sense (CS) and energy detection (ED). Compared with the LTE-U, LAA is concluded as a feasible alternative to increase the overall system throughput [8].

## 3    The Proposed Approach

In [5], the authors assumed that all UEs employ either random or scheduled access scheme to access the resource batches. In other words, the preference of UE is not considered. In [7], although the preference of UE is implicitly considered in allocating resource batches, the idea of coalition is not employed. Different from [5, 7], the author in [9] considered the downlink resource batch allocation problem. Inspired from [5, 7, 9], in this section, we will describe how the coalitions are formed, how the resource batches are allocated, and how the basic and premium UEs access the allocated resource batches. The analysis used to evaluate the performance of the proposed approach is also developed.

### 3.1    Coalition Formation

The key idea to form coalitions is inspired by the hedonic coalition [10]. In hedonic coalition, preference is strongly related to the formation of coalitions. A hedonic game is a pair $(N, \succeq)$ where $N = \{1, 2,..., N\}$ is the set of UEs and $\succeq$ is a preference profile that specifies a complete, reflexive, and transitive relation for every UE $x \in N$ in the coalitions that include UE $x$. The UEs are classified into two types: basic and premium. Basic UEs are with the preference to receive services at a normal cost while premium UEs are with the preference to receive services with extra payment. A UE joins a coalition based on its preference. A collection of disjoint coalitions that partitions $N$ is called a coalition structure. In this paper, a simple model of coalition formation is used by assuming that each UE only cares about the coalition it joins and only joins exactly one coalition.

Assume there are $P$ possible preferences. At time $i$, let $\Pi(i) = \{\Theta_1(i), \Theta_2(i),..., \Theta_P(i)\}$ be the coalition structure of the resulted coalitions, $\Theta_p(i) = \{C_{1,p}(i), C_{2,p}(i), C_{n_p(i),p}(i)\}$ be the set of coalitions with preference $p$, $C_{j,p}(i)$ be the $j$-th coalition in $\Theta_p(i)$, and $n_p(i)$ be the total number of coalitions in $\Theta_p(i)$. Besides, let $C_{max}$ be the maximum allowable number of UEs in a coalition. Hence, at time $i$, if the number of UEs in $C_j$,

$_p(i)$ reaches $C_{max}$, a new coalition $C_{(j+1),p}(i)$ is created to accommodate the UE that does not belong to any coalition yet. Based on the above descriptions, at time $i$, we have

$$\sum_{p=1}^{P}\sum_{j=1}^{n_p(i)} |C_{j,p}(i)| = N, \qquad (1)$$

where $|\cdot|$ is the cardinality of a set.

To simplify our study, only two preferences are considered, i.e., $p = 1, 2$, and are assigned to premium and basic UEs, respectively. For example, consider a network with 10 premium UEs and 30 basic UEs at time $i$. If $C_{max} = 10$, as demonstrated in Fig. 3, the 10 premium UEs form the coalition $C_{1,1}(i)$, while the 30 basic UEs form three coalitions $C_{1,2}(i)$, $C_{2,2}(i)$, and $C_{3,2}(i)$. Hence, the corresponding coalition structure is $\Pi(i) = \{ _1(i), \Theta_2(i)\}$, where $\Theta_1(i) = \{C_{1,\ 1}(i)\}$ and $\Theta_2(i) = \{C_{1,2}(i), C_{2,2}(i), C_{3,2}(i)\}$.

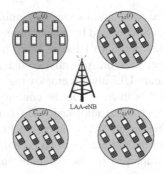

**Fig. 3.** Example of the hedonic coalition structure.

## 3.2 Resource Batch Allocation

The ideas of the coalition-based resource batch allocation are illustrated in Fig. 4. In Fig. 4, the time is divided into periods of two different lengths. The length of the short period is 20 μs. The short period is used to sense the availability of the channel, i.e., it is used to perform the CCA. As mentioned earlier, in the 5 GHz unlicensed spectrum, a UE can access a channel only when the report of CCA indicates that channel is available. As shown in Fig. 4, after each short period, a long period of length $\tau$ ms is used to perform the data transmission and is called an access opportunity. The value of $\tau$ can be either 4 in Japan or 10 in Europe and 4 is used in Fig. 4. Besides, as indicated on the right of Fig. 4, the consecutive resource blocks over an access opportunity is called a resource batch. In this paper, it is the resource batches that are allocated to the UEs and accessed by the UEs when CCA reports they are available.

Before allocating the resource batches to the UEs, all the radio batches of the considered 5 GHz unlicensed spectrum at the $i$-th access opportunity are divided into two sets $R_1(i)$ and $R_2(i)$. Specifically, at the $i$-th access opportunity, the resource batches

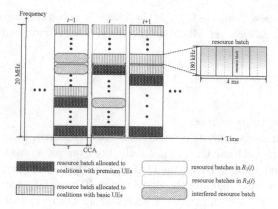

**Fig. 4.** Example of the resource batch allocation.

in $R_1(i)$ and $R_2(i)$ are allocated to coalitions whose members are premium and basic UEs, respectively. Since the QoS requested by the premium UEs is more rigid than that requested by the basic UEs, the premium UEs are given higher priority to access the allocated radio batches. Hence, to avoid potential collisions with other UEs, at any access opportunity $i$, the premium UEs always employ the scheduled access scheme to access the allocated radio batches in $R_1(i)$. On the contrary, at the $i$-th access opportunity, basic UEs can only access the allocated radio batches in $R_2(i)$ by utilizing random access scheme. In this paper, the resource batches are first allocated to the coalitions. After that, based on the preference of each coalition, scheduled access and random access schemes are employed by the premium and basic UEs to access the allocated resource batches, respectively. For simplicity, we assume each UE, regardless of premium or basic, requires only one resource batch at any access opportunity. Under this assumption, the number of resource batches allocated to a coalition is equal to the number of UEs in that coalition. When the total number of requested resource batches is higher than the total number of resource batches in the system, proportional fair allocation approach is employed. Besides, the floor function is used if the total number of resource batches in the system cannot be divided evenly by the total number of coalitions. In the following, $R_{j,p}(i)$ denotes the number of resource batches allocated to $C_{j,p}(i)$. Hence,

$$|R_p(i)| \geq \sum_{j=1}^{n_p(i)} |R_{j,p}(i)|, \tag{2}$$

where $p$ can be 1 or 2 in this paper. If the total number of resource batches in the system is $N_{RB}$, we have

$$N_{RB} \geq \sum_{p=1}^{2} |R_p(i)|. \tag{3}$$

As shown in Fig. 4, since the bandwidth of the considered 5 GHz unlicensed spectrum is 20 MHz, there are totally 100 resource batches at any access opportunity $i$. The sets $R_1(i)$ and $R_2(i)$ and the values of $n_1(i)$ and $n_2(i)$ are updated at the beginning of every access opportunity $i$.

## 3.3 Resource Batch Utilization (RBU)

Due to the hidden terminal problem in the LAA and Wi-Fi co-existence scenario as mentioned in Sect. 2.1, even if CCA reports that a particular resource batch is idle, it is possible for that particular resource batch to be interfered by Wi-Fi when a UE is utilizing it to transmit data. According to the assumption made in [5], the interference from Wi-Fi to a particular resource batch at any access opportunity $i$ is modelled as an independent and identical distribution (i.i.d.) with probability $q$. At any access opportunity $i$, since the resource batches are divided into two sets, $R_1(i)$ and $R_2(i)$, we need to derive the RBU of the resource batches allocated to these two sets, respectively.

First, at the $i$-th access opportunity, let $u_{j,1}(i)$ be the RBU of the resource batches in $R_{j,1}(i)$ and be defined as the expected number of interference-free resource batches in $R_{j,1}(i)$. A resource batch is regarded as successfully utilized by a premium UE to transmit data to the LAA-eNB only when this resource batch is not interfered by Wi-Fi. Since the scheduled access scheme is employed by the premium UEs in each $C_{j,1}(i)$ to access the resource batches, there is no need to consider the contention and collision issues among the premium UEs in each $C_{j,1}(i)$. Because each premium UE is assumed to request for only one resource batch at each access opportunity, we have the constraint $|C_{j,1}(i)| \geq |R_{j,1}(i)|$. Hence, $u_{j,1}(i)$ is given by

$$u_{j,1}(i) = (1-q)|R_{j,1}(i)|. \tag{4}$$

Let $U_1(i)$ be the RBU of the resource batches allocated to all the coalitions in $\Theta_1(i)$ at the $i$-th access opportunity. Hence, $U_1(i)$ is given by

$$U_1(i) = \sum_{j=1}^{n_1(i)} u_{j,1}(i). \tag{5}$$

Next, unlike the derivations in (4) and (5), since the random access scheme is employed by basic UEs in each $C_{j,2}(i)$ to access the allocated resource batches $R_{j,2}(i)$, in addition to the interference from Wi-Fi, the contention and collision issues among the basic UEs in the same $C_{j,2}(i)$ also need to be considered. Let $u_{j,2}(i)$ be the RBU of a resource batch in $R_{j,2}(i)$ at the $i$-th access opportunity and be defined as the expected number of basic UEs served by an interference-free and collision-free resource batch in $R_{j,2}(i)$ at the $i$-th access opportunity. First, similar to the derivations above, the probability for a resource batch in $R_{j,2}(i)$ to be interference-free is $(1-q)/|R_{j,2}(i)|$. Then, since the number of basic UEs in $C_{j,2}(i)$ is $|C_{j,2}(i)|$, the probability for a randomly selected resource batch in $R_{j,2}(i)$ to be interference-free and collision-free is given by

$$\eta_{j,2}(i) = |C_{j,2}(i)| \left( \frac{1-q}{|R_{j,2}(i)|} \right) \left( 1 - \frac{1-q}{|R_{j,2}(i)|} \right)^{|C_{j,2}(i)|-1}. \tag{6}$$

Since each basic UE is assumed to request for only one resource batch at each access opportunity, with $\eta_{j,2}(i)$ in (6), $u_{j,2}(i)$ is given by

$$u_{j,2}(i) = \eta_{j,2}(i)|R_{j,2}(i)| = |C_{j,2}(i)|(1-q)\left( 1 - \frac{1-q}{|R_{j,2}(i)|} \right)^{|C_{j,2}(i)|-1}. \tag{7}$$

Let $U_2(i)$ be the RBU of the resource batches allocated to all the coalitions in $\Theta_2(i)$ at the $i$-th access opportunity. Then, $U_2(i)$ can be obtained by

$$U_2(i) = \sum_{j=1}^{n_2(i)} u_{j,2}(i). \tag{8}$$

When random and scheduled access schemes are employed, the RBU at the $i$-th access opportunity $U(i)$ is defined as the total RBU obtained by (5) and (8) and is given by

$$U(i) = \sum_{p=1}^{2} U_p(i). \tag{9}$$

## 4    Numerical Results

The numerical results of the proposed approach are demonstrated in this section. The bandwidth of the considered 5 GHz unlicensed spectrum is assumed to be 20 MHz. Hence, there are 100 resource batches in each access opportunity. Each UE is assumed to request for only one resource batch.

### 4.1    The RBU if Only Random Access Scheme Is Allowed

First, we study the RBU under the scenario where all UEs can only use the random access scheme to access the allocated resource batches (i.e., $U_1(i) = 0$). We compared the RBU achieved 'with' and 'without' forming UEs into coalitions, respectively. In the case of 'without coalition', all UEs are conceptually in a coalition and the 100 resource batches are randomly accessed by all UEs, regardless of the type of UE. While, in the case of 'with coalition', although the UEs are grouped into coalitions based on their preferences, the resource batches allocated to each coalition can only be accessed by random access scheme. Based on the above-mentioned criterion, we study the RBU of the resource batches under different traffic load with the number of UEs being 50, 100, and 200, respectively. Hence, the green, red, and black lines shown in Fig. 5 are the results for 50, 100, and 200 UEs, respectively. Clearly, higher RBU can always be achieved when UEs are grouped into coalitions. Besides, reducing the size of a coalition provides another way to further improve the utilization.

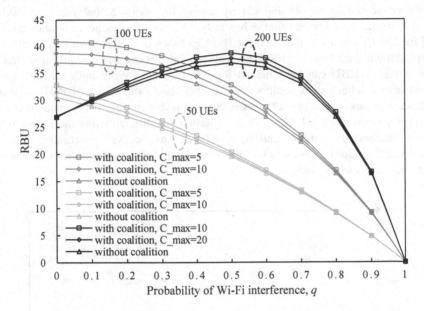

**Fig. 5.** The RBU if only random access scheme is allowed.

Next, Fig. 5 also demonstrated, when the number of UEs is smaller than the number of resource batches, the RBU is increased as the number of UEs is increased and achieved the maximum as the number of UEs equals the number of resource batches, i.e., 100 UEs in this case. However, when the number of UEs is greater than the number of resource batches, e.g., 200 UEs, an interesting observation can be made. As the interference from Wi-Fi to LAA is increased, we noticed that the RBU achieved when the number of UEs is 200 is increased also and is higher than that achieved when the number of UEs is 50 and 100 as $q \geq 0.4$. This is mainly because, when the number of UEs is 200 and the number of resource batches is 100, the probability for a randomly selected resource batch to be both interference-free and collision-free as given in (6) increases as the value of $q$ increases. Hence, it is recommended to use random access scheme to access the resource batches when UE is heavily interfered by Wi-Fi.

## 4.2 The RBU if Both Scheduled and Random Access Schemes Are Allowed

Now, we study the RBU achieved by 200 UEs consisting of 50 premium UEs and 150 basic UEs. By setting $C_{max}$ to 10, among the 20 formed coalitions, there are 5 and 15 coalitions formed by the premium and basic UEs, respectively. The RBU is calculated by changing the number of allocated resource batches in the sets $R_1(i)$ and $R_2(i)$ and is illustrated in Fig. 6. The RBU achieved when only scheduled (i.e., $U_2(i) = 0$) or random (i.e., $U_1(i) = 0$) access scheme is allowed for the 200 UEs are also depicted in Fig. 6. In the case when only scheduled access scheme is allowed, all UEs are scheduled by the LAA-eNB to access the allocated resource batches. Hence, the RBU is obtained according to (4) and (5) by letting $|R_{j,\ 1}(i)| = 5$ and $j = 1,\dots, 20$. In Sect. 4.1, we have mentioned that, when only random access scheme is allowed, the RBU for 200 UEs is lower than that for 100 UEs when $q \leq 0.3$. However, compared with the brown dash line for 100 UEs with random access scheme only depicted in Fig. 6, a higher RBU can be achieved for 200 UEs employing both scheduled and random access schemes. In addition, Fig. 6 also shows the achieved RBU of using scheduled and random access schemes is closing to that of only using random access scheme as $q$ approaches to 1. Hence, it is suggested that differentiating the access to the resource batches of premium and basic UEs at any access opportunity with the scheduled and random access schemes is a feasible approach to improve the utilization of the allocated resource batches.

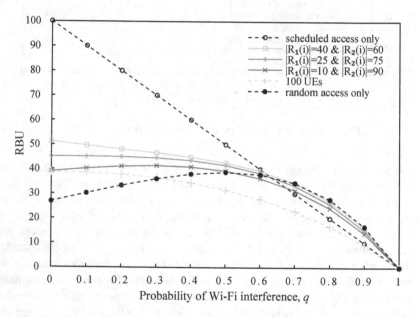

**Fig. 6.** The RBU if both scheduled and random access schemes are allowed.

## 5   Conclusions

Efficiently using the resource batches in the 5 GHz unlicensed spectrum is one of the important objectives in the design of LAA. When UEs are classified into premium and basic, this paper suggests that grouping UEs into coalitions based on their preferences before allocating resource batches is beneficial. After forming coalitions, differentiating the schemes for coalitions consisting of the premium and basic UEs to access the resource batches is further suggested. By allocating different number of resource batches to coalitions, the results show that, when the interference from the Wi-Fi is small, the RBU achieved by the proposed approach is higher than that achieved by using random access scheme only. In situations where the interference from Wi-Fi is high, the results also show that the RBU achieved by the proposed approach is very close to the maximum RBU that is achieved by using random access scheme only.

**Acknowledgement.** The authors would like to thank Jennifer Pounjeba. P for her help to this paper.

# References

1. Mukherjee, A., et al.: Licensed-assisted access LTE: coexistence with IEEE 802.11 and the evolution toward 5G. IEEE Commun. Mag. **54**(6), 50–57 (2016)
2. Bonanno, G.: Game Theory, 1st Edn, Chapter 1, p. 17 (2015)
3. https://cours.etsmtl.ca/mgr816/game_apC.pdf
4. Maglogiannis, V., Naudts, D., Shahid, A., Giannoulis, S., Laermans, E., Moerman, I.: Cooperation techniques between LTE in unlicensed spectrum and Wi-Fi towards fair spectral efficiency. Sensors **19**(9), 1–26 (2017). https://doi.org/10.3390/s17091994
5. Lien, S.-Y., Lee, J., Liang, Y.-C.: Random access or scheduling: optimum LTE licensed-assisted access to unlicensed spectrum. IEEE Commun. Lett. **20**(3), 590–593 (2016)
6. GPP TR 36.889 v13.0.0. Feasibility Study on Licensed-Assisted Access to Unlicensed Spectrum; 3GPP: Malmo, Sweden (2015)
7. Zhang, M., Zhang, X., Chang, Y., Yang, D.: Dynamic uplink radio access selection of LTE licensed-assisted access to unlicensed spectrum: an optimization game. IEEE Commun. Lett. **20**(12), 2510–2513 (2016)
8. https://www.qualcomm.com/invention/technologies/lte/laa
9. Jennifer Pounjeba, P.: Resource allocation in unlicensed spectrum for 5G: a hedonic coalition approach, Master Thesis, National Ilan University (2018)
10. Han, Z., Niyato, D., Saad, W., Baar, T., Hjrungnes, A.: Game Theory in Wireless and Communication Networks. 1 Edn, Chapter 12, p. 210 (2012)

# Comparative Study of Two Signal-to-Noise Ratio Calculation Methods in LTE Downlink Simulations

Yu-Sun Liu[1](✉), Shingchern D. You[2], Zong-Ru Jhan[3], and Meng-Fan Li[1]

[1] Department of Electronic Engineering,
National Taipei University of Technology, Taipei, Taiwan
ysliu@ntut.edu.tw
[2] Department of Computer Science and Information Engineering,
National Taipei University of Technology, Taipei, Taiwan
[3] Quanta Computer Inc., Taipei, Taiwan

**Abstract.** It is well-known that the bit error rate (BER) of a mobile communication system is strongly affected by the signal-to-noise ratio (SNR). Because the term SNR is so fundamental that most papers did not explain how SNR is calculatd in simulations. In this paper, we report the BER perfomrance for Long Term Evolution (LTE) downlink simulations with two different SNR calculation methods. It is found that using short-term SNR not only yields much smaller BER than using ensemble-average SNR, but also reverses the ordering of BER performance among the channel models. We thus suggest that in order to fully disclose their implications on performance, the BERs measured against the two SNRs should be presented side by side in LTE downlink simulation studies.

**Keywords:** Long term evolution · Signal-to-noise ratio · Simulated channel

## 1 Introduction

Nowadays almost all communication engineers rely on computer simulations to evaluate the performance of a digital communication system. To conduct simulations, one of the fundamental parameters for simulations is the signal-to-noise ratio (SNR). SNR is the ratio of signal power over noise power. The calculation of SNR seems so trivial that not too many technical papers have fully discussed how this value was obtained during simulations.

To calculate SNR, we need to know the signal power. When closely examining the calculation of signal power for a fading channel, we have two options. The first one is to average the transmitted power over multiple channel realizations. The SNR thus obtained is called ensemble-average SNR in the following. The

© ICST Institute for Computer Sciences, Social Informatics and Telecommunications Engineering 2019
Published by Springer Nature Switzerland AG 2019. All Rights Reserved
J.-L. Chen et al. (Eds.): WiCON 2018, LNICST 264, pp. 14–23, 2019.
https://doi.org/10.1007/978-3-030-06158-6_2

second one is to measure the short-term signal power for only one realization. The obtained SNR is called short-term SNR in the following. It seems reasonable to assume that either ensemble-average SNR or short-term SNR would not severely alter the observed performance. Therefore, most existing literature does not explicitly mention which SNR is used in the simulations. Previously, we also believed this conjecture. Later on, we found some interesting results when conducting simulations on the bit error rate (BER) performance of Long Term Evolution (LTE) downlink (DL) transmission [1–6] over three widely used channel models, known as Extended Pedestrian A model (EPA), Extended Vehicular A model (EVA), and Extended Typical Urban model (ETU) [7]. They are established by ETSI (European Telecommunications Standards Institute) to represent short, medium, and long delay spread environments, respectively. Our simulation results showed that the performance ranking of the three channels would be reversed if switching from ensemble-average SNR to short-term SNR. After an in-depth study, we found that the method used to calculate the SNR value significantly affects the BER performance in the mentioned ETSI channel models. In this paper, we would like to share our findings on this issue and give some recommendations on the use of SNR in simulations.

The rest of the paper is organized as follows. Section 2 presents the channel models and two different definitions of SNR, the ensemble-average SNR and short-term SNR. Section 3 describes the LTE DL physical layer. Section 4 presents the simulation method which uses ensemble-average SNR as the basis of comparison and analyzes the distributions of channel frequency responses. Section 5 presents the simulation method which uses short-term SNR as the basis of comparison and comments on the differences in BER performances based on the two different SNR calculation methods. Finally, conclusions are summarized in Sect. 6.

## 2    Channel Models and SNR Definitions

The multipath fading phenomenon in a mobile wireless channel is typically modeled as a tapped delay line with a constant delay for each tap. Specifically, the channel impulse response is modeled as

$$h(t) = \sum_{\ell=0}^{L-1} h_\ell \delta(t - \tau_\ell) \tag{1}$$

where $L$ is the number of paths in the channel, and $h_\ell$ and $\tau_\ell$ are the complex gain and the delay of path $\ell$, respectively. Each $\tau_\ell$ is a constant, and each $h_\ell$ is an outcome of a complex-valued random variable. As uncorrelated scattering among paths is usually assumed in channel modeling, all $h_\ell$ are outcomes of independent random variables. To generate a channel, the complex gains $h_\ell$, $\ell = 0, 1, \ldots, L - 1$, are obtained as outcomes from independent zero-mean complex Gaussian random variables $\boldsymbol{h_\ell}$. In the following, we call a set of $h_\ell$ produced in one probability trial as one realization (of the channel impulse response).

As mentioned previously, the ETSI defined three channel models, EPA, EVA, and ETU, for LTE DL simulations. The power-delay profiles of the models are listed in Table 1 [7]. In the table, the average power gain in a tap is defined as $P_\ell = E[\boldsymbol{h}_\ell \boldsymbol{h}_\ell^*]$. It is observed that the EPA model has a much shorter delay spread than the EVA and ETU models have. Not that although the sum of average powers over all taps is not 0 dB in the table, a widely acceptable implementation is to multiply each $h_\ell$ by a constant to ensure that the *expected* channel power gain is unity.

**Table 1.** Channel profiles

| Tap $\ell$ | EPA model $\tau_\ell$ (ns) | $P_\ell$(dB) | EVA model $\tau_\ell$ (ns) | $P_\ell$ (dB) | ETU model $\tau_\ell$ (ns) | $P_\ell$ (dB) |
|---|---|---|---|---|---|---|
| 1 | 0 | 0.0 | 0 | 0.0 | 0 | −1.0 |
| 2 | 30 | −1.0 | 30 | −1.5 | 50 | −1.0 |
| 3 | 70 | −2.0 | 150 | −1.4 | 120 | −1.0 |
| 4 | 90 | −3.0 | 310 | −3.6 | 200 | 0.0 |
| 5 | 110 | −8.0 | 370 | −0.6 | 230 | 0.0 |
| 6 | 190 | −17.2 | 710 | −9.1 | 500 | 0.0 |
| 7 | 410 | −20.8 | 1090 | −7.1 | 1600 | −3.0 |
| 8 | N/A | N/A | 1730 | −12.0 | 2300 | −5.0 |
| 9 | N/A | N/A | 2510 | −16.9 | 5000 | −7.0 |

At the receiver side, if the cyclic prefix (CP) is longer than the length of the multipath channel, the received signal within an OFDM (Orthogonal Frequency Division Multiplexing)symbol can be expressed as

$$y[m] = x[m] \otimes h[m] + w[m] \tag{2}$$

where $\otimes$ denotes the circular convolution, $x[m]$ and $h[m]$ are the sampled versions of transmitted OFDM signal and channel impulse response, respectively, and $w[m]$ is the complex-valued additive white Gaussian noise (AWGN) with mean zero and variance $N_0/2$. By applying discrete Fourier transformation (DFT) to $y[m]$, the frequency-domain representation of the received signal at OFDM symbol $n$ and subcarrier $k$ is given by

$$Y[n, k] = X[n, k]H[n, k] + W[n, k] \tag{3}$$

where $Y[n,k]$, $X[n,k]$, $H[n,k]$, and $W[n,k]$ are transformed results of $y[m]$, $x[m]$, $h[m]$, and $w[m]$, respectively. In this paper, we assume that perfect side information, namely channel impulse response, signal power, and noise power, is available to the receiver.

As mentioned previously, simulated channel models are probabilistic models. Therefore, the channel power gain

$$\sum_{\ell=0}^{L-1} h_\ell h_\ell^*$$  (4)

fluctuates from one particular channel realization to another. Only the (ensemble) average over infinitely many realizations approaches unity due to normalization. An SNR calculated based on ensemble-average power gain is called ensemble-average SNR. It has been shown that the resulting experimental BER performance closely matched to the analytical one [8–10].

It is also possible to use the individual channel power gain of each realization to compute SNR. We firstly compute the signal power at the receiver as

$$P_\mathrm{r} = \frac{1}{|\mathcal{M}|} \sum_{m \in \mathcal{M}} |x[m] \otimes h[m]|^2$$  (5)

where $\mathcal{M}$ is the set of sample indexes in a codeword, and $|\mathcal{M}|$ is its cardinality. SNR is then computed as the received signal power $P_\mathrm{r}$ over noise power. As this SNR is calculated based on a particular channel realization, and typically the codewords are short, we call it as short-term SNR. Note that in an experiment, if we want to generate channel realizations based on a given short-term SNR value and a fixed noise power (and thus a fixed $P_\mathrm{r}$), $h_{L-1}$ will depend on $h_0, h_1, \ldots, h_{L-2}$, which violates the assumption of uncorrelated scattering in the channel model. Therefore, the theoretical BER analysis developed in [8–10] cannot be directly applied in this case. However, in terms of user experience, the short-term SNR is a better indicator because it is the instantaneous SNR at the user's device, but not the average SNR over many devices. Considering these factors, we think it is worthy to study the performance discrepancy between these two SNR calculatio methods.

## 3  LTE DL Physical Layer

The LTE system uses 10 ms radio frames, with each frame containing 10 subframes of 1 ms duration. Each subframe is divided into two slots of equal length, where each slot is composed of seven OFDM symbols, namely, symbol 0 to symbol 6, if normal CP is used. The time-frequency representation of a DL subframe is depicted in Fig. 1, in which each small cell represents one subcarrier in one OFDM symbol period. Pilots, denoted by green cells, are inserted in the first and the third last OFDM symbols of each slot with a frequency domain spacing of six subcarriers. The basic unit for resource allocation is the physical resource block (PRB), which consists of 12 consecutive subcarriers in one slot. In this paper, the LTE system with 20 MHz bandwidth/100 PRBs which comprises of 1200 subcarriers (excluding DC) is considered.

In DL transmission, data are carried in PDSCH (Physical Downlink Shared Channel) in units of transport blocks. Each transport block is firstly segmented

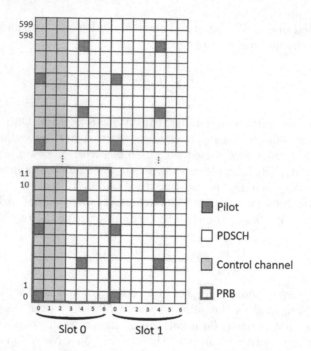

**Fig. 1.** Time-frequency representation of a DL subframe.

into code blocks if its size is larger than 6144 bits. Each code block is then encoded with a rate-1/3 symmetric turbo code which is the parallel concatenation of two identical 8-state (1, 15/13) constituent codes. Finally, coded sequence of each code block is processed by a rate matching module which matches the total number of coded bits in a transport block to the number of bits supported by the assigned PRBs. In the following simulation experiments, half a subframe which comprises 50 PRB/600 subcarriers in both slots is assigned to one transport block of length 1408 bits (which is transmitted using one codeword). Note that the resources available to the PDSCH do not include the pilots and the first three OFDM symbols in each subframe, as shown in Fig. 1, since these symbols are occupied by control channel. Finally, the coded bits are modulated with the QPSK scheme and then transmitted using OFDM with system parameters listed in Table 2. The resulting code rate is 0.11175, which is close to the lowest rate supported by the LTE standard.

## 4    Experiments with Ensemble-Average SNR

We now describe the experiment with ensemble-average SNR values. One experiment for a given SNR comprises 10,000 trials, and in each trial a new realization of the specified channel model is generated. The reported BER is the averaging BER over all trials, each having the duration of one DL frame. In the experiment, the noise power is calculated based on the the unity-channel-power-gain

**Table 2.** System parameters

| Parameter | Value |
|---|---|
| Channel bandwidth | 20 MHz |
| Carrier frequency | 1.8 GHz |
| Subcarrier spacing | 15 KHz |
| Sampling frequency | 30.72 M |
| FFT size | 2048 |
| CP duration (Normal CP) | 160 samples for symbol 0. 144 samples for symbols 1–6 |
| OFDM symbol duration | 66.6 μs |
| TX/RX antenna | SISO |
| PDSCH modulation scheme | QPSK |
| Code rate | 0.11175 |

assumption and the given SNR value. The obtained BER performance after demodulation are plotted in Fig. 2. It shows that all three channel models, as well as the analytic results, have identical demodulated BER.

When examining the BER after 6 decoding iterations of error correction decoding (decoded BER), we notice three channel models yield different curves, as shown in Fig. 3. Furthermore, the decoded BER for the EPA channel model is considerably larger than those for the other two channel models. The results are counter-intuitive. Firstly, as the three channel models yield the same demod-

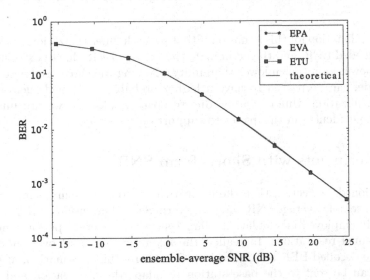

**Fig. 2.** Demodulated BERs using ensemble-average SNR as basis of comparison.

ulated BER performance, we would expect that they also have similar decoded BER performance. Secondly, if one channel model induces a much higher decoded BER than the other two, we would expect it to be ETU because ETU has a delay spread longer than CP and thus suffers from intersymbol interference (ISI). Note that our previous study on WiMAX (Worldwide Interoperability for Microwave Access) [9] also shows that different channel models yield similar decoded BER performances (within experimental uncertainty).

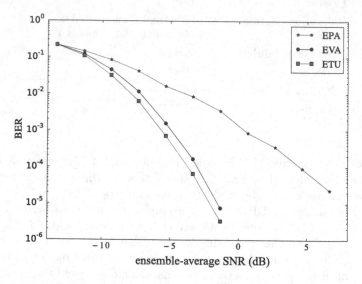

**Fig. 3.** Decoded BERs using ensemble-average SNR as basis of comparison.

One explanation for this situation is that some channel realizations have much higher decoded BER, and then dominate the average BER, due to extremely low channel power gain (much lower than unity). Among the three used models, the EPA model can be proved to have a higher probability to yield such a "bad" channel realization. Unfortunately, due to space limitation, we are unable to show more evidences in this paper to support our argument.

## 5    Experiments with Short-Term SNR

We mentioned in Sect. 2 that there are two different measurements of SNR, namely, ensemble-average SNR and short-term SNR. The ensemble-average SNR is typically employed in simulations, but it shows the average performance over many channel realizations. In reality, the instantaneous SNR over subcarriers affects the decoded BER at the receiver. Therefore, this information, after conversion, can be sent to the base station to adapt the modulation and coding scheme (MCS) [11,12]. Note that the short-term SNR discussed in this paper is closely related to the instantaneous SNR over subcarriers.

We now describe how to perform simulations with a given short-term SNR value. Basically, one experiment for a given SNR value comprises a large number of trials. In each trial, a new realization of the specified channel model is generated, and then, the noise power is calculated based on the received signal power and the given SNR value. The reported BER is computed by averaging BER over 10,000 trials. Using the above procedure, we obtain the demodulated BER and decoded BER (after 6 decoding iterations), which are plotted in Figs. 4 and 5, respectively. It is observed that the EPA model gives smaller demodulated BER than the other two channel models. It is because EPA has a shorter delay spread and then smoother channel frequency response. In terms of decoded BER, when comparing Fig. 5 with Fig. 3, we find that the BER results obtained based on short-term SNR are significantly smaller than those based on ensemble-average SNR. This is because in the short-term SNR case, all channel realizations have

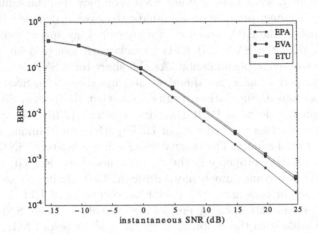

**Fig. 4.** Demodulated BERs using short-term SNR.

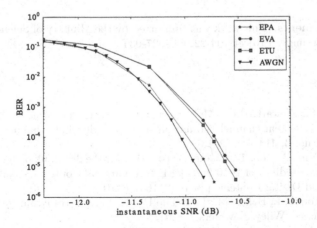

**Fig. 5.** Decoded BERs using short-term SNR.

comparable (per realization) SNR. Therefore, not a single codeword is transmitted through a channel (realization) with much lower SNR. Moreover, since source data are transmitted with very low code rate, the low BER results are understandable. Thus, the decoded BER performances of the three channel models in Fig. 5 are close to each other.

## 6 Conclusions

In this paper, we investigate how different SNR calculation methods affect simulated system performance for the EPA, EVA, and ETU channel models in LTE DL transmission. It is found that the received signal power averaged over a codeword can be very different from the power averaged over an ensemble of channel realizations. This disparity is especially evident for small Doppler-shift cases. Consequently, if ensemble-average SNR is employed in the simulations, the trials with low channel power gain dominate the overall decoded BER performance. As a result, the EPA model with a shorter delay spread exhibits higher decoded BER than the EVA and ETU models with longer delay spreads, an intuitively unreasonable phenomenon. As the short-term SNR is a better indicator of system performance, we therefore also use short-term SNR to evaluate the BER performance. Simulation results show that short-term SNR not only yields much smaller decoded BER than its counterpart for the same channel model, but also reverses the ordering of BER performance among the channel models as one would expect. The downsides of using short-term SNR is that the uncorrelated scattering property in the channel models is violated, and theoretical BER analysis becomes much more difficult. Considering these factors, we thus suggest that in presenting the performance results of LTE DL transmission, the BER results obtained by employing ensemble-average SNR should be presented alongside with those obtained by using short-term SNR. In this way, the reader can have a better understanding on the performance of the LTE DL transmission.

**Acknowledgements.** This work was supported by the Ministry of Science and Technology, Taiwan, under Project 104-2221-E-027-034.

## References

1. Adegbite, S., Stewart, B.G., McMeekin, S.G.: Least squares interpolation methods for LTE system channel estimation over extended ITU channels. Int. J. Inf. Electron. Eng. **3**, 414–418 (2013)
2. Weng, F., Yin, C., Luo, T.: Channel estimation for the downlink of 3GPP-LTE systems. In: Proceedings of 2010 2nd IEEE International Conference Network Infrastructure and Digital Content, pp. 1042–1046 (2010)
3. Sesia, S., Toufik, I., Baker, M.: LTE-The UMTS Long Term Evolution: From Theory to Practice. Wiley, New Jersey (2011)
4. Rumney, M.: LTE and the Evolution to 4G Wireless: Design and Measurement Challenges, 2nd edn. Wiley, New Jersey (2013)

5. You, S.D., Liu, Y.-S.: Comparative study of channel estimation methods for LTE downlink transmission. In: Proceedings of 2015 IEEE 4th Global Conference on Consumer Electronics, pp. 642–643 (2015)
6. Liu, Y.-S., You, S.D., Liu, Y.-M.: Iterative channel estimation method for long-term evolution downlink transmission. IET Commun. **9**, 1906–1914 (2015)
7. 3GPP: LTE; Evolved Universal Terrestrial Radio Access (E-UTRA); User Equipment (UE) Radio Transmission and Reception, 3GPP TS 36.101. (2014). 3GPP
8. You, S.D., Chen, K.-Y., Liu, Y.-S.: Cubic convolution interpolation function with variable coefficients and its application to channel estimation for IEEE 802.16 initial downlink. IET Commun. **6**, 1979–1987 (2012)
9. Liu, Y.-S., You, S.D., Wu, R.-K.: Burst allocation method to enable decision-directed channel estimation for mobile WiMAX downlink transmission. EURASIP J. Wireless Commun. Netw. **153** (2013) https://doi.org/10.1186/1687-1499-2013
10. Prasad, R.: OFDM for Wireless Communications Systems. Artec House, Washington, DC (2004)
11. 3GPP: System-level Evaluation of OFDM - Further Considerations, 3GPP TSG-RAN WG1 35, R1-031303. (2003). 3GPP
12. Donthi, S.N., Mehta, N.B.: An accurate model for EESM and its application to analysis of CQI feedback schemes and scheduling in LTE. IEEE Trans. Wireless commun. **10**, 3436–3448 (2011)

# Fractional Backoff Algorithm for the Next Generation WLAN

Xuewei Cai[1], Bo Li[1], Mao Yang[1(✉)], Zhongjiang Yan[1],
Bo Yang[1], Yi Jin[2], and Xiaobo Li[2]

[1] School of Electronics and Information,
Northwestern Polytechnical University, Xi'an, China
caixuewei@mail.nwpu.edu.cn,
{libo.npu,yangmao,zhjyan}@nwpu.edu.cn
[2] China Academy of Space Technology, Xi'an, China

**Abstract.** With the rapid popularization of wireless communication
devices, wireless local area network (WLAN) is ubiquitous in daily life.
However, the demand for wireless communication services is growing
rapidly and brings new challenges to WLAN technology. The problem
of performance degradation under dense deployment network scenarios is an important topic in the next generation WLAN (NGW). This
paper proposes fractional backoff algorithm, named eat-B, to enhance
area throughput. Eat-B introduces fractional backoff and enables the
nodes who provide more contributions for the area throughput to finish their backoff process faster. Simulation results indicate that the area
throughput of the eat-B algorithm outperforms the binary exponential
backoff (BEB) algorithm adopted by the traditional IEEE 802.11, especially under dense deployment scenarios.

**Keywords:** WLAN · IEEE 802.11 DCF · Binary exponential backoff ·
Dense deployment · Next generation WLAN

## 1 Introduction

With the development of information technology and wireless communication
devices, the demand for wireless communication, especially transmission data
rates, has keep rising. To meet the growing requirements, academia and industry are working on next-generation WLAN (NGW) standard amendment: IEEE
802.11ax towards high area throughput [1]. Highly dense deployment network [2]
such as residential areas or offices is the target scenarios of 802.11ax [3], where
many access points (APs) and non-AP stations (STAs) are distributed in geo-
graphically limited areas. IEEE 802.11ax modifies the physical layer (PHY) and
the medium access control layer (MAC) [4] to improve the average throughput
per station in dense deployment scenarios.

J.-L. Chen et al. (Eds.): WiCON 2018, LNICST 264, pp. 24–31, 2019.
https://doi.org/10.1007/978-3-030-06158-6_3

The distributed coordination function (DCF) protocol can be used to achieve fair access performance for multiple stations in IEEE 802.11 [5], but it also causes performance anomaly under multi-rate station conditions [6] (e.g., 802.11b supports four kinds of data rates [7]; 802.11a supports eight [8]) in which wireless channel are used by low-rate stations for a longer time than high-rate stations. This circumstance can inhibit network performance, especially in cases of dense deployment. Additionally, dense deployment poses great challenges for distributed channel access control due to fierce competition among a large number of stations.

The binary exponential backoff (BEB) algorithm is an important part of DCF to avoid simultaneous transmission and minimize interference. Each node needs to complete backoff process before accessing a channel. The backoff timer decreases when the clear channel assessment (CCA) and network allocation vector (NAV) indicate that the medium has been sensed to be idle for a DCF interframe space (DIFS) interval. The sensation granularity of the channel state in the BEB process is too coarse in dense deployment scenarios in which the channel state is complicated, only busy or idle. Similarly, the backoff action is also quite simple such that the backoff timer decreases by one when idle and hangs up when busy in one timeslot. Given these drawbacks of the BEB algorithm, Some researchers modified the minimum collision window to increase area throughput [9,10], but these method lacks efficiency in dealing with data frames of unequal length. A spatial reuse scheme proposed by Liu *et al.* [11] to enhance the average throughput, but falls short of setting backoff granularity reasonably.

To enhance area throughput, this paper proposes a fractional backoff algorithm called eat-B, in which the backoff process of each communication link dynamically adapts the channel state information (CSI) by refining the backoff granularity. It means the backoff counter of the node who may provide more contributions for the area throughput is probably decreased by a larger value, while that of the node who may provide less contributions for the area throughput is probably decreased by a smaller value. In other word, the nodes who provide more contributions for the area throughput will finish their backoff process faster. The simulation results confirm the performance advantages in area throughput.

The contribution of this research is as follows.

- To the best of our knowledge, this study is the first attempt to introduce a fractional backoff algorithm dynamically.
- This paper compares the eat-B and BEB algorithms through simulations, and the results indicate that the area throughput of the eat-B algorithm outperforms BEB, especially under dense deployment scenarios.

The reminder of this paper is as follows: Sect. 2 illustrates the motivation and key idea of backoff algorithm. Sect. 3 details the eat-B algorithm. Sec. 4 deploys several simulations and verifies the performance. Finally, Sect. 5 concludes the paper.

## 2   Motivation and Key Idea

### 2.1   Introduction to Backoff Mechanism and Analysis of Existing Problems

Two main problems plague the existing BEB mechanism. The first is that BEB has no unique ability to address the high collision probability resulting from fierce channel contention in dense deployment scenarios; reducing channel contention must be solved by NGWs in dense deployment circumstances. The second problem is that some parts of the BEB can inhibit area throughput for two reasons. First, WLANs contain multi-rate stations, but the probability of accessing the channels for each station is identical regardless of the station rate. The transmission time for a packet in a lower-rate station is longer than in a higher-rate station; thus, lower-rate stations occupy the channel for longer, limiting network performance and preventing proportional fairness. To solve this problem and improve channel utilization, an unfair channel access mechanism must be implemented to increase channel access opportunities for higher-rate stations. Second, even if the channel states across stations are similar, the contributions of communication link to area throughput may be different due to different link qualities.

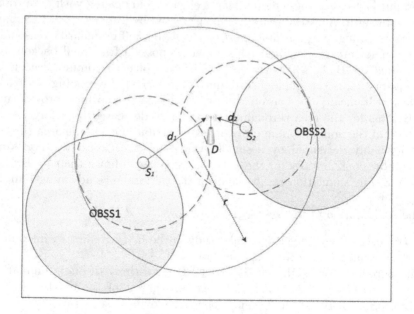

**Fig. 1.** Illustration of sample scenario.

As shown in Fig. 1, node $S_1$ and node $S_2$ have similar channel states, but the link quality of $S_2$ can be better than that of $S_1$ due to different transmission distances, which contributes more to area throughput. However, under the BEB mechanism, these nodes will have the same backoff speed and identical channel access opportunities, which cannot fully leverage good-quality links. Therefore, channel access opportunities should be adjustable depending on link quality so good-quality links have more opportunities to access the channel and thus improve area throughput.

## 2.2   Key Idea

The eat-B algorithm is assumed to solve problems related to performance degradation given dense deployment and performance anomalies under multi-rate station circumstances. The backoff granularity of each timeslot is not fixed at 1; rather, a fractional number in the eat-B algorithm can refine granularity, alleviate channel competition, and reduce the collision probability. The backoff granularity is determined by the contribution of the communication link to area throughput of each node, so stations making greater contributions can be provided more frequent channel access to make sufficient use of the wireless channel. For example, as shown in Fig. 1, $S_2$ has larger granularity than $S_1$ because the signal transmitted by $S_2$ can be received by $D$ at a higher signal to interference plus noise ratio (SINR) in which $S_1$ and $S_2$ have equal transmission power. Additionally, AP can adjust the backoff granularity factor to ensure fairness.

# 3   Description of Eat-B Algorithm

## 3.1   Overview

The most important question in the eat-B algorithm is how to apply the backoff granularity algorithm for each node. In each timeslot, the current channel state (e.g., interference power and communication link distance) is used to calculate the contribution of the link to the area throughput. Then, the backoff granularity of the current timeslot can be obtained, and the backoff process can be paused within this timeslot if necessary.

## 3.2   Specifications

The proposed eat-B algorithm is described as follows.

Step 1. The source node (denoted as $S$), which requires access to the channel and wants to send a data frame to the destination node (denoted as $D$), must query the maintained CCA range first; that is, $[-82dBm, CCA_{th}]$, where $CCA_{th}$ is the CCA threshold of each communication link; it may be a unique threshold for the whole network, or it could be obtained by the receiving node $D$ during the last transmission, in which case the $CCA_{th}$ of each node pair may be different.

Step 2. In each timeslot, $S$ detects the interference power of the channel, denoted as $I$. If $I > CCA_{th}$, then the backoff process becomes hung up within this timeslot. If so, Step 2 is repeated in the next timeslot; otherwise, proceed to Step 3.

Step 3. Calculate the estimated signal to interference ratio (SIR) as $SIR_e = Pr - I(dB)$, where $Pr$ is the receiving power of the last transmission from $S$ to $D$, such as the power of the RTS frame. Then, the corresponding data transmission rate $R_e$ can be obtained via mapping.

Step 4. The backoff granularity $\omega$ of the current timeslot can be calculated according to $\omega : \omega_{max} = \eta : \eta_{max}$, $\omega_{max}$ represents the maximum backoff granularity (the value can be either 1 or another positive number), $\eta$ represents the contribution of the communication link to the area throughput, and $\eta_{max}$ is the maximum value. Given a minimum interference area $\mathscr{A}_{min}$ and a maximum data rate $R_{max}$, then we have $\eta_{max} = \frac{R_{max}}{\mathscr{A}_{min}}$, similarly we have $\eta = \frac{R}{\mathscr{A}}$, where $\mathscr{A}$ represents the union of interference area of $S$ and $D$.

Step 5. The backoff timer counts down the value of $\omega$ , and $S$ transmits the frame when the backoff timer reaches 0; otherwise, return to Step 2 in the next timeslot.

### 3.3   Use Case

This section emulates the process of the eat-B algorithm using the scenario in Fig. 1.

Step 1. $S_1$ and $S_2$ each want to send a data frame to $D$. They have five and nine backoff timeslots at a CCA threshold of $-62dBm$ and $-60dBm$, respectively.

Step 2. Detect the interference power on the channel. Even if $S_1$ and $S_2$ have similar channel states, the backoff action may be different due to different CCA thresholds; for example, the backoff process of $S_1$ may get hung up when $I = -61dBm$, whereas that of $S_2$ continues.

Step 3. Calculate the corresponding data transmission rate $R_e$.

Step 4. The link quality of $S_2$ is better than that of $S_1$; thus, the backoff granularity of $S_2$ is assumed to be twice that of $S_1$.

Step 5. The backoff timer counts down, and the frame is sent if the timer reaches 0.

As indicated in this case, even if $S_2$ has twice as many backoff timeslots as $S_1$, $S_2$ which has a better channel state will still transmit the frame before $S_1$ due to having a larger backoff granularity and higher CCA threshold; therefore, resource utilization is enhanced.

## 4   Simulation

### 4.1   Simulation Environment

This section tests and compares the performance of the eat-B algorithm and BEB algorithm through simulations of the eat-B algorithm based on the NS-2 simulation platform developed for IEEE 802.11ax [12].

We deploy a multi-BSS network in which one AP and several STAs are served in each BSS and only the uplink traffic scenario is considered. We assume that the APs are deployed within a square area of with $120\,m \times 120\,m$. The STAs in each BSS are randomly deployed in an annular area with the AP as centre, an inner radius $r_a$ and outer radius $r_b$. We assume that $r_a = 10\,m$ and $r_b = 60\,m$ based on the condition of $r_a < r_b$ [13]. The path loss exponent $\alpha$ is set to 6 in the simulation. In the proposed eat-B algorithm, $\omega_{max} = 1$, $CCA_{th} = -62dBm$. The mapping relations between the SIR and transmission rate can be refereed as [14]. Performance is compared by testing the area throughput, collision probability, and average latency between the eat-B and BEB algorithms.

## 4.2   Performance Evaluation

Figure 2 illustrates that the area throughput of the proposed eat-B algorithm hardly changed with different numbers of STAs, and larger granularity avoided a high collision probability as the number of STAs in each BSS increased.

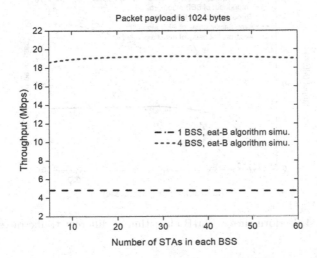

**Fig. 2.** Performance of eat-B algorithm with different numbers of STAs.

Figure 3 compares the area throughput and collision probability of the eat-B and BEB algorithms. As the number of BSS increased, the area throughput of the BEB algorithm was not perfectly linear because the collision probability also increased; the performance of the eat-B algorithm improved substantially with 24 BSS because the channel state for each station changed from simple to complex in this range and barely changed thereafter. The performance of eat-B and BEB followed the same trend with BSS above 4. Generally, the gap in area throughput and collision probability between the two algorithms was nearly 100% and 60%, respectively.

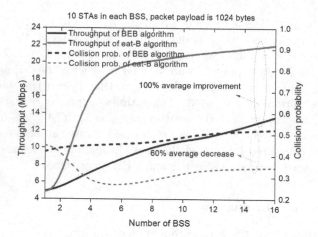

**Fig. 3.** Performance of eat-B algorithm with different numbers of BSS.

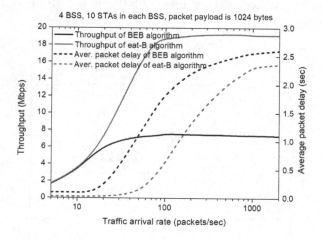

**Fig. 4.** Performance of eat-B algorithm at different traffic rates.

Fig. 4 compares the area throughput and average latency of the eat-B and BEB algorithms based on traffic rate. The latency of the eat-B algorithm declined by 15% compared to BEB, and the area throughput gain of eat-B became apparent at a traffic arrival rate exceeding channel capacity due to the gain is from its high channel utilization.

## 5    Conclusions and Future Work

This paper proposes fractional backoff algorithm called eat-B for dense deployment scenarios to improve NGW performance. Comparative simulations indicate this algorithm substantially enhanced area throughput by dynamically adapting the backoff granularity of each communication link. In the future, we plan to research the eat-B system model to enrich its theoretical foundation and extend it to multi-channel wireless networks [15].

**Acknowledgement.** This work was supported in part by the National Natural Science Foundations of CHINA (Grant No. 61771390, No. 61501373, No. 61771392, and No. 61271279), the National Science and Technology Major Project (Grant No. 2016ZX03001018-004, and No. 2015ZX03002006-004), and the Fundamental Research Funds for the Central Universities (Grant No. 3102017ZY018).

# References

1. IEEE 802.11 Wireless LANs: Proposed TGax draft specification. IEEE 802.11-16/002 4r1, March 2016
2. Kamel, M., Hamouda, W., Youssef, A.: Ultra-dense networks: a survey. IEEE Commun. Surv. Tutor. **18**(4), 25222545, Fourth quarter (2016)
3. IEEE: 802.11 HEW SQ Proposed PAR. IEEE, doc. IEEE 802.11-14/0165r1 (2014)
4. Bellalta, B.: IEEE 802.11ax: high-efficiency WLANs. IEEE Wirel. Commun. **23**(1), 38–46 (2016)
5. IEEE STD. 802.11: Wireless LAN Medium Access Control (MAC) and Physical Layer (PHY) Specifications (1999)
6. Heusse, M., Rousseau, F., Berger-Sabbatel, G., Duda, A.: Performance anomaly of 802.11b. In: IEEE INFOCOM 2003 Twenty-Second Annual Joint Conference of the IEEE Computer and Communications Societies (IEEE Cat. No.03CH37428), vol. 2, pp. 836–843 (2003)
7. IEEE W.G.: Supplement to part 11 : wireless LAN medium access control (MAC) and physical layer specifications: high-speed physical layer extension in the 2.4 GHz band. IEEE Std (1999)
8. IEEE. W.G.: Supplement to part 11 : wireless LAN medium access control (MAC) and physical layer specifications : high-speed physical layer extension in the 5 GHz band. IEEE Stda (1999)
9. Aad, I., Castelluccia, C.: Differentiation mechanism for IEEE 802.11. IEEE Infocom. Anchorage, AK **1**, 209–218 (2001)
10. Kim, H., Yun, S., Kang, I., Bahk, S.: Resolving 802.11 performance anomalies through QoS differentiation. IEEE Commun. Lett. **9**(7), 655–657 (2005)
11. Liu, J., Wu, T., Huang, R., Wang, J.: Prioritized channel access schemes with spatial reuse consideration. US 2016/0066257 A1, 3 March 2016
12. Lin, W., et al.: Integrated link-system level simulation platform for the next generation WLANIEEE 802.11 ax. IEEE GLOBECOM, pp. 1–7, December 2016
13. Liu, Y., Ding, Z., Elkashlan, M., Poor, H.V.: Cooperative non-orthogonal multiple access with simultaneous wireless information and power transfer. IEEE J. Sel. Areas Commun. **34**(4), 938–953 (2016)
14. Qiao, D., Choi, S., Shin, K.G.: Goodput analysis and link adaptation for IEEE 802.11a wireless LANs. IEEE Trans. Mobile Comput. **1**(4), 278–292 (2002)
15. Yang, B., Li, B., Yan, Z., Yang, M.: A distributed multi-channel MAC protocol with Parallel cooperation for the next generation WLAN. In: IEEE Wireless Communications and Networking Conference Workshops (WCNCW), pp. 327–332 (2016)

# A 60 GHz UWB-MIMO Antenna with Defected Ground for WPAN Applications

Syrine Lahmadi[1(✉)] and Jamel Bel Hadj Tahar[2]

[1] El Manar University, ENIT, Tunis, Tunisia
syrine.lahmadi@gmail.com
[2] Sousse University, NOCCS, Sousse, Tunisia

**Abstract.** The article presents a novel ultra-wideband (UWB) multi-input multi-output (MIMO) antenna with high isolation. The proposed MIMO antenna consists of four folded L-shaped strips patch which has very compact size of 2, $2 \times 2, 2 \ mm^2$. A line-slot is etched on the ground to reduce the mutual coupling on the 60 GHz band. Four other no-ended slots are etched on subtract to improve the impedance matching and to enlarge the bandwidth. Proposed antenna is resonating at 61 GHz. The mutual coupling is less than $-15$ dB throughout the 60 GHz band. The envelope correlation coefficient is less than 0.006 in the whole operating band. The performances of the proposed antenna indicate that it is a good candidate for UWB applications.

**Keywords:** Defected ground · UWB · ECC · MIMO

## 1 Introduction

The antenna is the most important element on the communication channel. It has the role of transmitting/receiving signal into free space. In old communication systems, a single antenna is used at the transmitter and a single one is used at the receiver. It's known as a single input/single output technology (SISO). This technology is very sensitive to multipath effects [1]. During the last years, in order to reduce this effect a new technology has been developed: multi input/multi output technology (MIMO). It consists on using multi antenna excited apart at the same frequency in the same antenna structure. This technology is an important solution to improve the capacity of wireless link [2].

However, MIMO antenna is affected by the radiation emission conductor and coupling losses caused by the radiating element which are placed on limited space. In literature, we can find many methods [3–5] to limit the mutual coupling and increase the efficiency and the gain of the system. One of the lowest cost method and less complicated to realize is to add slots [5]. The slots can be etched in different element of the patch antenna such in patch, in ground even in the subtract.

© ICST Institute for Computer Sciences, Social Informatics and Telecommunications Engineering 2019
Published by Springer Nature Switzerland AG 2019. All Rights Reserved
J.-L. Chen et al. (Eds.): WiCON 2018, LNICST 264, pp. 32–40, 2019.
https://doi.org/10.1007/978-3-030-06158-6_4

## 2  Antenna Configuration

Figure 1 shows the geometry of the proposed MIMO antenna. It is printed on the silicone subtract with compact size of 2, 2 × 2, 2 mm², thickness of 0, 2 mm and relative dielectric constant of 11,9. The top layer consist of four radiating elements which are placed on vertical and horizontal to cover signals in both directions to enhance the preciseness of the signals [6]. This diversity technique reduces space and limits the mutual coupling between the radiators. Each element is fed by a meander line of 50 Ω impedance. The radiator is divided symmetrically by the central line. At each side, there is one L-shaped strip. On the bottom layer, there is a narrow ground plane with line slot for each radiating element. On the middle layer (subtract), there are four no-ended slots to ameliorate the performance of the MIMO antenna. Thanks to an soft HFSS and parametric studies, we obtain this optimized values (millimeters) of the proposed antenna: Lg = 1.1, wg = 0.1, w1 = 0.1, w2 = 0.1, w3 = 0.98, ws = 2.2, WL = 0.6, L = 0.1, X1 = 0.1, X2 = 0.4, X3 = 0.5.

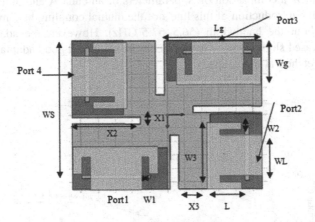

**Fig. 1.**  Configuration of the proposed antenna

## 3  Antenna Design

The proposed antenna was developed step by step. The good performance in terms of high isolation, broadband impedance and bandwidth are attended by etching a stepped slot on the ground and a line slot on the subtract. These performances are also realized thanks to the inverted ground branches. It is used to limit the direct linking current between radiators [7].

### 3.1  Line Slot

The coupling between the two ports (port1/port2 and port2/port3) can be enhanced by increasing the distance between the radiating elements, but it will increase the physical area of the proposed MIMO antenna. So to maintain the compactness of the antenna, a line slot of dimension Ls1 × Ws1 is etched at the ground plane of each radiating element (Fig. 2b).

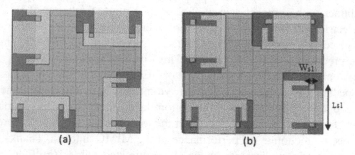

(a)                          (b)

**Fig. 2.** The configuration of (a) antenna A (b) antenna B

Figure 3 shows a comparison of |s| parameters of antenna A and antenna B. As it shown, due to the introduction of this line slot the mutual coupling become lower than −15 db throughout the bandwidth (56.5–67.5 GHz). However, the adaption of the antenna is increased slightly. So to have a better isolation and good adaptation four no-ended sots are etched at the subtract.

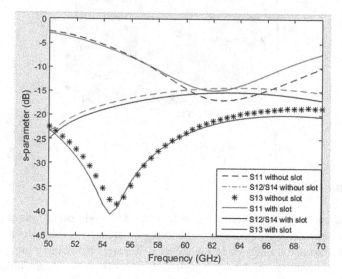

**Fig. 3.** The Simulated s-parameter

## 3.2    No-Ended Slot

To ameliorate the performance of the MIMO antenna (the impedance matching (sii) and the mutual coupling sij), a no-ended slot which is inspired from [8] is adopted as an element of the proposed antenna. The effect of different dimensions (x1, x2 and x3) of the no-ended slot was studied. For fixed length of the no-ended slots x2 = 0.1 mm and a position of x3 = 0.5 mm, the simulated reflection coefficient for different width x1 are shown in Fig. 4. As can be seen in Fig. 4, the bandwidth is more and more important when the width is narrower.

The effects of the slots lengths are also studied. Fig. 5 shows the simulated mutual coupling (s12/s14 and s13) at the length of the slots changed for width x1 = 0.1 mmn. the isolation increase with the increasing of the slots length.

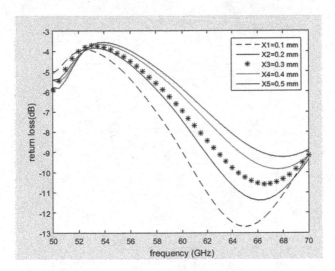

**Fig. 4.** The simulated S11 for different slot width

The slot position, x3 denote the spacing between the slot and the middle of the proposed MIMO antenna. By adjusting the position of the slot, the proposed MIMO antenna can achieve a good impedance matching. In Fig. 5, results for the parameter x3 is varied from 0.2 mm to 0.5 mm are shown.

As shown in Fig. 6, the simulated S11 is more interesting when the slot is nearer to the middle of the antenna. Good S11 is obtained when the position is x3 = 0.5 mm

## 4  Results

### 4.1  S-Parameter

From HFSS simulated s-parameters, we find that the return-loss at different ports is s11 = s22 = s33 = s44, and the mutual coupling between adjacent ports is s12 = s21 = s14 = s41 = s32 = s23 = s34 = s43, and at diagonal ports s13 = s31 = s42 = s24. The return loss is the same for different ports because the radiating elements are the same. As shown on Fig. 3, The MIMO antenna without slots on subtract (Fig. 2b) is having −10 db impedance band of 56.5–67.5 GHz .it resonate at 61 GHz frequency where the return loss is −15 db. In this case the achieved bandwidth is 10 GHz .When

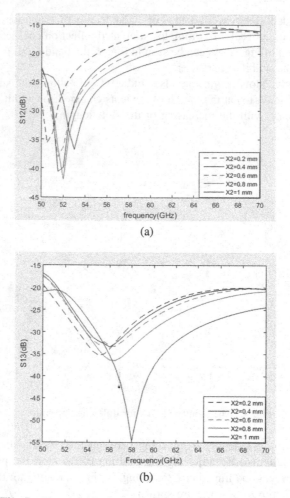

**Fig. 5.** The simulated (a) S12/s14 (b) S13for different slot

the proposed antenna (with slots on the subtract) having −10 db impedance band of 52–70 GHz. The bandwidth of 18 GHz is obtained here. In this case, the proposed antenna resonates at 61 GHz, where the return loss is −27 db. That means the fours slots made at the subtract improve the wideband and the impedance matching. Concerning the isolation, there is a good one along the 60 GHz band. As can see in Fig. 7, the mutual coupling is less than −15 db.

## 4.2 The Voltage Standing Wave Ration

The VSWR informs about the power reflected from the proposed MIMO antenna. It also indicate how efficient antenna input impedance is coordinate to the impedance of the transmitter line (in this case it is 50 Ω). Figure 8 shows the VSWR of the proposed antenna is less than 2 along the bandwidth. It attains 1.1 at 61 GHz.

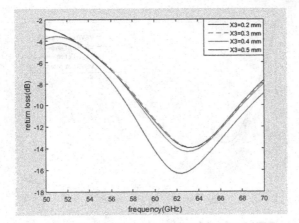

**Fig. 6.** The simulated S11 for different position X3

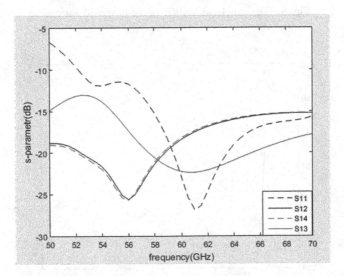

**Fig. 7.** The simulated S-parameter

## 4.3   The Radiation Efficiency

The radiation efficiency of a MIMO antenna must be important (about 0.9) to assure a good performance. The efficiency is affected by dielectric (especially when relative dielectric is very high like in this case), losses caused by conduction and losses due to the reflection. As shown in Fig. 9, the proposed MIMO antenna has a very high efficiency (high than 0.9) in the UWB frequency band.

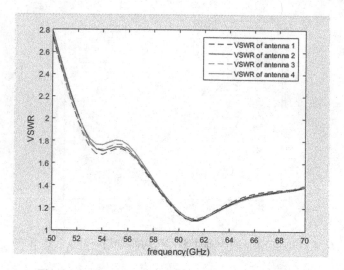

**Fig. 8.** The simulated VSWR of the proposed antenna

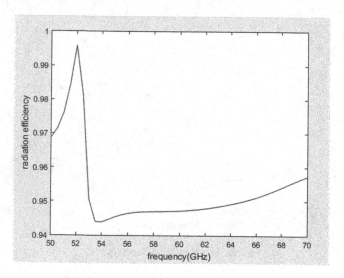

**Fig. 9.** The simulated radiation efficiency

## 4.4    The Envelope Correlation Coefficient

Orderly, to confirm the capability of the proposed antenna for MIMO application, it is obligatory to have a low envelope correlation coefficient (ECC). The envelope correlation coefficient describes how much the communication channels are isolated. To have a value of 0.5 as an envelope correlation coefficient is acceptable for diversity condition [9]. It can be calculated using the following formula [10]:

$$ECC(i,j,N) = \frac{\left| \sum_{n=1}^{N} S_{in}^{*} * S_{nj} \right|^2}{\prod_{k=(i,j)} \left[ 1 - \sum_{n=1}^{N} S_{in}^{*} * S_{nk} \right]} \tag{1}$$

where i, j are the antenna elements and N is the number of the antenna

Figure 10 shows the simulated envelope correlation coefficient (ECC) of the proposed antenna. As can be seen, the ECC of the proposed structure is less than 0.006 between any of the two ports.

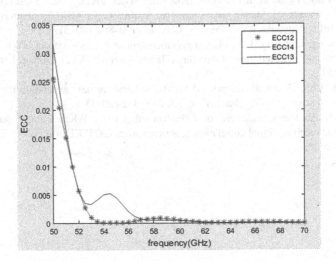

**Fig. 10.** The simulated ECC of the proposed antenna

## 5 Conclusion

A novel MIMO antenna with polarization diversity technique has been developed to limit the problem of multipath propagation. The proposed MIMO antenna offer a large bandwidth over 18 GHz which is enough to cover the 60 GHz band. With the optimized antenna geometry and the slots added to the ground, the proposed MIMO antenna provides good performances in term of good return loss, radiation efficiency and envelops correlation coefficient which is less than 0.06 in the whole operating band.

## References

1. Sharawi, Ms.: A dual-band dual-element compact MIMO antenna system for mobile 4G terminals. Microwav. Opt. Technol. Lett. **55**, 325–329 (2013)
2. Kaiser, T., Feng, Z., Dimitrov, E.: An overview of ultra-wideband systems with MIMO. Proc. IEEE **97**, 68–73 (2009)

3. Li, J.X., Ying, Z., He, S.: High isolation compact four-port MIMO antenna systems with built-in filters as isolation structure. In: 2010 Proceedings of the Fourth European Conference on Antennas and Propagation (EuCAP), pp. 1–4, April 2010

4. Lin, X.Q., Li, H., He, S., Fan, Y.: A decoupling technique for increasing the port isolation between two closely packed antennas. In: 2012 IEEE Antennas and Propagation Society International Symposium (APSURS), pp. 1–2, July 2012

5. Nandi, S., Mohan, A.: A compact dual-band slot antenna for WLAN application. IEEE Antennas Wirel. Propag. Lett. 52, 45–52 (2004)

6. Wong, H., Leung Lau, K., Man Luk, K.: Design of dual-polarized L probe pach antenna arrays with high isolation. IEEE Trans. Antennas Wirel. Propag. 52, 45–52 (2004)

7. Shoaib, S., Shoaib, I., Shoaib, N., Chen, X., Parini, C.G.: MIMO antennas for mobile handsets. IEEE Antennas Wirel. Propag. Lett. 14, 799–802 (2015)

8. Luo, C., Hong, J., Zhong, L.: Isolation enhancement of a very compact UWB-MIMO Slot antenna with two defected ground structures. IEEE Antennas Wirel. Propag. Lett. 14, 1766–1769 (2015)

9. Young, M., Chu, Q.: Small-size printed MIMO antenna for next generation mobile handset application. Microw. Opt. Technol. Lett. 53, 248–352 (2011)

10. Hallbjorner, P.: The significance of radiation efficiencies When using S-parameters to calculate the received signal correlation from two antennas. IEEE Ant. Wirel. Propag. Lett. 4, 97–99 (2005)

# Research and Performance Evaluation of Spatial Reuse Technology for Next Generation WLAN

Zhao Shen[1], Bo Li[1], Mao Yang[1]([✉]), Zhongjiang Yan[1], Xiaobo Li[2], and Yi Jin[2]

[1] School of Electronics and Information,
Northwestern Polytechnical University, Xi'an, China
{libo.npu,yangmao,zhjyan}@nwpu.edu.cn
[2] China Academy of Space Technology, Xi'an, China

**Abstract.** In order to improve the network performance in the high dense multi-BSSs, the next generation WLAN: IEEE 802.11ax introduces spatial reuse (SR) technology to improve the spectrum utilization, manage the multi-BSSs interferences and increase the possibility of simultaneous transmissions. This paper firstly introduces the SR technologies of IEEE 802.11ax in detail. After that, to fully verify the performance, we build a system & link level integrated simulation platform for IEEE 802.11ax and achieve the SR. Finally, we evaluate the performance of the SR through the built simulation platform, the simulation results clearly indicate that the network throughput is improved by 34.3% in uplink scenarios. To the best of our knowledge, this is the first work to introduce and evaluate the SR technologies for IEEE 802.11ax.

**Keywords:** WLAN · IEEE 802.11ax · Spatial reuse

## 1 Introduction

With wireless network and wireless services quickly developing, the demands for the quality of wireless services are also increasing [1]. According to CISCO's statistics and forecast, from 2016 to 2021, the total traffic of global wireless services has increased sharply by 47% annually. The traffics carried by wireless local area network (WLAN) will account for nearly 50% of the total traffic in 2021 [2]. WLAN becomes one important wireless network because of its advantages of high throughput, low cost and flexible deployment. However, the existing WLAN technologies are difficult to meet the growing user needs, so the next generation WLAN standard, IEEE 802.11ax, is currently being developed.

The high dense scenarios such as enterprises, shopping malls, gymnasiums and hospitals will become an important feature of future wireless network [3]. To satisfy the needs of the users in the future, a large number of access points (APs)

J.-L. Chen et al. (Eds.): WiCON 2018, LNICST 264, pp. 41–51, 2019.
https://doi.org/10.1007/978-3-030-06158-6_5

are required in a limited area to ensure the access of a large number of users, on the other hand, future wireless networks also need to support a lot of stations (STAs) in a basic service set (BSS), such as a large number of mobile phones in a gymnasium holding large football match and internet of things (IoT) terminals in families or enterprises. In view of the high dense scenarios and the technology requirement for IEEE 802.11ax in project authorization request (PAR) [4], IEEE 802.11ax has put forward a series of key technologies: multiple access technology based on orthogonal frequency division multiple access (OFDMA), enhanced physical layer (PHY) technologies, SR technology and uplink multi-user multiple-input multiple-output (UL MU-MIMO). Among them, SR technology provides the solutions to the high dense multi-BSSs scenarios.

At present, many studies focus on the key technologies and discuss about standard setting of IEEE 802.11ax from some different aspects, besides, some papers also introduce and evaluate SR technology. Among them, the [5,11] mainly discussed the standard setting of IEEE 802.11ax and predicted the possible key technologies. [5,7] summarized the current development of IEEE 802.11ax, pointed out the shortcomings of the traditional IEEE 802.11 in the high dense scenarios and discussed the possible technologies and challenges of medium access control (MAC) and PHY protocol for IEEE 802.11ax. In view of multi-user (MU) access in IEEE 802.11ax, [6] has analyzed and investigated the MU MAC protocol based on OFDMA and proposed a MU MAC protocol framework based on OFDMA. [10] introduced the MAC technologies of IEEE 802.11ax to well ensure QoS and user experience. [12,14] mainly introduced the key technologies of next generation WLAN - SR technology. [12] introduced key technologies of IEEE 802.11ax, such as PHY technologies based on OFDMA, uplink MU-MIMO, SR technology, etc. [13] outlined the SR technology based on OBSS power detection (OBSS_PD ) in IEEE 802.11ax. A power control algorithm is proposed to control the dynamicly changing of the clear channel assessment (CCA) threshold according to the state of the channel. The performance improvement is verified by simulating IEEE 802.11ac. The results of theoretical calculation model and actual simulations in [14] prove that optimizing the CCA threshold can increase the spatial utilization and improve the network performance. These related works provide deep analysis for the performance requirements and potential technologies of the IEEE 802.11ax. However, few of them focus on the analysis of the SR technology in IEEE 802.11ax and verify the performance improvement for IEEE 802.11ax.

In this paper, the SR of IEEE 802.11ax is fully analyzed and discussed in detail. After that, to verify the performance, we build the system & link level integrated simulation platform for IEEE 802.11ax and achieve the SR. Finally by the integrated platform, authors simulate the effect of changing the OBSS_PD level on the network throughput of IEEE 802.11ax with SR and select an OBSS_PD value that can maximize the network throughput; then we simulate the multi-BSSs scenarios and show the distribution of the network throughput of each BSS; moreover, authors use the integrated platform to evaluate the network throughput of the two schemes: IEEE 802.11ax without SR and IEEE 802.11ax with SR from uplink transmission, through the comparisons and analysis of the simulation results, under the 32 (8x4) BSSs scenario, the network throughput of uplink transmission is improved by about 34.3% by using SR technology for IEEE 802.11ax.

The main contributions of this paper are as followed:

(1) To the best of our knowledge, this is the first work to introduce and evaluate the SR technology for IEEE 802.11ax.
(2) According to the requirements for simulation platform requested by task group of IEEE 802.11ax (TGax) in evaluation methodology, authors build the system & link level integrated simulation platform for IEEE 802.11ax and achieve SR technologies on the platform. Based on the integrated simulation platform, the authors simulate two schemes: IEEE 802.11ax with SR and IEEE 802.11ax without SR in office scenarios and evaluate the performance improvement of uplink transmission caused by SR technology.

The reminders of this paper are arranged as follows: Sect. 2 introduces SR technologies of IEEE 802.11ax in detail and analyzes the implementation of SR through BSS color mechanism, Two NAV mechanism and OBSS_PD mechanism; Sect. 3 mainly introduces the architecture of the integrated platform and the function of modules forming the integrated simulation platform; In Sect. 4, based on the integrated simulation platform, the authors simulate two schemes: IEEE 802.11ax with SR and IEEE 802.11ax without SR in office scenarios and evaluate the performance improvement of uplink transmission caused by SR technology.

## 2   Introduction of IEEE 802.11ax SR Technology

Aiming at the high dense scenarios, technology requirement and performance target [4] in PAR, IEEE 802.11ax has put forward a series of key technologies: enhanced PHY technologies, such as new coding strategy to further improve the transmission rate and using the more finer subcarrier division technology to improve the spectrum utilization; multiple access technology based on OFDMA and UL MU-MIMO; MU-MAC enhancement technology, introducing MU-MAC technology to improve the efficiency of WLAN and parallel data transmission; SR technology, IEEE 802.11ax standard regards SR technology as the core technology to improve the spectrum utilization and manage signal interference among BSSs [15].

Because IEEE 802.11ax mainly focuses on high dense scenarios, it is a key problem how to improve the network performance, the SR technology in IEEE 802.11ax is used to improve the network performance in the high dense scenarios. Therefore, this paper analyzes the SR technology of IEEE 802.11ax and evaluates the performance improvement caused by the SR. The followings will introduce the SR in detail.

## 2.1  BSS Color Mechanism

The principle of SR technology in IEEE 802.11ax is to implement different operations for packets coming from different BSSs. In order to implement SR technology, firstly the received packet should be judged from which BSSs they come. Therefore, IEEE 802.11ax proposes the BSS color mechanism. The BSS color mechanism is concretely implemented as follows: for each packet the color field is inserted into the SIG field of PHY header and the range of value in the color field is $1 \sim 63$ with 8 bits, the value in the color field is used to distinguish different BSSs. When AP or STA receives a packet, it can be judged by the value of the color field if the packet is from the other BSSs (inter_BSS) or from this BSS (Intra_BSS).

## 2.2  Two NAV Mechanism

IEEE 802.11ax proposes a two NAV mechanism to alleviate the confusion of TXOP end. Figure 1 is shown as the single NAV mechanism, the Link2 is successfully built between STA1 and AP1 while STA3 is transmitting data to AP2; when STA1 ends up transmitting, it has to send CF_END frame to cancel TXOP duration, STA2 receives the CF_END frame and cancels NAV duration that is set by the Link1 to contend channel access again, packets from STA2 can interfere with the packets that STA3 is sending to AP2, so the Link1 is built failed. Figure 2 is shown as the two NAV mechanism, STA3 is transmitting data to AP2 while the Link2 is successfully built between STA1 and AP1; when STA1 ends up transmitting, it has to send CF_END frame to cancel TXOP duration, STA2 receives the CF_END frame and cancels Basic_NAV duration but the Intra_NAV is still busy, STA2 cannot contend channel access again, so the Link1 is built successfully. The specific implementation of the two NAV mechanism is as followed: each STA or AP needs to maintain two NAV period: Intra_NAV is used to record the period of the NAV carried by the packet from this BSS, the Basic_NAV is used to maintain the period of the NAV carried by the packet from other BSSs or some other unknown BSSs. When AP or STA receives a packet, it chooses to update Intra_NAV or Basic_NAV according to the color value carried by the packet. On the contrary, when AP or STA receives the CF_END frame, according to the color value, AP or STA determines to cancel Intra_NAV period or Basic_NAV period.

## 2.3  OBSS_PD Mechanism

OBSS_PD mechanism: this technology is used to increase the possibility of simultaneous transmission among BSSs and improve the network throughput. Figure 3 is shown as the traditional CCA mechanism, the Link1 is firstly successfully built, STA1 sends packets to AP1 and STA2 also receives the packets, if the received power is larger than CCA threshold ($-82\,\mathrm{dBm}$), the channel state is busy, so STA2 cannot contend channel access, the Link3 cannot be built. Figure 4 is shown as the OBSS_PD mechanism, the Link1 is firstly successfully built, STA1

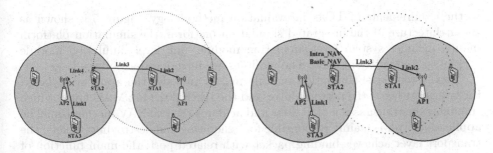

**Fig. 1.** Single NAV mechanism    **Fig. 2.** Two NAV mechanism

sends packets to AP1 and STA2 also receives the packets, if the received power is smaller than OBSS_PD level (OBSS_PD level is more larger than −82 dBm), the channel state is idle, so STA2 can contend channel access, the Link3 can be built successfully. The implementation of the OBSS_PD mechanism is that each STA or AP needs to maintain two CCA thresholds: one CCA threshold is the traditional CCA threshold value (−82 dBm) and the other CCA threshold value adopts a higher CCA level which is described as OBSS_PD level for channel sensing. When AP or STA successfully receives a packet and determines from which BSSs the packet come through the BSS color, if the packet comes from this BSS, the traditional CCA threshold (−82 dBm) is used to judge if channel is busy or idle; if the packet comes from the other BSSs, channel state is judged by the OBSS_PD Level. In general, the value of OBSS_PD level is larger than the traditional CCA threshold (−82 dBm), so that can greatly increase the possibility of simultaneous transmission among BSSs.

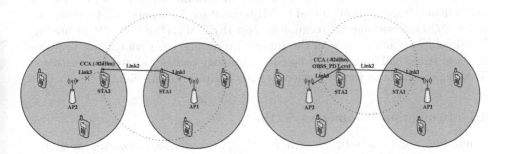

**Fig. 3.** Traditional CCA mechanism    **Fig. 4.** OBSS_PD mechanism

## 3  The Integrated Simulation Platform

In order to evaluate the throughput improvement caused by SR technology, this chapter mainly introduces the system & link level simulation platform based on network simulation version 2.0 (NS2). The simulation platform is built according to the requirements of TGax in evaluation methodology. Figure 5 is shown as the architecture of the integrated simulation platform, the simulation platform mainly includes system level simulation module, link level simulation module and integrated entity module. The modules are introduced as followed:

The system level simulation module mainly includes the application layer, the transport layer, the network layer and the IEEE 802.11ax MAC layer, which simulates the transmission of packets and achieves the two NAV mechanism. The application layer is mainly responsible for generating and destroying packets; the transport layer achieves binding packet with related port; the main function of the network layer is to find the next hop IP address; the IEEE 802.11ax MAC layer is mainly responsible for the implementation of the 802.11ax MAC protocol, including the queue module, the channel access module, channel state module and so on. The link level simulation module focuses on IEEE 802.11ax PHY layer and modeling for wireless channel. The PHY layer of IEEE 802.11ax mainly includes the power management module of resource unit (RU) and channel, channel sensing module and calculating SNR and PER module. Channel carrier sensing module mainly implements the OBSS_PD mechanism.

The integrated entity module is responsible for the integration of system level simulation and link level simulation, consisting of two modules: link level discretization and unified system & link level interface. The link level discretization module mainly manages all discrete events generated in network simulation. The unified system & link level interface module is regarded as the unified interfaces to deliver information between MAC layer and PHY layer.

## 4   Performance Evaluation

This chapter mainly focuses on using the simulation platform to evaluate the performance improvement caused by SR technology. In simulation, two schemes: IEEE 802.11ax without SR technology and IEEE 802.11ax with SR technology are simulated. Compared with the simulation results, the performance improvement of IEEE 802.11ax caused by SR technology can be clearly demonstrated. This paper simulates the two schemes from uplink transmission.

### 4.1   Simulation Parameters Setting

Simulation scenarios settings still follow the simulation scenarios document exported by TGax [16]. The specific parameter settings are shown in Table 1

### 4.2   Network Performance In High Dense Office Scenarios

In high dense office scenarios, this paper evaluates the performance improvement of IEEE 802.11ax caused by SR technology from uplink transmission

(1) The effect of changing OBSS_PD level on network throughput.

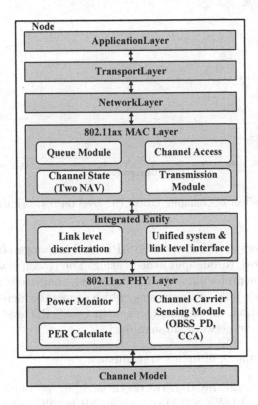

**Fig. 5.** Integrated simulation platform architecture

**Table 1.** Parameter setting for the simulation platform

| Parameter type | Parameter description |
| --- | --- |
| Traffic type/rate | CBR, 0.05 Mbps 3 Mbps |
| BSS number | 4, 8, 18, 24, 32 |
| STA number in BSS | 64 |
| STAs position | Uniform random distribution |
| MCS | 0, 1, 2, 3, 4, 5, 7, 8, 9, 10, 11 |
| Bandwidth | 20 MHz |
| Frequency | 5.57 GHZ |
| CCA Threshold | OBSS_PD level Traditional CCA level-82 dBm |

Figure 6 shows the effect of changing OBSS_PD level on network throughput in the high dense office scenarios. It can be seen from the graph that changing OBSS_PD level has great influence on the network throughput. When the value of OBSS_PD level is changed from −82 dBm to −70 dBm, the network throughput is increasing and the maximum network throughput can be obtained at

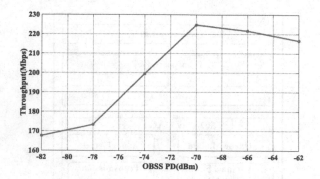

**Fig. 6.** The effect of changing OBSS_PD level on network throughput

about −70 dBm, however, when the OBSS_PD level is changed from −70 dBm to −62 dBm, the network throughput is decreasing. The reason is that if OBSS_PD level is too small, the probability of SR is decreased; conversely, the interferences between simultaneous links are increasing, which causes the increased packet loss. Through the simulation, the authors can get the OBSS_PD level value: −70 dBm that can maximize the network throughput.

(2) Network performance of uplink transmission

Figure 7 shows the saturated network throughput of both schemes: IEEE 802.11ax with SR and IEEE 802.11ax without SR in different scenarios, including 4 BSSs (2 × 2), 8 BSSs (4 × 2), 16 BSSs (4 × 4), 24 BSSs (6 × 4) and 32 BSSs (8 × 4). It can be clearly seen that when the number of BSSs is less, the probability of SR is very small and both of network throughput are almost same; with the number of BSSs increasing, such as 16 BSSs and 32 BSSs, the probability of SR is improved. In particular, in the case of 32 (8 × 4) BSSs, the network throughput of the uplink transmission is improved by about 34.3% by using SR technology for IEEE 802.11ax.

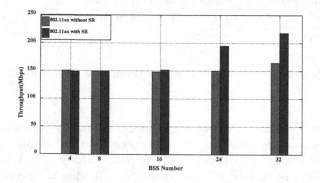

**Fig. 7.** Network throughput of uplink transmission in office scenarios

(3) The network performance of STA in office scenarios

Figure 8 shows the distribution of BSSs index. Figure 9 shows the distribution of the network throughput of each BSS in 32 (8 × 4) BSSs scenarios. From the simulation results, the more the BSS is near the center of the network scenario, the smaller the network throughput is; the more it is far away from the BSS in the center of the network scenario, the higher the network throughput is. Namely, the BSS is on the edge of the network scenario, the interference from other BSSs is relatively smaller; on the contrary, the interference is higher.

| 24 BSS | 25 BSS | 26 BSS | 27 BSS | 28 BSS | 29 BSS | 30 BSS | 31 BSS |
| --- | --- | --- | --- | --- | --- | --- | --- |
| 16 BSS | 17 BSS | 18 BSS | 19 BSS | 20 BSS | 21 BSS | 22 BSS | 23 BSS |
| 8 BSS | 9 BSS | 10 BSS | 11 BSS | 12 BSS | 13 BSS | 14 BSS | 15 BSS |
| 0 BSS | 1 BSS | 2 BSS | 3 BSS | 4 BSS | 5 BSS | 6 BSS | 7 BSS |

**Fig. 8.** The distribution of BSS index

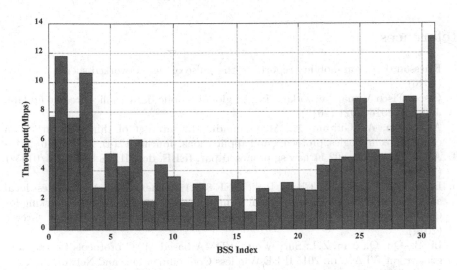

**Fig. 9.** The network performance of each STA in office scenarios

## 5 Conclusion

This paper firstly introduces the scenarios, key technologies and current researches for IEEE 802.11ax, discusses the SR technology in IEEE 802.11ax in detail and analyzes the shortcomings of the researches on SR technology of IEEE 802.11ax.

Based on the above studies, according to the technologies requirements of IEEE 802.11ax draft 2.0 for MAC layer and PHY protocol, we build a system & link level integrated simulation platform for IEEE 802.11ax and achieve the SR. Under the high dense office scenarios, firstly authors simulate the effect of changing the OBSS_PD level on the network throughput of IEEE 802.11ax with SR and select the OBSS_PD value that can maximize the network throughput; secondly authors simulate the multi-BSSs scenarios and show the distribution of the network throughput of each BSS; finally authors use the integrated platform to evaluate the network throughput of the two schemes: IEEE 802.11ax without SR and IEEE 802.11ax with SR from uplink transmission, through the comparisons and analysis of the simulation results, the network throughput of the uplink transmission is improved by about 34.3% by using SR technology for IEEE 802.11ax. It can be clearly demonstrated that the SR technology introduced by IEEE 802.11ax can significantly improve the network throughput.

**Acknowledgement.** This work was supported in part by the National Natural Science Foundations of CHINA (Grant No. 61501373, No. 61771392, No. 61771390, and No. 61271279), the National Science and Technology Major Project (Grant No. 2016ZX03001018-004, and No. 2015ZX03002006-004), and the Fundamental Research Funds for the Central Universities (Grant No. 3102017ZY018).

# References

1. Ericsson: Ericsson mobility report: on the pulse of the networked society. Journal (2016)
2. Cisco: Cisco Visual Networking Index: global mobile data traffic forecast update. Journal, 2016–2021 (2017)
3. Al-Fuqaha, A., Guizani, M., Mohammadi, M.: Internet of things: a survey on enabling technologies, protocols, and applications. Journal **17**(4), 2347–2376 (2015)
4. Aboul-Magd, O.: 802.11 hew sg proposed par, IEEE, doc. IEEE 802.11-14/0165r1 (2014)
5. Deng, D.J., Chen, K.C., Cheng, R.S.: IEEE 802.11ax: next generation wireless local area networks .In: 10th International Conference on Heterogeneous Networking for Quality, Reliability, Security and Robustness, pp. 77–82. IEEE, Rhodes. Greece (2014)
6. Li, B., Qu, Q., Yan, Z.J.: Survey on OFDMA based MAC protocols for the next generation WLAN. In: 2015 IEEE Wireless Communications and Networking Conference Workshops, pp. 131–135. IEEE, New Orleans, LA, USA(2015)
7. Khorov, E., Kiryanov, A., Lyakhov, A.: IEEE 802.11 ax: How to build high efficiency WLANs. In: 2015 International Conference on Engineering and Telecommunication (EnT), pp. 14–19. IEEE, Moscow, Russia (2015)
8. Bellalta, B.: IEEE 802.11ax: high-efficiency WLANs. IEEE Wirel. Commun. J. **23**(1), 38–46 (2016)
9. Gong, M.X., Hart, B., Mao, S.: Advanced wireless LAN technologies: IEEE 802.11 AC and beyond, 48–52. Journal **18**(4) (2014)

10. Deng, D.J., Lien, S.Y., Lee, J.: On quality of service provisioning in IEEE 802.11ax WLANs. 6086–6104. Journal **4** (2016)
11. Yang, H., Deng, D.J., Chen, K.C.: Performance analysis of IEEE 802.11ax UL OFDMA-based random access mechanism. In: 2017 IEEE Global Communications Conference, pp. 1–6, IEEE, Singapore, Singapore (2017)
12. Deng, D.J., Lin, Y.P., Yang, X.: IEEE 802.11ax: highly efficient WLANs for intelligent information infrastructure. Journal **55**(12), 52–59 (2017)
13. Ropitault, T.: NIST, N.G. :ETP algorithm: increasing spatial reuse in wireless LANs dense environment using ETX. In: IEEE 28th Annual International Symposium on Personal. Indoor, and Mobile Radio Communications (PIMRC), pp. 1–6. IEEE, Montreal, QC, Canada (2017)
14. Oteri, O., Sita, F.L., Yang, R.: Improved spatial reuse for dense 802.11 WLANs. In: 2015 IEEE Globecom Workshops (GC Wkshps), pp. 1–6, San Diego, CA (2015)
15. IEEE Draft 802.11ax/D2.0: WLAN medium access control (MAC) and physical layer (PHY) specifications amendment 6: Enhancements for high efficiency WLAN, Oct 2017
16. IEEE 802.11ax: TGax Simulation Scenarios. IEEE 802.11-14/0980r1

# CRJT: Channel Reservation Based Joint Transmission MAC Protocol for the Next Generation WLAN

Peng Tan, Ding Wang, Mao Yang[✉], Zhongjiang Yan, and Bo Li

School of Electronics and Information,
Northwestern Polytechnical University, Xi'an, China
tanpeng@mail.nwpu.edu.cn,
{wangd,yangmao,zhjyan,libo.npu}@nwpu.edu.cn

**Abstract.** In the past few decades, the rapid development of wireless local area networks (WLANs) provides great convenience to human lives. However, as the number of users and the complexity of deployment scenarios have increase, the next-generation WLANs face the unprecedented challenge of quality of service (QoS) and quality of experience (QoE) of cell-edge users. In response to this challenge, access point (AP) cooperation is supposed to be a promising solution. In this study, we propose a joint transmission medium access control (MAC) protocol based on channel reservation (CRJT). This protocol can make full use of the wireless channels to complete channel reservations and support joint transmissions effectively between APs. The simulation results show that this protocol provides a robust communication guarantee for edge users.

**Keywords:** WLAN · Channel reservation · Joint transmission (JT)

## 1 Introduction

Wireless local area networks (WLANs) are playing an increasingly important role in the global communication network [1]. Their rapid development and widespread application have resulted in a greater focus on the design of related protocols and the performance analysis. With the rapid growth of users' traffic, WLAN has become one of the most important ways of carrying data services. In order to meet the growing needs of users, both the academia and industrial focus on the key technologies for next-generation WLAN.

Quality of service (QoS) and quality of experience (QoE) of edge users are two of the key performance indicators (KPI) [2] of wireless networks. High-density deployment is an important trend for next-generation WLANs. On the one hand, high-intensive deployments increase the interference [3], making it

J.-L. Chen et al. (Eds.): WiCON 2018, LNICST 264, pp. 52–61, 2019.
https://doi.org/10.1007/978-3-030-06158-6_6

more difficult to guarantee the QoS and QoE of edge users. In particular, next-generation WLANs also need to support outdoor deployment scenarios, further aggravating the problem. Therefore, the service performance of the edge users in next-generation WLANs is an important research direction.

In response to these problems, many studies have proposed the idea of access point (AP) collaboration. Adachi and Kumagai [4] proposed the multi-AP cooperative diversity, which is formed between multiple APs in the surrounding area with poor channel quality. APs located in a collaborative diversity provide up link (UL) and down link (DL) traffic for the stations (STAs) simultaneously. The AP collaboration diversity can specify the traffic priorities that can be supported (for example, only high-priority traffic can be supported). Sirait et al. [5] proposed that in a densely deployed multi-AP network scenario, all APs are connected to a control center (CC). Depending on the transmission request of each STA, the beacon signal strength of each AP measured by the STA, and the interference intensity of each AP on each channel, the AP centrally plans the working channel for the AP and allocates the serving AP to the STA. However, this method has a great deal of overhead and complexity in implementation, especially because the AP frequently switches the working channel and the STA frequently switches the associated AP. In addition, to address the problem of inadequate resource utilization in WLANs due to hidden terminal and exposed terminal problems, Nishide et al. [6] proposed a method that can obtain information on hidden terminals and exposed terminals more accurately by cooperation between APs so that the access process can be performed more efficiently and the network performance can be improved. In summary, the existing research on the cooperation between APs is still at a preliminary stage. On the one hand, the information that is exchanged and shared between APs is far from enough to achieve deep cooperation. On the other hand, the achievements through AP cooperation are limited and far from diverse.

Coordinated multiple points (CoMP) is proposed in cellular networks, which is based on different degrees of sharing of the channel state information (CSI) and data information by each base station [7]. Through the cooperation of base stations between cells, the interference originally used by adjacent cells is converted into useful information, thereby improving the performance of users located at the edge of the cell. Cellular networks have X2 interfaces and are extremely time-critical networks. However, WLANs usually do not have X2 interfaces and have a distributed competition mode, whose time planning is not strict. Therefore, it is impractical to directly introduce CoMP into WLANs.

Therefore, in this paper, we propose joint transmission (JT) medium access control (MAC) protocol based on channel reservation, named CRJT, by combining the channel reservation mechanism and JT in the WLAN. The channel reservation guarantees the successful probability of JT. Specifically, in this study, we design the detailed MAC protocol for CRJT and verify its performance through simulation platforms. The simulation results show that the CRJT results in a 42.9% gain due to its maximum signal gain of 3 dB when there are two cooperative APs within the coverage distance of the APs service and when the STAs are located at the same distance from each other and far from each other. At the same time, regardless of the topology, the CRJT always has a lower packet loss rate than the non-CRJT. This gap is even more significant in a topology where the links are far away. This is a significant improvement in the QoS and QoE of the edge cell users.

The contributions of this paper is summarized as follows:

- As far as we know, this is the first work on the combination of channel reservation and JT in the design of the MAC protocol of the next generation WLAN. Meanwhile, the proposed method improves the edge users QoS significantly and guarantees the reliability of the JT.
- The results of this study demonstrate that the proposed protocol improves the QoS of the edge users using a simulation. In the topological structure in which the STAs are at the same distance from two cooperating APs, the distance covered by the AP is increased by 42.9%. At the critical case, the packet loss rate is reduced by more than 70%.

This structure of paper is as follows: Sect. 2 illustrates the proposed CRJT-MAC protocol. Section 3 depicts the simulation platform, Sect. 4 evaluate the performance. Section 5 lists some discussions, and Sect. 6 concludes this paper.

## 2   CRJT-MAC Description

### 2.1   Core Ideas

The CRJT is mainly aimed at cell-edge STAs and has the objective of increasing the signal-to-interference-plus-noise ratio (SINR) of the receiving STA through multi-AP JT to ensure the success rate of the reception, thereby increasing the edge users throughput.

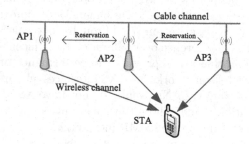

**Fig. 1.** CRJT scene schematic.

As shown in Fig. 1, the STA is an edge user of a cell and is far from the AP of the cell in which it is located (AP1). In addition to the dense deployment, the STA in this scenario cannot guarantee high throughput. In order to ensure that the AP1's DL traffic is accurately acquired by the STA, the JT MAC protocol based on the channel reservation schedules AP2, AP3, and AP1 for the JT.

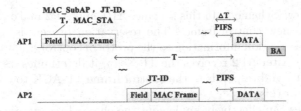

**Fig. 2.** CRJT flowchart (Scheme 1).

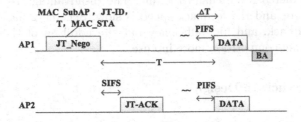

**Fig. 3.** CRJT flowchart (Scheme 2).

## 2.2 Protocol Process

The CRJT process is divided into two parts: channel reservation and JT. Figures 2 and 3 show the two implementation processes of the CRJT, whose main difference lies in the different methods of channel reservation.

Figure 2 shows Scheme one. In this scheme, AP1 and AP2 implement the channel reservation by adding a field in the data packet. The specific flow is as follows: (1) the principal AP (AP1) has information that needs to be jointly transmitted; it determines the subordinate AP (AP2) and the object to be transferred (STA) and then establishes an identifier(ID) for this reservation. (2) In the next data transmission of the AP1, the field is added to the data frame and the information such as the address of the AP, the address of the STA, the reservation time T, the reservation ID, etc. is added to the field and is sent along with the data packet. (3) After receiving a packet with a reserved field, AP2 parses the field, determines its own identity (subordinate AP), and determines whether it can participate in this JT according to its own traffic conditions. If possible, APs will add the same reservation ID to its own next packet to determine the reservation. (4) After receiving the reservation signal, AP1 sends the DATA frame to the STA according to the reservation time T. At the same time, AP2 also sends the same DATA. (5) After the STA receives this DATA, it sends an acknowledge packet (ACK) to AP1 to complete the joint transmission.

It should be noted that, in order to ensure that the JT is successfully performed at the scheduled time, the point coordination function interframe space (PIFS) duration is reserved prior to the transmission so that the AP can successfully obtain the channel use right. In addition, the peripheral traffic is set to remain within a period of time $\Delta T$ from the start of the PIFS timer to the transmission of the DATA frame to avoid collisions.

Figure 3 shows Scheme 2. In this scheme, AP1 and AP2 make channel reservations through new control frames. The reservation process is as follows: (1) AP1 adds the reservation information to the protocol control frame JT-Nego and sends it out. (2) After AP2 receives the JT-Nego, it determines its own identity (subordinate AP) and responds to the control frame JT-ACK to confirm that it can participate in this JT.

Both schemes can effectively implement the channel reservation. The advantage of Scheme 1 is that there is no need to add a new frame type to the protocol and it will not increase the channel traffic. The disadvantage is that the controllability is poor and the feedback speed is slow. Scheme 2 has good control effects, fast feedback, and high efficiency but the addition of the frame types makes the channel competition more intense.

## 2.3    Frame Structure Design

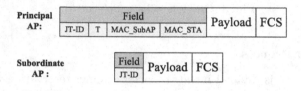

**Fig. 4.** CRJT frame structure (Scheme 1).

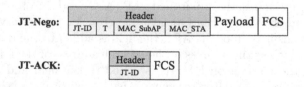

**Fig. 5.** CRJT frame structure (Scheme 2).

In Fig. 4, the channel reservation of Scheme 1 is shown. It consists of three parts, including the added field, payload, and frame check sequence. The newly added field includes a reservation ID, a reservation time T, the MAC address of the subordinate AP, and the MAC address of the receiving STA.

The channel reservation of Scheme 2 is shown in Fig. 5. Two types of frames are newly added. The JT-Nego frame sent by the principal AP includes information such as the reservation ID, the reservation time T, the MAC address of the subordinate AP, and the MAC address of the receiving STA. The JT-ACK frame returned from the subordinate AP contains the reservation ID.

# 3  Simulation Design

In order to evaluate the performance of the proposed design and verify the expected results, a simulation based on the NS-3 platform is conducted. NS-3 is a discrete event simulator [8]. Through serial configuration and code implementation, the protocol process design of the CRJT is completed.

## 3.1  Simulation Configuration

In this simulation, Scheme 2 is used. The design of the process (Fig. 3) is implemented in the NS-3 platform and the following parameters are configured [9]:

- Two cells are set; each cell has one STA and the scene is set as a diamond.
- The simulation time is set to 10 s.
- The modulation and coding scheme (MCS) of the data frame is set to an orthogonal frequency-division multiplexing (OFDM) rate of 36 millions of bits per second (Mbps) and the MCS of the control frame is set to an OFDM rate of 6 Mbps and remains fixed.
- The request to send/clear to send (RTS/CTS) are set to off.

## 3.2  Simulation Scene Design

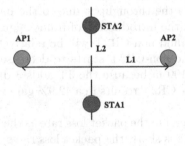

**Fig. 6.** Simulation scene.

The simulation scenario is shown in Fig. 6. There are two cells and each cell has one STA. A diamond structure is formed in which the distance between the APs is L1 and the distance between the STAs is L2. In the simulation, AP1 acts as a principal AP and has a UL traffic for STA1; AP2 as a subordinate AP needs to participate in the JT of the data frame based on the channel reservation.

In order to verify the effect of the protocol, the throughput and packet loss rate are used as indicators and the link distance and data rate are used as independent variables for the simulation verification.

In the simulation with the link distance as an independent variable, we set L1 as shown in Fig. 6 to be unchanged at 20 m. L2 is incrementally increased from 10 m to 120 m, that is, the link distance is increased from 11 m to 61

m. We set the data rate to 30 Mbps and the packet size to 1000 byte. AP1 is responsible for contracting in CRJT mode and mobilizing the AP2 assistance. We count the number of successfully received packets, calculate the packet loss rate based on the total number of packets sent, and calculate the throughput based on the simulation time.

In the simulation with the data rate as the independent variable, two kinds of topological structures are set. Topology one: L1 is 40 m, L2 is 70 m (link distance is 40 m); topology two: L1 is 40 m, L2 is 80 m (link distance is 45 m). The data rate is set to increase from 2 Mbps to 24 Mbps and the packet size is 1000 bytes. The two topologies are simulated separately to calculate the packet loss rate and throughput.

## 4   Performance Evaluation

### 4.1   Performance Trends for Different Link Distances

Figure 7a depicts the trend of the throughput as the link distance increases. The CRJT and non-CRJT exhibit similar trends as the distance increases, that is, the throughput remains stable when the link distance is short and drops sharply as the link distance continues to increase. The differences between the CRJT and the non-CRJT depend on the link distance. (1) When the link distance is short, the CRJT throughput is 79.4% of the non-CRJT throughput because the SINRs of both schemes are relatively high and thus the packet loss is small (Fig. 7b) but the CRJT scheme reduces the throughput due to the introduction of a certain overhead. Of course, with the introduction of frame aggregation technology, the difference between CRJT and non-CRJT will be relatively small. (2) When the link distance is longer, the non-CRJT starts to decrease at 70 m, whereas the CRJT only decreases at 100 m because the JT adds 3 dB of power gain to the signal. This shows that the CRJT results in a 42.9% gain in the coverage distance of the AP.

Figure 7b shows the trend in the packet loss rate as the link distance increases. (1) When the link distance is short, the packet loss rates are very similar for the two schemes and both are low. This is because the SINRs of both schemes are relatively high. (2) When the link distance is long, similarly, if the distance is about 70 m, the non-CRJT packet loss increases sharply; however, at this time, the CRJT still maintains a low packet loss rate. The CRJT shows a significant increase in the packet loss rate until about 100 m. This is also because the JT provides protection for the STAs to successfully receive data packets.

### 4.2   Performance Trends for Different Data Rates

Figures 8a and 9a show the trend of the throughput for different data rates. In terms of the throughput, the CRJT and non-CRJT exhibit a similar trend in the throughput for the different data rates. The differences are as follows. (1) Fig. 8a shows that the maximum throughput achieved by the CRJT in the

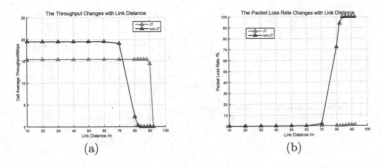

**Fig. 7.** Performance trends for different link distances

stationary phase is lower than that achieved by the non-CRJT (it is 92.1% of the non-CRJT). This is because the CRJT introduces a certain amount of reservation overhead. Similarly, under the frame aggregation technology, this gap will narrow. (2) For a very low throughput of the non-CRJT in Fig. 9a, the CRJT shows a throughput that is comparable to Fig. 8a. The CRJT has an approximately 7 times higher throughput than the non-CRJT in this topology. This is because in the scenario of topology 2, the link distance is very large. The non-CRJT can no longer guarantee the normal reception of the data packets, whereas the CRJT ensures the successful reception of data packets because of the power superposition. This shows that the CRJT can adapt more robustly to the change in the service rate of the AP and can provide several times the throughput of the non-CRJT in case of a long distance to the link.

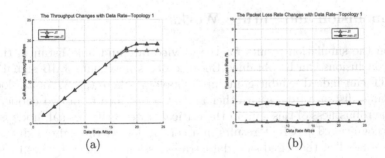

**Fig. 8.** Performance trends for different data rates (Topology 1)

Figures 8b and 9b show that the packet loss rate changes as the data rate increases. In both topologies, the packet loss rate is lower for the CRJT than the non-CRJT. Figure 8b shows that the packet loss rate of the CRJT is about 1.8% lower than that of the non-CRJT; Fig. 9b shows that the packet loss rate of the CRJT is about 72% lower than that of the non-CRJT. The simulation results indicate that the CRJT can exhibit greater gains with longer link distances.

 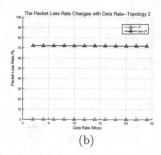

(a)                    (b)

**Fig. 9.** Performance trends for different data rates (Topology 2)

In summary, the CRJT significantly improves the QoS of the edge STAs.

## 5    Discussion

Based on the simulation results, it can be concluded that the MAC protocol based on the CRJT can play a significant role in the performance improvement of edge users in a high-density deployment environment. In the development of next-generation WLANs, if this protocol is used as a reference and a more appropriate protocol process is designed, the experience of edge users will be significantly improved [10,11]. Of course, this comes at the cost of an increase in the communication between APs, which will undoubtedly require higher data processing capabilities.

## 6    Conclusion and Future Works

Based on the simulation results for the service rate and link distance, the following conclusions can be obtained:Because of its maximum 3 dB signal gain, the CRJT can indeed exhibit gains in a topology where the STAs are located at the same distance from each other and at a distance from two cooperating APs. The robustness of this gain in the critical state of the normal mode is worthy of recognition.The CRJT results in a certain loss of throughput due to the added overhead of the wired-side data transmission and new frames.In future studies, the author will add simulation designs for more complex topologies, further observe the CRJT performance under non-specific topological structures, increase the number of APs, and discuss the strategies for screening the APs in order to further improve the protocol process.

**Acknowledgement.** This work was supported in part by the National Natural Science Foundations of CHINA (Grant No. 61771390, No. 61771392, No. 61501373, and No. 61271279), the National Science and Technology Major Project (Grant No. 2016ZX03001018-004, and No. 2015ZX03002006-004), and the Fundamental Research Funds for the Central Universities (Grant No. 3102017ZY018).

# References

1. Drieberg, M., Zheng, F.C., Ahmad, R., Olafsson, S.: An asynchronous distributed dynamic channel assignment scheme for dense wlans. In: International Conference on Information, Communications and Signal Processing, pp. 1–5 (2008)
2. Abinader, F.M., Almeida, E.P.L., Choudhury, S., Sousa, V.A.: Performance evaluation of IEEE 802.11n wlan in dense deployment scenarios. In: Vehicular Technology Conference, pp. 1–5 (2014)
3. Zhang, D., Mohanty, B., Sambhwani, S.D.: Scheduling based on effective target load with interference cancellation in a wireless communication system (2009)
4. Adachi, F., Kumagai, S.: Multi-ap cooperative diversity for disaster-resilient wireless lan. In: International Symposium on Wireless Personal Multimedia Communications, pp. 27–28 (2012)
5. Sirait, M.T.H., Matsumura, Y., Temma, K., Ishihara, K., Abeysekera, B.A.H.S., Kumagai, T., Adachi, F.: Ap cooperative diversity in wireless network using interference-aware channel segregation based dynamic channel assignment. In: IEEE International Symposium on Personal, Indoor, and Mobile Radio Communication, pp. 1185–1189 (2015)
6. Nishide, K., Kubo, H., Shinkuma, R., Takahashi, T.: Detecting hidden and exposed terminal problems in densely deployed wireless networks. IEEE Trans. Wirel. Commun. 11(11), 3841–3849 (2012)
7. Okamawari, T., Zhang, L., Nagate, A., Hayashi, H.: Design of control architecture for downlink comp joint transmission with inter-enb coordination in next generation cellular systems. In: Vehicular Technology Conference, pp. 1–5 (2011)
8. El-Sayed, H., Jaseemuddin, M., Kidwai, H., Lakas, A.: Simulation and analysis of an integrated gprs and wlan network. Int. J. Environ. Anal. Chem. 54(4), 299–314 (2005)
9. Ha, D.V.: Network simulation with ns3 (2010)
10. Bae, D., Kim, J., Park, S., Song, O.: Design and implementation of IEEE 802.11i architecture for next generation WLAN. In: Feng, D., Lin, D., Yung, M. (eds.) CISC 2005. LNCS, vol. 3822, pp. 346–357. Springer, Heidelberg (2005). https://doi.org/10.1007/11599548_30
11. Chan, Z.H.: Investigation of next generation ieee 802.11n wireless local area networks (wlan) (2009)

# Artificial Intelligence

# Deep Learning for Smartphone-Based Human Activity Recognition Using Multi-sensor Fusion

Charlene V. San Buenaventura, Nestor Michael C. Tiglao$^{(\boxtimes)}$,
and Rowel O. Atienza

Electrical and Electronics Engineering Institute, University of the Philippines,
Velasquez St. Diliman, 1101 Quezon City, Philippines
charlene.san_buenaventura@upd.edu.ph,
{nestor, rowel}@eee.upd.edu.ph

**Abstract.** In the field of ubiquitous computing, machines need to be aware of the present context to enable anticipatory communication with humans. This leads to human-centric applications that have the primary objective of improving the Quality-of-Life (QoL) of its users. One important type of context information for these applications is the current activity of the user, which can be derived from environmental and wearable sensors. Due to the processing capabilities and the number of sensors embedded in a smartphone, this device exhibits the most promise among other existing technologies in human activity recognition (HAR) research. While machine learning-based solutions have been successful in past HAR studies, several design struggles can be easily resolved with deep learning. In this paper, we investigated Convolutional Neural Networks and Long Short-Term Memory Networks in dealing with common challenges in smartphone-based HAR, such as device location and subject dependency, and manual feature extraction. We showed that the CNN model accomplished location- and subject-independent recognition with overall accuracy of 98.38% and 90.61%, respectively. The LSTM model also performed location-independent recognition with an accuracy of 97.17% but has a subject-independent recognition accuracy of only 80.02%. Finally, optimal performance of the network was achieved by performing Bayesian Optimization using Gaussian Processes in tuning the design hyperparameters.

**Keywords:** Deep learning · Human activity recognition · Sensor fusion
Hyperparameter optimization

## 1 Introduction

For any system that requires human-machine interaction (HMI), user and environmental context are necessary to enable machines to better serve humans and improve their quality of life. An important behavioral context for HMI is the current activity being performed by the user, which can be useful for anticipatory communications between machines and humans.

It is also becoming more essential to add some form of intelligence to systems that involve HMI. For human activity recognition (HAR), pattern recognition and machine learning strategies have been the most prevalent and widely implemented solutions.

© ICST Institute for Computer Sciences, Social Informatics and Telecommunications Engineering 2019
Published by Springer Nature Switzerland AG 2019. All Rights Reserved
J.-L. Chen et al. (Eds.): WiCON 2018, LNICST 264, pp. 65–75, 2019.
https://doi.org/10.1007/978-3-030-06158-6_7

Although classical machine learning strategies have made remarkable progress in the field of HAR, they require domain knowledge and thus prohibit generalization across multiple application domains. Furthermore, machine learning algorithms have inadequate capabilities in modelling input data dependencies and are limited to recognition of simple tasks.

Unlike traditional shallow learning based activity recognition, deep learning algorithms accomplish sensor fusion naturally and do not require combining multi-sensor signals prior to feeding it into the network. Moreover, features are automatically learned in a hierarchical manner to accurately perform recognition. One category of deep learning networks, called Convolutional Neural Network (CNN), has been shown to be more effective in classifying data that have inherent order in them, such as time series sensor data. Another type of deep learning, called Recurrent Neural Networks (RNN), is also commonly used for time series data since learning is done through time.

Although deep learning algorithms are generally better than shallow ones, their performance greatly depends on the hyperparameters set before training. Therefore, careful tuning of design hyperparameters is crucial in determining the success of these networks. While hyperparameters are usually set by the designer manually before training, finding the optimal hyperparameter settings can be done in a more automated manner that is based on the actual data to be processed.

In this study, we used CNN to model more complex dependencies in the raw sensor input and perform accurate activity recognition in smart phones. Moreover, since CNNs have been shown to capture local dependencies and extract scale-invariant features, this paper investigates the network's ability to perform subject and device location independent recognition. We also examined RNN in its capability to model the inter-temporal dependencies within time series data. Furthermore, the recognition performance, through the network's innate ability to automatically extract hierarchical features, was improved by leveraging on sensor fusion. Lastly, hyperparameter optimization was performed by employing Bayesian Optimization using Gaussian Processes.

The rest of the paper is structured as follows. Section 2 summarizes relevant work on human activity recognition in literature. Section 3 presents the methodology in building the system. In Sect. 4, experimental results are reported and analyzed to give further insights to the current HAR problem. Finally, conclusion is drawn in Sect. 5 along with recommendations and future work.

## 2 Human Activity Recognition

Human activity recognition (HAR) is defined as identifying the physical activity of a person at a desired instant. It obtains its significance in several applications such as healthcare, sports and fitness, and assisted living systems.

Action recognition has been used in assessing the physical well-being of an individual as well as monitoring the rehabilitation progress of patients, such as paraplegics. In previous studies, gait analysis was used to detect step frequency and assess individuals for diagnosis, prognosis and progress of their rehabilitation [1]. Activity recognition also finds its way in the domain of sports and fitness since some people, such as athletes, are required to perform a set of activities that should be strictly followed, to maintain a healthy body [2]. Similarly, obese people have to execute certain exercises and movements that would help in their calorie consumption [2]. Application of HAR in fitness is particularly relevant today since two-thirds of the world population is obese [3]. In all of these applications, further conclusions can be drawn for critical decision-making.

## 2.1 Ambient-Assisted Living (AAL)

It has been projected that 20% of the world population will belong to the senior citizen age group by the year 2050 [4], which opens up several challenges to the society. Since the elderly are more prone to diseases, this will cause a rapid increase in the diseases that our current healthcare systems can support. Due to shortage of caregivers and nursing homes, a huge majority of the elderly would still prefer to live independently in the comfort of their own homes. Hence, it is necessary to build systems and create services that assist this population while they age in place.

The general term that refers to concepts, products and services that have the goal of improving the quality-of-life (QoL) of individuals is ambient-assisted living (AAL). AAL systems usually employ intelligent technologies to assist individuals and ensure a better and a safer living environment. In AAL systems, monitoring the habitual physical activity is important for several reasons. By recording the daily activities of individuals, patterns and abnormalities in their behavior can be detected and aid into making inferences about their physical, mental and physiological well-being. Furthermore, by tracking their activities, a probabilistic model can be created to guide the intelligent system serving them.

## 2.2 State-of-the-Art in HAR

In this section, we discuss existing technologies used in HAR based on the platform used to gather data and infer human activity.

### Vision-Based HAR

Vision-based systems have long been used in recognizing human activities and analyzing motion in general since they provide accurate characterization of the entire body [5, 6]. However, ideal results can only be obtained in controlled environments since video-based systems tend to suffer from problems such as data-association for multiple subjects. In addition, these systems are generally not immune to varying ambient conditions [6] and are computationally expensive due to the large amount of data being processed. Cameras also have limited fields of view, thus requiring installation of multiple cameras within an area. In most cases, the use of cameras is not practical in many environments because of their intrusiveness.

### Sensor-Based HAR

In human activity recognition, human action can be inferred from a single sensor or from a set of sensors. Many HAR studies utilize sensor measurements from several locations on the body. However, most of these systems require the sensors to be attached firmly. Thus, wearing a network of sensors can be obtrusive and limits their real-world practicability.

There are also several attempts in using a single sensor for recognition and most of them make use of one tri-axial accelerometer. Accelerometers are widely used in motion sensing because of their low-power requirement and non-intrusiveness [7]. However, the classification performance is lower compared to when using multiple sensors. The most commonly used mobile sensors in HAR literature are accelerometers, gyroscopes, and magnetometers [7].

### Smartphone-Based HAR

The smartphone is the latest technology that is being utilized for activity recognition due to its widespread use across various groups of people. Since smartphones are more integrated than other existing technologies in HAR, they can gain more acceptance due to their pervasiveness and non-intrusiveness. Hence, smartphones can be used as a cost-effective tool in pervasive healthcare to cut down healthcare costs due to the increasing population of the elderly [8].

Although HAR has been an active field of research over the past decade, very few works have successfully been deployed in mobile phones. There are still several challenges in designing a smartphone-based HAR system [9]. Two common challenges encountered in mobile-HAR are the variations in which smartphones can be positioned on the body as well as inherent diversity among humans. In previous studies, HAR models are usually only valid for a specific smartphone orientation and location. Since smartphones can be placed on different locations on the body at random placement orientations, these models are not valid in real-life scenarios. Thus, this warrants a learning algorithm that is independent of these variations. Furthermore, the manner in which different activities are performed varies from human-to-human. In most studies, the model is trained by the subject's own data, resulting to a subject-dependent prediction. However, it is sometimes inconvenient to retrain the system for each new user since collection of data can become difficult or nearly impossible in some scenarios. For example, a large volume of activities may need to be recognized, activities may be difficult to be simulated by the user, or subjects could be suffering from different medical conditions.

## 3 Deep Learning for Smartphone-Based HAR

In this study, the deep learning models used for classifying human activities based on sensor data from smartphones are Convolutional Neural Networks (CNN), and Long Short-Term Memory (LSTM) Networks which is a class of Recurrent Neural Networks (RNN). CNN is popular for time-series data or any data that has an underlying local dependency among its samples [10]. Likewise, LSTM is also capable of modelling the inherent dependencies in a time series data. Both models have the ability to automatically extract features from the raw data [10] which are more representative of the true nature of the input data. Unlike hand-engineered features, these features are better at discriminating between classes, since they are based on the data itself. For CNN, higher level features and hierarchical representations of the input are formed as you go deeper into the network.

## 3.1 Convolutional Neural Network

For convolutional neural networks, weights are shared across the input of each layer. A filter of weights is applied on a portion of the input and is replicated across the entire input space. This process is called convolution. The convolution process searches the occurrence of a certain feature associated with one filter in the input and outputs it into a feature map. One layer can output multiple feature maps that represent the presence of different features. The output of a convolutional layer is

$$x_i^{l,j} = \sigma\left(b_j + \sum_{a=1}^{m} w_a^j x_{i+a-1}^{l-1,j}\right) \tag{1}$$

where $x_i^{l,j}$ is the output at the $l$th and $j$th feature map. The non-linear mapping $\sigma$ is usually a ReLu function which is element-wise rectification.

After the convolutional and ReLu layers, a statistical vote is carried out over local regions in the input feature maps. We used max pooling as the statistical tool in this study. To perform max-pooling on top of a convolutional layer, the maximum value in a certain partition is obtained for all partitions of the convolved input. This operation gives rise to scale-invariant features of the input which is useful in recognizing activities that can be performed with varying intensities. The output of one max-pooling layer is given by

$$x_i^{l,j} = \max_{k=1}^{r}\left(x_{(i-1)\times s+k}^{l-1,j}\right) \tag{2}$$

Several stacks of these convolutional, ReLu and max-pooling layers in different permutations can be constructed depending on the application. Next, the output of the last layer will be flattened and fed into dense layers or fully-connected layers, similar to regular deep neural networks. Finally, the output layer is a softmax layer that will perform the final classification.

## 3.2 Long-Short Term Memory

Long-Short Term Memory (LSTM) is a recurrent neural network that allows us to model the temporal dynamics of the input signal more effectively since it addresses the problem of vanishing gradients. The problem of vanishing gradients arises when the output error is back propagated through several time steps. Updating the training parameters through each time step involves multiplying all the gradients. Hence, if the gradients are very small, the total product will be almost zero, and this will correspond to a zero improvement in the weights. Therefore, no learning takes place.

To regulate the problem of vanishing gradients, extra interactions are added. An LSTM cell has four main components namely, an input gate, a forget gate, an output gate and an intermediate cell state. The equations for these four components are

$$f_t = \sigma(W_f S_{t-1} + W_f X_t) \tag{3}$$

$$i_t = \sigma(W_i S_{t-1} + W_i X_t) \tag{4}$$

$$o_t = \sigma(W_o S_{t-1} + W_o X_t) \tag{5}$$

$$C_t = tanh(W_c S_{t-1} + W_c X_t) \tag{6}$$

Each of these gates is sum of old the state and the current input, each multiplied with their respective weights, and are passed to a sigmoid activation function. This allows us to control how far back in the past we want to recall. The intermediate cell state is obtained in a similar manner, but using *tanh* for the activation function.

The current cell state is computed as the sum of intermediate cell state times the input gate and the previous cell state times the forget gate. The new state will be the *tanh* of the cell state multiplied by the output gate.

$$c_t = (i_t * C_t) + (f_t * c_{t-1}) \tag{7}$$

$$h_t = o_t * tanh(c_t) \tag{8}$$

## 3.3  Bayesian Optimization Using GP

Bayesian optimization is a type of a sequential model-based optimization (SMBO) algorithm that uses previous observations of the loss function $f$ in determining the next point in the hyperparameter space to sample $f$ for. It relies on sequentially building a model for $f$ for varying hyperparameter sets, by using smooth functions called Gaussian processes. This allows us to predict the expected performance of the network for a certain set, as well as the uncertainty of the prediction.

The posterior distribution of $f$ is updated for every observed value of $f(x)$ corresponding to a hyperparameter set x that maximizes an acquisition function until desired convergence is reached. The most common acquisition function found in literature is the expected improvement (EI) which is defined as

$$EI(\mathrm{x}) = E[\max\{0, f(\mathrm{x}) - f(\hat{x})\}] \tag{9}$$

where $\hat{x}$ is the current optimal hyperparameter set. Maximizing this function gives us the set that improves $f$ the most.

We can compute the expected improvement for the GP model by using integration by parts

$$EI(\mathrm{x}) = \begin{cases} (\mu(\mathrm{x}) - f(\hat{x}))\Phi(z) + \sigma(\mathrm{x})\Phi(z), & \sigma(\mathrm{x}) > 0 \\ 0, & \sigma(\mathrm{x}) = 0 \end{cases} \tag{10}$$

$$z = \frac{\mu(\mathrm{x}) - f(\hat{x})}{\sigma(\mathrm{x})}$$

where $\mu(\mathrm{x})$ is the expected value of $f$, while $\Phi(z)$ and $\Phi(z)$ are the cumulative distribution and probability density function of the standard normal distribution, respectively.

From this closed form solution, we see that the EI is high when the expected value of the loss, $\mu(x)$, is greater than the current best value $f(\hat{x})$. Likewise, EI is high when the uncertainty $\sigma(x)$ is high around x. Hence, by maximizing EI, we get the points that gives a higher value of $f$ as well as points in the region of the hyperparameter space that were not explored yet. This allows us to build the model for hyperpameter performance more efficiently.

## 4 Simulation Results

### 4.1 Dataset

Sensor Activity Dataset [11] is a publicly available dataset which consisted of accelerometer, gyroscope, and magnetometer readings by five Samsung Galaxy SII (i9100) from ten participants, while performing seven ambulatory activities. The participants performed walking, sitting, standing, jogging, biking, walking upstairs and walking downstairs for 3–4 min, while the smartphones are placed in five on-body locations namely, belt, left trousers pocket, right trousers pocket, upper arm and wrist.

Data was collected at a sampling rate of 50 Hz, which was observed to be sufficient in recognizing physical activities in the past [12]. The sensor stream was segmented by a sliding time window of 2 s with 50% overlap. The choice of both the time window length and the amount of overlap has been shown to be effective in physical activity recognition [12].

### 4.2 Location-Independent Prediction

Table 1 shows the summary of the recognition performance of CNN for different smartphone locations, as well as the overall performance. It can be seen that the best-performing smartphone location is the left pocket location with an accuracy of 98.78%. The overall performance for all locations is 97.37%. Similarly, Table 2 shows the summary of the recognition rates of the LSTM model. It can be observed that both left and right pockets gave the most accurate predictions having recognition rates of 98.38% and 97.49%, respectively. In this case, the recorded per-location results of both

**Table 1.** Classification rates for each location using CNN

|          | Belt   | Left pocket | Right pocket | Upper arm | Wrist  | Overall |
|----------|--------|-------------|--------------|-----------|--------|---------|
| Accuracy | 97.01% | 99.07%      | 97.89%       | 96.88%    | 96.27% | 97.37%  |

models listed in Tables 1, 2 tell us that ambulatory motion is best captured when sensor data is collected from the trousers pocket of the subject.

### 4.3 Subject-Independent Prediction

In this section, we test the generalization ability of the models using the leave-one-subject-out validation. Using CNN, Table 3 lists the test accuracy for each subject,

**Table 2.** Classification rates for each location using LSTM

|          | Belt   | Left pocket | Right pocket | Upper arm | Wrist  | Overall |
|----------|--------|-------------|--------------|-----------|--------|---------|
| Accuracy | 96.51% | 98.38%      | 97.49%       | 96.03%    | 95.17% | 97.17%  |

**Table 3.** Leave-one-subject-out classification rates using CNN

| Test subject | Classification rate |
|--------------|---------------------|
| Subject 1    | 85.49%              |
| Subject 2    | 93.33%              |
| Subject 3    | 90.73%              |
| Subject 4    | 91.04%              |
| Subject 5    | 92.44%              |
| Overall      | 90.61%              |

when the model is trained with the data, from while the remaining subjects. The overall accuracy of 90.61% is the average of the five classification rates for each of the five test subjects, verifying the subject-independent recognition ability of CNN.

On the other hand, it can be seen from Table 4 that LSTM has significantly lower classification rates for the leave-one-subject-out recognition compared to CNN. Hence, it is less capable of providing subject-independent recognition. This is due to the fact that CNN has convolutional and max-pooling layers that inherently extract scale- and

**Table 4.** Leave-one-subject-out classification rates using LSTM

| Test subject | Classification rate |
|--------------|---------------------|
| Subject 1    | 77.07%              |
| Subject 2    | 80.88%              |
| Subject 3    | 83.04%              |
| Subject 4    | 81.10%              |
| Subject 5    | 78.02%              |
| Overall      | 80.02%              |

shift-invariant features, while LSTM is only concerned with the temporal dependencies in the data. Both models were only trained for eight epochs, and the performance can still improve by training the models further.

### 4.4   Hyperparameter Optimization

In this study, we use *gp_minimize* from the Scikit-Optimize, or skopt, library, which is an implementation of Bayesian Optimization using Gaussian Processes.

The network is first evaluated at an initial set of hyperparameters, with 1000 hidden neurons, 2 hidden layers, and $1 \times 10^{-3}$ learning rate. The network is then updated and evaluated on each of the hyperparameter setting at each call. The valid range of the

**Table 5.** List of valid ranges of hyperparameters to search in during optimization

|  | Lower bound | Upper bound |
|---|---|---|
| No. of hidden neurons | 10 | 1000 |
| No. of hidden layers | 1 | 5 |
| Learning rate | 1.00E-06 | 1.00E-02 |

**Table 6.** Summary of validation accuracy during hyperparameter optimization

| No. of hidden neurons | No. of hidden layers | Learning rate | Validation accuracy |
|---|---|---|---|
| 559 | 5 | 5.70E-04 | 0.9886 |
| 1000 | 5 | 7.60E-04 | 0.9857 |
| 1000 | 1 | 1.70E-04 | 0.9839 |
| 1000 | 5 | 5.13E-05 | 0.9839 |
| 1000 | 5 | 1.30E-04 | 0.9838 |
| 1000 | 1 | 3.73E-05 | 0.982 |
| 425 | 2 | 3.10E-04 | 0.981 |
| 1000 | 1 | 2.30E-05 | 0.981 |
| 1000 | 5 | 1.60E-04 | 0.981 |
| 24 | 4 | 8.20E-04 | 0.9801 |

three hyperparameters that were considered are listed in Table 5. The hyperparameter setting that gave the highest validation accuracy of 98.86% is a network of 559 hidden neurons, 5 hidden layers and learns at a rate of $5.7 \times 10^{-4}$. Table 6 shows the summary for different calls during optimization while exploring the hyperparameter space, listing the top ten optimal hyperparameter settings. By plotting the results in a table, trends in the data will be more apparent, for which Gaussian processes are satisfactorily used.

## 5 Conclusion and Future Work

Smartphones can be an unobtrusive means of gaining contextual information from the user. In this study, Convolutional Neural Networks and Long-Short Term Memory Networks were examined in classifying activities of daily living (ADL) from three smartphone sensor signals.

Using CNN, we were able to achieve location- and subject-independent recognition which can be attributed to the presence of the convolutional and max-pooling layers in the network. The CNN model achieved an overall accuracy of 98.38% and 90.61% for location- and subject-independent recognition, respectively. For the LSTM model, we were able to achieve a location-independent recognition accuracy of 97.17%, which is slightly lower than that obtained with CNN. However, the overall accuracy of LSTM for the subject-independent recognition using the leave-one-subject-out training is 80.02%, which proves that LSTM is generally less capable of generalizing to different subjects compared to CNN. Finally, we investigated the application of Bayesian Optimization Using Gaussian Processes in finding the optimal or near-optimal hyperparameter values.

In the future, we wish to recognize higher level activities, as well as composite ones, to challenge the classification ability of deep learning models. Furthermore, computational and resource expenditures during training and testing can also be considered, and different regularization methods can be explored.

**Acknowledgement.** The authors acknowledge the financial support of the University of the Philippines and Department of Science and Technology through the Engineering for Research and Development for Technology (ERDT) Program.

# References

1. Zhang, Y., Markovic, S., Sapir, I., Wagenaar, R.C., Little, T.D.: Continuous functional activity monitoring based on wearable tri-axial accelerometer and gyroscope. In: 2011 5th International Conference on Pervasive Computing Technologies for Healthcare and Workshops, Pervasive Health 2011, pp. 370–373 (2011). https://doi.org/10.4108/icst. pervasivehealth.2011.245966
2. Yamansavascilar, B., Amac Guvensan, M.: Activity recognition on smartphones: efficient sampling rates and window sizes, 1–6 (2016). https://doi.org/10.1109/percomw.2016. 7457154
3. Altini, M., Penders, J., Amft, O.: Energy expenditure estimation using wearable sensors: a new methodology for activity-specific models. In: Proceedings—Wireless Health 2012, WH 2012 (2012). https://doi.org/10.1145/2448096.2448097
4. Rashidi, P., Mihailidis, A.: A survey for ambient-assisted living tools for older adults. IEEE J. Biomed. Health Inform. **17**(3) (2013)
5. Khan, A.M., Tufail, A., Khattak, A.M., Laine, T.H.: Activity recognition on smartphones via sensor-fusion and KDA-based SVMs. Int. J. Distrib. Sens. Netw. 1–14 (2014). https://doi. org/10.1155/2014/503291
6. Zhu, C., Sheng, W.: Multi-sensor fusion for human daily activity recognition in robot-assisted living. In: Proceedings of the 4th ACM/IEEE International Conference on Human Robot Interaction—HRI 2009 (2009). https://doi.org/10.1145/1514095.1514187
7. San Buenaventura, C., Tiglao, N.: Basic human activity recognition based on sensor fusion in smartphones. In: IFIP/IEEE IM 2017 Workshop: 1st Workshop on Protocols, Applications and Platforms for Enhanced Living Environments (2017)
8. Vavoulas, G., Pediaditis, M., Chatzaki, C., Spanakis, E., Tsiknakis, M.: The mobifall dataset: fall detection and classification with a smartphone. Int. J. Monit. Surveill. Technol. Res. **2**, 44–56 (2016). https://doi.org/10.4018/ijmstr.2014010103
9. Pires, I., Garcia, N., Pombo, N., Flórez-Revuelta, F.: From data acquisition to data fusion: a comprehensive review and a roadmap for the identification of activities of daily living using mobile devices. Sensors **16**(2), 184 (2016). https://doi.org/10.3390/s16020184
10. Zebin, T., Scully, P.J., Ozanyan, K.B.: Human activity recognition with inertial sensors using a deep learning approach. In: 2016 IEEE Sensors (2016). https://doi.org/10.1109/ icsens.2016.7808590
11. Shoaib, M., Bosch, S., Incel, O., Scholten, H., Havinga, P.: Fusion of smartphone motion sensors for physical activity recognition. Sensors **14**(6), 10146–10176 (2014). https://doi. org/10.3390/s140610146

12. Wen, J., Loke, S., Indulska, J., Zhong, M.: Sensor-based activity recognition with dynamically added context. In: Mihaela, U., Valeriy, V. (eds) 12th EAI International Conference on Mobile and Ubiquitous Systems: Computing, Networking and Services MOBIQUITOUS 2015. International Conference on Mobile and Ubiquitous Systems: Computing, Networking and Services, pp. e4.1–e4.10, Coimbra, Portugal, 22–24 July 2015 (2015). https://doi.org/10.4108/eai.22-7-2015.2260164

# An Efficient MapReduce-Based Apriori-Like Algorithm for Mining Frequent Itemsets from Big Data

Ching-Ming Chao[1], Po-Zung Chen[2], Shih-Yang Yang[3(✉)], and Cheng-Hung Yen[1]

[1] Department of Computer Science and Information Management, Soochow University, Taipei 100, Taiwan
[2] Department of Computer Science and Information Engineering, Tamkang University, Taipei, Taiwan
[3] Department of Media Art and Management of Information System, University of Kang Ning, Taipei, Taiwan
shihyang@ukn.edu.tw

**Abstract.** Data mining can discover valuable information from large amounts of data so as to utilize this information to enhance personal or organizational competitiveness. Apriori is a classic algorithm for mining frequent itemsets. Recently, with rapid growth of the Internet as well as fast development of information and communications technology, the amount of data is augmented in an explosive fashion at a speed of tens of petabytes per day. These rapidly expensive data are characterized by huge amount, high speed, continuous arrival, real-time, and unpredictability. Traditional data mining algorithms are not applicable. Therefore, big data mining has become an important research issue.

Clouding computing is a key technique for big data. In this paper, we study the issue of applying cloud computing to mining frequent itemsets from big data. We propose a MapReduce-based Apriori-like frequent itemset mining algorithm called Apriori-MapReduce (abbreviated as AMR). The salient feature of AMR is that it deletes the items of itemsets lower than the minimum support from the transaction database. In such a way, it can greatly reduce the generation of candidate itemsets to avoid a memory shortage and an overload to I/O and CPU, so that a better mining efficiency can be achieved. Empirical studies show that the processing efficiency of the AMR algorithm is superior to that of another efficient MapReduce-based Apriori algorithm under various minimum supports and numbers of transactions.

**Keywords:** Data mining · Frequent itemsets · Big data · MapReduce Apriori

## 1 Introduction

Currently in the age of information explosion, data are used in various aspects of one's daily life. However, the speed of data generation and storage has far exceeded that of analysis and digestion people could achieve. Therefore, it is an important issue of how

J.-L. Chen et al. (Eds.): WiCON 2018, LNICST 264, pp. 76–85, 2019.
https://doi.org/10.1007/978-3-030-06158-6_8

to use information technology to analyze large amounts of data to discover and apply valuable information in order to enhance personal or organizational competitiveness. Data mining comes into the play. One of the important problems in data mining is discovering frequent itemsets from a set of transactions where each transaction contains a set of items [1]. A frequent itemset is a set of items that frequently occur together in a set of transactions. Apriori is a classic algorithm for mining frequent itemsets [2].

With rapid growth of the Internet as well as fast development of information and communications technology, such as the emergence of Web 3.0, the amount of data is augmented in an explosive fashion at a speed of tens of petabytes (1 PB = 1024 TB) per day. The global big data research report published by McKinsey Global Institute in May 2011 indicated that global enterprise data had increased 7 exabytes (1 EB = 1024 PB) while the new data consumers stored in their personal computers (including notebooks) and mobile devises had exceeded 6 exabytes in 2010 alone [3]. According to statistics by International Data Center, the information capacity of digital world will grow from 0.8 zettabytes (1 ZB = 1024 EB) in 2009 to 44 zettabytes in 2020, i.e. a growth of 1 PB in every 15 s and an annual compound growth rate up to 40% [4]. These rapidly expansive data are characterized by huge amount, high speed, continuous arrival, real-time, and unpredictability, which suggest that manual analysis methods and conventional data mining algorithms are no longer applicable [2, 5–7]. Therefore, big data mining has become an important research issue.

The emergence of big data, the pervasion of networks, and the rapid development of personal computers, servers, and mobile devices all together have called for the needs of applying cloud computing to big data mining. It is a great challenge to properly distribute and manage resources, effectively analyze data to discover interesting patterns, and promptly respond to the user. Applying cloud computing to big data mining can have many practical applications. For example, it can be used in medical treatment to analyze examined items (blood, urine, X-ray, magnetic resonance imaging, etc.) and medicine prescriptions, as instructional materials of examined items and medicine prescriptions to a specific disease for interns [8]. The network management personnel may rapidly analyze to reveal user behavior and abnormal flow through monitoring the cloud network flow to insure the quality of networks as well as to find out the primary reasons for internet instability from analyzed results to insure the stable and smooth operation of networks [9].

Clouding computing is a key technique for big data. In this paper, therefore, we study the issue of applying cloud computing to mining frequent itemsets from big data. We proposed MapReduce-based Apriori-like frequent itemset mining algorithm called Apriori-MapReduce (AMR). The salient feature of AMR is that it deletes the items of itemsets lower than the minimum support from the transaction database. In such a way, it can greatly reduce the generation of candidate itemsets to avoid a memory shortage and an overload to I/O and CPU, so that a better mining efficiency can be achieved. Empirical studies show that the processing efficiency of the AMR algorithm is superior to that of another efficient MapReduce-based Apriori algorithm under various minimum supports and numbers of transactions.

## 2   AMR Algorithm

The AMR algorithm is an improvement of the Apriori algorithm [1]. It overcomes the drawback of generating too many candidate itemsets of the traditional Apriori algorithm by deleting the items of itemsets lower than the minimum support from the transaction database each time after generating frequent itemsets of a certain length. It is safe to do so because any itemsets generated by adding more items to itemsets lower than the minimum support cannot be frequent.

The basic approach of the AMR algorithm is generally the same as that of the traditional Apriori algorithm. The difference is that AMR uses MapReduce to distribute transaction data to multiple Map nodes that separately find candidate itemsets and combine the candidate itemsets returned from these nodes to generate frequent itemsets. Then, the items of itemsets lower than the minimum support are deleted from the transaction database. If the transaction database is empty or no frequent itemsets can be generated, the algorithm stops execution.

### 2.1   Details of Algorithm

Figure 1 shows the AMR Algorithm proposed in this paper. Input a transaction database and a prespecified minimum support, the AMR Algorithm will output all of the frequent itemsets in the transaction database.

```
Algorithm:  Apriori-MapReduce (AMR)
Input:
■    D, a transaction database;
■    min_sup, the prespecified minimum support
Output: L, frequent itemsets in D.
Method:
   k=0;
   repeat {
(1)k++;
   //Map-function:
(2) uniformly distribute transactions in D to each Map node m;
(3) C_mk = {candidate itemsets of length k at node m};
   // Reduce-function:
   // compute C_k with all C_mk
(4) C_k = {candidate itemsets of length k};
   // remove itemsets with support < min_sup from C_k
(5) L_k = {frequent itemsets of length k};
(6) remove items of itemsets with support < min_sup from D;
(7)} until (D == φ) or (L_k == φ)
   return L = ∪_k L_k;
```

**Fig. 1.**  AMR algorithm

Definitions of parameters in the algorithm are as follows:

k: length of an itemset

m: Map node

Cmk: candidate itemsets of length k generated by the Map node m

Ck: candidate itemsets of length k

Lk: frequent itemsets of length k

Steps of the algorithm are described as follows:

(1) Start with itemsets of length 1.
(2) Uniformly distribute transactions in the transaction database to each Map node.
(3) Separately compute candidate itemsets of length k in the transactions of each node Cmk.
(4) Combine candidate itemsets generated by each node to generate candidate itemsets of length k Ck.
(5) Eliminate candidate itemsets lower than the minimum support from Ck to generate frequent itemsets of length k Lk.
(6) Delete the items of itemsets lower than the minimum support from the transaction data-base.
(7) If there are no transactions in the transactions database or no frequent itemsets in Lk, terminate the execution the algorithm; otherwise, increase the length of itemsets by 1 and repeat steps 2 to 6.

## 2.2   Example

Table 1 shows a transaction database consisting of 10 transactions. Suppose the minimum support is 3 and there are 3 Map nodes

**Table 1.** Transaction database

| TID  | List of items |
|------|---------------|
| T001 | cookies, cola, pizza |
| T002 | milk, coffee, bread |
| T003 | cookies, bread |
| T004 | bread, milk, coffee |
| T005 | cookies, bread, milk |
| T006 | coffee, cookies, cola |
| T007 | pizza, cola, beer |
| T008 | cookies, coffee, cola |
| T009 | beer, milk, |
| T010 | cookies, milk, bread |

First, start with itemsets of length 1. Uniformly distribute the 10 transactions in the transaction database to 3 Map nodes, so that Map1 has transactions T001, T002, T003, and T004, Map2 has T005, T006, and T007, and Map3 has T008, T009, and T010. Each node separately computes candidate itemsets of length 1 Cm1.

C11 = {<bread, 3>, <coffee, 2>, <cola, 1>, <cookies, 2>, <milk, 2>, <pizza, 1>}

C21 = {<beer, 1>, <bread, 1>, <coffee, 1>, <cola, 2>, <cookies, 2>, <milk, 1>, <pizza, 1>}

C31 = {<beer, 1>, <bread, 1>, <coffee, 1>, <cola, 1>, <cookies, 2>, <milk, 2>}

Combine C11, C21, and C31 to generate candidate itemsets of length 1 C1

C1 = {<beer, 2>, <bread, 5>, <coffee, 4>, <cola, 4>, <cookies, 6>, <milk, 5>, <pizza, 2>}

Eliminate candidate itemsets lower than the minimum support from C1 to generate frequent itemsets of length 1 L1

L1 = {<bread, 5>, <coffee, 4>, <cola, 4>, <cookies, 6>, <milk, 5>}

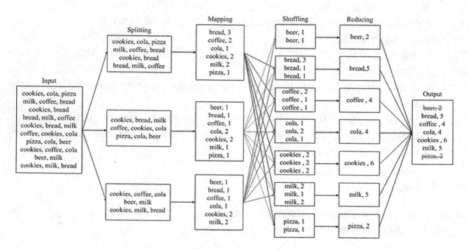

**Fig. 2.** Generating frequent itemsets of length 1

Figure 2 shows the process of generating frequent itemsets of length 1.

Delete the items in $C_1$ that are lower than the minimum support from the transaction database. Since there are transactions in the transaction database and frequent itemsets in $L_1$, increasethe length of itemsets by 1 to become 2. Uniformly distribute the 10 transactions in the transaction database to 3 Map nodes, so that Map1 has transactions T001, T002, T003, and T004, Map2 has T005, T006, and T007, and Map3 has T008, T009, and T010. Each node separately computes candidate itemsets of length 2 $C_{m2}$.

$C_{12}$ = {<{bread, coffee}, 2>, <{bread, cookies}, 1>, <{bread, milk}, 2>, <{coffee, milk}, 2>, <{cola, cookies}, 1>}

$C_{22}$ = {<{bread, cookies}, 1>, <{bread, milk}, 1>, <{coffee, cola}, 1>, <{coffee, cookies}, 1>, <{cola, cookie}, 1>, <{cookies, milk}, 1>}

$C_{32}$ = {<{bread, cookies}, 1>, <{bread, milk}, 1>, <{coffee, cola}, 1>, <{coffee, cookies}, 1>, <{cola, cookie}, 1>, <{cookies, milk}, 1>}

Combine $C_{12}$, $C_{22}$, and $C_{32}$ to generate candidate itemsets of length 2 $C_2$.

$C_2$ = {<{bread, coffee}, 2>, <{bread, cookies}, 3>, <{bread, milk}, 4>,<{coffee, cola}, 2>, <{coffee, cookies}, 2>, <{coffee, milk}, 2>, <{cola, cookies}, 3>, <{cookies, milk}, 2>}

Eliminatecandidate itemsets lower than the minimum support from $C_2$ to generate frequent itemsets of length 2 $L_2$.

$L_2 = \{<\{bread, cookies\}, 3>, <\{bread, milk\}, 4>, <\{cola, cookies\}, 3>\}$

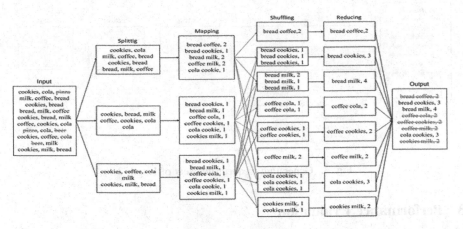

**Fig. 3.** Generating frequent itemsets of length 2

Figure 3 shows the process of generating frequent itemsets of length 2.

Delete the itemsof itemsets in $C_2$ that are lower than the minimum support from the transaction database. Since there are transactions in the transaction database and frequent itemsets in $L_2$, increasethe length of itemsets by 1 to become 3. Uniformly distribute the 10 transactions in the transaction database to 3 Map nodes, so that Map1 has transactions T001, T002, T003, and T004, Map2 has T005, T006, and T007, and Map3 has T008, T009, and T010. Each node separately computes candidate itemsets of length 3 $C_{m3}$.

$C_{13} = \{\}$

$C_{23} = \{\}$

$C_{33} = \{\}$

Combine $C_{13}$, $C_{23}$, and $C_{33}$ to generate candidate itemsets of length 3 $C_3$.

$C_3 = \{\}$

Eliminatecandidate itemsets lower than the minimum support from $C_3$ to generate frequent itemsets of length 3 $L_3$.

$L_3 = \{\}$

Figure 4 shows the process of generating frequent itemsets of length 3.

Since there is no frequent itemset in L3, terminate the execution the algorithm. Finally, by using the AMR algorithm, the frequent itemsets generated from the transaction database in Table 1 are as follows:

$L = L1 \cup L2 \cup L3 = \{<bread, 5>, <coffee, 4>, <cola, 4>, <cookies, 6>, <milk, 5>,$
$<\{bread, cookies\}, 3>, <\{bread, milk\}, 4>, <\{cola, cookies\},$
$3>\}$

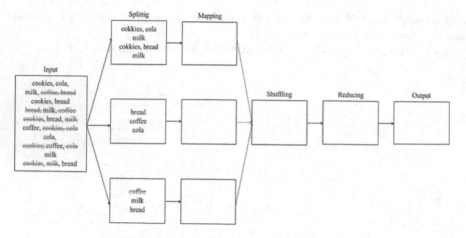

**Fig. 4.** Generating frequent itemsets of length 3

# 3  Performance Evaluation

## 3.1  Experiment Environment and Data

The experiment environment uses two HP servers to generate eight virtual computers for performance test. One of the virtual computers serves as Master and the remaining seven virtual computers as Slaves. Each virtual computer is equipped with one CPU (2 thread) and 2 GB memory. The development tool Eclipse is used to write programs.

We use the 2013 whole year meteorological data at Taipei, Danshui, Keelung, and Branchial from Central Weather Bureau as the realdataset for experiments.It consists of 52600 data records and each data record includes atmospheric pressure, air temperature, dew point temperature, relative moisture, average wind speed, maximum average wind speed, and maximum instantaneous wind speed. In addition, we use IBM Quest Synthetic Data Generator to generatesynthetic datasets. A synthetic dataset has three parameters, of which T denotes the number of transactions, L denotes the average length of transactions, and N denotes the number of different kinds of items. For example, T1000KL5N0.5 K denotes that this synthetic dataset consists of one million transactions, the average length of transactions is 5, and there are 500 different kinds of items.

## 3.2  Comparison and Analysis

Because both Apriori-Map/Reduce and AMRare MapReduce-based Apriori-like algorithms for mining frequent itemsets, we compare and analyze these two algorithms with respect to their processing efficiency under various minimum supports and numbers of transactions, respectively.

**Processing efficiency under various minimum supports.** Figures 5 and 6 show the comparison of processing efficiency between AMR and Apriori-Map/Reduce under various minimum supports, where the X-axis is the minimum support (%) and the Y-axis is the execution time in seconds. The experiment data for Fig. 5 is a synthetic database T1000KL6N0.5 K. The experiment data for Fig. 6 is taken from the real dataset with 52000 data records and of data length 7. As shown in Figs. 5 and 6, the processing efficiency of AMR is superior to that of Apriori-Map/Reduce under various minimum supports. It is because that AMR deletes the items of itemsets lower than the mini-mum support from the transaction database, which can greatly reduce the generation of candidate itemsets so as to reduce database scanning time.

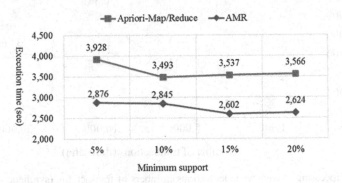

**Fig. 5.** Processing efficiency under various minimum supports (synthetic dataset)

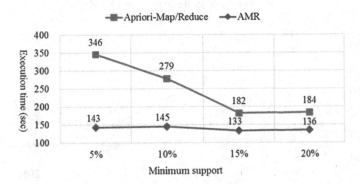

**Fig. 6.** Processing efficiency under various minimum supports (real dataset)

**Processing efficiency under various numbers of transactions.** Figures 7 and 8 show the comparison of processing efficiency between AMR and Apriori-Map/Reduce under various numbers of transactions, where the X-axis is the number of transactions in thousands and the Y-axis is the execution time in seconds. The experiment data for Fig. 7 are four synthetic datasets T1000KL8N0.5 K, T5000KL8N0.5 K, T10000 K L8N0.5 K and T20000KL8N0.5 K. The experiment data for Fig. 8 are four datasets taken from the real dataset with 5000, 10000, 25000, and 52000 data records, respectively, and a data length 7. As shown in Figs. 7 and 8, the processing efficiency of AMR is superior to that of Apriori-Map/Reduce under various numbers of transactions, and the difference becomes more prominent as the number of transactions gets larger. It is because that AMR deletes the items of itemsets lower than the minimum support from the transaction database, which can greatly reduce the generation of candidate itemsets so as to reduce database scanning time.

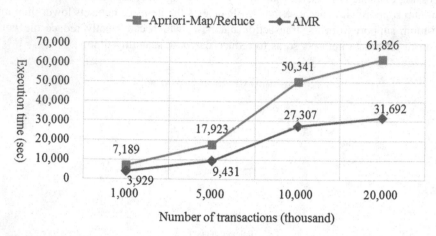

**Fig. 7.** Processing efficiency under various numbers of transactions (synthetic dataset)

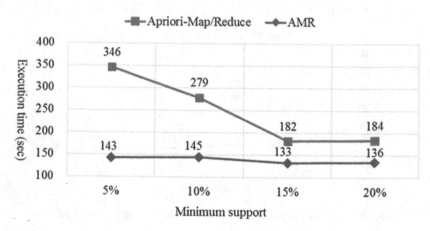

**Fig. 8.** Processing efficiency under various numbers of transactions (real dataset)

## 4    Conclusion

In this paper, we have proposed the AMR algorithm that applies cloud computing to big data mining. It can efficiently mine big data under the framework of MapReduce. AMR differs from Apriori-Map/Reduce in that, after the generation of frequent itemsets, it deletes the items of itemsets lower than the minimum support from the transaction database to avoid a memory shortage and an overload to I/O and CPU, so that a better mining efficiency can be achieved. Empirical studies show that the processing efficiency of the AMR algorithm is superior to that of the Apriori-Map/Reduce algorithm under various minimum supports and numbers of transactions.

# References

1. Agarwal R., Srikant, R.: Fast algorithms for mining association rules in large database. In: Proceedings of the 20th International Conference on Very Large Data Bases, pp. 487–499, Santiago de Chile (1994)
2. Babcock, B., Babu, S., Datar, M., Motwani, R., Widom, J.: Models and issues in data stream systems. In: Proceedings of the 21st ACM SIGMOD-SIGACT-AIGART Symposium on Principles of Database Systems, pp. 1–16, Madison, WI, June 2002
3. Manyika, J., Chui, M., Brown, B., Bughin, J., Dobbs, R., Roxburgh, C., Byers, A.H.: Big data: the next frontier for innovation, competition, and productivity. McKinsey Global Institute, New York (2011)
4. Turner, V., Gantz, J.F., Reinsel, D., Minton, S.: The digital universe of opportunities: rich data and the increasing value of the internet of things. In: International Data Corporation, White Paper, IDC_1672, May 2014
5. Gaber, M.M., Zaslavsky, A., Krishnaswamy, S.: Towards an adaptive approach for mining data streams in resource constrained environments. In: Proceedings of the 2004 International Conference on Data Warehousing and Knowledge Discovery, pp. 189–198, Zaragoza, Spain, September 2004
6. Gaber, M.M., Zaslavsky, A., Krishnaswamy, S.: Mining data streams: a review. ACM Sigmod Record **34**(2), 18–26 (2005)
7. Golab, L., Ozsu, T.M.: Issues in data stream management. ACM Sigmod Record **32**(2), 5–14 (2003)
8. Wang, F., Ercegovac, V., Syeda-Mahmood, T., et al.: Large-scale multimodal mining for healthcare with MapReduce. In: Proceedings of the 1st ACM International Health Informatics Symposium, pp. 479–483, New York, November 2010
9. Lin, R.C.H., Liao, H.J., Tung, K.Y., Lin, Y.C., Wu, S.L.: Network traffic analysis with cloud platform. J. Internet Technol. **13**(6), 953–961 (2012)

# Using Long-Short-Term Memory Based Convolutional Neural Networks for Network Intrusion Detection

Chia-Ming Hsu, He-Yen Hsieh, Setya Widyawan Prakosa, Muhammad Zulfan Azhari, and Jenq-Shiou Leu[(✉)]

National Taiwan University of Science and Technology, Taipei, Taiwan
{d10402101,m10502103,d10702804,
d10702805,jsleu}@mail.ntust.edu.tw

**Abstract.** The quantity of internet use has grown dramatically in the last decade. Internet is almost available in every human activity. However, there are some critical obstacles behind this massive development. Security becomes the hottest issue among the researchers. In this study, we focus on intrusion detection system (IDS) which is one of the solutions for security problems on network administration. Since intrusion detection system is a kind of classifier machine, it is allowed to engage with machine learning schemes. Related to this reason, the number of studies related to utilizing machine learning schemes for intrusion detection system has been increased recently. In this study, we use NSL-KDD dataset as the benchmark. Even though machine learning schemes perform well on intrusion detection, the obtained result on NSL-KDD dataset is not satisfied enough. On the other hand, deep learning offers the solution to overcome this issue. We propose two deep learning models which are long-short-term memory only (LSTM-only) and the combination of convolutional neural networks and LSTM (CNN-LSTM) for intrusion detection system. Both proposed methods achieve better accuracy than that of the existing method which uses recurrent neural networks (RNN).

**Keywords:** Intrusion detection system · Deep learning · Long-short term memory · NSL-KDD dataset

## 1 Introduction

With increasing the number of internet users, the global internet use has escalated. The internet is very helpful almost in every human activity. However, it has a lot of vulnerability in term of security. The researchers have been handling the vulnerability, but the attacks become more dangerous day by day. An Intrusion Detection System (IDS) is one of the best inventions in computer security because the number of researchers who work for developing the performance of

J.-L. Chen et al. (Eds.): WiCON 2018, LNICST 264, pp. 86–94, 2019.
https://doi.org/10.1007/978-3-030-06158-6_9

intrusion detection is high. Furthermore, intrusion detection is the most fundamental part for network system administrator to monitor various malicious behavior inside a computer networking. Then, based on the method that is used by intrusion detection, it is considered as a classifier machine. Intrusion detection identifies every single network traffic and classifies it into which kind of category it belongs to, normal or malicious traffic. Thus, intrusion detection is able to utilize machine learning schemes to enhance its accuracy during classifying.

Even though conventional machine learning schemes are highly used for intrusion detection, they cannot present the result optimally. So, it triggers the researchers to apply deep learning to overcome this such an issue. The result that they can achieve is outstanding. Many of researchers use NSL-KDD dataset [1, 2] as the benchmark as for the validation and evaluation of their implementation. In this study, we utilize two deep learning models in intrusion detection and NSL-KDD dataset as the benchmark as well. The first model is Long short-term memory (LSTM) which is used as the baseline and basic model. The second is the combination of convolutional neural networks (CNN) and LSTM is applied in this study. As a result, both our proposed methods achieve better accuracy than that of existing methods, particularly for KDDTest$^{-21}$.

We organize this paper as follows: Sect. 2 list of existing works related to the machine learning and deep learning implementation on intrusion detection. Next is Sect. 3 which describes our proposed methods. Afterward, Sect. 4 presents result and evaluation. The last section infers the work that we have done and discusses future works of our implementation.

## 2   Related Work

There are many researchers that employ various machine learning schemes. For instance, Kuang et al. [3] propose a novel support vector machine (SVM) which combine kernel principal component analysis (KPCA) and genetic algorithm (GA) for intrusion detection and use KDD Cup99 [4] as the dataset. Then, Reddy et al. [5] also use SVM as well for intrusion detection. Then, they adopt effective discriminant function to increase the accuracy.

Meanwhile, Ingre et al. [6] analyze the performance of NSL-KDD using Artificial Neural Networks (ANN). Then, Farnaaz et al. [7] propose intrusion detection system using Random Forest (RF) and NSL-KDD datasets to evaluate the performance of their model. In addition, Zhang et al. [8] build network intrusion detection system which is also based on RF but they use KDD Cup99 to assess the achievement of their model. However, there are some weaknesses in machine learning scheme. For instance, feature engineering and selection do not perform well for extracting the most representative features in big data and cause the decreasing of accuracy [9]. Since the intrusion detection encounters massive data in the traffic network, these classical machine learning schemes do not yield a better result.

Recently, the number of research on deep learning which is a branch of machine learning has risen. It induces deep learning implemented in many fields

[10–12] and intrusion detection system is no exception. For instance, the study of classifying intrusion detection using deep learning has been done by performing Recurrent Neural Networks (RNN) [13]. Authors have constructed the approach for classification task on NSL-KDD dataset and confirmed that deep learning scheme promises better result compared to traditional machine learning schemes.

From the fact that RNN can be used for Intrusion Detection System (IDS) and it gives promised result for classification the intrusion. The scheme to employ Long Short-Term Memory (LSTM) [14] for intrusion detection is proposed in this paper. The proposed scheme is evaluated on NSL-KDD dataset and we also compare it with RNN-IDS proposed by [13].

## 3  Methodology

In this study, we propose two deep learning models that we have evaluated on NSL-KDD dataset. The first model is an LSTM-only model which views the dataset as the time series while another model is CNN-LSTM which is basically almost the same as LSTM-only but in this model, we perform extracting important features vectors by using CNN.

### 3.1  Dataset Description

The NSL-KDD dataset was developed in 2009 and it has been utilized massively by researchers for the benchmark of intrusion detection experiments. The NSL-KDD dataset has refined KDD Cup99 dataset which has some drawbacks [15] that can affect the accuracy of the model. In addition, NSL-KDD has some the advantages such as training set not containing redundancy records and test set not containing duplicate records [1]. The NSL-KDD dataset consists of the KDDTrain+ as the training set while for the testing set, it has KDDTest+ and KDDTest-21. There are 41 features and 1 additional feature as a label for each record. For the experiments, we apply two models of classification. The first model is binary classification which consists of two categories which are normal and abnormal illustrated in Table 1 while another model is five-categories classification which contains data such as normal, DoS (Denial of Service attacks), R2L (Root to Local attacks), U2R (User to Root attacks), and Probe (Probing attacks) as shown in Table 2. Moreover, KDDTest-21 is more difficult to be classified than that of KDDTest+.

**Table 1.** Binary classification in NSL-KDD dataset-2 categories

|            | Total   | Normal | Abnormal |
|------------|---------|--------|----------|
| KDDTrain+  | 125973  | 67343  | 58630    |
| KDDTest+   | 22544   | 9711   | 12833    |
| KDDTest-21 | 11850   | 2125   | 9698     |

**Table 2.** Different classification in NSL-KDD dataset-5 categories

| | Total | Normal | DoS | Probe | R2L | U2R |
|---|---|---|---|---|---|---|
| KDDTrain[+] | 125973 | 67343 | 45927 | 11656 | 995 | 52 |
| KDDTest[+] | 22544 | 9711 | 7460 | 2421 | 2885 | 67 |
| KDDTest[-21] | 11850 | 2125 | 4344 | 2402 | 2885 | 67 |

## 3.2 Data Preprocessing

Since LSTM is a variant of RNN, the input value must be a numerical value. NSL-KDD dataset contains three non-numerical features namely, protocol_type, service, and flag. These three features are converted into numerical form by using one-hot-encoding. Furthermore, the range of value in some features varies widely such as in duration, src_byte, and dst_byte. Thus, we need to normalize these features by employing feature scaling.

## 3.3 Long-Short Term Memory (LSTM)

LSTM is a special variant of RNN architecture which is able to learn long-term dependencies. LSTM is a network which is composed of cells (LSTM units) that are connected to each other. An LSTM unit consists of three kinds of the gate such as input gate, output gate, and forget gate as illustrated in Fig. 1.

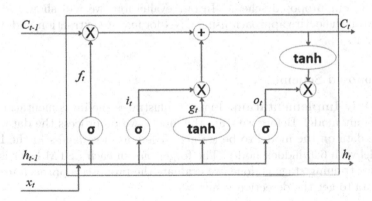

**Fig. 1.** LSTM Unit

Based in Fig. 1, a LSTM unit gets three input from the last step. The first is $x_t$ which is a feature at time step $t$. The next is $h_{t-1}$ which is the hidden unit from the last time step and the last is a memory cell that is represented by $C_{t-1}$ which containts the information of previous steps. Then, input, output, and forget gate are represented by $i_t$, $o_t$, and $f_t$ respectively at time step $t$ and each gate has its own function. The forget gate gets rid of the information from the cell state based on $h_{t-1}$ and $x_t$. Then, the input gate updates the information of memory cell by using $i_t$ and $g_t$ which is a hyperbolic tangent *(tanh)*. $C_t$ is the new value of memory cell. The last is output gate that decides what the output looks like. The equation of all computation in a LSTM unit can be written as follows:

$$f_t = \sigma(W_{xf}x_t + W_{hf}h_{t-1} + b_f) \tag{1}$$

$$i_t = \sigma(W_{xi}x_t + W_{hi}h_{t-1} + b_i) \tag{2}$$

$$g_t = tanh(W_{xc}x_t + W_{hc}h_{t-1} + b_c) \tag{3}$$

$$C_t = f_t * C_{t-1} + i_t * g_t \tag{4}$$

$$o_t = \sigma(W_o x_t + W_{ho}h_{t-1} + b_o) \tag{5}$$

$$h_t = o_t * tanh(C_t) \tag{6}$$

Where $W$ represents the weight of the gate and $b$ denotes the bias.

### 3.4 Convolutional Neural Networks

CNN is a feed-forward artificial neural networks that can be applied to various schemes including classification and feature extraction. In this work, CNN is designed to be the feature extraction method. To obtain a robust feature that represents each class in the database, CNN is utilized before applying LSTM. Furthermore, LSTM receives a representative feature that can enhance the performance of our proposed scheme. In our evaluation, we will show the difference between the entire approach using CNN for feature extraction and without employing it.

### 3.5 Proposed Schemes

**LSTM-Only Implementation.** Figure 2 illustrates the implementation steps of LSTM-only model. Before we train the model, we preprocess the data. Then, we fit the data on the model to be trained. There are two layers in the LSTM-only model with 640 hidden nodes. The forget bias of each LSTM layer is set to 1. Once the training stage is done, we evaluate the proposed approach using the testing data to get the detection result.

**CNN-LSTM Implementation.** Figure 3 shows the implementation steps of CNN-LSTM model. We use the convolutional neural networks to obtain a set of robust features before applying LSTM. There are two convolutional layers with 32 kernel filters in each layer following by max pooling layer. Furthermore, we apply LSTM described above with the extracted features from convolutional neural networks.

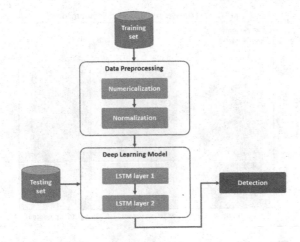

**Fig. 2.** Diagram of proposed method LSTM-only

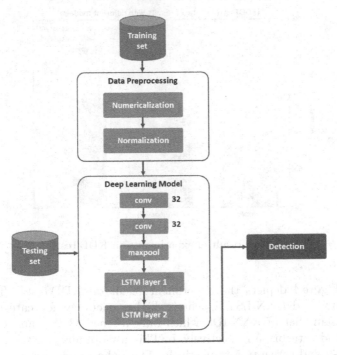

**Fig. 3.** Diagram of proposed method LSTM-only

## 4    Result and Discussion

After conducting experiments on NSL-KDD dataset, we compare our proposed methods to RNN-IDS [13] and the outcome of proposed methods perform higher accuracy both of KDDTest$^+$ and KDDTest$^{-21}$ which is more complicated to

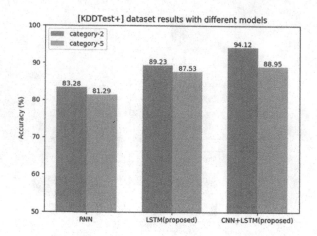

**Fig. 4.** The result of experiments on KDDTest⁺

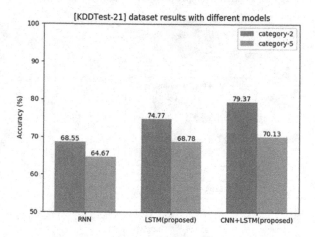

**Fig. 5.** The result of experiments on KDDTest⁻²¹

be tested. Figure 4 depicts the experiment result on KDDTest⁺. The result of LSTM-only and CNN-LSTM achieve higher accuracy for category-2 and category-5 than that of RNN-IDS which only reaches 83.28% and 81.29% for category-2 and category-5 respectively. LSTM-only obtains 89.23% and 87.53% for category-2 and category-5 respectively. Then, the second proposed method, CNN-LSTM gets higher accuracy with 94.12% and 88.95% for category-2 and category-5 respectively.

Figure 5 presents the experiment result on KDDTest⁻²¹. Even though it is difficult to do classifying on KDDTest⁻²¹, the proposed methods can perform well and surpass the performance of RNN-IDS. CNN-LSTM still obtains the highest accuracy with 79.37% and 70.13% for category-2 and category-5 respectively.

Then, LSTM-only also outpaces the outcome of RNN-IDS with 74.77% and 68.78% while RNN-IDS cannot gain 70% of the accuracy.

## 5  Conclusion

In this paper, we propose two deep learning models which are LSTM-only and CNN-LSTM to classify the packet traffic. To evaluate proposed methods, we conduct the experiment on NSL-KDD dataset which is often used by researchers for the benchmark. NSL-KDD dataset contains two test sets named KDDTest[+] and KDDTest[-21] which is hard to be classified. By utilizing LSTM, we can achieve higher accuracy on both test sets than that of the existing method. Moreover, after implementing CNN for feature extraction before LSTM layer, the accuracy of proposed method increases significantly.

## References

1. Revathi, S., Malathi, A.: A detailed analysis on NSL-KDD dataset using various machine learning techniques for intrusion detection. Int. J. Eng. Res. Technol. **2**, 1848–1853 (2013)
2. Dhanabal, L., Shantharajah, S.P., Dr.: A study on NSL-KDD dataset for intrusion detection system based on classification algorithms. In: International Journal of Advanced Research in Computer and Communication Engineering, vol. 4, pp. 446–452 (2015)
3. Kuang, F., Xu, W., Zhang, S.: A novel hybrid KPCA and SVM with GA model for intrusion detection. Appl. Soft Comput. **18**, 178–184 (2014)
4. Hettich, S., Bay, S.D.: The UCI KDD Archive, University of California, Department of Information and Computer Science, Irvine, CA (1999). http://kdd.ics.uci.edu
5. Reddy, R.R., Ramadevi, Y., Sunitha, K.V.N.: Effective discriminant function for intrusion detection using SVM. In: International Conference on Advances in Computing, Communications and Informatics (ICACCI), pp. 11481153 (2016)
6. Ingre, B., Yadav, A.: Performance analysis of NSL-KDD dataset using ANN. In: International Conference on Signal Processing and Communication Engineering Systems (SPACES), pp. 9296 (2015)
7. Farnaaz, N., Jabbar, M.A.: Random forest modeling for network intrusion detection system. Procedia Comput. Sci. **89**, 213217 (2016)
8. Zhang, J., Zulkernine, M., Haque, A.: Random-forests-based network intrusion detection systems. IEEE Trans. Syst. Man Cybern. Part C (Appl. Rev.) **38**, 649–659 (2008)
9. Niyaz, Q., Sun, W., Javaid, A.Y., Alam, M.: A deep learning approach for network intrusion detection system. EAI Endorsed Trans. Secur. Saf. **16**, 21–26 (2015)
10. Xu, Y., Shi, L., Ni, Y.: Deep-learning-based scenario generation strategy considering correlation between multiple wind farms. J. Eng. **2017**, 2207–2210 (2017)
11. Wu, B.-F., Lin, C.-H.: Adaptive feature mapping for customizing deep learning based facial expression recognition model. IEEE Access **6**, 12451–12461 (2018)
12. Wang, T., Wen, C.-K., Wang, H., Gao, F., Jiang, T., Jin, S.: Deep learning for wireless physical layer: opportunities and challenges. China Commun. **14**, 92–111 (2017)

13. Yin, C., Zhu, Y., Fei, J., He, X.: A deep learning approach for intrusion detection using recurrent neural networks. IEEE Access **5**, 21954–21961 (2017)
14. Hochreiter, S., Schmidhuber, J.: Long short-term memory. Neural Comput. **9**, 1735–1780 (1997)
15. Kaushik, S.S., Deshmukh, P.R., Dr. Prof.: Detection of attacks in an intrusion detection system. Int. J. Comput. Sci. Inf. Technol. **2**(3), 982–986 (2011)

# Intrusion Detection for WiFi Network: A Deep Learning Approach

Shaoqian Wang[1,2], Bo Li[1], Mao Yang[1(✉)], and Zhongjiang Yan[1]

[1] School of Electronics and Information,
Northwestern Polytechnical University, Xi'an, China
{libo.npu,yangmao,zhjyan}@nwpu.edu.cn
[2] Science and Technology on Communication Networks Laboratory,
Shijiazhuang 053200, China

**Abstract.** With the popularity and development of Wi-Fi network, network security has become a key concern in the recent years. The amount of network attacks and intrusion activities are growing rapidly. Therefore, the continuous improvement of Intrusion Detection Systems (IDS) is necessary. In this paper, we analyse different types of network attacks in wireless networks and utilize Stacked Autoencoder (SAE) and Deep Neural Network (DNN) to perform network attack classification. We evaluate our method on the Aegean WiFi Intrusion Dataset (AWID) and preprocess the dataset by feature selection. In our experiments, we classified the network records into 4 types: normal record, injection attack, impersonation attack and flooding attack. The classification accuracies we achieved of these 4 types of records are 98.4619%, 99.9940%, 98.3936% and 73.1200%, respectively.

**Keywords:** Wi-fi network · Network intrusion detection ·
Deep learning

## 1 Introduction

With the development of Internet related technology and the enhancement of network demand, WLAN technology has developed rapidly day by day. There are many kinds of Wi-Fi networks, such as home wireless local area network, campus network, enterprise network, etc. Users can use mobile phones to access the Internet at any time, as long as they are in the range of signal reception. However, with the increasing number of wireless network users, the problem of network security is becoming more and more serious. Many large wireless local networks, such as campus network and enterprise network, contain a large number of important information, and any network security problems may cause huge

© ICST Institute for Computer Sciences, Social Informatics and Telecommunications Engineering 2019
Published by Springer Nature Switzerland AG 2019. All Rights Reserved
J.-L. Chen et al. (Eds.): WiCON 2018, LNICST 264, pp. 95–104, 2019.
https://doi.org/10.1007/978-3-030-06158-6_10

losses. In contrast to the wired networks, Wi-Fi network with wireless propagation characteristics is relatively less secure and more vulnerable to attack. Packets are easily intercepted and tampered when they are propagating from source address to destination address. In order to protect the confidentiality, integrity and security of network system resources in a Wi-Fi network, the application of intrusion detection technology is very necessary.

Intrusion Detection System (IDS) can monitor the running status of network and system in real time, and detect various kinds of attack. There have been many studies related to the use of intrusion detection technology in large-scale wireless local area networks such as campus networks and enterprise networks. Deep learning techniques can also be adopted to improve the performance of IDS and classify the attacks from the mass data of the wireless network.

A large number of records including various network attack patterns are important for deep learning techniques. In previous papers, KDDCUP99 [1] and NSLKDD [2] datasets have been used for many times. These two are very classic Wi-Fi network datasets, which have 4 categories and 39 attack types. However, because of the rapid development of network technology, network records more than a decade ago have apparently been unable to adapt to today's Wi-Fi network. In this paper, we use the Aegean WiFi Intrusion Dataset (AWID) [3] to validate our proposed approach. The dataset was published in 2015 and it contains normal records and different attack records. In recent years, more and more research literatures on intrusion detection have cited the AWID dataset.

Kolias et al. [3] used the AWID dataset to perform intrusion detection based on various machine learning algorithms. They introduced AWID and network attack types in great detail, but the accuracy of classification using machine learning techniques is not ideal. Aminanto et al. [4–6] proposed several novel methods to detect impersonation type attack and showed a detection rate of 99.918% and a false alarm rate of 0.012%. But their models can not detect other attacks except impersonation attack. Thing [7] compared the classification accuracies under the SAE model with different activation functions and achieved optimal results based on the Parametric Rectified Linear Unit (PRelu) [8] function. However, in the above-mentioned papers, only two-layer or three-layer models were used in the deep learning model, and no attempt was made in a neural network with more hidden layers.

In this paper, we analyse several kinds of network attacks in Wi-Fi networks and utilize Deep Neural Network (DNN) and Stacked Autoencoder (SAE) to perform attack classification. We validate our approach using AWID dataset after the feature selection. In our experiments, our proposed approach classified the network records into 4 categories, and we achieved great classification accuracies of the injection, flooding and impersonation attacks.

In the rest of this paper, the second part introduces some common network attacks in Wi-Fi networks. The third part introduces the AWID dataset and the data preprocessing. The fourth part introduces our SAE model and DNN model. The fifth section shows the test results and analysis. The sixth part summarizes the full text.

# 2 Attacks for Wireless Network

Attacks in Wi-Fi networks generally fall into two categories. One is attacks against data confidentiality protection, network access control, and data integrity protection; the other is attacks based on a unique approach to wireless network deployment, design, and maintenance. In addition, network attacks in Wi-Fi networks can also be subdivided into the following seven categories:

## 2.1 Injection

In a Wi-Fi network, an attacker can implement message injection by installing related attack software. An attacker can implement forged data packets, modify the header or end of the data packet, and can tamper with any field of the data packet. After the packet is injected into the relevant data transmission, the attacker can control the entire transmission process of the message.

## 2.2 Eavesdropping Adversary and Network Traffic Analysis

Because of the characteristics of Wi-Fi network, its transmission medium is open. Attackers can eavesdrop the network information in Wi-Fi networks through related tools. Even if the message has been encrypted, as long as there are certain rules or vulnerabilities in the message, the attacker can perform analysis and calculation on the information packet to obtain some or all of the messages from the specific message.

## 2.3 Unauthorized Access

In a Wi-Fi network, signals are transmitted by electromagnetic waves. Within the service area formed by the access point (AP), any wireless terminal may access the AP. Unauthorized access means that the user accesses the wireless terminal device through the AP, but this access is not allowed by the AP. Wi-Fi network encryption and authentication methods need to be improved, there are still some loopholes. The Wi-Fi network uses a unidirectional authentication mechanism, the wireless terminal sends a authentication request to the AP, and the AP does not authenticate the wireless terminal. Unidirectional authentication will give the intruder the opportunity to enter the network through the AP. Illegal users can constantly send authentication requests to AP. A large number of authentication requests can cause AP to be paralyzed and not work properly. And then, the attacker can steal network data or information on the network terminal device after access to the network.

## 2.4 Session Hijacking

Session hijacking attacks generally consist of two parts. First, the attacker uses some method to force the station (STA) to disconnect from the AP. After that, the attacker will establish a connection with the AP as a faked STA, steal the message session, and control the sending and receiving of the session. Session hijacking attacks are also generally divided into two forms: passive hijacking and active hijacking. Passive hijacking is actually monitoring the data flow between two parties in the background to get sensitive data. Active hijacking is to replace a host in the session with an attacker and take over the conversation.

## 2.5  Forged AP

AP's MAC address is included in the header of the packet in Wi-Fi networks. The data packet header exists in clear text during data transmission. The attacker can obtain the MAC address of the AP and change his MAC address to the address of a valid AP.

## 2.6  Man-in-the-Middle Attack

Man-in-the-middle attack is an indirect attack. This attack mode is to place a computer controlled by an intruder between two communication computers that are network-connected through various technical means. This computer is called a "Man-in-the-Middle". This computer can intercept and tamper with the normal network communication data, but both parties of the communication are unaware of it. When host A and B communicate, they are forwarded by host C. There is no real direct communication between A and B. The information transfer between them is done by C as an intermediary. In this way, host C is able to eavesdrop and tamper with the information from the communication, and achieve its own goals by sending the malicious information to A or B.

## 2.7  Dos

Dos attack is a very serious and most common type of attack in wired networks and wireless networks. Its purpose is to make the network unable to serve legitimate users. Attackers can initiate multiple forms of denial of service attacks. Attackers can broadcast a large number of radio frequency interference signals. The wireless channel is always busy. As a result, legitimate users cannot use the channel to send normal requests. An attacker can also send a large number of invalid association messages to the AP. As a result, the AP resources are exhausted and crashed, and normal wireless access services cannot be provided. This affects the establishment of relationships between other legal STAs and APs.

## 3  Datasets and Attributes Selecting

AWID dataset is collected in a real local area network. Compared with the dataset generated by simulation software, AWID dataset has higher reliability and authenticity. AWID dataset can be classified into AWID-CLS dataset and AWID-ATK dataset. There are 4 types of labels in AWID-CLS dataset and 16 types of labels in AWID-ATK dataset. In this paper, we select the AWID-CLS-R dataset, which contain 4 classes namely normal, injection, impersonation and flooding. The training dataset contains 1795575 records and the test dataset contains 575643 records. The distribution of normal records and various attack records are shown in Table 1.

**Table 1.** Data distribution

|                | Normal  | Injection | Impersonation | Flooding |
| -------------- | ------- | --------- | ------------- | -------- |
| AWID-CLS-R-Trn | 1633190 | 65379     | 48522         | 48484    |
| AWID-CLS-R-Tst | 530785  | 16682     | 20079         | 8097     |

The records in AWID have 154 attributes, but not all of them contribute to the training of the model. In addition, there are also some question mark ("?") for unavailable values for the corresponding attributes in the dataset. Therefore, the preprocessing of the datasets is necessary. In the first step, string attribute and the attributes which consist of the same value are removed. In the second step, we removed some attributes according to the amount of the question marks. All the attributes which have too many "?" were removed, while the rest of the question marks in the dataset were set to zero [9] value. Based on these steps, 71 attributes were selected. In the third step, we transformed all the data into numerical values and normalize the attributes. Equation (1) shows the formula of normalizing.

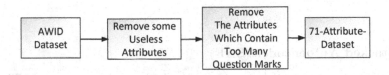

**Fig. 1.** Preprocessing of the dataset

$$y_i = \frac{x_i - min(x)}{max(x) - min(x)} \tag{1}$$

In this formula, $y_i$ expresses the normalized value, $x_i$ expresses the attribute values, and $max(x)$ and $min(x)$ express the maximum and minimum values of the attribute $x$. In the last step, because the size of normal records is much larger than the size of attack records, the amount of normal type records should be reduced. We balanced the train dataset by selecting only 10% of the normal type records randomly. Table 2 shows the data distribution of the final training dataset.

**Table 2.** Remaining records

| Category | Number |
|---|---|
| Normal | 163319 |
| Injection | 65379 |
| Impersonation | 48522 |
| Flooding | 48484 |

## 4    Deep Learning Model

In this paper, SAE and DNN are used to build intrusion detection classification models. They both use PRelu as the activation function. In PReLU, parameter $a$ can be learnt during the training phase.

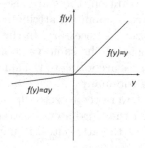

**Fig. 2.** Parametric Rectified Linear Unit(PRelu)

### 4.1    Stacked Autoencoder (SAE)

SAE is a deep learning model composed of multi-layered autoencoders. The output of the previous autoencoder can be used as the input of the next autoencoder. SAE is widely used in model pre-training and non-label supervised learning. Figure 3 briefly shows the a single-layer autoencoder. Based on the principle of input equal to output, the input data will be encoded and decoded. After many times of training, the input data encoded result can be used as the input of the next layer.

The SAE model we utilized in this paper is composed of three hidden layers, the number of neurons in each layer are 128, 96 and 64. After the training step, we utilized Softmax regression to classify the records.

### 4.2    Deep Neural Networks (DNN)

The DNN model is a deep back propagation (BP) neural network model. A larger number of hidden layers provide a higher level of abstraction for the model, and

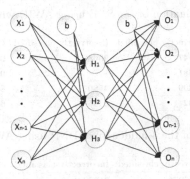

**Fig. 3.** Autoencoder

improve the ability of the model. In this paper, we use the DNN with more hidden layers to train and test the dataset. We used mini-batch gradient descent and dropout [10] algorithm to further improve the performance of DNN model.

We proposed two kinds of DNN models, one is composed of 3 hidden layers, the number of neurons in each layer are 128, 64 and 32; the other is composed of 7 hidden layers, and the number of neurons in each layer are 94, 112, 128, 96, 72, 48 and 24. They both utilize Softmax regression to classify the records.

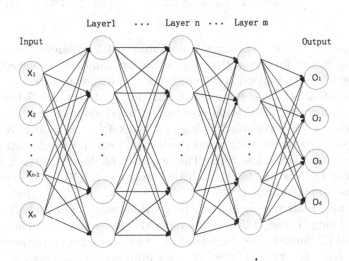

**Fig. 4.** Deep Neural Network (DNN)

# 5  Performance Evaluation

Based on SAE and DNN models, training and testing were conducted on 71-attribute dataset. We achieved the classification accuracies of the normal records and the three types of attack records. Tables 3, 4, 5 show the classification results for the three models we proposed.

**Table 3.** The Evaluation of the SAE using AWID with 71 Attributes

| Category | Number | Correctly classified | Incorrectly classified | Classification accuracy (%) |
|---|---|---|---|---|
| Normal | 530785 | 521477 | 9308 | 98.2464 |
| Injection | 16682 | 16681 | 1 | 99.9940 |
| Impersonation | 20079 | 16499 | 3580 | 82.1704 |
| Flooding | 8097 | 5602 | 2495 | 69.1861 |

**Table 4.** The evaluation of the 3-hidden-layer DNN using AWID With 71 attributes

| Category | Number | Correctly classified | Incorrectly classified | Classification accuracy (%) |
|---|---|---|---|---|
| Normal | 530785 | 509697 | 21088 | 96.0270 |
| Injection | 16682 | 16681 | 1 | 99.9940 |
| Impersonation | 20079 | 1278 | 18801 | 6.3649 |
| Flooding | 8097 | 5974 | 2123 | 73.7804 |

**Table 5.** The evaluation of the 7-hidden-layer DNN using AWID With 71 attributes

| Category | Number | Correctly classified | Incorrectly classified | Classification accuracy (%) |
|---|---|---|---|---|
| Normal | 530785 | 522621 | 8164 | 98.4619 |
| Injection | 16682 | 16681 | 1 | 99.9940 |
| Impersonation | 20079 | 19757 | 322 | 98.3963 |
| Flooding | 8097 | 5927 | 2170 | 73.1200 |

By comparing the results showed from Tables 3, 4, 5, it can be found that the classification accuracies of injection type attack are same. We achieved an accuracy of 99.994%, only 1 injection type record was classified incorrectly. Although the impersonation attack is the most challenging to detect, our 7-hidden-layer DNN showed a great classification accuracy of impersonation type attack. The accuracy of impersonation attack is high to 98.3963%, it is a obvious improvement, compared to the 82.1704% and the 6.3649% which we achieved based on the 3-hidden-layer DNN and SAE. The accuracy of flooding attack based on 7-hidden-layer DNN is 73.12%, it is a little lower than the 73.7804% we achieved based on the 3-hidden-layer DNN.

We compared our results against the previous work by Thing [7] as shown in Table 6. Thing [7] tested 2-hidden-layer SAE model and 3-hidden-layer SAE model on AWID dataset. The 2-hidden-layer SAE showed a better performance, and it achieved a accuracy of 99.8050%. Our proposed method showed a drop in the normal record classification by 1.343%, but we achieved a improvement in the classification accuracies of the injection and flooding attacks by 17.2761% and 15.642%, respectively. Our proposed approach has the advantage of detecting injection type attack and flooding type attack.

**Table 6.** Result comparing

|            | Normal(%) | Injection (%) | Impersonation (%) | Flooding (%) |
|------------|-----------|---------------|-------------------|--------------|
| Thing [7]  | 99.8050   | 82.7179       | 98.4959           | 57.4780      |
| Our result | 98.4619   | 99.9940       | 98.3963           | 73.1200      |

# 6 Conclusion

In this paper, we analyze theoretically the various types of attacks that exist in Wi-Fi networks and proposed a deep learning approach for the attack classification problem. We validate our approach using AWID dataset and select 71 attributes after the feature selection. We adopt SAE and DNN to perform attack classification. The experimental results showed that our 7-hidden-layer DNN model achieved a high accuracy for all categories. The classification accuracy of normal, injection attack, impersonation attack and flooding attack are 98.4619%, 99.9940%, 98.3936% and 73.1200%, respectively.

**Acknowledgment.** This work was supported in part by the National Natural Science Foundations of CHINA (Grant No. 61771390, No. 61501373, No. 61771392, and No. 61271279), the National Science and Technology Major Project (Grant No. 2016ZX03001018-004, and No. 2015ZX03002006-004), the Fundamental Research Funds for the Central Universities (Grant No. 3102017ZY018), and the Science and Technology on Communication Networks Laboratory Open Projects (Grant No. KX172600027).

# References

1. KDDCUP99, Kdd cup99 data set (1999). http://kdd.ics.uci.edu/databases/kddcup99/kddcup99.html. Accessed 15 Jan 2018
2. NSL-KDD, NSL-KDD data set for network-based intrusion detection systems (2009). http://www.unb.ca/research/iscx/dataset/iscx-NSL-KDD-dataset.html. Accessed 15 Jan 2018
3. Kolias, C., Kambourakis, G., Stavrou, A., et al.: Intrusion detection in 802.11 networks: empirical evaluation of threats and a public dataset [J]. IEEE Commun. Surv. Tutor. **18**(1), 184–208 (2016)
4. Aminanto, M.E., Choi, R., Tanuwidjaja, H.C., et al.: Deep abstraction and weighted feature selection for Wi-Fi impersonation detection [J]. IEEE Trans. Inf. Forensics Secur. **PP**(99), 1–1 (2018)
5. Aminanto, M.E., Tanuwidjaja, H.C., Yoo, P.D., et al.: Wi-Fi intrusion detection using weighted-feature selection for neural networks classifier [C]. In: International Workshop on Big Data and Information Security, pp. 99–104 (2018)
6. Aminanto, M.E., Kim, K.: Detecting impersonation attack in WiFi networks using deep learning approach. In: Choi, D., Guilley, S. (eds.) WISA 2016. LNCS, vol. 10144, pp. 136–147. Springer, Cham (2017). https://doi.org/10.1007/978-3-319-56549-1_12

7. Thing, V.L.L.: IEEE 802.11 network anomaly detection and attack classification: a deep learning approach [C]. In: Wireless Communications and Networking Conference, pp. 1–6. IEEE (2017)
8. He, K., Zhang, X., Ren, S., et al.: Delving deep into rectifiers: surpassing human-level performance on ImageNet classification [J]. pp. 1026–1034 (2015)
9. Larose, D.T.: Data Preprocessing, Discovering Knowledge in Data: An Introduction to Data Mining, pp. 27–40. Wiley (2014)
10. Srivastava, N., Hinton, G., Krizhevsky, A., et al.: Dropout: a simple way to prevent neural networks from overfitting [J]. J. Mach. Learn. Res. 15(1), 1929–1958 (2014)

# Audio Event Detection Using Wireless Sensor Networks Based on Deep Learning

Jose Marie Mendoza, Vanessa Tan[✉], Jr. Vivencio Fuentes, Gabriel Perez, and Nestor Michael Tiglao

Electrical and Electronics Engineering Institute,
University of the Philippines - Diliman, Quezon City, Philippines
{jose.marie.mendoza,vanessa.tan,
vivencio.fuentes,gabriel.perez,nestor}@eee.upd.edu.ph

**Abstract.** Wireless acoustic sensor network is useful for ambient assisted living applications. Its capability of incorporating an audio event detection and classification system helps its users, especially elderly, on their everyday needs. In this paper, we propose using convolutional neural networks (CNN) for classifying audio streams. In contrast to AAL systems using traditional machine learning, our solution is capable of learning and inferring activities in an end-to-end manner. To demonstrate the system, we developed a wireless sensor network composed of Raspberry Pi boards with microphones as nodes. The audio classification system results to an accuracy of *83.79%* using a parallel network for the Urban8k dataset, extracting constant-Q transform (CQT) features as system inputs. The overall system is scalabale and flexible in terms of the number of nodes, hence it is applicable on wide areas where assisted living applications are utilized.

**Keywords:** Audio event detection · Ambient assisted living

## 1 Introduction

Advancements in sensor node technologies allowed the development of low-cost and low-power multipurpose devices. These are usually integrated in a Wireless Sensor Network (WSN), where multiple sensor nodes communicate with each other to monitor the environment and gather data periodically. WSNs are already being utilized in different applications such as environment sensing, health monitoring, and smart homes [1].

The main goal of this paper is to create a wireless sensor network that could help in assisted living applications. In this work, audio streams are gathered by the sensor nodes then the sink node analyzes the data to detect different events in the environment. This paper has two main contributions: the exploration

J.-L. Chen et al. (Eds.): WiCON 2018, LNICST 264, pp. 105–115, 2019.
https://doi.org/10.1007/978-3-030-06158-6_11

of techniques using Convolutional Neural Networks (CNNs) for audio and the utilization of different audio input representations in audio event detection.

The rest of the paper is organized as follows. In Sect. 2, the related works are presented. Section 3 describes the WSN set-up while Sect. 4 briefly mentions the dataset used in the audio event detection. Section 5 presents the different CNN architectures that were implemented and a thorough discussion of the results in Sect. 6. Lastly, a summary of the findings and recommendations can be seen in Sect. 7.

## 2  Related Work

Ambient Assisted Living (AAL) is being used to monitor elderly in health care institutions [2]. A variety of sensors could be used such as mobile, wearable or static (e.g. pressure sensors, cameras, and microphones) to create a reliable system. For this application, microphones are more recommended since they are less invasive compared to wearable and cameras. Early stages of AAL using Wireless Acoustic Sensor Networks (WASN) implemented algorithms to lower the computational complexity of audio recognition by introducing a hybrid time-frequency approach [3]. While other methods increase efficiency of the system in terms of distribution and power consumption using real-time and scalable networks [4,5]. Detecting a few audio classes is one of the prominent limitations of these methods. Fortunately, homeSound, a distributed network where each node deployed reports to a GPU-enabled concentrator, is capable of classifying fourteen different indoor events [6]. It results to a more secured reporting mechanism to the sink since detection and classification is done locally before reporting to the server. This type of implementation is scalable by enabling indoor appliances to have specific alerts to report to a sink. This is possible in a smart home with devices sending alerts to an Android application, providing assistance whenever elderly people are left alone in the house [7].

Recently, classification using deep learning show exceptional results compared to traditional machine learning algorithms. The simplest architecture that can be constructed is the fully connected Deep Neural Networks (DNN). It is used in the Detection and Classification Acoustic Scenes and Events (DCASE) challenge. The DNN is used as baseline, using Mel-Frequency Cepstral Coefficients (MFCCs) for input features [8]. The problem of using MFCC is that it is more appropriate in speech processing applications, because it discards characteristics of environmental sounds. For this reason, features such as spectrogram and Constant-Q Transform (CQT) gave better performance in the DCASE challenge while using convolutional neural networks (CNN) [9,10,12]. CNN proved to be more effective than DNN on audio classification tasks, achieving approximately 10% improvement in classification using spectrogram inputs [11]. However, CQT input features produced an equal error rate of 16.6%, which is the best system proposed for DCASE Challenge 2016 on domestic audio tagging [10].

Pre-processing techniques introduce additional computation time to arrive to a prediction. Because of this, end-to-end networks using CNN extracts useful feature maps from input data on image classification architectures [12]. Similarly, this option is explored for environmental audio classification, where instead of 2-dimensional inputs, a time-domain windowed signal is used [13]. This paper discusses experiments using different input data to evaluate CNN architectures in audio classification.

## 3    WSN Raspberry-Pi Setup

A Wireless Sensor Network (WSN), composed of multiple nodes and a central base station, was implemented to facilitate the gathering and processing of audio signals over an enclosed area. These wireless acoustic sensor nodes would capture environmental audio signals, while a desktop computer would act as a base station which receives all signals captured. Data processing techniques would then be applied in the base station to detect specific audio events. A sample of the implemented network is illustrated in Fig. 1a showing three nodes and the main computer connected to the router.

Wireless sensor nodes used by the system are Raspberry Pi 3 devices, which are interfaced with a microphone using an integrated sound card. Raspberry Pi devices were chosen as the nodes for the network as it runs on a free open-source Linux operating system. These devices offer good computing power and are easily interfaced with audio components [14]. The devices record audio data via a microphone and is set to do so continuously. Recordings are done every 3 s, and audio is generated with a sampling rate of 44.1 kHz as Waveform Audio File Format. The audio data have meta-data, such as time stamps, in order to prepare the data for analysis in the server.

Transfer of the audio files are done via Secured Shell (SSH) through a WiFi network. Files are then retrieved by the server where classification using DNN takes place. As each audio file comes from different source nodes, their energy signatures would then be estimated to generate a consensus on which file would be used for the analysis of the signal at a given time [15]. The set-up of the system is shown in Fig. 1b, where a microphone is connected to the Raspberry-Pi and encodes the audio data received that is immediately sent to the computer.

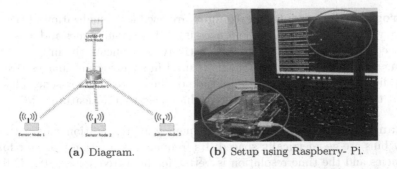

(a) Diagram.              (b) Setup using Raspberry- Pi.

**Fig. 1.** Wireless sensor network implementation

## 4    Dataset

The audio dataset used for training the classification model is the Urban Sound Dataset [16]. It contains 8,732 sound sources with 10 classes. The sounds included in the dataset are listed in Table 1. The audio data was split into 80% training set and 20% test set. All audio files were converted to mono, sampled at 44.1 kHz, and reduced to 3 s if the original data is too long and appended with silence if shorter than 3 s.

**Table 1.** Classes of the urban sound dataset

| Class | Label | Class | Label |
|-------|-------|-------|-------|
| 0 | Air conditioner | 5 | Engine idling |
| 1 | Car horn | 6 | Gunshot |
| 2 | Children playing | 7 | Jackhammer |
| 3 | Dog bark | 8 | Siren |
| 4 | Drilling | 9 | Street music |

## 5    Audio Classification

### 5.1    Sound Representations

Features are extracted using the Short-Time Fourier Transform (STFT) where each frame is 30 ms long. Overlap of each frames are 15 ms and extracts 1024 Fast Fourier Transform (FFT) points to compute for the spectrogram at the same frequency resolution.

**Spectrogram Features** are used as representation of a signal strength over time at different frequencies. It expresses the signal in its time-frequency representation, where the presence of frequencies are extracted per time frame.

**Spectrogram Representative Images** are used for visualization of the spectrogram which is common in audio processing, where time frames and frequencies are placed in the x-axis and y-axis respectively. To indicate the intensity of the frequency components, a color scheme is used in spectrogram images [18]. The lighter the color, the higher the amplitude of the intensity is present. This type of input turned out to be more effective than spectrogram features alone.

**Constant-Q Transform** is a time-frequency representation where the frequency bins are geometrically spaced. Its frequency resolution is better for low frequencies and the time resolution is better for high frequencies [10]. Different parameters are set in this feature, with a hop length of 512 samples with 12 bins per octave. Hamming window is used for short-time processing.

## 5.2 CNN Architectures

The following CNN architectures use 2-D convolutional layers for feature mapping. It is followed by fully connected layers which increases the capacity of the network during classification.

**Sequential CNN** is illustrated in Fig. 2. This implementation is similar with the sequential layers in [9]. Batch normalization and dropout layers are also included to explore their effects on the network. Moreover, dropout is implemented in the fully connected layers to provide regularization for training.

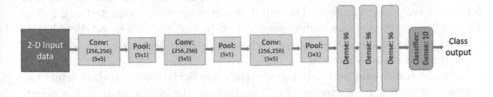

**Fig. 2.** A sequential CNN using a combination of 2D convolutional and fully-connected layers.

**Parallel CNN** is based on DeXpression architecture, a facial expression recognition system [19]. Some of the convolutional and pooling layers in the architecture are done in parallel. In this case, batch normalization replaced the local response normalization layer of the architecture. Dropout was also added at the fully-connected layers similar to sequential CNN.

**CNN for End-to-End Classification** is also explored, which uses raw audio as input by implementing a 1-D convolutional layer that acts similarly as a short-time pre-processing technique [13]. The network is shown in Fig. 3. It involves pooling layers for regularization and reshaping to allow the signals to be processed using 2-D feature mapping. In this case, the audio feature representation is extracted within the CNN architecture.

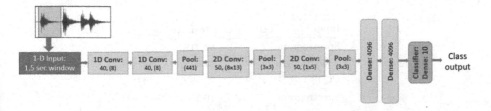

**Fig. 3.** An end-to-end CNN accepting a 1.5 s window for classification.

## 5.3   Experiments

A 5-fold cross validation was done on the training set to tune and evaluate the performance of the networks on different inputs. The batch size is set to 64, running for 30 epochs. A dropout of 0.5 on the fully-connected layers is also implemented. Rectified Linear Units (ReLU) are used for activation and the ADAM optimizer to boost training. All architectures are implemented in Keras using a NVIDIA GTX 960Ti GPU [20]. Training time took 2–3 h to finish for each architecture.

**Classification.** The 3-second audio recorded at the nodes are sent to the sink for audio event classification. The input features are then extracted and fed to the network to predict the audio event sensed by the nodes. The predicted class belongs to one of the classes in the Urban8k dataset. Moreover, the sink gives an output for each 1 s interval.

For the end-to-end network, the system accepts the 3-second data while the network extracts a 1.5-s window of raw audio from the initial input with an overlap of 200 ms. The class of the initial audio input is determined using probability voting [21]. Furthermore, the latency for providing output classes depends of the number of windows processed by the system, $n_{windows} \times delay_{network}$.

# 6   Results and Analysis

## 6.1   Classification Accuracy

For evaluation, the average accuracy of each class is calculated to get an overall accuracy of the network. Each CNN architecture will test the effects of batch normalization (BN) and dropout (DO) to the performance of the system.

**Feature-Based: Sequential Convolutional Neural Network.** It can be seen in Table 2 that the network with CQT input and with batch normalization yields the highest mean accuracy of 72.98%. This is the effect of accelerating the training that has regularization given that the model is trained for 30 epochs.

**Table 2.** Classification accuracies of the sequential CNN architecture on the Urban8K test set

| Input | BN | DO | Mean Acc. |
|---|---|---|---|
| Spectrogram | ✓ | | 62.41% |
| Spec. Images | ✓ | | 57.91% |
| CQT | ✓ | | 72.98% |
| Spectrogram | | ✓ | 10.30% |
| Spec. Images | | ✓ | 34.83% |
| CQT | | ✓ | 21.62% |

**Feature-Based: Parallel Convolutional Neural Network.** Different results were obtained using the parallel CNN. In Table 3, CQT input with dropout in training yields 86.17%, beating the previous network with batch normalization. It is also observed that spectrogram inputs are not effective when using dropout. This regularization technique does not work if inputs are not images causing it to have accuracies below 15%.

**Table 3.** Classification accuracies of the parallel CNN architecture on the Urban8K test set

| Input | BN | DO | Mean Acc. |
|---|---|---|---|
| Spectrogram | ✓ | | 62.27% |
| Spec. Images | ✓ | | 77.36% |
| CQT | ✓ | | 73.32% |
| Spectrogram | | ✓ | 11.91% |
| Spec. Images | | ✓ | 82.59% |
| CQT | | ✓ | 83.79% |

**End-to-End: 1-D and 2-D Combination of Sequential CNN.** The end-to-end network performance is shown in Table 4. It is noticeable that if the model is trained with dropout, it gives the best performance at 36.81% but not near the performance of systems with initial pre-processing. The reason for its low performance is the uneven distribution of data of Urban8k.

**Table 4.** Classification accuracies of the end-to-end CNN architecture on the Urban8K test set

| Input | BN | DO | Mean Acc. |
|---|---|---|---|
| Raw audio | ✓ | ✓ | 28.70% |
| Raw audio | ✓ | | 11.14% |
| Raw audio | | ✓ | 36.81% |

## 6.2 Discussion

Among the three input representations, Constant-Q Transform is the most significant feature for urban sound classification. Because of its advantage of mimicking the human auditory system, this feature captures the low and mid-to-low frequencies better than spectrogram. This results to a classification system achieving the best performing accuracy.

As shown in Tables 2 and 3, the parallel CNN architecture is more stable and yields high accuracies for models with batch normalization and dropout. However, it fails the configuration where the model has dropout and uses spectrogram features as input. The regularization caused by dropout have been proven to work on images, but if it is a spectrogram which is time-frequency data important information may be omitted at times leading to unstable training. Similar experiments are also performed for the end-to-end network. The highest accuracy is observed with batch normalization shown in Table 4. Good performance with batch normalization is caused by the reduction of the dependencies of the gradients to the scale of the parameters when it is added.

A brief summary of the highest accuracies per architecture is shown in Table 5. The CQT-based parallel architecture achieves the highest accuracy while the end-to-end architecture has the lowest accuracy. The architectures are also compared to an implementation of a very deep CNN classifying the Urban8k dataset. For the end-to-end network, it is anticipated that it could be improved if CQT related features could be extracted from the raw audio signal.

**Latency** of each network is also observed to determine the practicality of the system. Compared to feature-based networks, the end-to-end approach have its pre-processing qualities within the network which lessens the run time of the system. Execution speed are seen in Table 5 where the parallel architecture performed slowest because of the wide structure of the network.

### 6.3   Overall Performance

Figure 4 shows the confusion matrix for the evaluation of the test set using the highest performing model which is the parallel CNN architecture with CQT as input and dropout for regularization. The class with the highest accuracy is *engine idling* (class 5) while the class with the lowest accuracy is *children playing* (class 2). The network finds difficulty in classifying *children playing* due to its wide difference of samples and relates it to *street music* because of the same set-up environment during data collection.

**Table 5.** Classification accuracies and execution time of the best architectures per implementation. Note that for the end-to-end network, multiple labels are obtained from 1 s of audio

| Network | Mean Acc. | Time |
|---|---|---|
| Sequential | 72.98% | 0.67 s |
| Parallel | **83.79%** | 0.75 s |
| End-to-end | 36.81% | **0.56 s** (0.055 s/win) |
| Deep CNN [22] | 71.80% | – |

The combination of the deep learning systems and the wireless sensor network is illustrated in Fig. 1b. This scene depicts real-time processing, where the audio event is captured by the microphone and the predicted class label is displayed on the monitor.

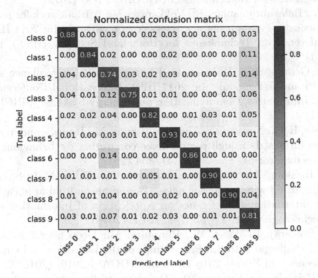

**Fig. 4.** Confusion matrix of parallel CNN architecture, best performing system, on the Urban8K dataset using CQT input features and dropout layers.

## 7    Conclusion and Recommendation

Deep learning techniques such as CNN used in wireless acoustic sensor networks for audio event detection proved that the system could be reliable. Results show that Constant-Q transform inputs are more appropriate to use in the system. This feature transform may also improve the end-to-end implementation if the features can be extracted within the network. The number of Raspberry-Pi nodes could also be increased to check for the reliability of the system if it is scalable. The continuous operation of the sensor nodes suggests that an energy efficiency algorithm could also be explored.

**Acknowledgments.** The authors would like to acknowledge the support of the University of the Philippines Diliman and the Department of Science and Technology through the Engineering Research and Development for Technology (ERDT) Consortium.

## References

1. Ramson, S.R.J., Moni, D.J.: Applications of wireless sensor networks-a survey. In: 2017 International Conference on Innovations in Electrical, Electronics, Instrumentation and Media Technology (ICEEIMT), pp. 325–329. IEEE (2017)

2. Erden, F., Velipasalar, S., Alkar, A.Z., Cetin, A.E.: Sensors in assisted living: a survey of signal and image processing methods. IEEE Signal Process Mag. **33**(2), 36–44 (2016)
3. Martalò, M., Ferrari, G., Malavenda, C.: Wireless Sensor Networks and Audio Signal Recognition for Homeland Security. CRC Press (2012)
4. Dhawan, A., Balasubramanian, R., Vokkarane, V.: A framework for real-time monitoring of acoustic events using a wireless sensor network. In: 2011 IEEE International Conference on Technologies for Homeland Security (HST), pp. 254–261. IEEE (2011)
5. Sruthy, S., George, S.N.: WiFi enabled home security surveillance system using raspberry Pi and IoT module. In: 2017 IEEE International Conference on Signal Processing, Informatics, Communication and Energy Systems (SPICES), pp. 1–6. IEEE (2017)
6. Alsina-Pagès, R.M., Navarro, J., Alías, F., Hervás, M.: HomeSound: real-time audio event detection based on high performance computing for behaviour and surveillance remote monitoring. Sensors **17**(4), 854 (2017)
7. Nisar, K., Ibrahim, A.A.A., Wu, L., Adamov, A., Deen, M.J.: Smart home for elderly living using wireless sensor networks and an android application. In: 2016 IEEE 10th International Conference on Application of Information and Communication Technologies (AICT), pp. 1–8. IEEE (2016)
8. Kong, Q., Sobieraj, I., Wang, W., Plumbley, M.: Deep neural network baseline For DCASE challenge 2016. In: Proceedings of the Detection and Classification of Acoustic Scenes and Events 2016 Workshop (DCASE2016) (2016)
9. Cakir, E., Heittola, T., Virtanen, T.: Domestic audio tagging with convolutional neural networks. In: IEEE AASP Challenge on Detection and Classification of Acoustic Scenes and Events (DCASE 2016) (2016)
10. Lidy, T., Schindler, A.: CQT-based convolutional neural networks for audio scene classification and domestic audio tagging. In: Proceedings of the Detection and Classification of Acoustic Scenes and Events 2016 Workshop (DCASE2016), DCASE2016 Challenge, vol. 90 (2016)
11. Hershey, S., Chaudhuri, S., Ellis, D.P.W., Gemmeke, J.F., et al.: CNN architectures for large-scale audio classification. In: 2017 IEEE International Conference on Acoustics, Speech and Signal Processing (ICASSP), pp. 131–135. IEEE (2017)
12. Krizhevsky, A., Sutskever, I., Hinton, G.E.: ImageNet classification with deep convolutional neural networks. In: Advances in Neural Information Processing Systems, pp. 1097–1105 (2012)
13. Tokozume, Y., Harada, T.: Learning environmental sounds with end-to-end convolutional neural network. In: 2017 IEEE International Conference on Acoustics, Speech and Signal Processing (ICASSP), pp. 2721–2725. IEEE (2017)
14. Vujović, V., Maksimović, M.: Raspberry Pi as a wireless sensor node: performances and constraints. In: 2014 37th International Convention on Information and Communication Technology, Electronics and Microelectronics (MIPRO), pp. 1013–1018 (2014)
15. Bahari, M.H., Plata-Chaves, J., Bertrand, A., Moonen, M.: Distributed labelling of audio sources in wireless acoustic sensor networks using consensus and matching. In: 2016 24th European Signal Processing Conference (EUSIPCO), pp. 2345–2349. IEEE (2016)
16. Salamon, J., Jacoby, C., Bello, J.P.: A dataset and taxonomy for urban sound research. In: Proceedings of the 22nd ACM International Conference on Multimedia, pp. 1041–1044. ACM (2014)

17. Mysore, G., Smaragdis, P.: Relative pitch estimation of multiple instruments. In: IEEE International Conference on 2009 Acoustics, Speech and Signal Processing, ICASSP 2009, pp. 313–316. IEEE (2009)
18. Nanni, L., Costa, Y.M.G., Lucio, D.R., Silla, C.N. Jr., Brahnam, S.: Combining visual and acoustic features for audio classification tasks. In: Pattern Recognition Letters, pp. 49–56, vol. 88 (2017)
19. Burkert, P., Trier, F., Afzal, M.Z., Dengel, A., Liwicki, M.: DeXpression: deep convolutional neural network for expression recognition (2015). arXiv preprint arXiv:1509.05371
20. Chollet, F. et al.: KERAS. In: GitHub (2015). https://github.com/fchollet/keras
21. Piczak, K.J.: Environmental sound classification with convolutional neural networks. In: 2015 IEEE 25th International Workshop on Machine Learning for Signal Processing (MLSP), pp. 1–6. IEEE (2015)
22. Dai, W., Dai, C., Qu, S., Li, J., Das, S.: Very deep convolutional neural networks for raw waveforms. In: 2017 IEEE International Conference on Acoustics, Speech and Signal Processing (ICASSP), pp. 421–425. IEEE (2017)

# Security

# A Robust Remote Authentication Scheme for M-Commerce Environments

Shih-Yang Yang[1]([✉]), Jian-Wen Peng[2], Wen-Bing Horng[3],
and Ching-Ming Chao[4]

[1] Department of Media Arts, University of Kang Ning, Taipei 11485, Taiwan, ROC
shihyang@ukn.edu.tw
[2] Department of Commerce Technology and Management,
Chihlee University of Technology, Taipei 22050, Taiwan, ROC
pchw8598@mail.chihlee.edu.tw
[3] Department of Computer Science and Information Engineering,
Tamkang University, Taipei 25137, Taiwan, ROC
horng@mail.tku.edu.tw
[4] Department of Computer Science and Information Management,
Soochow University, Taipei 10048, Taiwan, ROC
chao@csim.scu.edu.tw

**Abstract.** With the rapid growth of electronic and mobile commerce today, how to design a secure and efficient remote user authentication scheme with resource-limited devices over insecure networks has become an important issue. In this paper, we present a robust authentication scheme for the mobile device (a non-tamper-resistant device in which the secret authentication information stored in it could be retrieved) to solve the challenging lost device problem. It tries to satisfy the following advanced essential security features: (1) protecting user privacy in terms of anonymity and non-traceability, (2) supporting session keys with perfect forward secrecy, and (3) secure even for the case of lost devices, in addition to the conventional security requirements. The security of our scheme is based on the quadratic residue assumption, which has the same complexity as in solving the discrete logarithm problem. However, the computation of the quadratic congruence is very efficient. It only needs one squaring and one modular operations in the mobile device end, which is much cheaper than the expensive modular exponentiation used in those schemes based on the discrete logarithm problem. Thus, using the quadratic congruence, our scheme can achieve robustness and efficiency, even for the non-tamper-resistant mobile device.

**Keywords:** Authentication · Quadratic congruence · Security

© ICST Institute for Computer Sciences, Social Informatics and Telecommunications Engineering 2019
Published by Springer Nature Switzerland AG 2019. All Rights Reserved
J.-L. Chen et al. (Eds.): WiCON 2018, LNICST 264, pp. 119–128, 2019.
https://doi.org/10.1007/978-3-030-06158-6_12

# 1   Introduction

Today is at the era of the rapid growth in electronic and mobile commerce. At this age, how to design a secure and efficient remote user authentication with resource-limited portable devices, such as cellular phones or smart cards, has become an important issue to keep communications confidential and to protect user privacy. Since Lamport [1] proposed the first password authentication scheme over insecure networks, many research works [2–8] have been proposed to improve security and efficiency on the remote authentication used in, for example, electronic toll collection and online financial transactions.

According to the remote authentication schemes proposed so far, it could be summarized that a robust, complete, and efficient remote authentication scheme must satisfy the following criteria:

(1) The remote server does not need to store password or verification tables.
(2) The users can freely choose and change their own passwords.
(3) The scheme must be efficient and practical.
(4) The scheme must provide mutual authentication.
(5) The scheme must provide session key agreement with perfect forward secrecy.
(6) The scheme must protect user privacy in terms of anonymity and non-traceability.
(7) The scheme must withstand various kinds of attacks, such as replay attack, offline password guessing attack, man-in-the-middle attack, user/server impersonation attack, and so on.
(8) The scheme must be secure even for the non-temper-resistant smart card.

Recently, Chung et al. [5] proposed a remote user authentication scheme for resource-limited devices to fulfill the above criteria. However, the scheme suffers from two drawbacks. First, it does not protect user privacy, because static ID is used. Second, it is inefficient for the resource-limited devices, since the scheme is based on the discrete logarithm problem and the expensive modular exponentiation needs to be performed in such devices.

In this paper, we propose a new robust and efficient remote user authentication scheme trying to satisfy all the above security features even for the non-tamper-resistant resource-limited devices. To achieve the same security strength as those using the costly modular exponentiation while releasing the computation burden from the resource-limited devices, we utilize the quadratic congruence. In our scheme, it is very efficient in computing the quadratic congruence because the mobile device only needs to perform one squaring and one modular operations. On the other hand, solving a quadratic congruence modulo a composite needs to factorize the modulus, which has the same complexity as solving the discrete logarithm problem for the factorization. One of the distinguished features of our scheme, as compared to Chung et al.'s scheme, is that our scheme can preserve user anonymity and provide non-traceability by utilizing dynamic ID to protect user privacy. In addition, because our scheme can provide session keys with perfect forward secrecy, which makes our scheme more secure because all communications (including past ones) are confidential.

The rest of the paper is organized as follows. Section 2 presents our proposed authentication scheme. Section 3 analyzes the security of our scheme. Section 4 gives a performance comparison with other related schemes. Finally, the last section concludes this paper.

# 2 Our Proposed Scheme

Our proposed scheme consists of five phases: (1) initial setup phase, (2) registration phase, (3) login phase, (4) authentication phase, and (5) password change phase.

## 2.1 Initial Setup Phase

The server $S$ first selects two distinct large prime numbers $p$ and $q$. It then computes $n = p \times q$. In addition, $S$ selects a random number $x$ as its long-term secret key and a secure one-way hash function $h(\cdot)$. Note that $p$, $q$, and $x$ are kept secretly in the server.

## 2.2 Registration Phase

This phase is invoked whenever a new user $U$ initially registers to $S$. The user $U$ first chooses his/her identity $ID$ and submits it to $S$ through a secure channel. After receiving $ID$, the server $S$ first computes $Y = h(ID \| x) \oplus h(PW_o)$, where $PW_o$ is a random default password for user $U$. Then, the server $S$ stores $\{Y, n, h(\cdot)\}$ into a smart card and sends it together with the default password $PW_o$ to $U$ (or directly sends $\{Y, n, h(\cdot), PW_o\}$ to $U$'s mobile device) via a secure channel. Before the user $U$ begins to use his/her new smart card (or mobile device), he/she is requested to change his/her default password $PW_o$ into a new one, say $PW$, as performed in the password change phase, described in Sect. 2.5.

## 2.3 Login Phase

When user $U$ wants to login with server $S$, he/she inserts his/her smart card into the card reader of a terminal (or uses his/her mobile device) and inputs his/her $ID$ and $PW$. The user $U$'s portable device first generates a random number $a$ and computes $C_0 = Y \oplus h(PW)$, $X = (T_1 \| ID \| a)^2 \bmod n$, and $C_1 = h(X \| T_1 \| C_0 \| a)$, where $T_1$ is the current timestamp. It then sends the login request message $\{X, C_1, T_1\}$ to server $S$.

## 2.4 Authentication Phase

**User Authentication.** After receiving the login request message $\{X, C_1, T_1\}$ at time $T_1'$, the server $S$ performs the following steps to authenticate the user $U$.

1. Verify whether $(T_1' - T_1) < \Delta T$, where $\Delta T$ is a predefined transmission delay. If it is not, reject the login request to avoid the replay attack.

2. Solve $X = (T_1 \| ID \| a)^2 \bmod n$ with $p$ and $q$ to obtain four roots $(r_1, r_2, r_3, r_4)$ [9,10]. Check which root $r_i$ (for $i = 1, 2, 3, 4$) containing the prefix $T_1$ to determine the correct root $r = (T_1 \| ID \| a)$. Then, $ID$ and $a$ will be determined from the correct root $r$.

3. Check the validity of $ID$. If it fails, stop the verification procedure.

4. Check if $h(X \| T_1 \| h(ID \| x) \| a) = C_1$. If they are not equal, terminate the current session. Otherwise, $U$ is authenticated as a legal user.

5. Generate a random number $b$ and compute $R = a \oplus b$ and $C_2 = h(R \| h(ID \| x) \| b \| T_2)$, where $T_2$ is the current timestamp of the server $S$.

6. Send the reply message $\{R, C_2, T_2\}$ to the user $U$'s smart card.

**Server Authentication.** At the receipt of the message $\{R, C_2, T_2\}$ from the server $S$ at time $T_2'$, the user $U$'s smart card performs the following steps to authenticate the server $S$.

1. Check the freshness of $T_2$ by verifying whether $(T_2' - T_2) < \Delta T$. If it is not, terminate the current session.

2. Compute $b = R \oplus a$, and check if $h(R \| C_0 \| b \| T_2) = C_2$. If they are not equal, terminate the current session. Otherwise, $S$ is authenticated as the legal server.

**Session Key Establishment.** After mutual authentication is complete, the user $U$ calculates the session key $SK = h(a \| C_0 \| b)$ and the server $S$ computes the session key $SK = h(a \| h(ID \| x) \| b)$. Note that these two session keys are exactly the same since $C_0 = h(ID \| x)$ and they are used for securing transmissions by encrypting/decrypting subsequent transmitted messages during the current session.

### 2.5 Password Change Phase

If the user $U$ wants to change his/her password, he/she first inserts his/her smart card into the card reader of a terminal and enters his/her $ID$ and $PW$. The login and authentication phases, as described before (Sects. 2.3 and 2.4), are performed first. After successful mutual authentication, the smart card asks the user $U$ to enter a new password $PW_n$. It then computes $Y_n = Y \oplus h(PW) \oplus h(PW_n)$ and replaces $Y$ with $Y_n$.

## 3   Security Analysis

In this section, we analyze the security of our proposed authentication scheme. Note that in our scheme we allow the authentication information stored in the portable device can be retrieved (i.e., the portable device is non-tamper-resistant). Because the security of our scheme is based on the quadratic residue assumption, we describe it first.

**Assumption 1. (Quadratic Residue Assumption)** *Let $p$ and $q$ be two large primes and $n = p \times q$. If $y = x^2 \bmod n$ has a solution, then $y$ is called a quadratic residue modulo $n$. Let $QR_n$ denote the set of all quadratic residues in $\mathbf{Z}_n$ (i.e., $[1, n-1]$). Then, the quadratic residue assumption can be described as follows. Let $y \in QR_n$. Because of the difficulty of factoring the composite modulus $n$, it is computationally infeasible to find $x$ such that $y = x^2 \bmod n$ without knowing $p$ and $q$ [9, 10].*

**Lemma 1.** *In the proposed scheme, the random numbers $a$ (generated by the user's portable device) and $b$ (generated by the server) cannot be derived by an adversary.*

*Proof.* In this scheme, we apply the quadratic residue assumption to protect the random number $a$ in $X$ during the login phase, where $X = (T_1 \,\|\, ID \,\|\, a)^2 \bmod n$. An adversary can eavesdrop on $X$ from the login request $\{X, C_1, T_1\}$ transmitted over the network. Note that $n = p \times q$, where $p$ and $q$ are two large primes which are kept secretly in the server. Without knowing $p$ and $q$, it is difficult to factor the composite modulus $n$ by the quadratic residue assumption. Therefore, it is computationally infeasible for the adversary to solve $X$ to obtain $a$ even if he knows $T_1$ from the login request. On the other hand, due to the one-way property of the secure hash function $h(\cdot)$, it is computationally infeasible to obtain $a$ from $C_1 = h(X \,\|\, T_1 \,\|\, C_0 \,\|\, a)$ and $b$ from $C_2 = h(R \,\|\, C_0 \,\|\, b \,\|\, T_2)$, where $C_2$ can be intercepted from the reply message $\{R, C_2, T_2\}$. Although $R = a \oplus b$, without knowing $a$, it is impossible to derive $b$ from $R$, and vice versa. Therefore, the random numbers $a$ and $b$ cannot be compromised by an adversary.

**Proposition 1.** *The proposed scheme can withstand the offline password guessing attack.*

*Proof.* A remote user authentication scheme which is vulnerable to the offline password guessing attack must satisfy the two conditions: (1) the users password is weak and (2) there exists a piece of password-related information used as a comparison target for the password guessing. In our scheme, only $Y = h(ID \,\|\, x) \oplus h(PW)$ stored in a user $U$'s portable device involves the password information, $PW$. To launch a password guessing attack, it is assumed that an adversary has obtained $Y$ from $U$'s portable device and has intercepted the login request $\{X, C_1, T_1\}$ and the reply message $\{R, C_2, T_2\}$ over the network. The adversary then guesses a password $PW^*$ and computes $C_0^* = Y \oplus h(PW^*)$. As mentioned previously, the adversary must find a piece of password-related information to verify whether the guessed password $PW^*$ is correct or not. In our scheme, it would be $C_1 = h(X \,\|\, T_1 \,\|\, C_0 \,\|\, a)$ or $C_2 = h(R \,\|\, C_0 \,\|\, b \,\|\, T_2)$, in which $a$ and $b$ are two random numbers generated by the portable device and the server, respectively. By Lemma 1, the adversary cannot derive $a$ and $b$. Therefore, although $X$, $R$, $T_1$, and $T_2$ are known, without correct $a$ and $b$, the adversary cannot verify whether the guessed password $PW^*$ is correct or not by comparing $h(X \,\|\, T_1 \,\|\, C_0^* \,\|\, a)$ with the intercepted $C_1$ (or $h(R \,\|\, C_0^* \,\|\, b \,\|\, T_2)$ with $C_2$). Thus, our scheme can resist the offline password guessing attack.

**Proposition 2.** *The proposed scheme can preserve user privacy.*

*Proof.* User privacy can be divided into two parts for discussion: anonymity and non-traceability. In our scheme, the login request $\{X, C_1, T_1\}$ and the reply message $\{R, C_2, T_2\}$ do not contain explicit static-ID information of the user $U$. Thus, an adversary cannot easily know which user is connecting with the server from these authentication messages. However, $X$, $C_1$, and $C_2$ indeed implicitly contain user $U$'s $ID$ information. Let us examine whether or not they might reveal $ID$ information. First, consider $X = (T_1 \parallel ID \parallel a)^2 \bmod n$. By the quadratic residue assumption, it is computational infeasible to solve $X$. Thus, an adversary cannot obtain $ID$ from $X$. Next, we consider $C_1 = h(X \parallel T_1 \parallel C_0 \parallel a)$ and $C_2 = h(R \parallel C_0 \parallel b \parallel T_2)$, where $C_0 = h(ID \parallel x)$. However, it is computational infeasible to derive $ID$ from $C_1$ and $C_2$ owing to the one-way property of the hash function $h(\cdot)$. Moreover, $X$, $R$, $C_1$, and $C_2$ are different at each session due to random numbers $a$ and $b$ and timestamps $T_1$ and $T_2$. Hence, the adversary cannot trace a specific user just by eavesdropping on $X$, $R$, $C_1$, and $C_2$ from the exchanged login messages.

On the other hand, an adversary may want to find $U$'s $ID$ by performing the offline identity guessing, just like the offline password guessing. However, $X$, $R$, $C_1$, and $C_2$ contain random numbers $a$ or $b$. By Lemma 1, an adversary cannot derive them without knowing $p$ and $q$. Thus, the adversary cannot verify whether a guessed identity $ID^*$ is correct or not. Hence, he cannot obtain $U$'s $ID$ and use it to trace the user $U$. Note that $ID$ is not stored in $U$'s portable device in our proposed scheme. Even if an adversary can extract $Y = h(ID \parallel x) \oplus h(PW)$ from $U$'s portable device, he still cannot know $U$'s $ID$ because $Y$ contains three unknown parameters $x$, $ID$ and $PW$. From above observations, we conclude that our scheme can provide user anonymity and non-traceability. Hence, our scheme can protect user privacy.

**Proposition 3.** *The proposed scheme can withstand the insider attack.*

*Proof.* In our scheme, the user $U$ only submits his/her $ID$ to the server $S$ during the registration phase. After $U$ receives his/her new authentication information $\{Y, n, h(\cdot), PW_o\}$ stored in a portable device, he/she needs to change the default password, $PW_o$, to a new one, $PW$, before using it. Since the update of password is executed by the user $U$ only after successful mutual authentication with the server $S$, the insider of $S$ cannot know $U$'s true password. Thus, the insider attack will not take place in our scheme.

**Proposition 4.** *The proposed scheme can provide perfect forward secrecy for session keys.*

*Proof.* In our scheme, we exchange the session key $SK = h(a \parallel h(ID \parallel x) \parallel b)$ in each session, where $a$ and $b$ are two random numbers generated by the user $U$'s portable device and the server $S$, respectively. Perfect forward secrecy is a very important property in that if some user's long-term secret values, e.g. $ID$ and $PW$ in our scheme, are compromised, session keys used before still cannot be derived. By Lemma 1, $a$ and $b$ cannot be obtained by an adversary. Even if both $U$'s identity $ID$ and password $PW$ are compromised, the adversary still cannot derive any session keys used in previous sessions without knowing $p$ and $q$. Hence, our scheme provides perfect forward secrecy for session keys.

**Proposition 5.** *The proposed scheme can withstand the user impersonation attack.*

*Proof.* If an adversary wants to impersonate the user $U$, he/she has to send the server $S$ a proper login request either by replaying an old one $\{X, C_1, T_1\}$ intercepted from the network or by forging a new one $\{X^*, C_1^*, T_1^*\}$ to pass the authentication of $S$. In our scheme, we employ the timestamp mechanism (i.e., $T_1$) to prevent the replay attack. Thus, replaying previous login requests is impossible. On the other hand, to forge a new login request $\{X^*, C_1^*, T_1^*\}$, the adversary needs to have $U$'s $ID$ and $C_0 = h(ID \| x)$ so that he/she can counterfeit $X^* = (T_1^* \| ID \| a^*)^2 \bmod n$ and $C_1^* = h(X^* \| T_1^* \| C_0 \| a^*)$ from forged $T_1^*$ and $a^*$. However, as shown in Proposition 2, the adversary cannot obtain $U$'s $ID$. Furthermore, as shown in Proposition 1, the adversary cannot guess the correct password $PW$. Thus, he cannot compute $C_0 = h(ID \| x) = Y \oplus h(PW)$, even though $Y$ stored in $U$'s portable device can be obtained by the adversary. Therefore, without $ID$ and $C_0$, the adversary cannot forge proper login request $\{X^*, C_1^*, T_1^*\}$. Hence, our scheme can withstand the user impersonation attack.

**Proposition 6.** *The proposed scheme can withstand the server impersonation attack.*

*Proof.* If an adversary wishes to masquerade as the server $S$, he/she needs to send the user $U$ a proper reply message either by replaying an old one $\{R, C_2, T_2\}$, intercepted over the network, or by forging a new one $\{R^*, C_2^*, T_2^*\}$ to pass the authentication of $U$. Similarly, the timestamp mechanism is used to avoid the replay attack. On the other hand, to forge a new proper reply message $\{R^*, C_2^*, T_2^*\}$, the adversary has to know the random number $a$ generated by $U$'s portable device and $C_0 = h(ID \| x)$ so that he/she can fake $R^* = a \oplus b$ and $C_2* = h(a \| C_0 \| b^* \| T_2^*)$ from bogus $b^*$ and $T_2^*$. However, as shown in Lemma 1, the adversary cannot derive $a$. Similarly, as demonstrated in Proposition 5, the adversary cannot compute $C_0$. Therefore, without knowing $a$ and $C_0$, the adversary cannot forge proper reply message $\{R^*, C_2^*, T_2^*\}$. Therefore, our scheme can resist the server impersonation attack.

**Corollary 1.** *The proposed scheme can achieve mutual authentication.*

*Proof.* By Propositions 5 and 6, our scheme can withstand both the user and server impersonation attacks. Thus, the scheme can achieve mutual authentication.

**Corollary 2.** *The proposed scheme is secure for the non-tamper-resistant portable device.*

*Proof.* When the portable device is lost, the authentication information stored in the portable device can be obtained by an adversary. As stated in Propositions 1, 2, 4, 5, and 6, we have shown that our scheme can withstand the offline password guessing attack, can achieve mutual authentication, can preserve user privacy in terms of anonymity and non-traceability, and can provide session keys with perfect forward secrecy even if the adversary has obtained the secret information stored in the portable device. Therefore, we can conclude that our scheme is secure even for the non-tamper-resistant portable device.

## 4    Performance Comparisons

In this section, we give a comparison of our proposed scheme with two other schemes specially designed for non-tamper-resistant portable devices to provide more security in terms of security features and computation cost. The first one is Fan et al.'s scheme [3], which is also based on the quadratic congruence as ours, in addition to using some symmetric cryptosystems. The second one is Chung et al.'s scheme [5]. It is based on the modular exponentiation to achieve its security, which is the most secure scheme.

Table 1 shows the comparison of computation cost of our scheme with the other two schemes. During the login and verification phases, the computation cost in the portable device of our scheme has one additional hash operation as compared to Fan et al.'s scheme, in which the portable device only needs to perform light-weight operations such as arithmetic operation, random number generation, and one-way hash function. As compared to Chung et al.'s scheme, it needs one heavy-weight modular exponentiation in each of the login and verification phases. Because Fan et al.'s scheme requires one additional symmetric decryption in the server during the authentication phase, our scheme is more efficient than the other two schemes in terms of computation cost.

**Table 1.** Comparison of computation cost at the server and device end.

| Phase | End | Fan et al.'s scheme | Chung et al.'s scheme | Our scheme |
|-------|-----|---------------------|------------------------|------------|
| Registration | Server | 1S+1H+1R | 3H+1R+1M | 2H |
| Login | Portable device | 1R+2M | 1E+2H+1R | 2H+1R+2M |
| Verification | Portable device | 3H | 1E+4H+1M | 2H |
| Verification | Server | 1Q+1S+2H+1R | 2E+6H+1R+1M | 1Q+3H+1R |

Note: E: modular exponentiation, S: symmetric encryption/decryption,
H: one-way hash function, Q: solving the quadratic congruence,
R: random number generation, M: multiplication/division.

As shown in Table 2, Fan et al.'s scheme can withstand the offline password guessing attack even if the portable device is lost. Unfortunately, Rhee et al. [6] has shown that Fan et al.'s scheme is vulnerable to the server impersonation attack. In addition, Fan et al.'s scheme does not protect user privacy because it uses static ID. Besides, it does not provide session key agreement as well as password change procedure. On the other hand, Chung et al.'s scheme provides almost all the security features, except that is uses static ID when sending login requests. Like Fan et al.'s scheme, it also does not protect user privacy in terms of anonymity as well as non-traceability. Apparently, our proposed scheme can provide all security features listed in Table 2.

**Table 2.** Comparison of security properties.

| Security property | Fan's | Chung's | Ours |
|---|---|---|---|
| Without verification table in the server | Yes | Yes | Yes |
| Resistant to offline password guessing attack | Yes | Yes | Yes |
| Resistant to insider attack | Yes | Yes | Yes |
| Resistant to user impersonation attack | Yes | Yes | Yes |
| Resistant to server impersonation attack | No | Yes | Yes |
| Providing user anonymity | No | No | Yes |
| Providing non-traceability | No | No | Yes |
| Providing mutual authentication | No | Yes | Yes |
| Providing session key agreement | No | Yes | Yes |
| Providing perfect forward secrecy for session keys | – | Yes | Yes |
| Providing secure password change phase | – | Yes | Yes |
| Secure for non-tamper-resistant portable device | No | Yes | Yes |

Note: The symbol "–" stands for "not supported."

## 5   Conclusion

In this paper, we presented a robust and efficient remote authentication scheme with resource-limited portable devices for M-commerce environments. The security of our scheme is based on the quadratic congruence assumption, which has the same security strength as the discrete logarithm problem, while it uses much less computation cost in computing the quadratic congruence in the portable devices as comparing to the modular exponentiation. By robustness, we mean that our scheme can support the following security features: (1) without verification tables, (2) freely choosing and updating passwords, (3) providing mutual authentication, (4) providing session keys with perfect forward secrecy, (5) protecting user privacy in terms of anonymity and non-traceability, (6) withstanding various kinds of attacks, and (7) secure even for non-tamper-resistant portable devices. By efficiency, we mean that the resource-limited device in our scheme only needs to execute light-weight operations, such as bitwise exclusive-or operations, arithmetic operations, secure one-way hash functions, and pseudo random number generations, rather than the heavy-weight modular exponentiations. Because of the robustness and efficiency, these make our scheme more secure and practical.

# References

1. Lamport, L.: Password authentication with insecure communication. Commun. ACM **24**(11), 770–772 (1981)
2. Hwang, M.S., Lee, C.C., Tang, Y.L.: A simple remote user authentication scheme. Math. Comput. Model. **36**(1–2), 103–107 (2002)
3. Fan, C.I., Chan, Y.C., Zhang, Z.K.: Robust remote authentication scheme with smart cards. Comput. Secur. **24**(8), 619–628 (2005)
4. Shieh, W.G., Wang, J.M.: Efficient remote mutual authentication and key agreement. Comput. Secur. **25**(1), 72–77 (2006)
5. Chung, H.R., Ku, W.C., Tsaur, M.J.: Weaknesses and improvement of Wang et al.'s remote user password authentication scheme for resource-limited environments. Comput. Stand. Interfaces **31**(4), 863–868 (2009)
6. Rhee, H.S., Kwon, J.O., Lee, D.H.: A remote user authentication scheme without using smart cards. Comput. Stand. Interfaces **31**(1), 6–13 (2009)
7. Li, X., Nju, J.W., Ma, J., Wang, W.D., Liu, C.L.: Cryptanalysis and improvement of a biometrics-based remote user authentication scheme using smart card. J. Netw. Comput. Appl. **34**(1), 73–79 (2011)
8. Wen, F., Li, X.: An improved dynamic ID-based remote user authentication with key agreement scheme. Comput. Electr. Eng. **38**(2), 381–387 (2012)
9. Patterson, W.: Mathematical Cryptology for Computer Scientists and Mathematicians. Rowman (1987)
10. Rosen, K.H.: Elementary Number Theory and its Applications. Addison-Wesley, Reading (1988)

# MIH-Based eNB Selection for Untrusted Networks

Fang-Yie Leu[1(✉)], Kun-Lin Tsai[2], and Rui-Ting Hung[1]

[1] Department of Computer Science, Tunghai University, Tunghai, Taiwan
leufy@thu.edu.tw, tom813813@gmail.com
[2] Department of Electric Engineering, Tunghai University, Tunghai, Taiwan
kltsai@thu.edu.tw

**Abstract.** In recent years, some mobile phones are equipped with more than one Radio Access Technology (RAT) to make themselves adapt to a heterogeneous environment which comprises networks of different technologies. Also, during a User Equipment's (UE's) handover, it would be better if we can choose a suitable eNB as the next eNB (NeNB) to serve this UE. Generally, this can be achieved with the help of Common Radio Resource Management (CRRM). In this study, we propose a NeNB selection scheme, called eNB Selection System (eSeS), for two adjacent networks, e.g., Q and R, to select an appropriate eNB in R for UE before UE hands over from Q, i.e., source network, to R, i.e., target network. In order to enable the communication between different types of RATs, such as Long Term Evolution Advanced (LTE-A) and Wireless Local Area Network (WLAN), we utilize the IEEE 802.21 Media Independent Handover (MIH) as their common data exchange mechanism. With the CRRM, the load balance in a heterogeneous network environment can also be maintained. In our simulation, the performance of this scheme in untrusted network handover cases is better than that of PMIPv6 and FMIPv6.

**Keywords:** MIH · CRRM · Untrusted networks · LTE-A · WLAN

## 1 Introduction

In recent years, some mobile phones are equipped with more than one Radio Access Technology (RAT) to make themselves adapt to a heterogeneous environment which comprises networks of different technologies. A typical example is that one is 802.16 Wimax [1] and others are 802.11 (WLAN) [2] and Long Term Evolution Advanced (LTE-A) [3]. Further, when UE hands over from a wireless system of model A to another one of model B, the delay time is relatively long [4].

On the other hand, two adjacent networks, e.g., Q and R, may be trustable or untrusted. The former is defined as that Q and R have signed a contract with which Q (R) offers R's (Q's) users with the same network services that these users receive when staying in R (Q), while the latter is the case in which Q (R) can only provide basic network services to R's (Q's) users, no matter what network services the users can receive from R (Q).

© ICST Institute for Computer Sciences, Social Informatics and Telecommunications Engineering 2019
Published by Springer Nature Switzerland AG 2019. All Rights Reserved
J.-L. Chen et al. (Eds.): WiCON 2018, LNICST 264, pp. 129–140, 2019.
https://doi.org/10.1007/978-3-030-06158-6_13

In 2008, the IEEE 802.21 (Media Independent Handover, MIH) protocol [5] was proposed for helping UE to hand over, aiming to shorten the handover delay and reduce packet loss rates. However, MIH works only when source network (S-Net for short) and target network (T-Net for short) are trustable. The handover based on MIH has been discussed in many studies [6–8].

Basically, during handover, it would be better if we can choose a suitable base station as NMAG to serve UE, and this choice truly balances network load [9] and supports session QoS. In fact, Common Radio Resource Management (CRRM) [10] as a network resource management scheme can help us to achieve this. Houda et al. [11] proposed a scheme to optimize handover decision in an LTE-A network by using MIH and CRRM. But CRRM entity and MIIS server need to exchange information frequently. Also, CRRM is applicable only when S-Net and T-Net are trustable.

Therefore, in this study, we propose a next eNB (NeNB) selection scheme, named eNB Selection System (eSeS), for two adjacent networks, e.g., Q and R, to select an appropriate eNB in R before UE hands over from Q to R. The selection is performed by LMA. Once S-Net eNB (i.e., PMAG) discovers that UE's signal is weak, it requests S-Net LMA autonomously choosing one of eNBs in T-Net as the UE's NMAG. A part of the results of this study was published in [12].

Also, in current wireless network, some terms are names of the same items, e.g., MN and UE. MAG, eNB and base station are the other example. In this study, we use MN and UE (MAG, eNB and base station) interchangeably, even though they are used in different systems, like PMIPv6, MIPv6 and LTE-5G/4G.

The remaining portion of this paper is structured as follows. Section 2 overviews the background and related work of this study. Section 3 presents the eSeS. The simulation and results are, respectively, performed and discussed in Sect. 4. Section 5 concludes this study and addresses our future studies.

## 2 Background and Related Studies

In this section, we introduce background and related work of this study

### 2.1 Related Work

Recent researchers have tried to improve handover performance for a heterogeneous environment by using IEEE 802.21 MIH standard. Mussabbir *et al.* [13] proposed a scheme to optimize FMIPv6 in a vehicular network. They designed a cross-layer mechanism for making an intelligent handover decision and creating a repository to store neighbor-network information. Its advantage is reducing network-prediction time. But MN's power consumption is high because the prediction is done by MN. This may seriously shorten the available time of battery. The scheme proposed by Ha *et al.* in [14] balanced network loads by using a traffic balancing architecture for heterogeneous wireless networks. But serious interference among base stations cannot be avoided. Wang *et al.* [15] proposed a framework which enhances MIH by developing a function providing seamless mobility management. Nevertheless, it may bring heavy signaling overheads to users. Buiati *et al.* [16] proposed a hierarchical MIIS architecture to diminish MIIS response time and reduce the latency of heterogeneous vertical handover.

## 2.2    Signals of FMIPv6 Handover

The primitives exchanged in FMIPv6 [17] for handover are that at first, each MN and MAG in the system periodically send their information, such as Signal-to-Interference-plus-Noise Ratio (SINR), Received Signal Strength Indication (RSSI), etc., to CRRM. The information is conveyed in some primitives defined in IEEE802.21 MIH standard. MN's MIHF sends MIH_Get_Information.request to CRRM to acquire the statuses of neighbor base stations. CRRM replies MN with MIH_Get_Information.response. When MN's RSSI is lower than RSSIth, MN's MIHF sends MIH_Link_Going_Down to the mobile user to indicate that an event will occur. The user then sends MIH_MN_HO_Candidate_Query.request back to its MIHF. MN's MIHF passes this primitive to MIIS Server through AP MIHF to enquire nearby base-station information which is then conveyed in the MIH_MN_HO_Candidate_Query.response sent by MIIS server to MN's MIHF through AP's MIHF. With this information, MN chooses its NMAG.

After that, MN sends MIH_MN_HO_Commit.request to CRRM through the serving MAG to request handover. On receiving this primitive, CRRM sends MIH_Resource_Reservation.request to NMAG to reserve the required resources (e.g., wireless uplink and downlink channels, backhaul transmission bandwidth, etc.) for MN. When NMAG receives this primitive, it internally delivers MIH_Resource_Allocation.request to its own RRC for resources allocation since in an eNB/MAG, wireless resources are managed by RRC. After that, MIH_Resource_Allocation.response will be sent to eNB's MIHF by RRC. Then the NMAG sends a MIH_Resource_Reservation.response primitive to CRRM. CRRM replies MN with MIH_MN_HO_Commit.response. When MN enters the communication area of the NMAG and attaches to it, NMAG sends a MIH_Resource_Report.request to CRRM telling CRRM the arrival of this MN, and CRRM replies NMAG with MIH_Resource_Report.response as an acknowledgement.

## 2.3    Signals of PMIPv6 Handover

In PMIPv6 [18], those primitives originally designed for handover and sent by MN in FMIPv6 are now delivered by previous MAG (i,e., PMAG), since PMAG is the proxy of MN. The main difference between FMIPv6 and PMIPv6 is which network entity decides to hand over. When MN's RSSI is lower than $RSSI_{th}$, PMAG sends MIH_MN_HO_Candidate_Query.request to CRRM to acquire the statuses of neighbor base stations with which to choose a suitable NMAG for MN. CRRM will deliver MIH_MN_HO_Candidate_Query.response, which carries the statuses of neighbor base stations, to PMAG. In FMIPv6, this primitive is issued by MN. The remaining sections of resources reservation are almost the same as those of FMIPv6. We do not redundantly describe them.

# 3 The eSeS Scheme

In the eSeS, MIH is utilized to assist handover in a heterogeneous environment and CRRM is used to balance network burden

## 3.1   eNB-Collection Subsystem

The main function of eNB-collection Subsystem is mediating the working processes of $n$ untrusted networks, i.e., T-Net LMA, S-Net LMA and so on, $n > 1$. This subsystem basically is created by a trustable third party. In fact, S-Net LMA cannot directly enquire the information of T-Net MAGs. Generally, there are two types of eNB status collection policies. The first one is that eNB-collection Subsystem on demand dynamically requests its nearby network LMAs transferring the statuses of all candidate eNBs near the S-Net MAG to it. The disadvantage, as a dynamic inquiry approach, is that the information available time is relatively longer since the inquiry lasts longer. Its advantages are that the information is provided in a real time manner. Therefore, its statuses accuracy is higher. The storage required to store data is smaller. The second type is that it retrieves the information from its MIIS database or cloud system, indicating eNB-collection Subsystem needs to periodically gathers nearby eNBs' statuses. The disadvantage is that we need to prepare a large database or cloud system to keep eNB statuses that have been so far collected. Maintaining the data and database is another problem. Of course the information accuracy is a little poor, and LRRMs need to periodically collect eNB statuses and send the statuses to eNB-collection Subsystem, consequently increasing network loads. But the information available time is shorter since it accesses data from its local database or cloud system. In this study, we choose the cloud approach. It means we need to prepare a cloud system and periodically collect data from eNBs. This subsystem retrieves eNBs' statuses and then passes these statuses to S-Net LMA. S-Net LMA chooses an appropriate eNB as the NMAG for MN, and delivers related information to MN. With the help of eNB-collection Subsystem, the handover can be smoothly performed.

## 3.2   The Signaling of the eSeS

Assume that S-Net and T-Net are two adjacent untrusted networks, the primitives exchanged among network entities are shown in Fig. 1. MN is currently staying in S-Net. MN's serving MAG (i.e., PMAG) periodically sends MIH_Net_Measurement_Report which carries the status of the link between MN and PMAG (also called an active link) to S-Net LMA. When MN has to hand over to T-Net, the S-Net LMA sends the MIH_HO.Indication.request to eNB-collection Subsystem to request a suitable MAG for MN.

After receiving this request, eNB-collection Subsystem transmits this request to T-Net LMA. T-Net LMA delivers Authentication.request to T-Net AAA server. This server in turn requests S-Net AAA server to authenticate MN. After that, when receiving Authentication response from S-Net AAA server, T-Net AAA server passes this primitive to T-Net LMA, which then chooses an appropriate MAG as NMAG for MN and sends MIH_Resource_Reservation.request to NMAG. On receiving this

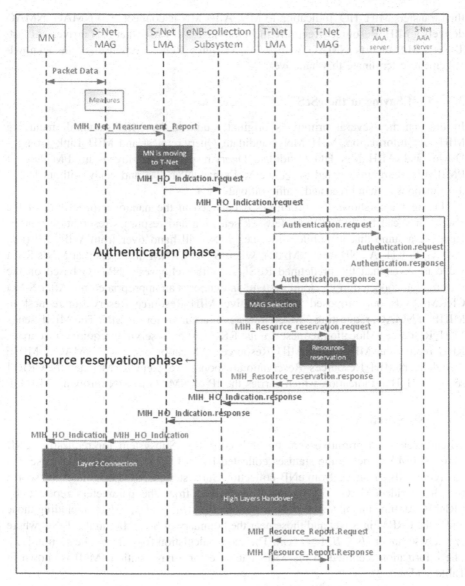

**Fig. 1.** The primitives exchanged in untrusted networks handover case (MN hands over from S-Net to T-Net) [12].

request, NMAG transmits a MIH_Resource_Allocation.request (not shown) to its RRC to reserve network resources for MN.

Then, NMAG sends a MIH_Resource_Reservation.response to T-Net LMA. T-Net LMA passes MIH_HO_Indication.response carrying IP of NMAG to eNB-collection Subsystem, which then delivers this primitive to CRRM in S-Net LMA. S-Net LMA transmits MIH_HO_Indication.response containing IP of NMAG to PMAG, which then transfers MIH_HO_Indication to MN. After MN is connected to NMAG, NMAG delivers a MIH_Resource_Report.request telling T-Net LMA that MN arrives. At last, T-Net LMA reports NMAG with MIH_Resource_Report.response as an acknowledgement to terminate this handover.

### 3.3    Cost Saving of the eSeS

In our scheme, several primitives originally utilized by MIH standard, including MIH_Get_Information, MIH_MN_Candidate_Query.request and MIH_Link_Going_-Down and MIH_MN_HO_Candidate_Query.response employed in FMIPv6 or PMIPv6 system, are deleted to reduce MN's handover cost and delay without losing the functions of handover and traffic offload.

Figure 1 also shows the primitives exchanged in the handover procedure of the eSeS. They can be divided into network selection and resources reservation phases. Here we assume that a mobile node, i.e., MN, will hand over from WiFi AP (i.e., PMAG) to LTE-A eNB (i.e., NMAG). When S-Net CRRM discovers that MN's RSSI value is lower than the predefined $RSSI_{th}$, it either chooses a NMAG based on the information collected in its cloud system, and chooses an appropriate one. After S-Net CRRM sends our proposed new primitive MIH_Resource_Reservation.request to MIHF of NMAG, requesting NMAG to reserve resources for the MN. The MIHF sends MIH_Resource_Allocation.request to its RRC. After reserving required resources, RRC replies the MIHF with MIH_Resources_Allocation.response. NMAG's MIHF then delivers MIH_Resources_Reservation.response to S-Net CRRM. Then the CRRM sends MIH_HO_Indication which carries the IP of NMAG to MN through PMAG.

### 3.4    eNB Selection

When receiving a primitive sent by eNB-collection Subsystem for requesting eNB statuses, LMA retrieves the statuses collected by its LRRM from MIIS database. On receiving eNB's statuses from eNB-collection Subsystem, CRRM calculates the scores for all provided MAGs. The scores are derived from the parameters reported by LRRMs. Assume that there are $m$ base stations $B = \{b_1, b_2, b_3, ..., b_m\}$, including those under the CRRM in S-Net and those near the boundary of S-Net but in the T-Net where $b_i$ is a base station, $b_i \in B$, $1 \leq i \leq m$. The score calculation formula can be seen in [12]. The information recorded in the MIIS database for a base station (MN) is shown in Table 1 (Table 2).

**Table 1.**  Information recorded in the MIIS Server or MIH cloud for a base station.

| Parameters | Weight |
|---|---|
| Location | 0 |
| Bandwidth | 0.3 |
| End-to-end delay | 0.1 |
| Throughput | 0.1 |
| Drop rate | 0.1 |

**Table 2.** Information recorded in the MIIS Server or in MIH cloud for MN.

| Parameters | Weight |
|---|---|
| RSS | 0.1 |
| MN's moving direction | 0 |
| $Angle_{MN,MAG}$ | 0.2 |
| $Distance_{MN,MAG}$ | 0.1 |

## 4    Simulation and Discussion

In the study, two experiments were performed. The eSeS and current untrusted-network handover scheme (i.e., reactive mode) were simulated by using NS-2 and its mobility extension developed by National Institute of Standards and Technology (NIST) [19]. In the first experiment, the three tested schemes were evaluated given two untrusted homogeneous networks, including two LTE-As. An MN is equipped with two network interface cards, each of which is assigned a unique IP and channel. That is, it is a two-connections SCTP association. MN hands over from LTE-A to the other LTE-A. The second compared the performance of eSeS algorithm and current algorithm (based on RSS).

Three test metrics are employed, including throughput defined as the bit rate received, end-to-end delay defined as the time required by a packet to travel from sender to receiver, and drop rate defined as the number of packets received over the number of packets sent. The specifications and network parameters of the test-bed used are illustrated in Table 3. Figure 2 shows the simulation topology.

**Table 3.** The specifications and default parameters of our tested.

| Network parameter | Value |
|---|---|
| LTE-A bandwidth | 200 Mbps |
| Bandwidth of a wired link | 100 Mbps |
| Data rate | 80 Mbps |
| MN's moving speed | 1 m/s |
| Simulation time | 10 s |

### 4.1    An Untrusted Homogeneous Network

In the first experiment, the three schemes are evaluated in an untrusted-homogeneous environment. At the beginning, MN is connected to an LTE-A, and it hands over to another LTE-A network at about the 10th sec. Figure 3 shows the throughputs. Owing to the employment of eNB-collection Subsystem and SCTP's multi-streaming and multi-homing characteristics, the performance of the eSeS is better than those of

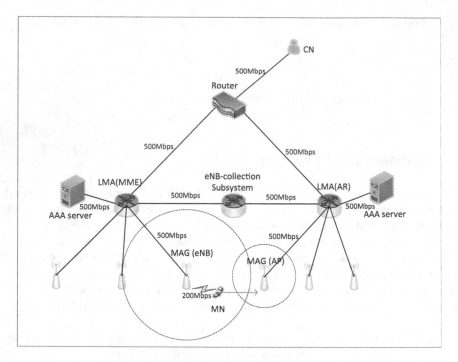

**Fig. 2.** The topology of our simulation.

FMIPv6 and PMIPv6. Figure 4 illustrates the drop rates. Because of active link disconnection, the drop rates of FMIPv6 (PMIPv6) are 100% between the 10th and 10.15th (between 10th and 10.10th) sec. The end-to-end delays are illustrated in Fig. 5. Because before connecting to NMAG, MN must disconnect its current active link. It is the reason why the end-to-end delays of FMIPv6 and PMIPv6 are higher than those of the eSeS.

## 4.2    The Performance of eSeS and Current Scheme

In the second experiment, MN hands over from S-Net to T-Net and there are 10 MAGs in T-Net. The topology of this experiment is shown in Fig. 6. Each MAG provides multiple parameters, the values of which are set randomly on each time of test. This experiment was performed ten times. Each time the direction of MN is randomly chosen and the scores of the 10 MAGs are calculated.

Table 4 shows the throughputs, drop rates and end-to-end delays of the eSeS and current scheme (used by PMIPv6 and FMIPv6) in this experiment. The throughput of eSeS is better than those of the current schemes which select NMAG only based on RSS. But the eSeS calculates multiple parameters for all MAGs and then chooses the one with the highest score as NMAG. The eSeS's drop rates is lower than the current

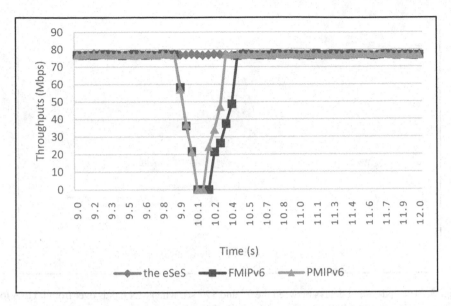

**Fig. 3.** The throughputs between the 9ᵗʰ and 12ᵗʰ sec when MN hands over from LTE-A to LTE-A in an untrusted-homogeneous network environment

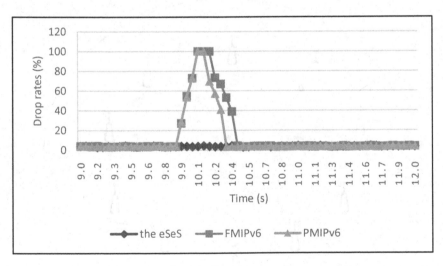

**Fig. 4.** The drop rates between the 9ᵗʰ and 12ᵗʰ sec when MN hands over from LTE-A to LTE-A in an untrusted-homogeneous network environment.

scheme's. Its End-to-end delay is shorter than that of current schemes. It is clear that multi-parameters reflecting current statuses of candidate MAGs are helpful in choosing an appropriate NMAG.

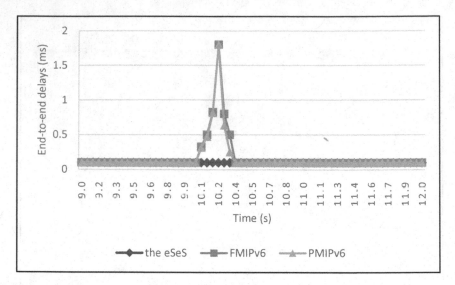

**Fig. 5.** The end-to-end delays between the 9$^{th}$ and 12$^{th}$ sec when MN hands over from LTE-A to LTE-A in an untrusted-homogeneous network environment.

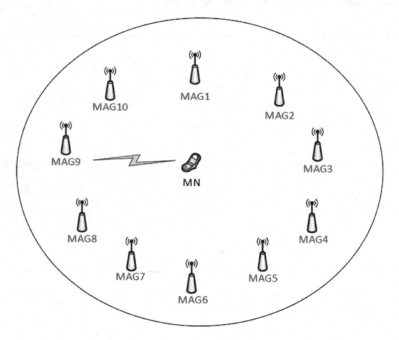

**Fig. 6.** The topology of performance test.

Table 4. The performance of the eSeS and current scheme.

| Metric | eSeS | Current scheme (PMIPv6/FMIPv6) |
|---|---|---|
| Throughput (Mbps) | 94.11 | 88.35 |
| Drop rates (%) | 5.88 | 11.64 |
| End-to-end delay (ms) | 0.24 | 0.69 |

## 5  Conclusions and Future Work

In this study, we propose a scheme to mitigate the network handover problem for two adjacent untrusted networks by introducing the eNB-collection Subsystem which constructed by a trustable third party is the mechanism helping two networks' LMAs to communicate with each other and mutually exchange network information. Due to the help of eNB-collection Subsystem and the feature of SCTP, the link between MN and NMAG will be established before handover starts. The association between MN and network will not disconnect during the handover. With the CRRM, NMAG can allocate resources required by MN before MN connects to it. CRRM can also help us to accomplish congestion control and network load balance. Considering the untrusted relationship between two adjacent networks, we can choose an appropriate MAG as NMAG with the help of eNB-collection Subsystem.

In the future, we will deal with another situation. Our proposed scheme only considers the case in which S-Net is MN's Home network. When stays in a foreign network and MN needs to hand over to another network, the problem is that T-Net's AAA server should communicate with S-Net's AAA server and MN's AAA server. The relationship among the three AAA servers may be heterogeneous/homogeneous and/or trustable/untrusted. In fact, the relationship among them is complicated. We hope we can propose a mechanism to solve this problem. Also, we would like to derive the behavior and reliability models so that users can predict its behaviors and reliability before using it. These constitute our future studies.

## References

1. Leung, K.: WiMAX Forum/ 3GPP2 proxy mobile IPv4, IEFT RFC 5563. https://tools.ietf. org/html/rfc5563 (2010). Accessed 15 Jan 2018
2. Stanley, D.: Control and provisioning of wireless access points (CAPWAP) protocol binding for IEEE 802.11, IETF RFC 5416. https://tools.ietf.org/html/rfc5416 (2009). Accessed 27 Aug 2018
3. Xia, F.: DHCPv6 prefix delegation in long-term evolution (LTE) networks, IETF RFC 6653. https://tools.ietf.org/html/rfc6653 (2012). Accessed 10 Aug 2018
4. Begerow, P., Krug, S., Rubaye, A.A., Renhak, K., Seitz, J.: Delay tolerant handover for heterogeneous networks. In: 39th Annual IEEE Conference on Local Computer Networks, pp. 370–373 (2014)
5. IEEE Standard for Local and metropolitan area networks.: Part 21: Media independent handover services. http://ieeexplore.ieee.org/document/4769367/ (2009). Accessed 04 Aug 2018

6. Mzoughi, H., Zarai, F., Kamoun, L.: Interference—Limited radio resources allocation in LTE_A system with MIH cooperation. In: The Asia-Pacific Conference on Communications (APCC), pp. 174–179 (2016)

7. Wang, G., Chen, L.: Performance comparison between utility based and MIH schemes in vertical handover. In: The 9th IEEE Conference on Industrial Electronics and Applications, pp. 203–207 (2014)

8. Kim, P.S., Jang, M.S., Lee, E.H.: An IEEE 802.21 MIH functionality assisted proxy mobile IPv6 for reducing handover latency and signaling cost. In: 2013 10th International Conference on Information Technology: New Generations, pp. 692–695 (2013)

9. Chiu, D.M., Jain, R.: Analysis of the increase and decrease algorithms for congestion avoidance in computer networks. Comput. Netw. ISDN Syst. 17(1), 1–14 (1989)

10. Wu, L., Sandrasegaran, K.: A survey on common radio resource management. In: The 2nd International Conference on Wireless Broadband and Ultra Wideband Communications (2007)

11. Houda, M., Zarai, F., Obaidat, M.S., Kamoun, L.: Optimizing handover decision and target selection in LTE-A network-based on MIH protocol. In: IEEE International Conference on Communications, pp. 299–304 (2014)

12. Leu, F.Y., Cheng, C.C.: MIH-based Congestion control with seamless handover in untrusted heterogeneous networks. In: The 11th International Conference on Innovative Mobile and Internet Services in Ubiquitous Computing (IMIS 2017), pp. 502–510 (2017)

13. Mussabbir, Q.B., Yao, W., Niu, Z., Fu, X.: Optimized FMIPv6 using IEEE 802.21 MIH services in vehicular networks. IEEE Trans. Veh. Technol. 56(6), 3397–3407 (2007)

14. Ha, J., Kim, J.Y., Kim, J.U., Kim, S.H.: Dynamic load balancing architecture in heterogeneous wireless network environment. In: The 9th International Symposium on Communications and Information Technology (ISCIT 2009), pp. 248–253 (2009)

15. Wang, Y., Yuan, J., Zhou, Y., Li, G., Liu, F., Zhang, P.: Handover management in enhanced MIH framework for heterogeneous wireless networks environment. Wirel. Pers. Commun. 52(3), 615–636 (2010)

16. Buiati, F., Villalba, L.J.G., Corujo, D., Sargento, S., Aguiar, R.L.: IEEE 802.21 information services deployment for heterogeneous mobile environments. IET Commun. 5(18), 2721–2729 (2011)

17. Koodli, R.: Mobile IPv6 fast handovers, IETF RFC 5568. https://tools.ietf.org/html/rfc5568 (2009). Accessed 09 Aug 2018

18. Devarapalli, V.: Proxy Mobile IPv6, IETF RFC 5213. https://tools.ietf.org/html/rfc5213 (2008). Accessed 09 Mar 2018

19. Seamless and secure mobility. https://www.nist.gov/publications/seamless-and-secure-mobility. Accessed 17 Mar 2018

# Using Instant Messaging for Collaboration: A Study of the Relationships Among Organizational Trust, Justice, and Spirituality

Huang Neng-Tang and Lee Hui-Lin[✉]

Department of Technology Application and Human Resource Development,
National Normal University, 162, Sec.1, Heping E. Rd, Taipei, Taiwan
{nthuang, swim}@ntnu.edu.tw

**Abstract.** Enterprises must use human resource management to create the difference in the fierce competition of today's business environment. Employees are an enterprise's most important assets, and it is important for administrators to grasp the psychology of their staff. Modern technology provided by mobile instant messaging (IM) has created a communication revolution, creating a culture of "texting rather than talking" through the use of smart phone mobile applications, such as WhatsApp, Line, and WeChat. Therefore, it is important for researchers to consider the influence of IM on work relationships and communication. This study explores the relationships between organizational trust, organizational justice, and organizational spirituality in the context of IM communication. Structural equation modeling was used to analyze questionnaire data, showing that organizational spirituality predicted organizational trust and organizational justice. The findings suggested that organizations should utilize the benefits of IM, create an organizational justice strategy, offer better human resource management, and create an environment in which employees' organizational spirituality can be enhanced.

**Keywords:** Instant messaging · Organizational trust · Organizational justice Organizational spirituality

## 1 Introduction

Modern enterprises must satisfy their customers in order to survive. In competitive markets, high quality goods and services are not enough to sustain an advantage, so enterprises must look to innovation. Currently, more than 30 billion people use smartphones, and instant messaging (IM) has become a primary activity among smartphone utilities (Embrain 2014; Smith 2015). The convenient application of IM has already been extensively employed in industry, for example, chat groups and direct messaging may be used during collaboration. Research has shown that technology use has beneficial effects on relationships and satisfaction with life (Reinecke and Trepte 2014). Technology could offer similar beneficial effects in work relationships. Human resources are the most important assets in an organization, only people cannot lack the advantage that cannot replace in enterprises either. Internal marketing has recently become an important strategy in business administration. Executives know that

J.-L. Chen et al. (Eds.): WiCON 2018, LNICST 264, pp. 141–147, 2019.
https://doi.org/10.1007/978-3-030-06158-6_14

employing satisfactory staff may increase customer satisfaction. For this reason, it is important for employers to understand their staff's ideas and attitudes.

Many researchers have investigated satisfaction, commitment, and identification to understand whether an employee's positive view of their company has influenced their performance and efficiency. Organizational trust began to receive the attention of researchers in the 1990s. Organizational trust can be defined as the trust a member of staff has for their colleagues, executives, and organization. The more organizational trust an employee has, the more they may be willing to contribute to the organization. In addition, organizational justice theory has received attention in the literature in the last ten years. This posits that justice within an organization can be distributive, procedural, or interactional and if an employee assesses organizational activities as unjust, then they may be more suspicious of the enterprise in the future.

Organizational spirituality is a new topic. Originating from the concept of spirituality in religious groups, it explains staff's inner life, the energy they devote to enterprises, and the meaning they find in work and in their community. The effects of a technology communication tool such as IM on organizational spirituality would offer value to studies on work collaboration. To date, there has been no discussion of the relationships between organizational, organizational justice, and organizational spirituality, which have been addressed by the current study.

## 2  Literature Review

### 2.1  Organizational Trust

When conceptualized as a psychological state, trust has been defined in terms of several interrelated cognitive processes and orientations (Blau 1964). Trust can be characterized as a set of socially learned and socially confirmed expectations that people have of each other, of the organizations and institutions in which they work, and of the natural and moral social orders that form fundamental understandings in their lives. Several organizational researchers have argued that it is useful to conceptualize trust in terms of individual choice behavior in various trust dilemma situations (Meyer 1994). The accumulation of social capital requires a significant amount of trust within and between all levels of an organization (Sashittal et al. 1998).

### 2.2  Organizational Justice

Organizational justice was first described by Greenberg (1990), who defined it as an individual's perception of, and reaction to, fairness in an organization. Much earlier, Adam (Adams 1965) proposed equity theory, in which conditions of unfairness are said to create tension within a person, which he or she will attempt to resolve. The concept of justice is one important variable in organizational behavior. Organizational justice has been defined as the processes and procedures has measured, regular and is said to be present when staff view their leaders as impartial, sincere, and logical (Niehoff et al. 1993).

## 2.3   Organizational Spirituality

Interest in spirituality and religion has grown considerably in scientific and professional communities over the past three decades. However, the bulk of this interest has focused on the relation of religion and spirituality to general health and well-being (Ashmos and Duchon 2000). Inner life is the strength that an individual produces from the inside, which they may rely on to overcome personal challenges, and the values through which they perceive themselves. When engaged in meaningful work, staff feel that they are making a contribution to society that affirms the value and meaning of their life. Individuals may find a sense of community in linking with each other through work, and cooperating with each other may encourage a sense of mutuality between peers.

## 2.4   Organizational Trust, Organizational Justice, and Organizational Spirituality

Understanding organizational trust and organizational justice through review of the relevant literature may provide some explanation of organizational spirituality. Many findings have confirmed that increasing organizational trust can improve performance in whole enterprises (Liu and Ding 2012; Mitchell et al. 2012; Nambudiri 2012; Wong et al. 2012). The current research has addressed the following hypotheses:

*H1: Organizational trust has a significant influence on organizational spirituality.*

*H2: Organizational justice has a significant influence on organizational spirituality.*

## 2.5   IM and Work Collaboration

Previous studies have investigated whether automatic feedback systems improved organizational performance better than face-to-face feedback. Certain studies have suggested that workplace performance may be enhanced by electronically-mediated communication, which may be valuable, as it allows employees to self-disclose (Valkenburg and Peter 2007). Employees may take advantage of electronic communication by engaging actively in self-presentation through IM and text messaging (Reid and Reid 2010).

# 3   Research Design

## 3.1   Research Structure

The theoretical model upon which this research has been based is as follows.

## 3.2   Participants

A questionnaire was administered to small and medium-sized enterprises in Taiwan using IM (mostly Line) as a communication instrument. Of the 500 questionnaires sent, 210 responses were received, giving a response rate of 42%.

### 3.3  Research Tool

Organizational trust has two dimensions: cognitive and affective, while organizational justice has three: distributive, procedural, and interactional justice. Organizational spirituality refers to an employee's inner life, community, and their sense of meaningful work. In order to examine the reliability and validity of each assumption, AMOS version 20.0 was used (Fig. 1).

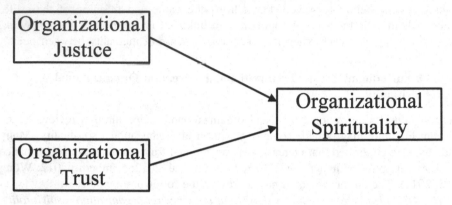

**Fig. 1.**  Research structure chart

## 4  Findings and Discussion

### 4.1  Confirmatory Factor Analysis

Confirmatory factor analysis was conducted for organizational trust, organizational justice, and organizational spirituality under the effects of IM. This showed the composite reliability of organizational trust (0.8673), organizational justice (0.8294), and organizational spirituality (0.9154), and the average variances extracted in each were 0.7657, 0.6214, and 0.7836, respectively. Convergent validity of the three constructs was very good, and comparing the square root of the average variance extracted and all correlations showed discriminant validity (Table 1 and Fig. 2).

**Table 1.**  AVE & correlation

|  | Organizational Justice | Organizational Trust | Organizational Spirituality |
|---|---|---|---|
| Organizational Justice | 0.7882 | | |
| Organizational Trust | 0.6081 | 0.8750 | |
| Organizational Spirituality | 0.6511 | 0.5693 | 0.8852 |

Note: The diagonal number value is the square root of AVE

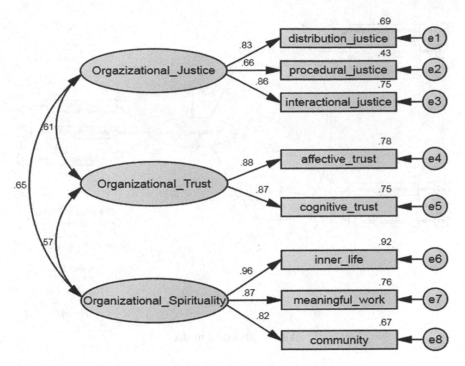

**Fig. 2.** Confirmatory factor analysis

## 4.2 Structure Model and Hypothesis

After confirmatory factor analysis, further examination of the hypotheses found that the structure model was a good fit. Chi-square was 20.692, GFI was 0.978, AGFI was 0.952, CFI was 0.978, NNFI was 0.994, IFI was 0.997, and RMSEA was 0.032. All indicators reached the standard number value. In addition, bootstrapping was used to estimate standardized regression coefficients, which were statistically significant, suggesting that both hypotheses were supported (Table 2 and Fig. 3).

**Table 2.** Standardized regression coefficients and significance

| Parameter | | | Estimate | Lower | Upper | P |
|---|---|---|---|---|---|---|
| Organizational Spirituality | <— | Organizational Justice | .4839*** | .2889 | .6849 | .0007 |
| Organizational Spirituality | <— | Organizational Trust | .2750* | .0619 | .4743 | .0120 |
| distribution justice | <— | Organizational Justice | .8335 | .7330 | .9001 | .0018 |
| procedural justice | <— | Organizational Justice | .6585 | .5573 | .7392 | .0008 |
| interactional justice | <— | Organizational Justice | .8635 | .7883 | .9188 | .0024 |
| affective trust | <— | Organizational Trust | .8830 | .7840 | .9622 | .0014 |
| cognitive trust | <— | Organizational Trust | .8672 | .7931 | .9363 | .0011 |
| inner life | <— | Spirituality | .9617 | .9236 | .9911 | .0017 |
| meaningful work | <— | Spirituality | .8723 | .8064 | .9226 | .0014 |
| community | <— | Spirituality | .8206 | .7284 | .9004 | .0010 |

*p<0.05, ** p<0.01, ***p<0.001

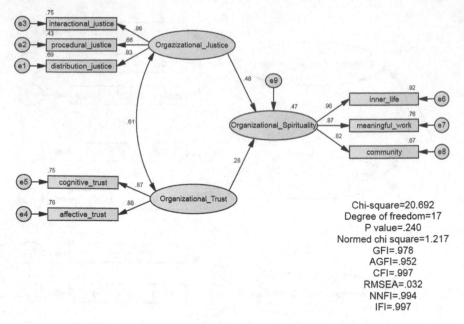

**Fig. 3.**  Structural model

## 5  Conclusions

Under the advantages of IM, this study showed that organizational trust and organizational justice had a forward significant influence on organizational spirituality. Therefore the hypotheses were supported. The function of organizational justice is important, so enterprises should make efforts to increase it, for example, through the use of IM. In order to improve competitiveness, enterprises should avail themselves of IM technologies and combine strategy with human resource management to strengthen organizational trust, organizational justice, and ultimately, organizational spirituality. It may be helpful for future research to investigate mediators or moderators of the relationships shown in this model.

## References

Adams, J.S.: Inequity in social exchange. In: Berkowitz, L. (ed.) Advances in Experimental Social Psychology, vol. 2, pp. 267–299. Academic Press, New York (1965)

Ashmos, D., Duchon, D.P.: Spirituality at work: a conceptualization and measure. J. Manag. Inq. **9**(2), 134–145 (2000)

Blau, P.M.: Exchange and power in social life. Wiley, New York (1964)

Embrain.: Survey on utilization of smartphone functions (2014). Retrieved from https://www. trendmonitor.co.kr/tmweb/trend/allTrend/detail.do?bIdx=1193&code=0102&trendType= CKOREA&prevMonth=&currentPage=1, 14 February 2017

Greenberg, J.: Organization justice: yesterday, today, and tomorrow. J. Manag. **6**, 399–432 (1990)

Liu, N.T., Ding, C.G.: General ethical judgments, perceived organizational support, interactional justice, and workplace deviance. Int. J. Hum. Resour. Manag. **23**(13), 2712–2735 (2012)

Meyer, R.: Universal optimality of rank constrained matrix approximation. In: Bock, H.H., Lenski, W., Richter, M.M. (eds.) Information Systems and Data Analysis: Prospects—Foundations-Applications. Studies in Classification, Data Analysis, and Knowledge Organization, vol. 4, pp. 335–342. Springer, Berlin (1994)

Mitchell, J.I., Gagne, M., Beaudry, A., Dyer, L.: The role of perceived organizational support, distributive justice and motivation in reactions to new information technology. Comput. Hum. Behav. **28**(2), 729–738 (2012)

Nambudiri, R.: Propensity to trust and organizational commitment: a study in the Indian pharmaceutical sector. Int. J. Hum. Resour. Manag. **23**(5), 977–986 (2012)

Reid, F.J.M., Reid, D.J.: The expressive and conversational affordances of mobile messaging. Behav. Inf. Technol. **29**(1), 3–22 (2010)

Reinecke, L., Trepte, S.: Authenticity and well-being on social network sites: a two-wave longitudinal study on the effects of online authenticity and the positivity bias in SNS communication. Comput. Hum. Behav. **30**, 95–102 (2014)

Robbins, S.P.: Organizational behavior, 9th edn. Prentice Hall Press, Eaglewood Cliffs, NJ (2001)

ERupp, D, Cropanzano, R.: The mediating effects of social exchange relationships in predicting workplace outcomes from multifoci or organizational justice. Organ. Behav. Hum. Decis. Process. **89**(1), 925–946 (2002)

Sashittal, H.C., Berman, J., Selim, I.: Impact of trust on performance evaluations. Mid-Atlantic J. Bus. **34**(2), 163–184 (1998)

Smith, A.: U.S. Smartphone use in 2015 (2015). Retrieved from http://www.pewinternet.org/2015/04/01/us-smartphone-use-in-2015/, 14 Feb 2017

Valkenburg, P.M., Peter, J.: Preadolescents' and adolescents' online communication and their closeness to friends. Dev. Psychol. **43**(2), 267–277 (2007)

Wong, Y.T., Wong, C.S., Ngo, H.Y.: The effects of trust in organisation and perceived organisational support on organisational citizenship behaviour: a test of three competing models. Int. J. Hum. Resour. Manag. **23**(2), 278–293 (2012)

Cohen-Charash, Y., Spector, P.E.: The role of justice in organizational a meta-analysis. Organ. Behav. Hum. Decis. Process **86**(2), 278–321 (2001)

# Application and Challenges of Blockchain Technology to Big Data-Based Credit Reference in China

Cheng-yong Liu[1(✉)] and Cheng Chen[2(✉)]

[1] Beijing Institute of Technology, Zhuhai 519088, Guangdong,
People's Republic of China
liucyl3@126.com
[2] Taiwan University, Taipei, Taiwan, China
legalcici@126.com

**Abstract.** Big data-based credit reference gradually attracts wide attention due to its ad-vantages in remedying the shortages of traditional credit reference and dealing with new challenges arising from financial credit management. Nevertheless, this new method is also adapted through different studies and experiments to be problematic with island of credit information and information security. Some researchers begin exploring the possibility of applying blockchain technology to the individual credit reference field. The business links in the individual credit reference can be innovated through the blockchain mechanism so that credit data from different industries get collected through peering points, secure communication and anonymous protection on the basis of such techniques as distributed storage, point-to-point transmission, consensus mechanism and encryption algorithm. In this way, it is feasible to solve island of information and enhance the protection of user information security. A promising future can be expected about the big data-based credit reference, but there are also many problems with blockchain-based credit reference in China.

**Keywords:** Big data · Blockchain · Credit reference · Islands of information

## 1 Foreword

The operation of modern financial system can never be separated from the credit support. Big data-based credit reference gradually attracts wide attention due to its advantages in remedying the shortages of traditional credit reference and dealing with new challenges arising from financial credit management. Nevertheless, this new method is also adapted through different studies and experiments to be problematic with island of credit information and information security. Some researchers begin exploring the possibility of applying blockchain technology to the individual credit reference field. In this way, it is feasible to solve island of information and enhance the protection of user information security. A promising future can be expected about the big data-based credit reference, but there are also many problems with blockchain-based credit reference in China. Future research is required to find corresponding solutions and verify their feasibility.

© ICST Institute for Computer Sciences, Social Informatics and Telecommunications Engineering 2019
Published by Springer Nature Switzerland AG 2019. All Rights Reserved
J.-L. Chen et al. (Eds.): WiCON 2018, LNICST 264, pp. 148–155, 2019.
https://doi.org/10.1007/978-3-030-06158-6_15

## 2    Problems Concerning Big Data-Based Credit Reference in China

Big data-based credit reference means the employment of such new technical means as big data, deep algorithms (incl. cloud computing), mobile terminal, and artificial intelligence to re-design a credit rating model, both structural and non-structural data to analyze the credit information of enterprises and individuals [1], portrait of credit subjects from different dimensions to present their default rate and credit conditions so as to form credit evaluation of higher reference value [2]. As the big data-based credit reference is to collect, arrange, save, process and release the information about credit subjects in essence, it is still within the credit reference business scope defined in Credit reference Management Regulations of China. The development of big data-based credit reference still faces following outstanding challenges.

### 2.1    Islands of Credit Information

There isn't any information sharing mechanism among big data-based credit service agencies. What's more, the credit information between financial industry and non-financial industries are scattered around different agencies [3] so that a number of problems arises, such as difficult data integration and islands of information [4]. The possible causes include: firstly, the ownership of data in our country is not defined yet, and all the agencies involved view such data as their own core assets and are unwilling to share the data or providing distorted data, which result in the islands of information; secondly, out of consideration about privacy protection, all the agencies prefer securing the information under control to sharing them with others; thirdly, besides the mechanical and institutional reasons, data can't be securely shared among different agencies and industries due to the technical architecture of traditional credit service industry so that the problem about islands of information is not solved in the traditional credit reference work.

### 2.2    Infringement of Privacy and Consent Rights

During the information collection process, big data-based credit service agencies frequently infringe the privacy right, consent right and other rights and interests of the information subjects because of the asymmetrical information. Hereby the phenomena are explained as follows: In the first place, information collection against the big data background features elusiveness and block box processing. The information subjects can never know whether the collected personal sensitive data contains any information forbidden to be collected by relevant laws and regulations[1] and whether the collected information is true and accurate [5–7]. Secondly, even if the users give consent, it is hardly to acknowledge the scope of collection, intended use, and the time and place of

---

[1] It is specified in Article 2 and 14 of Credit service industry Management Regulations, personal information acquisition is limited to credit-related information, and the scopes of personal information that can and can't be collected by the credit service agencies are defined.

copying and transmission under present "package authorization" mode [8], and the consent right can't fulfill the designed purpose. Thirdly, the credit report resulting from analysis by big data-based credit service agencies is in nature a kind of personal information, and its output and use should be based on the consent from information subjects[2]. In China, some big data-based credit service agencies extend the credit evaluation results to all sorts of social living scenes without gaining the prior consent of information subjects.

# 3  Application of Blockchain to Big Data-Based Credit Reference in China

Now there are mainly two modes through which the blockchain technology is applied to the big data-based credit service industry in China [9–14].

## 3.1  Scenes of Application

**Data exchange platform mode**
In the data exchange platform mode, all the participants independently maintain the original databases and submit only some limited abstract information to third party data exchange platform for safekeeping through the blockchain technology. The inquirer can send inquiry application to the original data supplier through the platform so that a sea of external data is available for inquiry and the core business data are protected from being disclosed. For instance, GXB data exchange is a decentralized data transaction platform based on blockchain technology [15, 16]. Its representative clients include a number of industrial enterprises that have data exchange demand in such industries as internet, finance, government agencies, banking, insurance and securities. On the other hand, it takes the financial performance data produced by such clients as the major assets in data transaction in order to solve the data sharing and exchange problem among different industries.

**Common construction and sharing data platform mode**
As for the common construction and sharing data platform mode, the generation, recording and inquiry of credit are completely dependent on blockchain technology [12]. It creates decentralized credit inquiry, credit performance, and default records, and offers such data for all the credit reference users and consumption financial partners that use client credit records. In this platform mode, once such data and information as personal credit performance and default records are generated and distributed to all the

---

[2] It is specified that "when credit service agency or information supplier or user obtain the permission from information subject through contractual terms and conditions, prompt that can attract the attention of information subject shall be offered in the contract in combination with explicit explanation" in Article 19 of Credit Service Industry Management Regulations, and "information user shall use the personal information for the proposes agreed with the information subject instead of using it for any other purpose, or provide the information for a third party without gaining the permission from the information subject" in Article 20.

nodes of network, every credit behavior will become personal assets with definite ownership. The members can use and share the open and transparent user credit data that are protected from being falsified or denied. This is a relatively radical mode in the application of blockchain technology to credit. Chinese Cloud Prism credit system has devoted itself to the blockchain-based credit reference business of this mode since 2014 [17].

**Analysis of two modes in terms of advantages and disadvantages**
Though having a low construction cost, the data exchange platform mode has many demerits. More specifically, this mode focuses more on the combination of existing technologies with data in credit service industry, so it is easier in operation, low in cost, and more possible in achieving a success. Nevertheless, it still fails to solve following problems perplexing the present credit service industry, though it does use the blockchain technology: 1. difficulty in data acquisition; 2. authenticity of data; and 3. data monopoly.

The common sharing and construction data platform mode is hard in construction but advantageous in many aspects. However, since blockchain technology gets radially applied to the generation, recording and inquiry of credit in this mode, following credit application problems can be solved: 1. Difficult data acquisition; 2. Information monopoly.

## 3.2 Application Strengths

The combination of big data-based credit reference system with "blockchain technology" is helpful in solving such issues as islands of information and credit security.

**Solve islands of information**
The distributed storage of blockchain offers a physical foundation of information sharing which is exactly an effective means for solving the islands of information. We analyze first the data exchange platform with "alliance chain". Some academicians believe it is impossible to avoid data abuse in the completely decentralized information sharing system, thus only the credit reference and sharing mechanism built on the basis of the incompletely decentralized "alliance chain" technology can implement the information sharing functions of credit reference system within a more secure scope [5]. Then, it sets to analyze the common construction and sharing data platform of "public chain" mode. In this mode, the information ownership belongs to individuals [6] so that platform architecture can connect the enterprises with public sections so as to carry out user data authorization, solve the issue about islands of information, and achieve common sharing, communication, construction and use of information resources.

**Maintain information safety**
The combined use of "blockchain technology" with "encryption algorithm" in the big data-based credit reference system may be able to alleviate the conflict between information sharing and information protection.

(1) The "asymmetrical encryption function" of the blockchain is helpful in protecting the confidentiality of information and data, whereas its "distributed function" can

assure their completeness. In the first place, after personal information is input into the blockchain-based credit reference system, personal information will be deeply encrypted and protected with the asymmetrical encryption algorithm [18–21]. Then, the blockchain information network can hardly be attacked. Moreover, the blockchain exists in the whole network in a distributed way, which means every complete node in the platform is involved in the system maintenance and the information completeness won't be affected by an attack of single node by computer virus or any artificial mis-operation.

(2)  In the alliance chain-based credit reference system, not all the data are broadcast to the whole network, and not all of them are open and transparent. Except for the parties involved in data sharing and transaction, no other third party can obtain the data.

(3)  The common construction and sharing data platform of public chain appears to be relatively weak in information security protection. The transaction data are made visible to the whole network and traceable by the general public, when such data are maliciously explored or utilized, the legal information rights and interests of individual or agencies will be harmed. It is, thus, proper to take following measures to avoid the possible risks [11].

## 4  Challenges for the Development of Blockchain-Based Credit Reference in China

### 4.1  Contradiction Between Blockchain Technology and User's Right to Be Forgotten

The blockchain technology has the feature of permanent recording, which contradicts with the "right to be forgotten" in information protection in existing Chinese legislation system. To put it more specifically, in accordance with Article 16 in Credit reference Management Regulations of China, the personal credit records saved in the blockchain should be kept for only 5 years, and the adverse credit information that has been kept for over 5 years should be deleted. However, the credit reference system constructed with blockchain as the core technology is a network of data that can permanently record all the input information. This poses a great challenge to the execution of users' "right to be forgotten".

### 4.2  Unsuitability of Traditional Credit Reference Regulation to Blockchain-Based Credit Reference

The present credit reference regulation system in China is mainly arranged with traditional credit service industry, demanding further improvement in both legislation and means. First of all, the present credit reference regulatory system remains weak and ineffective in spite of the existing hierarchic institutional system.

Secondly, the anonymity and decentralization of blockchain form certain challenge to the traditional regulatory mode and makes the latter even more difficult to adapt to the regulation demand against the new situation [22].

## 4.3  Damage on Information Subjects' Rights and Interests Caused by Missing of Private Key

Once the private key of user to blockchain-based credit reference system is lost, forgotten or disclosed, the user won't be able to get an access to the information stored in the block and the information ownership will be thus affected [23]. Let's take the blockchain-based credit reference system as an example, once the user loses the private key, he/she will have no right to authorize the credit service agencies to user his/her information. Even if he/she re-joins the blockchain, the credit service agencies still can't trace his/her previous credit data. This does affect the credit assets of the user and cause some loss of interest.

## 4.4  Non-compliance of Public Chain Architecture with Safety Protection Criteria

The blockchain-based credit reference architecture of public chain can't meet the information safety protection evaluation criteria for domestic credit reference information system [24]. More specifically, in accordance with Article 21 and 31 in Network Security Law of the country[a] and Article 30 of Credit service agencies Management Regulations[3], the state enforces hierarchical network safety protection system [24]. As the public chain system allows several nodes to lose effect or retreat from it in essence, and even indulges the existence of malicious nodes. This is believed by some to be possible to cause severe consequence to the blockchain-based credit reference system. Therefore, it fails to comply with the national classified protection of information security in terms of physical access control, cyber security guarantee, service performance, and system operation reliability [5].

# 5  Conclusion

The traceability of blockchain enables all related steps from data collection to transaction, circulation, computation and analysis to be kept in the blockchain and the data quality to become unprecedently trustable. The correctness of data analysis outcome and data mining effect are also better guaranteed. Now the blockchain technology has been applied to the big data-based credit service industry of China, including the data exchange platform mode and common construction and sharing data platform mode, in order to achieve data sharing and conquer the problem about islands of information. But when it comes to the practical employment and development, there are still many challenges in front of blockchain-based credit service industry in China. Active endeavors are needed in terms of technology and legislation in order to meet the future market demand.

---

[3] In accordance with Article 30 of Credit Service Agencies Management Methods, "the credit service agencies shall assess the safety of the credit information system according to national classified information security protection criteria. The information systems of level 2 security protection shall be assessed once every two years while those of level 3 or above shall be assessed every year".

**Acknowledgement.** The paper is a periodical achievement of the 2018 school-supported scientific research program A Study on Liability Theories about Insider Trading of Financial Derivatives of Beijing Institute of Technology, Zhuhai (XK-2018-19).

# References

1. Xinhai, L.: Dingwei: application of big data-based credit reference and the revelation–with American internet financial company zestfinance as an example. Tsinghua Financ. Rev. **10**, 98 (2014)
2. Mingsheng, S.: A study of big data credit reporting and the protection of personal information subjects' rights and interests. Credit Ref. **5**(220), 38–39 (2017)
3. Yongqian, T.: Wang Xiaotian. Improvement of legislation about individual credit information against big data background, China internet **5**, 43 (2017)
4. Qiang, W., Sude, Q., Jieru, B.: Discussion about application of blockchain to credit service industry. Telecommun. Netw. Technol. **6**, 38 (2017)
5. Guomao, S., Meng, L.: A study on application of blockchain technology to individual credit field–based on digital inclusive finance perspective. Stud. Corp. Financ. **1**(15), 121 (2017)
6. Tong, L., et al.: Hadoop-based visual deep web acquisition platform design. Comput. Eng. Sci. **2**, 217–233 (2016)
7. Liu, Y., Chenghuan, Z.: Scrapy-based deep web crawler study. Eng. Res. Appl. **7**, 112 (2017)
8. Harper, J.: Reputation under regulation: the fair credit reporting act at 40 and lessons for the internet privacy debate, cato institute policy analysis, No. 690. https://ssrn.com/abstract= 2033360 (2011). Last accessed 8 May 2018
9. Jie, H.: Application of blockchain technology and smart contract in intellectual property determination and transaction and corresponding laws and regulations. Intel. Prop. **2**, 14–15 (2018)
10. Hailong, W., et al.: Rights ascertainment plan for big data in blockchain. Comput. Sci. **2**, 16–17 (2018)
11. China blockchain technology and industrial development forum: china blockchain technology and application progress whitepaper, released at the website of Informatization and Software Service Industry Office, Ministry of Industry and Informatization (in October of 2016) http://www.gongxiangxueshe.com/forum.php?mod=attachment&aid=Nzkwf GJIOGNINjZifDE0Nzc0NjcxMzJ8Mjg5OXw2OTc3 (2016). Last accessed 8 May 2018
12. Zhongbin, Z., Yansong, L.: Application practice of blockchain technology to credit service industry and future prospect. Credit Ref. **7**(222), 47 (2017)
13. Chunming, T., Long, G.: Multi-parties key agreement protocol in block chain. Netinfo Secur. **12**, 19 (2017)
14. Desheng, L., Jianping, G., Yibin, D.: A tentative discussion about the application of blockchain technology to book copyright protection. Science-Technology & Publication, vol. 6, p. 77 (2017)
15. GXB data exchange: GXB Dapp whitepaper, released by GXB website. http://static.gxb.io/ files/GXS_Dapp_Whitepaper_V1.0.pdf (2016). Last accessed 8 May 2018
16. Yong, Z., Xiaohui, L.: Study on and achievement of an improved blockchain consensus mechanism. Electron. Des. Eng. **1**, 38–39 (2018)
17. Cloud prism credit: blockchain credit service released at. http://www.yintongzhengxin.com/ blockchain/index.html?ver=17.5.107. Last accessed 8 May 2018

18. Linming, G., Shundong, L., Jiawei, D., Yimin, G., Daoshun, W.: Homomorphic encryption scheme and a protocol on secure computing a line by two private points. J. Softw. **12**, 3275 (2017)
19. Xian, Z., Yuzhao, J., Ying, Y.: A glimpse at blockchain: from the perspective of privacy. J. Inf. Secur. Res. **11**, 985 (2017)
20. Kang, L., Yi, S., Jun, Z., Jun, L., Jihua, Z., Zhongcheng, L.: Technical challenges in applying zero-knowledge proof to blockchain. Big Data **1**, 59–60 (2018)
21. Huaqun, W., Tao, W.: Cryptography on blockchain. J. Nanjing Univ. Posts Telecommun. (Nat. Sci.) **6**, 64–65(2017)
22. Ruijue, Z.: Legal supervision of blockchain technology. J. Beijing Univ. Posts Telecommun. (Soc. Sci.) **3**, 39–43 (2017)
23. Si, Z.: The Technology Principle, Application and Suggestion of Block Chain, Software, vol. 11, p. 52 (2016)
24. China National Standardization Management Committee: Information Security Technology–Baseline for Classified Protection of Information System Security (GB/T 22239-2008) (released in June of 2008). http://www.gb688.cn/bzgk/gb/newGbInfo?hcno=D13C8CD02A FC374BC31048590EB75445. Last accessed 8 May 2018

# A Trust Evaluation Gateway for Distributed Blockchain IoT Network

Hsing-Chung Chen[1,2(✉)]

[1] Department of Computer Science and Information Engineering,
Asia University, Taichung, Taiwan
shin8409@ms6.hinet.net
[2] Department of Medical Research, China Medical University Hospital,
China Medical University, Taichung, Taiwan

**Abstract.** As the number of Internet of massive Things (IoT) applications in vehicles, factory machinery, smart buildings and city infrastructure grows, a secure and automated solution of enabling a mesh network for transactional processes is an important demand. However, the trust evaluation among those unknown IoT devices which communicate and trade to each other is still the high demand in distributed BC IoT network. The idea of the trust evaluation gateway is first proposed for distributed BC IoT network. Finally, the three types of trust evaluation functionfor Machine to Individual (M2I), Machine to Machine (M2M), and Individual to Individual (I2I), selectively, are proposed and provided an appropriate solution for solving the online authentication problem in distributed BC IoT network.

**Keywords:** Internet of things · Blockchain · Trust evaluation
Gateway

## 1 Introduction

As the number of Internet of massive Things (IoT) applications in vehicles, factory machinery, smart buildings and city infrastructure grows, a secure and automated solution of enabling a mesh network for transactional processes is an important demand. IoT is in search of a secure method for automating processes and exchanging data in real time to speed transactions, Blockchain (BC) technology could be one of the perfect appropriate approaches [1, 2]. Blockchain is a kind of distributed ledger technology that uses smart contract to offer a standardized method for accelerating data exchange and enabling processes between IoT devices by removing the central server [1, 2]. In a distributed Blockchain IoT network, the IoT devices on a peer-to-peer network could authenticate transactions and execute transactions based on pre-determined rules without the central server. In the other words, BC technology consolidating the cryptocurrency have been recently used to provide security and privacy on transaction domain in peer-to-peer networks with similar topologies to IoT. However, the trust evaluation among those unknown IoT devices which communicate and trade to each other is still the high demand in distributed BC IoT network. A trust evaluation gateway is then proposed for distributed BC IoT network. Finally, the three

© ICST Institute for Computer Sciences, Social Informatics and Telecommunications Engineering 2019
Published by Springer Nature Switzerland AG 2019. All Rights Reserved
J.-L. Chen et al. (Eds.): WiCON 2018, LNICST 264, pp. 156–162, 2019.
https://doi.org/10.1007/978-3-030-06158-6_16

types of trust evaluation functionfor Machine to Individual (M2I), Machine to Machine (M2M) [3–6], and Individual to Individual (I2I), selectively, are proposed and provided an appropriate solution for solving the online authentication problem in distributed BC IoT network.

The remainder of this paper is organized as follows: the related work is introduced in Sect. 2. The system architecture of BCTEG is first proposed for distributed BC IoT network in Sect. 3. The trust evaluation is proposed in Sect. 4. In addition, the discussions and there types of trust evaluation tables are presented in Sect. 5. Finally, the conclusion is drawn in Sect. 6.

## 2 Related Work

Blockchain is already a payment system for the Internet, and it could be considered as the "Internet of Money" [2]. The transactions in Blockchain can be sourced and completed directly between two parties over the Internet. The assets to be allocated and traded between two parties could be tokenized as cryptocurreny in a decentralized, distributed, and global way [2]. The Blockchain network can be a programmable open network for decentralized trading of all assets, in which the functionality of cryptocurrency is beyond the traditional currency and payments [2]. Therefore, Blockchain 1.0 for currency and payments is already extended into Blockchain 2.0 to take advantage of the more robust functionality of programmable cryptocurrency. Blockchain 1.0 is for decentralization of currency and payments, whereas Blockchain 2.0 is more generally for decentralization of markets, and concerns the transfer among other kinds of assets beyond fiat currency [2]. Some terminologies of Blockchain 2.0 includes Bitcoin 2.0, Bitcoin 2.0 Protocols, smart contract, smart property, Dapp (decentralized applications), DAOs (decentralized autonomous organizations), and DACs (decentralized autonomous corporations) [2].

Public Key Cryptography is an essential part of cryptocurrency protocol and is used in several places to ensure the integrity of messages created in the protocol [7]. Wallet creation and signing of transactions, which are the core components of any currency rely heavily on public key cryptography [7]. The cryptocurrency protocol creates a new set of private key and corresponding public key [7]. For example, the public key is then used with a hash function to create the public address that Bitcoin users use to send and receive funds. The private key is kept secret and is used to sign a digital transaction to make sure the origin of the transaction is legitimate [7].

## 3 BCTEG System Architecture

In this section, the system architecture of the proposed trust evaluation gateway for distributed BC IoT network is shown in Fig. 1 in which the system architecture consists of Blockchain Trust Evaluation Gateway (BCTEG), Electrical Wallet (E-Wallet), Trust Evaluation Database (TE-DB), BC Network (BCN), Local IoT Network and IoT devices is illustrated in this section. In addition, the basic elements in BCTEG are described below.

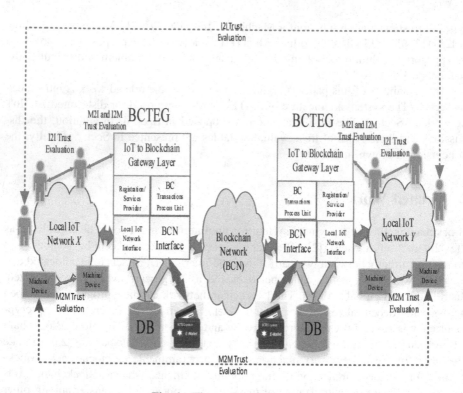

**Fig. 1.** The system architecture.

BCTEG is a Blockchain gateway server in Fig. 1. It supports BC protocol and serves as a BC node in BC Network. BCTEG consists of IoT to BC Gateway Layer, Registration Services Provider, Local IoT Network Interface, BC Transaction Process Unit, and BC interface. IoT devices are the digital assets belonging to the BCTEG which divided into two types: machine IoT devices and non-machine devices called individual IoT devices. Each IoT device is not a BC node in Fig. 1. Thus, BCTEG in this system architecture is proposed and designed that it could not only issue but also manage the identities for each IoT device. Moreover, BCTEG will assign a distinct as well as unique BC address according to his BC E-Wallet to each IoT device, separately. At first, each IoT device will register BCTEG using his basic identity (ID) to be a member via a secret channel. After receiving the registration request, BCTEG will generate and assign to him a private key, a public key and the corresponding BC address via the cryptocurrency wallet belonging to BCTEG. Second, each IoT device will then receive and store the information of registration. Third, each IoT device could do the BC transaction via the assigned registration information consisting ID, a private key, a public key, and a BC address.

Because each IoT device uses the distinct registration information to do any BC transaction, BCTEG will then record its activities and behaviors to TE-DB. In addition, consumers increasingly want to know that the ethical claims companies make about their products are real. Distributed ledgers provide an easy way to certify that the backstories of the things we buy are genuine. Transparency comes with Blockchain-based timestamping of a date and location—on ethical diamonds, for instance—that corresponds to a product number. Thus, BCTEG will collect all transaction information and their proof of works for each IoT device via access the distributed ledgers in BCN. Finally, BCTEG will collect all information consisting of the behaviors in local IoT network and transaction information in BCN for his all transaction records of each IoT device not only Individual but also machine IoT device via BC interface. Then, the reputation for each IoT device will be calculated via BC Transaction Process Unit and stored in TE-DB.

## 4   Trust Evaluation

The idea of cooperation in the three types of trust evaluation is from the terminology of Blockchain 2.0 including DAOs and DACs. Therefore, there are three types of trust evaluation function are proposed and designed in BCTEG to solving the online authentication problem in distributed BC IoT network. **Type 1** is Machine to Machine (M2M); **Type 2** is non-machine individual IoT device (called as Individual IoT device) to Individual IoT device (I2I); **Type 3** is Machine to Individual (M2I). The trust evaluation function which could deal with three types trust evaluation operations is proposed in Eq. (1) could provide an appropriate solution for distributed BC IoT network.

In Fig. 1, there are two local IoT networks, one is the local IoT network $X$ and another is the local IoT network $Y$, where the local IoT network $Y$ is the remote IoT network for the local IoT network $X$. In turn, the local IoT network $X$ is the remote IoT network for the local IoT network $Y$.

Assume that $x \in X$ is a machine IoT device or individual IoT device and $y \in Y$ is also a remote machine IoT device or individual IoT device. The evaluation function between the local IoT device and its remote IoT device is represented as Eq. (1).

$$f(x \rightarrow y) = x \vec{\Theta} y = E_{xy}, \forall x \neq y, \tag{1}$$

where $x \rightarrow y$ means $y$ is evaluated by $x$ and $\vec{\Theta}$ is the evaluation operation, e.g. the trust evaluation function proposed in Refs. [4, 5] for $x \rightarrow y$.

The two properties of the evaluation function are descripted below.

1. $E_{xy} \neq E_{yx}, \forall x \in X, y \in Y$.
2. $E_{xx} = 1, \forall x \in X$ and $E_{yy} = 1, \forall y \in Y$.

## 5   Discussions

All collaboration evaluation results will be collected and recorded in system's TE-DB shown in Fig. 1. The trust evaluation tables will then be maintained by each BCTEG according to the collaboration evaluation results. In this section, the three types of trust evaluation tables are discussed below.

**Type 1.** The result of $f(x \to y) = f(m_x \to m_y) = m_x \vec{\Theta} m_y = E_{m_x m_y}$ according to Eq. (1) is represented as $Em_1 m_2$ when $y = m_y$ is a remote machine IoT device evaluated by a local machine IoT device $x = m_x$. Then, the evaluation table shown in Table 1 is corrected the all results evaluated by Eq. (1) among any two IoT devices $x = m_x \in X$ and $y = m_y \in Y$.

**Table 1.** The all evaluation results computed by Eq. (1) between any a machine IoT device in local IoT network $X$ and a machine IoT device in local IoT network $Y$.

| $m_x \in Y$ | $m_y \in Y$ | | | | | |
|---|---|---|---|---|---|---|
| | $m_1$ | $m_2$ | $m_3$ | $\cdots$ $m_x$ | $\cdots$ | $m_z$ |
| $m_1$ | $-$ | $Em_1 m_2$ | $Em_1 m_3$ | $\cdots$ $Em_1 m_x$ | | $Em_1 m_z$ |
| $m_2$ | $Em_2 m_1$ | $-$ | $Em_2 m_3$ | $\cdots$ $Em_2 m_x$ | | $Em_2 m_z$ |
| $m_3$ | $Em_3 m_1$ | $Em_3 m_2$ | $-$ | $\cdots$ $Em_3 m_x$ | | $Em_3 m_z$ |
| $\vdots$ | $\vdots$ | $\vdots$ | $\vdots$ | $-$ $\vdots$ | $\vdots$ | $\vdots$ |
| $m_x$ | $Em_x m_1$ | $Em_x m_2$ | $Em_x m_3$ | $\cdots$ $-$ | | $Em_x m_z$ |
| $\vdots$ | $\vdots$ | $\vdots$ | $\vdots$ | $\vdots$ | $-$ | $\vdots$ |
| $m_z$ | $Em_z m_1$ | $Em_z m_2$ | $Em_z m_3$ | $\cdots$ $Em_z m_x$ | | $-$ |

**Type 2.** The result of $f(x \to y) = f(i_x \to m_y) = i_x \vec{\Theta} m_y = E_{i_x m_y}$ according to Eq. (1) is represented as $Em_x i_y$, when $y = i_y$ is a remote individual IoT device evaluated by a local machine IoT device $x = m_x$. Next, the bit-map evaluation table shown in Table 2 is corrected the all results evaluated by Eq. (1) among any two IoT devices $x = m_x \in X$ and $y = i_y \in Y$.

**Table 2.** The all evaluation results computed by Eq. (1) between any an individual IoT device in local IoT networks $X$ and a machine IoT device in local IoT networks $Y$.

| $m_x \in X$ | $i_y \in Y$ | | | | | |
|---|---|---|---|---|---|---|
| | $i_1$ | $i_2$ | $i_3$ | $\cdots$ $i$ | $\cdots$ | $i_n$ |
| $m_1$ | $-$ | $Em_1 i_2$ | $Em_1 i_3$ | $\cdots$ $Em_1 i_x$ | | $Em_1 i_n$ |
| $m_2$ | $Em_2 i_1$ | $-$ | $Em_2 i_3$ | $\cdots$ $Em_2 i_x$ | | $Em_2 i_n$ |
| $m_3$ | $Em_3 i_1$ | $Em_3 i_2$ | $-$ | $\cdots$ $Em_3 i_x$ | | $Em_3 i_n$ |
| $\vdots$ | $\vdots$ | $\vdots$ | $\vdots$ | $-$ $\vdots$ | $\vdots$ | $\vdots$ |
| $m_x$ | $Em_x i_1$ | $Em_x i_2$ | $Em_x i_3$ | $\cdots$ $-$ | | $Em_x i_n$ |
| $\vdots$ | $\vdots$ | $\vdots$ | $\vdots$ | $\vdots$ | $-$ | $\vdots$ |
| $m_z$ | $Em_z i_1$ | $Em_z i_2$ | $Em_z i_3$ | $\cdots$ $Em_z i_x$ | | $-$ |

**Type 3.** The result of $f(x \to y) = f(i_x \to i_y) = i_x \vec{\Theta} i_y = E_{i_x i_y}$ according to Eq. (1) is represented as $Ei_1 i_2$ when $y = i_y$ is a remote machine IoT device evaluated by a local

machine IoT device $x = i_x$. Finally, the bit-map evaluation table shown in Table 3 is corrected the all results evaluated by Eq. (1) among any two IoT devices $x = i_x \in X$ and $y = i_y \in Y$.

**Table 3.** The all evaluation results computed by Eq. (1) between any an individual IoT device in local IoT networks $X$ and a individual IoT device in local IoT networks $Y$.

| $i_x \in X$ | $i_y \in Y$ | | | | | | |
|---|---|---|---|---|---|---|---|
| | $i_1$ | $i_2$ | $i_3$ | $\cdots$ | $i$ | $\cdots$ | $i_n$ |
| $i_1$ | $-$ | $Ei_1i_2$ | $Ei_1i_3$ | $\cdots$ | $Ei_1i_x$ | | $Ei_1i_n$ |
| $i_2$ | $Ei_2i_1$ | $-$ | $Ei_2i_3$ | $\cdots$ | $Ei_2i_x$ | | $Ei_2i_n$ |
| $i_3$ | $Ei_3i_1$ | $Ei_3i_2$ | $-$ | $\cdots$ | $Ei_3i_x$ | | $Ei_3i_n$ |
| $\vdots$ | $\vdots$ | $\vdots$ | $\vdots$ | $-$ | $\vdots$ | $\vdots$ | $\vdots$ |
| $i_x$ | $Ei_xi_1$ | $Ei_xi_2$ | $Ei_xi_3$ | $\cdots$ | $-$ | | $Ei_xi_n$ |
| $\vdots$ | $\vdots$ | $\vdots$ | $\vdots$ | $\vdots$ | $\vdots$ | $-$ | $\vdots$ |
| $i_z$ | $Ei_zi_1$ | $Ei_zi_2$ | $Ei_zi_3$ | $\cdots$ | $Ei_zi_x$ | | $-$ |

# 6 Conclusion

In distributed BC IoT network, the trust evaluation among those unknown IoT devices which communicate and trade to each other is still the high demand. In this paper, the trust evaluation gateway is then proposed for the distributed BC IoT network in order to solve the problem mentioned above. Therefore, the three types of trust evaluation functionfor Machine to Individual (M2I), Machine to Machine (M2M), and Individual to Individual (I2I), selectively, are proposed and provided an appropriate solution for solving the online mutual trust evaluation in the proposed distributed BC IoT network.

**Acknowledgments.** This study was supported by the Ministry of Science and Technology (MOST), Taiwan, Republic of China, under the grants of MOST 106-2632-E-468-003 and MOST 107-2221-E-468-015.

# References

1. D'Aliessi, M.: How does the blockchain work? The blockchain technology explained in simple words. a medium corporation, US (2016). https://medium.com/@micheledaliessi/how-does-the-blockchain-work-98c8cd01d2ae#.x4eu0wtnz
2. Swan, M.: Blockchain: Blueprint for a New Economy. O'Reilly Media, CA (2015)
3. Chen, H.-C., You, I., Weng, C.-E., Cheng, C.-H., Huang, Y.-F.: A security gateway application for end-to-end M2M communications. Comput. Stand. Interfaces **44**, 85–93 (2016)
4. Chen, H.-C.: A trusted user-to-role and role-to-key access control scheme. Soft. Comput. **20** (5), 1721–1733 (2016)

5. Chen, H.-C.: TCABRP: a trust-based cooperation authentication bit-map routing protocol against insider security threats in wireless ad hoc networks. IEEE Syst. J. **11**(2), 1–11 (2015)
6. Chen, H.-C.: A multi-issued tag key agreement with time constraint for homeland defense sub-department in NFC. J. Netw. Comput. Appl. **38**, 88–98 (2014)
7. Sharma, T.K.: How does blockchain use public key cryptography? Retrieved from https://www.blockchain-council.org/blockchain/how-does-blockchain-use-public-key-cryptography/

# Personal Data and Identifiers: Some Issues Regarding General Data Protection Regulations

Sung Chunhsien[✉] and Lu Shangchien

School of Civil and Commercial Law, Beijing Institute of Technology,
No.6 Jinfeng Road, Zhuhai, Guang Dong, China
scotsung@gmail.com

**Abstract.** This paper investigates the identifier in general data protection regulations in relation to personal information and privacy matters. The paper compares different legal systems regarding protection of personal information, taking the system of general data regulation (as adopted by the EU and by China) as the most influential protective regime. Because general data is defined as any information related to a person, the key term "identifier" becomes excessively broad in its application. The second half of this paper contributes to the discussion about identifiers and the de-identification process envisaged in the regulations, addressing certain criticisms of the identifier provisions.

**Keywords:** Data protection · Personal data identifiers · GDPR

## 1 Introduction

This paper has as its subject matter the regulation of the protection of personal data, i.e., the forms of information that are included in the personal data protection schemes used in the EU and in China. Generally, personal data protection regulations employ in-sequence protective schemes: measures relating to the data subject, to data processing (including data collectors and controllers), to security, and to aftermath (response and compensation); the concept of the "data subject" is the key to these other protective schemes. Therefore, entities involved in data processing are required to comply with the personal data protection regulations if the processed data falls under the scope of the data subject. In particular, the internet has created a difficult environment, because it is easy to identify a person via a search engine.

### 1.1 Protection in Different Systems

Personal data protection and privacy matters are worldwide issues, and international organizations including the United Nations, the Organization for Economic Co-operation and Development, and Asia-Pacific Economic Cooperation have created similar framework provisions for their member states to comply with. Protective schemes commonly use one of two modes. The first mode is protection in functionality (i.e., different regulations apply to different forms of personal data usage); the second

J.-L. Chen et al. (Eds.): WiCON 2018, LNICST 264, pp. 163–169, 2019.
https://doi.org/10.1007/978-3-030-06158-6_17

mode is general protection (i.e., an identical regulation applies to each individual). The former mode corresponds to the US pattern; the latter mode corresponds to the pattern used in the EU and in China.

These patterns have different protective purposes. The US functionality-directed mode focuses primarily on user privacy, which is a fundamental right according to the US constitution. However, the EU regards all personal information as general data and is more concerned about rights relating to personal information, regardless of the nature of the information. This major difference corresponds to a difference in the scope of the concept of data subject in each protective scheme. As a result of this difference, entities involved in data processing easily fall within the scope of EU protective jurisdiction.

## 1.2   Territorial Scope and Worldwide Influence of General Data Protection Schemes

The European General Data Protection Regulation (GDPR) came into force in May 2018 [1]. The implementation of the GDPR has had a worldwide influence because of its provisions under "territorial scope", which give worldwide jurisdiction over any entity involved in using the personal data of European residents. In other words, regardless of the location of an entity, its access to European personal data would put the entity under the control of the GDPR. In particular, use of the internet, which is considered to be a space without territorial limitations, may lead to unforeseen consequences because of the difficulty of managing internet users [2].

Since EU Data Protection Directive 95/4630 (GDPR Predecessor) established "the most influential international policy instrument" [3] in the field of data protection, the EU personal data protection regime has inspired many data protection provisions in different regions. In the case of China, although the Cybersecurity Law came into force in June 2017, the authority began to apply personal data protection policies in 2000 with a decision of congress safeguarding internet security. The first explicit ruling was the 2005 amendment of the Criminal Law (Art. 253-1) regarding the infringement of citizens' personal information. The territorial scope was later established in the aforementioned Cybersecurity Law.

## 1.3   The Substance of This Paper: Personal Data Subjects in the EU and China

On account of the worldwide implications of general data protection regulations, this paper focuses on the role of the data subject in regulation in the EU and China, the world's two biggest personal data protection jurisdictions in terms of population and economic scale.

The concept of the personal data subject (i.e., the definition of personal data and the nature of that data) is the fundamental issue at stake. This paper therefore provides a comprehensive analysis of the data subject as conceptualized in the EU and China regulations.

Information related to personal data is classified into general information, identifiers, and sensitive data. This classification closely corresponds to different levels of security and their corresponding safeguarding measures.

# 2 Data Subjects: General Personal Information

## 2.1 Any Information

Personal data is a broad concept that can cover any form of information used to recognize a natural person. Accordingly, the term "any information" needs to be taken literally; in other words, any information related to a person that may have an impact on his or her privacy rights is the subject matter of data protection regulations. As a result, any element involved in verification of identity, including physical, biometrical, or factual information, falls within the category of general data. Under personal data regulations, identity verification also refers to the use of a combination of information to identify a person. Therefore, if a single piece of information can with the help of other information be used to identify a person, these pieces of information are subject to personal data regulations.

The identification of an individual using multiple pieces of information is known as "internet doxing" or re-identification.

## 2.2 General Data Related to a Person

Personal general data is a broad term, and it is difficult to give a clear definition. Generally speaking, it refers to any information related to a person, including the following:

- physiological features, such as appearance, eye color, height, weight, health status, and genetics (including medical history, genetic data, and information about sick leave)
- personal circumstances, such as social security or ID numbers, phone numbers, residential address, email addresses, location data, and economic status
- habits or behavior, such as character traits, religion, cultural factors, political opinions, and geotracking data
- biographical information, such as date of birth, workplace data, level of education, salary, tax information, and student ID number.

However, owing to policy considerations, not every type of information listed above is included in the regulations. The EU and China have also used different terminology for the various types of personal data in their respective regulations.

## 2.3 Data Protection Regulations

The EU GDPR defines personal data as "any information relating to an identified or identifiable natural person." The GDPR gives certain forms of information as examples, including but not limited to "a name, an identification number, location data, an online identifier or to one or more factors specific to the physical, physiological, genetic, mental, economic, cultural or social identity of that natural person." In the case of China, the Provisions on Protecting the Personal Information of Telecommunications and Internet Users (Internet Provision China) [4] define personal data as "information with which the identity of the user can be distinguished independently or in combination with other information." Internet Provision China gives certain forms of information as examples, including but not limited to "a user's name, date of birth, identity card number, address, telephone number, account number, passwords."

In connection with the China Internet Provision, it should be noted that the scope of personal data is a successor to the GB/Z 28828–2012 Guideline for personal information protection within information systems for public and commercial services.

## 2.4    Rights in Relation to Personal Information in China

Another important aspect of the China regulation is the latest reform of the General Provisions of the Civil Law, which came into effect on 1 October 2017. The reform specifies "right of personal information" as an independent measure within civil rights. Article 111 states that "Natural persons' personal information shall be protected by law. Any organizations and individuals who need to obtain personal information of others shall obtain the information according to law and shall ensure the safety of the information. It is not permitted to illegally collect, use, process, or transfer the personal information of others. It is illegal to buy and sell, supply, or publish the personal information of others." Although the latest reform and implementation of Article 111 in Civil Law have led to some updating of cybersecurity standards in the privacy domain, the term "personal information" as used in Article 111 is not clearly defined, and no further interpretation is provided. Thus, the issue of whether the forms of personal data listed in Internet Provision China are regarded as a civil right or are protected by civil law remains unclear.

# 3    Data Subjects: Identifiers

## 3.1    Identifiable Data Subjects

In most data protection schemes, several types of data are categorized as personal because they enable the singling out or identification of a natural person. Identification of this sort is not evaluated purely in terms of individual pieces of information; it covers any combination of pieces of information that may directly or indirectly identify a person. Since identification may take place on the basis of one or more pieces of information, once the person is singled out, these pieces of information, taken singly or jointly, are defined as "identifiers" [5].

Although the concept of identifier is at the core of the concept of the personal data subject, it is controversial. In the context of personal general data, the regulations only govern personal information that is identifiable. Therefore, an identified data subject is a person who can be clearly known, named, or recognized; directly identifiable examples include a person's full name or appearance; indirectly identifiable examples include a person's mobile phone number, email address, or any form of ID number.

Nevertheless, the consequences of information combination result in an ambiguity in the term "indirectly identify a person." To take a practical example, a list of first names does not enable the singling out of a person; however, the addition of further information, such as residential address, workplace data, or surname, allows a particular group of people to be extracted by means of the combination of information. Accordingly, when an individual can be recognized from the group on the basis of a combination of information, that combination of information is regarded as an identifier.

## 3.2 Online Identifiers

Consequently, information combination may give rise to a large number of potential identifiers, and given the possibilities of the internet, more online identifiers are likely to emerge. The EU GDPR clarifies online identifiers in its Recital 30, which covers information from a number of sources that may single out a person, such as devices, applications, cookies, radio frequency identification tags, and tools and protocols (including IP addresses).

It should be noted that traces of such sources may become identifiable by means of other information (either online or offline). For instance, the keywords entered into a search engine are temporally saved in cookies, which may indicate a tendency or behavior on the part of the user. This sort of information may, in combination with identifiers or other information, single out a person.

## 3.3 De-Identification

Anonymous information falls outside the scope of general data regulations. In other words, data processors who are not willing to be governed by the regulations must understand and make use of the principles of data protection concerning identifiers and de-identification.

In Article 4(5), the GDPR defines pseudonymization as follows:

'pseudonymisation' means the processing of personal data in such a manner that the personal data can no longer be attributed to a specific data subject without the use of additional information, provided that such additional information is kept separately and is subject to technical and organizational measures to ensure that the personal data are not attributed to an identified or identifiable natural person.

However, it is not easy to ensure treatment of data that makes personal information no longer identifiable; as long as the information can be combined with other information (e.g., in case of failure to keep the additional information separate), such a combination may suffice to narrow the range to a specific group or to single out a person.

In Recital 26 of the GDPR, even though personal data have undergone a process of pseudonymization, if a person can be singled out by the use of additional information, that processed information should be considered as an identifier. In other words, anonymous information must afford no possibility of identifying the data subject.

## 3.4 Appropriate Measures and Data Doxing

In most cases, general data protection regulations recommend that the process of de-identification should take the form of appropriate technical and organizational measures that are able to ensure ongoing confidentiality and integrity. However, the authorities provide no specific information about what counts as "appropriate measures." For example, in the case of the GDPR, apart from pseudonymization, the only measure suggested is data encryption. This suggestion offers very limited help to entities involved in data processing. Data encryption is commonly associated with concerns about data leaking or hacking; identifiers are more commonly associated with concerns about data "doxing" on the internet (i.e., combination of information).

Data doxing involves narrowing the scope so that a particular person can be singled out. Thus, in order to single out an individual, the conditions used to narrow down the possibilities are vital and unpredictable factors. For example, a surname is regarded as personal information; however, a surname on its own usually indicates nothing and is therefore not regarded as an identifier. However, once a surname is combined with workplace information, these two conditions taken together indicate a particular group of people. If the surname is rare or unique, or if the workplace is very small, these two conditions may be sufficient to single out a person, regardless of any additional information. Therefore, unpredictability is an outcome of the characteristics of personal data, not of the form of personal data.

## 4   Conclusions: Some Thoughts on Re-Identification

With reference to distinguishing identifiers from personal information, the GDPR offers the following guidance to data processors in its Recital 26:

> To ascertain whether means are reasonably likely to be used to identify the natural person, account should be taken of all objective factors, such as the costs of and the amount of time required for identification, taking into consideration the available technology at the time of the processing and technological developments.

Therefore, objective factors and technological considerations are crucial to distinguishing identifiers.

The previous section approached unpredictability in terms of whether internet information is capable of doxing. This section takes a technical approach: the best method of taking personal information outside the scope of identifiers is to incorporate de-identification (or pseudonymization) as a fundamental process. Regardless of the forms or catalogues of personal information, de-identification must take account of the "directivity" of the information. Four sorts of directivity are described as follows:

1. Personal information that directly indicates a single person, such as full name or appearance. The data processor should treat this sort of information using strict de-identification or pseudonymization approaches (i.e., completely anonymous treatment).
2. Personal information that indirectly indicates a single person, such as social security or ID numbers and mobile phone numbers. The data processor should treat this sort of information using pseudonymization approaches (i.e., blocking part of the information).
3. Personal information that can be used for cross-examination (doxing), which includes most information, such as part of a name, date of birth, home phone number, residential address, and workplace. The data processor should treat this sort

of information using pseudonymization or isolation approaches (i.e., keeping the types of information separate).

4. Personal information presented with pure numbers and without directivity, such as weight and height. This sort of information apparently falls outside the scope of identifier, because without any further identifiable information, mere numbers would not suffice to identify anything. It is nevertheless necessary to isolate this numerical data from identities.

Personal data protection is a critical issue in the context of the internet, as it has become more difficult to isolate one piece of information from another. Thus, the scope of the concept of identifier is broader than it first appears. In particular, as most forms of e-commerce involve personal information, the establishment of safeguards regarding identifiers is a difficult task that must be reconsidered.

# References

1. Commission Regulation 2016/679, 2016 O. J. (L119) 1(EU)
2. Voss, W.: European Union Data Privacy Law Reform: General Data Protection Regulation, Privacy Shield, and the Right to Delisting, vol. 72, The Business Lawyer (2016–2017)
3. Bennett, C., Raab, C.: The Governance of Privacy: Policy Instruments in Global Perspective. MIT Press (2006)
4. Provisions on Protection of Personal Information of Telecommunications and Internet Users, MIIT Order No. 24 (2013)
5. Elliot, M., Mackey, E., O'Hara, K., Tudor, C.: The Anonymization Decision-Making Framework. UKAN, Manchester (2016)

# Internet of Things

# A Channel Selection Method for Device to Device (D2D) Communication Using the Mobile Edge Computing (MEC) Paradigm

Chung-Ming Huang[1], Rung-Shiang Cheng[2(✉)],
and Hsing-Han Chen[1]

[1] Department of Computer Science and Information Engineering, National
Cheng Kung University, Tainan, Taiwan, R.O.C.
huangcm@locust.csie.ncku.edu.tw
[2] Department of Information Technology, Overseas Chinese University,
Taichung, Taiwan, R.O.C.
rscheng@ocu.edu.tw

**Abstract.** Nowadays, LTE (Long Term Evolution) had been developed stably and can support large scale communication services to mobile devices, the traffic offloading in core network and mobile devices is still an issue. Besides, the intensive collision between mobile devices is also an issue because they need to compete the finite network resources with each other. Mobile Edge Computing (MEC) is a promising technique applied to network edge, which can assist the edge device to offload the data traffic and decrease the gigantic computation effort through sending the complicated tasks to remote MEC before sending to core network. To solve the traffic and location issues, this paper proposed a channel selection scheme for MEC-assisted Device to Device Communication Offloading (MD2DO) which can help the peered mobile devices to confirm the location of the mobile device and efficiently have Wi-Fi D2D through channel selection for traffic offloading.

**Keywords:** Mobile edge computing (MEC) · Device to device communication (D2D) · Channel selection · Offloading

## 1 Introduction

LTE cellular network can provide large-scale communication services and support users to access network ubiquitously. With the high increase rate of mobile users, it always has heavy loading and congestion in cellular network. To tackle the afore-mentioned problems of cellular network, many methods and studies of offloading cellular network traffic were proposed and discussed, such as Wi-Fi offloading [1, 2] and Device to Device Communication (D2D) [3, 4]. With the techniques of Wi-Fi offloading and D2D communication, mobile devices can utilize other communication way's available bandwidth to relieve the heavy load in cellular network.

Current Wi-Fi offloading has the mobile device to switch from attaching with a Base Station (BS) of cellular network to attaching with an AP of the Wi-Fi network when a Wi-Fi AP is available and vice versa when the Wi-Fi AP is unavailable. Thus, it

© ICST Institute for Computer Sciences, Social Informatics and Telecommunications Engineering 2019
Published by Springer Nature Switzerland AG 2019. All Rights Reserved
J.-L. Chen et al. (Eds.): WiCON 2018, LNICST 264, pp. 173–182, 2019.
https://doi.org/10.1007/978-3-030-06158-6_18

belongs to the infrastructure-based approach. When a mobile device switches from cellular network to Wi-Fi network or from Wi-Fi network to cellular network, it needs to have some signal transmission for automatic switch or some manual operation from the corresponding user. To have the signal transmission and control for automatic switch between Wi-Fi network and cellular network, 3GPP of the International Telecommunication Union (ITU) devised the standard of LTE WLAN Aggregation (LWA) [5]. Using LWA, Mobile Network Operators (MNOs) can adjust the usage ratio of LTE and Wi-Fi according to the using status of the mobile devices for downloading data; but, users can only use LTE for uploading. Thus, the LWA technique has the potential of increasing network utilization and system capacity and the peak throughput users can experience.

The other offloading method technique is based on D2D communication, which belongs to the un-infrastructure communication way. D2D communication allows direct communication between proximate mobile devices to reduce the load of the core network. LTE D2D [6] and Wi-Fi D2D [7] are two well-known D2D communication techniques, which can offload the infrastructure-based traffic of cellular network. LTE D2D has advantages of larger signal coverage, fast device discovery and high privacy. But LTE D2D utilizes licensed bandwidth of LTE cellular network and therefore it may not be free. In contrast, Wi-Fi D2D can enable quick connection and direct communication of two mobile devices using the unlicensed band. That is, Wi-Fi D2D utilizes unlicensed band and thus can offload cellular network's traffic more effectively.

MEC is a new computing paradigm that can provide cloud computing in network edge to meet some real time requirements [8, 9]. MEC is considered as a key enabler to help resource-limited mobile devices to process gigantic volume of data before sending these data to the core network, support delay-sensitive applications and services and remedy high bandwidth requirement of current cellular network. The deployment of a MEC server is expected to be placed at the edge of mobile network, e.g. each eNB is associated with an MEC server that plays the role of a centralized manager and offers high virtualized computation and storage. The MEC technique not only improves the edge network utilization but also alleviates cellular traffic. Thus, instead of using the remote cloud server, mobile devices can have the heavy tasks that need complicated calculation, e.g., collect edge network information, to the near powerful MEC server for saving cellular traffic.

When the peered mobile devices are communicating with each other using the cellular network, each mobile node's Wi-Fi interface switches to each Wi-Fi channel periodically. Let each mobile node report its context, which contains the sensed Wi-Fi APs in each Wi-Fi channel, to the MEC server periodically. When the MEC server finds that the peered mobile devices sensed the same Wi-Fi AP in a specific channel $m$, for which they did not switch to the same channel to sense at the same time, it implies that the peered mobile devices are proximate with each other. Thus, the MEC server notifies these two peered mobile devices to go to channel $n$, which has the better networking situation calculated by the MEC server, to try Wi-Fi D2D offloading in channel $n$. Although there are researches exploring how to apply MEC for the access technologies of network, researches of applying MEC to measure channel quality and have Wi-Fi D2D offloading are still insufficient.

The rest of this thesis are organized as follows. Section 2 presents related works, including D2D communication, LWA, MEC and traffic offloading. Section 3 presents details of the proposed MD2DO method. Section 5 presents performance analysis. Finally, Sect. 6 summarizes and has conclusion remarks.

## 2  Related Work

LTE-WLAN aggregation (LWA) is a standard made by International Telecommunication Union (ITU) [5, 10]. Through the integration of LTE mobile network and Wi-Fi wireless network, mobile devices can simultaneously access two kinds of network services, for which uploading is through LTE and downloading is through either Wi-Fi or LTE. This communication paradigm solves the contention problem of wireless network and meanwhile efficiently performs downloading using both licensed band and unlicensed band. Comparing with the past technique, on which users have to manually switch between LTE and Wi-Fi to select the preferred network service, mobile network operators can provide appropriate services through the diagnosis of the network status that users are using and achieve network optimization based on LWA.

In [11], the authors proposed a Self-Organizing Network (SON) algorithm according to the network status, i.e., the quality of LTE communication link (SINR) and RSSI of wireless network (WLAN) of each user, to adjust the control parameter of the LWA transmission mode. The proposed SDN algorithm not only provides higher transmission rate but also guarantees better service quality, and thus enhances user satisfaction.

In [12], the authors adopted a new comprehensive optimization framework to solve the increasing demand of downloading large data on cellular network. Using the proposed method, a base station sends different chunks of contents to a group of Mobile Devices (MD), and then some MDs multicast these chunks to other MDs in the same group using D2D. The framework optimizes the chunk distribution and multi-hop cooperation while keeping the fairness constrains on the power consumption of the MDs and multicast transmission. The optimization problem is a NP-complete problem. The authors obtained computationally fast solutions with the close-to-optimal performance using the polynomial time greedy method.

In [13], the authors proposed a dynamic channel assignment method based on a regret learning algorithm (DCA-LA), which takes co-channel interference (CCI) power, the average CCI power estimation and the utility estimation into account, for base stations (BSs). In the algorithm, BSs learn nearby BSs' channels by altering their channels and minimizing their regrets if they do not select other available channels. A BS distributes a non-zero probability to each channel and the higher probability is assigned to one with more regret. In this way, it can decrease the chance of two adjacent cells selecting the same channel. The algorithm is processed in a fully distributed manner, therefore, it does not need to exchange signal information between BSs.

# 3   The Proposed Scheme- MD2DO Method

In this section, the control flow of the proposed MD2DO scheme, for which phase 1 is D2D Peer Discovery and Channel Selection and phase 2 is Association and Offloading, is presented in detail.

**A. The Control Flow**

Initially, each mobile node that is using cellular network reports its context, including the collected network information, to the MEC server periodically using cellular network. The MEC server uses the contexts sent by mobile devices to coordinate the infrastructure communication using cellular network and the Wi-Fi D2D communication using Wi-Fi network. Let mobile devices MN1 and MN2 be communicating with each other using cellular network. When the MEC server finds that mobile devices MN1 and MN2 can receive the beacon sent by the same AP in the same Wi-Fi channel, it indicates that MN1 and MN2 are proximate with each other because they are in the signal coverage of the same Wi-Fi AP. When the MEC server confirms MN1 and MN2 are proximate with each other, the MEC server calculates each Wi-Fi channel's quality according to the networking information sent from Wi-Fi AP and mobile devices and then assigns the better Wi-Fi channel for MN1 and MN2 to try Wi-Fi D2D communication; otherwise, MN1 and MN2 keep using cellular network.

**B. D2D Peer Discovery and Channel Selection**

When two mobile devices are proximate with each other, having Wi-Fi D2D communication can further improve the performance of the network and reduce the burden of cellular network and even Wi-Fi APs. The first issue to have Wi-Fi D2D communication is to confirm the location of mobile devices because mobile devices keep moving. In this paper, each mobile device, which is using cellular network, uses the collected network information to make a Carrier Sense Information (CSI) record, which includes current time, MAC addresses of nearby mobile devices, i.e., the ones that the mobile device can sense, MAC address of nearby Wi-Fi APs, sensed RSSI of nearby mobile devices, and its own Frame Error Rate (FER), Contention Window (CW) Size, and sends it to the MEC server to judge the networking situation.

Each mobile device would utilize passive scanning for listening to beacon frames in each Wi-Fi channel because passive scanning does not require any signal transmission from the mobile device, i.e., it is an action of passively receiving and thus the mobile device can save power. A mobile device would switch from one Wi-Fi channel to the other Wi-Fi channel and wait for the beacon frames sent from Wi-Fi APs that are using the corresponding channel currently.

In this paper, in addition to have passively scanning, i.e. receiving beacon frames sent by Wi-Fi APs to know the MAC addresses of Wi-Fi APs, each mobile device would overhear the received data packets, which are sent by surrounding mobile devices, to record related data, i.e., MAC addresses of nearby mobile devices and sensed RSSI of nearby mobile devices. Besides the aforementioned data, each mobile device measures its own FER and CW to compose the CSI (Carrier Sense Information) record. The MEC server estimates the channel quality of each Wi-Fi channel and selects the best one for peered mobile devices to try to have Wi-Fi D2D communication using the *Channel Selection algorithm*, which will be presented in the next section.

**C. Association and Offloading**

After the calculation of channel quality and the selection of a suitable Wi-Fi channel, the MEC server notifies the peered mobile devices to start the association process in the assigned channel. The association process is used to confirm that the peered mobile device MN1/MN2 is in MN2's/MN1's Wi-Fi signal coverage and can communicate with each other directly using Wi-Fi D2D communication in the assigned channel. If the association is successful, then the peered mobile devices can have Wi-Fi D2D communication. When Wi-Fi D2D communication ends, MN1 and MN2 switch to the cellular network to continue scanning and reporting. However, if the association process is failed, the peered mobile devices MN1 and MN2 keep using the cellular network to communicate with each other and send the failed result to the MEC server.

# 4   The Functional Scenario of the Proposed MD2DO Scheme

The aforementioned problem can be resolved using the MEC paradigm. Let (1) each mobile device report its CSI record, which contains MAC addresses of nearby mobile devices, MAC address of nearby Wi-Fi APs, the sensed RSSI of nearby mobile devices, and its own Frame Error Rate (FER) and its own Contention Window (CW) Size, and (2) each Wi-Fi AP report its context, which contains its FER and CW, to the MEC server. The MEC server can analyze each channel's situation based on the aforementioned contexts reported from mobile devices and Wi-Fi APs.

| | |
|---|---|
| 1. | The MEC server creates *ChannelQualityList*. |
| 2. | **for** each channel $k$, $k = 1, 6, 11$, |
| 3. | Calculate the channel quality for $x$ $(C_x^k)$ and $y$ $(C_y^k)$ at channel $k$. |
| 4. | Add $min\{C_x^k, C_y^k\}$ to *ChannelQualityList[k]*. |
| 5. | **end for** |
| 6. | The MEC server selects channel $m$ that has the maximal channel quality value $Q^m$ among all *ChannelQualityList[k]*, $k = 1, 6, 11$, as the suitable channel for Wi-Fi D2D communication. |
| 7. | MEC server notifies the peered mobile devices $x$ and $y$ to use the Wi-Fi channel to try Wi-Fi D2D communication. |

Let mobile devices $x$ and $y$ be the peered mobile devices that have the chance to try Wi-Fi D2D communication. Two part of the *Channel Selection algorithm*, are (1) channel quality calculation, which calculates the quality of each channel based on the reported CSI records of mobile devices and the reported contexts of Wi-Fi APs and (2) channel selection, which chooses the suitable channel that will be assigned to the peered mobile devices for having Wi-Fi D2D communication. The formula for channel quality calculation is as follows:

$$\text{Channel Quality} = \frac{1}{\emptyset}, where \emptyset = \left[ \frac{\sum_{i=1}^{N} \left( FER_i \times CW_i \times \left| \frac{1}{RSSI_i} \right| \right)}{N} \right]$$

$N$ is the number of nearby mobile devices that are sensed by each one of the peered mobile devices in the corresponding channel. That is, the bigger/smaller $N$ is, the more/less mobile devices there are in the corresponding channel could be influenced. FER indicates the frame error ratio, which is equal to the number of retransmission times is dividing by the number of total transmission times in each mobile device. The value indicates the probability of unsuccessfully transmitting packets and can be used to indicate the channel networking situation. Each mobile device, which connects to the Wi-Fi AP or Wi-Fi D2D communication, needs to calculate its $FER$ value after sending a packet and then reports the $FER$ value to the MEC server. The value of $CW$ indicates the average contention window size of all of the transmitted packets' contention window size and is used to imply the delay time of accessing a channel. Each mobile device, which has connected to the Wi-Fi AP or Wi-Fi D2D, needs to report its $CW$ value to the MEC server periodically for measuring the delay time of accessing the channel. After a mobile device scans all of the Wi-Fi channels and needs to report, it calculates how many packets the mobile device has been sent since the most recent report, and then calculates a new $CW$ value to report. $RSSI$ is an indicator to measure the intensity of received energy of mobile devices. Through this measurement, the distance between the receiving end and the transmitting end can be inferred.

The higher the RSSI value is, (1) the stronger the energy of the received signal is and (2) the shorter the distance between the receiving end and the transmitting end is, meanwhile, the mutual influence of these two neighboring entities, i.e., the receiving end and the transmitting end is stronger. To select a channel with less influence, it can calculate the absolute value of $RSSI$ and finds the inverse of the calculated number as an index. The lower the value is, the longer the distance between the receiving end and the transmitting end is and the influence between neighboring devices is weaker.

After calculating all channels quality's value, these channels will be separated into two exclusive groups. If the channel that the peered mobile devices sensed has no nearby mobile devices, the channel will be classified to the first group; otherwise, the channel will be classified to the second group. Then, the MEC server selects the channel from the first group because the channel in the first group have no node and thus the channel quality is the best.

## 5  Performance Analysis

This section presents the performance analysis and simulation results for the proposed scheme. The configured parameters that are used in the simulation are listed in Table 1. To present the results in a more comprehensive way, the simulation is divided into two parts, in which one is associated with eleven Wi-Fi channels, i.e., channel $1 \sim 11$, and the other one is associated with three Wi-Fi channels, i.e., channel 1, 6 and 11.

**Table 1.** The parameters used in the experiment.

| Simulation parameters | Value |
|---|---|
| MAC protocol | 802.11 g |
| Propagation model | Two ray |
| Slot time | 9 μsec |
| SIFS time | 10 μsec |
| PIFS time | 19 μsec |
| DIFS time | 28 μsec |
| Packet size | 1024 byte |
| ACK size | 14 byte |
| Queue length | 1024 packets |
| Min. contention windows | 32 |
| Max. contention windows | 1024 |

To explain the channel's networking situation conveniently, two terminologies are defined as follows:

- *Good channel*: If the channel is called a good channel, wherein two mobile nodes have Infrastructure-based Wi-Fi communication using the channel for transmitting data, the collision is less and channel loading is low.
- *Bad channel*: If the channel is called a bad channel, wherein thirty mobile nodes have Infrastructure-based Wi-Fi communication using the channel for transmitting data, and the collision in is critical and the channel's loading is high.

To verify that the mobile nodes using the proposed the MD2DO can have Wi-Fi D2D using good channels and always achieve higher network performance when the number of new arrival nodes increases, two networking situations are discussed. In case A, channel 6 and 11 are good channels and channel 1 is a bad channel. In case B, to observe the node number, transmission rate and throughput of each channel in the simulation process, the environment setting are that channel 6 and 11 are good channel and channel 1 is a bad channel and the number of new arrival nodes is thirty-six.

## 5.1   The Performance Analysis

**Case A: Channel 6 and 11 are good channels and channel 1is a bad channel**
Figures 1(a) and 2(a) depict the transmission rate comparison of Case A with the increasing number of new arrival nodes. It can be observed that the trend of transmission rate of channel 6 and channel 11 gradually close to channel 1 using the MD2DO method. The reason is that new arrival nodes can use the better channels, which are selected by the MEC server, for having Wi-Fi D2D. When new arrival nodes enter into the network, the MEC server assigned the good channel (channel 6 and 11) to them for having efficient Wi-Fi D2D such that new arrival nodes can avoid using the bad channel to have Wi-Fi D2D. Since new arrival nodes that are having Wi-Fi D2D can use good channels, the trend of transmission rate of channel 1 maintains stable. In

the Normal D2D scheme, the trend of transmission rate of channel 6 and channel 11 does not gradually close to channel 1. The channel that two new arrival nodes, which are communicating with each other, used is the one that the same Wi-Fi AP they sensed is using. If the corresponding Wi-Fi channel that the Wi-Fi AP is using is a bad channel, then they have Wi-Fi D2D in a bad channel. Even if there were still other good channels to choose, they can not use because there is no channel selection mechanism. Therefore, the transmission rate of three channels decrease simultaneously, which results in the lower network performance. The same situation happened in the comparison of the throughput and collision rate. Referring to Figs. 1(b)(c) and 2(b)(c), since MD2DO can choose better channels for Wi-Fi D2D, it can balance the loading of channel 1, 6 and 11, and thus it can have higher average throughput and lower average collision rate in these three Wi-Fi channels.

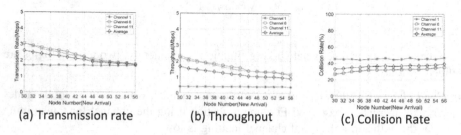

(a) Transmission rate          (b) Throughput          (c) Collision Rate

Fig. 1. The simulation results of using MD2D in case A.

## Case B: Channel 6 and 11 are good channels and channel 1 is bad channel

Figures 3(a) and 4(a) show the number of mobile nodes in each channel. In MD2DO, the number of mobile nodes in channel 1 is stable because the MD2DO method can let new arrival nodes use the better channel. Therefore, the number of the other two channels increases. In the normal D2D method, the number of mobile nodes in each channel is randomly increased. The reason is that no channel selection mechanism is used, i.e., new arrival mobile nodes used the channel that the same Wi-Fi AP both peered mobile nodes sensed is using. Thus, new arrival nodes were randomly scattered in these three channels.

Figure 3(b) and (c) depict the transmission rate and throughput of MD2DO. Initially, the transmission rate and throughput of channel 6 and 11 increase because new arrival node use channel 6 and 11 and avoid using channel 1 for having Wi-Fi D2D. Therefore, the transmission rate and throughput of channel 1 maintain stable. Figure 4 (b) and (c) depict the transmission rate and throughput of Normal D2D. Since new arrival nodes spread randomly in these three channels, transmission rate and throughput of these three channels varied. The transmission rate and throughput of channel 1 decrease because some new arrival nodes have Wi-Fi D2D using channel 1, which deteriorates the channel competition and results in lower network performance.

MD2DO can reduce the burden of bad channel and offload data traffic to good channels. Thus, MD2DO can enhance the channel utilization and shorten the simulation time. In this experiment, the proposed MD2DO improves about 15% simulation

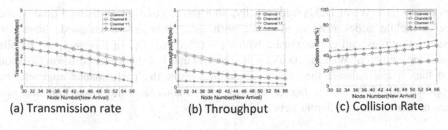

**Fig. 2.** The simulation result of using normal D2D in case A.

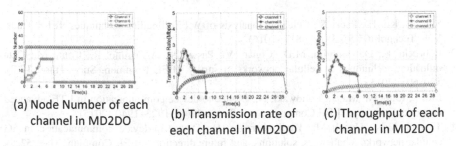

**Fig. 3.** The simulation results of using MD2D in case B.

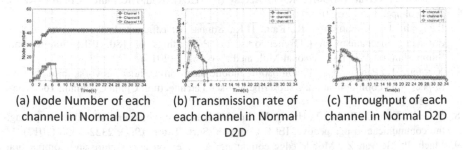

**Fig. 4.** The simulation result of normal D2D in case B.

time. However, the channel utilization is uneven using the Normal D2D, which may have new arrival nodes use the bad channels for having Wi-Fi D2D. Thus, the normal D2D exacerbates the network performance and prolongs the simulation time.

## 6 Conclusion

This paper proposed a scheme called MD2DO, which combines the MEC mechanism and Wi-Fi D2D to enhance the capacity of network and offload cellular traffic. The main concept of MD2DO is to have mobile nodes to collect the network information and send to the MEC server periodically to confirm the location of mobile nodes, calculate the channel quality and then assign the suitable channel for the peered mobile devices to have Wi-Fi D2D. Additionally, after the calculation of channel quality, the peered mobile nodes need to associate with each other in the assigned channel to confirm that they can communicate with each other directly. In this way, the mobile nodes have efficient Wi-Fi D2D using the channel that has the lower collision situation and thus it can balance the channels' loading. From the performance analysis, the proposed MD2DO has the higher network performance and the lower collision rate than normal D2D in different networking situations.

# References

1. Suh, D., Ko, H., Pack, S.: Efficiency analysis of WiFi offloading techniques. IEEE Trans. Veh. Technol. **65**(5), 3813–3817 (2016)
2. Rebecchi, F., De Amorim, M.D., Conan, V., Passarella, A., Bruno, R., Conti, M.: Data offloading techniques in cellular networks: a survey. IEEE Commun. Surv. Tutor. **17**(2), 580–603 (2015)
3. Liu, J., Kato, N., Ma, J., Kadowaki, N.: Device-to-device communication in LTE-advanced networks: a survey. IEEE Commun. Surv. Tutor. **17**(4), 1923–1940 (2015)
4. Tehrani, M.N., Uysal, M., Yanikomeroglu, H.: Device-to-device communication in 5G cellular networks: challenges, solutions, and future directions. IEEE Commun. Mag. **52**(5), 86–92 (2014)
5. GPP TS 36.331 V14.4.0 Release 14, Technical Specification Group Radio Access Network; Evolved Universal Terrestrial Radio Access (E-UTRA); Radio Resource Control (RRC); Protocol specification, 2017/9
6. Panigrahi, B., Ramamohan, R., Rath, H.K., Simha, A.: Efficient device-to-device (D2D) offloading mechanism in LTE networks. In: Proceedings of 18th IEEE International Symposium on Wireless Personal Multimedia (WPMC) (2015)
7. Xiaofeng, L., Pan, H., Lio, P.: Offloading mobile data from cellular networks through peer-to-peer WiFi communication: a subscribe-and-send architecture. China Commun. **10**(6), 35–46 (2013)
8. Mao, Y., You, C., Zhang, J., Huang, K., Letaief, K.B.: A survey on mobile edge computing: the communication perspective. IEEE Commun. Surv. Tutor. **19**(4), 2322–2358 (2017)
9. Mach, P., Becvar, Z.: Mobile edge computing: a survey on architecture and computation offloading. IEEE Commun. Surv. Tutor. **19**(3), 1628–1656 (2017)
10. GPP TS 36.360 version 14.0.0 Release 14, LTE; Evolved Universal Terrestrial Radio Access (E-UTRA); LTE-WLAN Aggregation Adaptation Protocol (LWAAP) specification, 2017/4
11. Balan, I., Perez, E., Wegmann, B., Laselva, D.: Self-optimizing adaptive transmission mode selection for LTE-WLAN aggregation. In: Proceedings of Personal, Indoor, and Mobile Radio Communications (PIMRC), 2016 IEEE 27th Annual International Symposium, pp. 1–6
12. Al-Kanj, L., Poor, H.V., Dawy, Z.: Optimal cellular offloading via device-to-device communication networks with fairness constraints. IEEE Trans. Wirel. Commun. **13**(8), 4628–4643 (2014)
13. Arani, A.H., Mehbodniya, A., Omidi, M.J., Adachi, F.: Learning-based joint power and channel assignment for hyper dense 5G networks, In: Proceedings of Communications (ICC), 2016 IEEE International Conference, pp. 1–7

# Using Internet of Things Technology to Improve Patient Safety in Surgical Instrument Sterilization Control

Lun-Ping Hung[1]([✉]), Cheng-Jung Peng[1], and Chien-Liang Chen[2]

[1] Department of Information Management, National Taipei
University of Nursing and Health Sciences, Taipei, Taiwan
lunping@ntunhs.edu.tw
[2] Department of Computer Science and Information Engineering,
Aletheia University, Taipei, Taiwan

**Abstract.** Medical services influence the people's health and lives. It is a sacred and professional work with the features that do not allow errors and cannot be redone. Therefore, the quality of medical services directly affects the health and safety of patients. In the operating room, the central supply room is responsible for sterilizing surgical instruments. It is also an important place for infection control. Once incompletely sterilized medical devices are used, it may lead to nosocomial infections, thus affecting the safety and quality of the surgical patients. Therefore, to ensure the integrity of the sterilization process and to avoid the use of unsafe surgical instruments. This study uses the sensing technology of the Internet of Things to monitor the sterilization process of surgical instruments sterilization with using the automatic monitoring system to alarm the validity period of surgical instruments pack, and to calculate the required safety stock of surgical instruments packing. With the system, it reduces the additional cost of emergency sterilization when surgical instruments packs are out of supply. Ensure the safety of the patient's use of surgical instruments, so that patients can be treated in a safer medical environment to achieve a win-win benefit.

**Keywords:** Surgical instrument sterilization · Patient safety · Internet of things

## 1 Introduction

The purpose of medical services is to alleviate the suffering or injury of patients, but medical services have incredibly complex professional techniques, uncertainties in conditions, and characteristics that do not allow mistakes, so medical services are not as safe as they are supposed to be. Medical services have the characteristics of "no mistakes, no redoing," so the quality of medical services directly affects the health and safety of patients. Patient safety is an important topic that has been concerned by the World Health Organization and the international community in recent years. The research on the frequency of adverse medical events in foreign countries shows that the incidence of adverse medical events is between 2.9% and 16.6% [1]. Moreover, in the ratio of adverse medical events, surgical adverse events are about 40%–50% [2, 3] of

J.-L. Chen et al. (Eds.): WiCON 2018, LNICST 264, pp. 183–192, 2019.
https://doi.org/10.1007/978-3-030-06158-6_19

adverse medical events in the hospital and adverse events caused by surgical equipment supply are about 15% [4, 5] of surgical adverse events. In Taiwan, about 8,000 people die directly or indirectly due to nosocomial infections which are causing huge financial losses in hospitals. Therefore, in 2009, the World Health Organization began to advocate "safe surgery, save lives" and called on countries around the world to improve operational safety as an essential medical quality policy [6]. The Joint Commission of Taiwan promotes hospital medical quality and patient safety as the annual target and strategy. Medical institutions will implement infection control and improve operational safety [7].

The hospital supply center is the unit responsible for the sterilization of surgical instruments. It is also an important place for infection control. Once Incompletely sterilized medical devices are used in clinically, it may occur nosocomial infections, which may affect the safety and medicinal quality of surgical patients. Today, with the fierce competition and cost-oriented medical institutions, the service quality and effectiveness of the operating room have received considerable attention. In the operating room, all treatments are invasive. Therefore, the control of surgical infection and the quality assurance of instrument sterilization are important tasks for maintaining patient safety. In [8], the Meyer et al. point out one of the future research areas of medical services is the practice of stock management in hospitals. One of the most significant challenges for clinical care managers is to balance costs and maintain proper stock and immediate patient care. In the pursuit of low-cost, high-efficiency best performance in medical institutions, we must face various uncertainties and risks. Therefore, to ensure the safety of the instruments used by surgical patients and reduce the number of emergency sterilization of the surgical instruments packing, reduce labor costs and improve effectiveness.

In the light of the above arguments, IoT technology is used to improve the sterilization and sterilization process of surgical instruments, to ensure the safety of the sterilization process, and to notify and handle the errors immediately, to improve patient safety and reduce the incidence of errors. Use the wireless temperature sensor with system monitoring to reduce the infection caused by the use of incompletely sterilized instruments and reduce the additional cost of emergency sterilization of the supply center instrument pack by systematic safety stock management and labor cost. It effectively improves the safety of patients, so that patients are in a safer medical environment, to achieve a win-win benefit of medical care.

## 2 Related Work

### 2.1 Surgical Instrument Sterilization Safety

Proper sterilization is a significant part of infection control, which affects the infection rate and the length of stays of surgical patients. Infection may be caused by human error or insufficient concept of sterilization of medical devices, so it is necessary to strengthen the standardized operation process and correct sterilization concept [9]. An active sterilization process can prevent the occurrence of surgical infections or other related costs due to surgical infections and It also can improve patient safety.

The monitoring of sterilization quality should be based on the guidelines of the Hospital Infection Control Society and the supply center experts to set up the guidelines for sterilization monitoring, including the load control – it's based on the Process Challenge Device (PCD) to know whether the sterilization conditions meet the sterilization standards, and to issue or recycle the sterilization items [10, 11]. Equipment control – It is mainly divided into mechanical and chemical monitoring to confirm the temperature, permeability, humidity, sterilization cycle time, air removal efficiency. The purpose of equipment control is to ensure the complete function of the sterilize boiler and consistent results of sterilization [12–14]. Pack control: When wrapping the pack, a chemical indicator is placed inside the pack to monitor the sterilization pressure, temperature, humidity, time, etc. during the sterilization process. All of the above four conditions are effective to achieve sterilization standards. When the user opens the sterilization pack, it is visually judged whether the color of the chemical indicator in the pack is changed or whether the color is changed to monitor whether the sterilization succeeds or fails [9, 15]. Exposure control – The chemical indicator outside the pack is mainly in the process of inspection. It can be divided into tape and label type. It can quickly identify the items that have been sterilized or not sterilized by color change [16, 17]. Record keeping control – All the data generated during the sterilization process should be preserved. In the future, as the reference point for the function and maintenance of the sterilizing device flow tracking and sterilize boiler, the above five major controls monitor the sterilization quality to provide patient-safe medical equipment and reduce the risk of infection [15, 16, 18].

The failed of medical device sterilization in medical institutions is an important reason of infection in hospitals. In-hospital infections can cause treatment difficulties and high mortality rates, prolong the hospitalization days and increase the waste of medical resources [19]. Therefore, the quality of medical device sterilization monitoring is critical, and the purpose of the analysis of the monitoring results of sterilization items is to monitor the disinfection and sterilization effect of the disinfected and sterilized items. So as, we can detect the problems in real time, analysis the reason and propose the improvement methods. To ensure the quality of hospital disinfection and sterilization items and it can effectively control hospital infections.

## 2.2    Medical Service Quality and Patient Safety

The purpose of medical services is to relieve the suffering or injury of patients. Because of the complexity, uncertainty, and refusal to make mistakes, medical services are not as safe as they are supposed to be. Medical services are different from the general industry. Their services are a sacred and professional work because of the health and life of people. They have the characteristics of "no mistakes, no redoing," so the quality of medical services directly affects national health and safety. The people are on demand for medical service quality, with the improvement of knowledge and the rise of consciousness. The demands of the people's self-rights are getting higher and higher, and they are no longer limited to the treatment of diseases. The expectation of medical quality is increasingly emphasized, so the pursuit of medical service quality has become the focus of hospital management. Therefore, how to ensure that patients receive excellent service quality is a top priority for hospitals.

Among the various departments of the hospital, the operating room is a highly specialized department with the primary task of performing surgery. The workload of medical staff in the operating room is numerous and high-risk, and the situation of medical disputes in the process of service is also endless. In 2000, Thomas et al. [20] found in 15,000 medical records in Utah and Colorado in the United States that 83.8% of all adverse events occurred in hospitals, of which 39.5% occurred in operating rooms. Compared with other departments, the occurrence of adverse events in the operating room is higher. Research indicates that the operating room is indeed a high-risk service place. To prevent accidental injuries and implement patient safety, it creates a safe medical environment by planning a sound operating system to reduce errors, improve patient safety and promote the quality of medical services.

According to the above literature, the incidence of adverse medical events in the operating room is high, and human error causes many medical errors. The occurrence of adverse events is predictable and avoidable. Therefore, the medical service should have a monitoring design that prevents errors or can immediately detect and effectively handle the control when the error occurs, to minimize the chances of errors and failures in the medical service process, to prevent and reduce medical negligence, and to improve the patient safety.

## 2.3 Sensing Technology Application Research

The rapid development of Internet technology and applications have changed the way people live and communicate. With the innovation of network and communication technologies and the advancement of Micro-electromechanical Systems (MEMS) technology, perceptual and IoT technologies have enabled sensors and wireless communication chips to be incorporated into physical materials. The sensor is a crucial component for receiving signals or reacting with a variable amount of braking and can convert the physical quantity or chemical quantity to be measured into a data output. Its application function is mainly used to detect human senses and then detect external information, including sight, hearing, touch, smell, taste and so on. Some sensors can also detect messages that humans cannot judge. Through the integration of sensing technology, they can also be applied to the value-added services of smart medical care. In the automatic control of food logistics, it is necessary to monitor factors such as temperature, humidity and time continuously. If the temperature is too high, the humidity is too oppressive, or the delivery time is too long, it may cause the food to deteriorate and produce bacteria, which may affect the consumer. This phenomenon is very similar to the sterilization of surgical instruments. The management of the sterilization process must also control the above factors to avoid sterilization failure or incomplete sterilization process.

Scholars use RFID sensing technology to control food logistics and combine wireless temperature and humidity sensors for wireless monitoring. During the logistics delivery process, various influencing factors in the product storage environment are monitored, and food tracking is performed by RFID sensing technology [21]. However, in the sterilization process of the surgical instrument, the control of the sterilization device can be effectively performed through the application of the sensing device, so that the hospital can monitor the sterilization process and can immediately handle the error occurrence event.

Through the literature mentioned above, it can be found that the knowledge of the field of Internet of Things technology and medical services is applied to the operating room supply center environment. The supply center with many instruments, limited medical and human resources, can improve the complexity of the sterilization process, and the integrity of the sterilization process can be ensured, and the resources can be maximized, which not only prevents and reduces medical negligence but also enhances the safety of the patient.

## 3 Methodology

This study aims to improve the safety of surgical patients, ensure the safe sterilization of surgical instruments, optimize the surgical instrument sterilization process, and design the device management information system. The key points include the pairing of the sensor and the pack, and the sterilization in the sterilization boiler to monitor the sterilization process; the automatic monitoring validity period of the pack after sterilization and the calculation of the safety stock of the pack. As mentioned above, the system will be divided into three functions: sterilization error monitoring function, validity monitoring function, and safety stock calculation function. The system will be described in detail below.

The system architecture will be divided into the base layer, the sensing layer, the transport layer, the backend data layer and the application layer as a discussion, as shown in Fig. 1. The base layer and the sensory layer collect information from device sterilization. The transport layer will sent/transmit data and transmit the information in wireless transmission mode. The data layer converts and stores the received

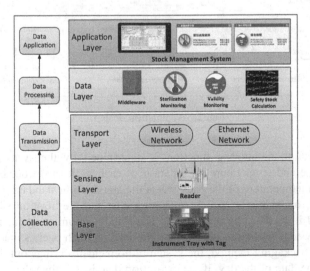

**Fig. 1.** System architecture

information. The sterilization error monitoring function, the validity monitoring function and the safety stock calculation function will read the information in the database for the judgment of sterilization standards, to determine whether it has expired, and calculate the quantity of the safety stock before storing it to the database. The application layer is responsible for providing different users to view different screens. The system will present different screens according to different user rights.

As shown in Fig. 2, the sterilization stock control assistance mechanism will be divided into three parts: the sensor end that sends the information, the core program that performs the information calculation and processing judgment, and the web end show the results. The sensor at the sensor end collects information on the time and temperature changes of the instrument pack in the sterilizing boiler and transmits the information stored in the memory to the reader using the 2.4 GHz wireless transmission technology, and the reader transmits the received information to the system via Ethernet transmission. The relay software in the core program converts the received information into a database after being converted by the data format. The database contains information such as the sterilization time and temperature information of each sensor, the pack barcode and the ID number corresponding to the sensor, and the expiration date of the pack.

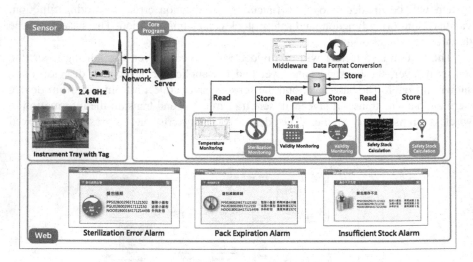

**Fig. 2.** Application design

The sterilization monitoring function is determined by the system reading the sterilization time and temperature information of each pack in the database. Whether the sterilization temperature of the pack meets the sterilization standard, if the standard is not reached, an alarm is issued, indicating that the sterilization of the pack is incomplete and it needs to be resterilized. The validity monitoring function is determined by the system reading database when the label of each pack is made. According to the selected packaging method, the system automatically brings out the set expiration date and the date of the day, if the expiration date is less than the date of the day.

Then it issues an expired alarm. The safety stock calculation function reads the information in the database that the status is expired and the sterilization fails, calculates the average incidence rate of the two, and brings it into the safety stock calculation formula. It is more appropriate to calculate the safety stock quantity. When the safety stock is less than the safety stock, the system will issue an alarm that the inventory quantity is too small and it needs to be sterilized. System alarms and quantity of stock are presented in the form of web browsers. Monitor the sterilization process through the Internet of Things technology, match the system monitoring alarm reminder pack expiration, and optimize the safety stock calculation, reduce the sterilization error rate and expiration rate found only when the pack is in use, and calculate the clinical safety stock amount to avoid the lack of supply of the pack cause the operation time is delayed. The following describes each system function in detail.

## 4 Results

This study optimizes the surgical instrument sterilization process and combines the system background judgment. When the sterilization failure, the pack expires, and the stock is insufficient, an alarm will be issued to remind the supply center medical staff that the condition of the instrument pack is up to standard. The system usage features are described in detail below.

### 4.1 Pack Sterilization Error Alarm Interface

The following Fig. 3 shows the alarm interface of the pack sterilization error. The system reads the information of the sterilization process of the pack stored in the database, and judges whether the pack is successfully sterilized according to the sterilization standard of the pack. If it is found that the sterilization of the pack is a failure, an alarm will be issued to remind the supply center medical staff which tray pack sterilization failure and failure reasons, and the pack must be resterilized.

**Fig. 3.** Pack sterilization error alarm

### 4.2 Pack Expiration Alarm Interface

The following Fig. 4 shows the alarm interface for the expiration of the pack. When the pack is in the warehousing operation, the system will automatically read the validity period of all the packs in the database and compare the date of the day. If the pack is overdue after the comparison, the medical staff will be reminded which pack has expired and need to be re-sterilized.

**Fig. 4.** Pack expired alarm

The system will also start a warning reminder two days before the expiration date of the pack, to inform the medical staff that the time limit for the pack is close. The pack should be used as soon as possible within the service period. As shown below (Fig. 5).

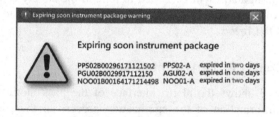

**Fig. 5.** Nearly expired alarm

## 4.3    The Insufficient Stock Alarm Interface

The following Fig. 6 shows the alarm interface for the shortage of the stock of the pack. When the system is in the warehousing operation, the amount of the existing stock and the safety stock calculated by the system is compared, and judges whether the existing stock quantity has less than the safety stock quantity. If the existing stock quantity is small, it will remind the medical staff which packs insufficient stock, it

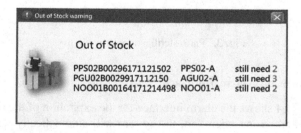

**Fig. 6.** Insufficient stock of the pack alarm

needs to be sterilized again, and it will reduce the existing stock according to the calculated safety stock. It shows how many packs need to be sterilized, which is enough to supply the pack requirements.

# 5 Conclusion

Medical services have characteristics that do not allow errors and cannot be redone. Therefore, delays in surgery or the use of surgical instruments that are not thoroughly sterilized may affect the treatment of the disease. Severe cases are more likely to cause worsening of the condition and even death. The anxiety caused by the patients and their families due to long waits also affects their satisfaction with hospital satisfaction and trust. Therefore, in the supply of surgical instruments, the appropriate stock should be maintained to meet the needs of patients, and When using the pack, it can make sure that the pack is fully sterilized.

This study uses the Internet of Things sensing technology to improve the disinfection and sterilization process of surgical instruments to ensure the integrity and safety of the sterilization process, and to achieve instant notification and handling when an error occurs, to improve the safety of the devices used by patients, and to reduce the error rate of sterilization equipment. Moreover, with the system monitoring, whether the alarm device pack has expired and coming soon to expire. It reduces infections caused by patients using expired or incompletely sterilized instruments. At the same time, through the system's safety stock management, the additional cost and labor cost incurred in the emergency sterilization of the supply center equipment pack are reduced, and the patient's safety is effectively improved. So that it effectively improves the safety of patients, patients are in a safer medical environment, and achieve a win-win benefit.

# References

1. Wilson, R.M., Harrison, B.T., Gibberd, R.W., Hamilton, J.A.: An analysis of the causes of adverse events from the quality in australian health care study. Medi. J. Aust. **170**(9), 411–415 (1999)
2. Cuschieri, A.: Nature of human error: implications for surgical practice. Ann. Surg. **244**(5), 642–648 (2006)
3. de Vries, E.N., Ramrattan, M.A., Smorenburg, S.M., Gouma, D.J., Boermeester, M.A.: The incidence and nature of in-hospital adverse events: a systematic review. Qual. Saf. Health Care **17**(3), 216–223 (2008)
4. Arora, S., Hull, L., Sevdalis, N., Nestel, D., Woloshynowych, M., et al.: Factors compromising safety in surgery: stressful events in the operating room. Am. J. Surg. **199**(1), 60–65 (2010)
5. Gawande, A.A., Zinner, M., Studdert, D., Brennan, T.A.: Analysis of errors reported by surgeons at three teaching hospitals. Surgery **133**(6), 614–621 (2003)
6. WHO News: Safe surgery saves lives: the second global patient safety challenge. Int. J. Risk Saf. Med. **20**(3), 181–182 (2008)

7. The Joint Commission of Taiwan. Annual target and strategy for hospital patient safety in 107 and 108 (2017). http://www.jct.org.tw/FrontStage/index.aspx
8. Rosales, C.R., Magazine, M., Rao, U.: The 2Bin system for controlling medical supplies at point-of-use. Eur. J. Oper. Res. **243**(1), 271–280 (2015)
9. Chang, Y.-Y., Chang, S.-C., Chen, Y.-C., Huang, P.-H.: Taiwan sterilization monitoring measures guide. J. Infect. Control **15**(1), 27–44 (2005)
10. Acosta-Go, E., Mata-Portuguez, V.H., Herrero-Faras, A., Sanchez, L.: Biologic monitoring of dental office sterilizers in mexico. Am. J. Infect. Control **30**(3), 153–157 (2002)
11. Kelkar, U., Bal, A.M., Kulkarni, S.: Monitoring of steam steril ization process by biologic indicatorsa necessary surveillance tool. Am. J. Infect. Control **32**(8), 512–513 (2004)
12. Rutala, W.A., Weber, D.J.: Disinfection and sterilization in health care facilities: an overview and current issues. Infect. Dis. Clin. North Am. **30**(3), 609–637 (2016)
13. Spry, C.: Understanding current steam sterilization recommendations and guidelines. Assoc. Oper. Room Nurses J. **88**(4), 537–554 (2008)
14. Veerabadran, S., Parkinson, I.M.: Cleaning, disinfection and sterilization of equipment. Anaesth. Intensiv. Care Med. **11**(11), 451–454 (2010)
15. Rutala, W.A., Weber, D.J.: Disinfection and sterilization: an overview. Am. J. Infect. Control **41**(5, Supplement), S2–S5 (2013)
16. Wang, W.: Hospital Supply Center Business Manual. Farseeing Publishing Group (1999)
17. Huang, P.-H.: Monitoring and storage management of device sterilization. Med. Preview **4**(17), 11–12 (2002)
18. Mohapatra, S.: Sterilization and disinfection. In: Essentials of Neuroanesthesia, pp. 929–944. Elsevier (2017)
19. Diekema, D.J., Beekmann, S.E., Chapin, K.C., Morel, K.A., Munson, E., Doern, G.V.: Epidemiology and outcome of nosocomial and community-onset bloodstream infection. J. Clin. Microbiol. **41**(8), 3655–3660 (2003)
20. Thomas, E.J., Studdert, D.M., Burstin, H.R., Orav, E.J., Zeena, T., Williams, E.J., Howard, K.M., Weiler, P.C., Brennan, T.A.: Incidence and types of adverse events and negligent care in Utah and Colorado. Med. Care **38**(3), 261–271 (2000)
21. Zou, Z., Chen, Q., Uysal, I., Zheng, L.: Radio frequency identification enabled wireless sensing for intelligent food logistics. Philos. Trans. R. Soc. A Math. Phys. Eng. Sci. **372**(2021), 20130313 (2014)

# Reporting Mechanisms for Internet of Things

Chia-Wei Chang, Yi-Bing Lin, and Jyh-Cheng Chen[✉]

Department of Computer Science, National Chiao Tung University,
Hsinchu 300, Taiwan
{chwchang,liny,jcc}@cs.nctu.edu.tw

**Abstract.** Energy saving is one of the most important issues for Internet of Things (IoT). An intuitive way to save energy of IoT devices is to reduce the reporting frequency to the IoT server. However, to do so, the time-variant values are distorted, which may be influential to the measured results. In this letter, we take PM2.5 application as an example to discuss the relation between energy efficiency and data accuracy. Through analyzing PM2.5 concentration collected via LoRa at National Chiao Tung University (NCTU) from 2016 to present, two reporting mechanisms based on timer and threshold, respectively, are proposed. The experimental results demonstrate that the threshold-based reporting outperforms the timer-based reporting by more than 37% in energy saving when the accuracies of these two reporting mechanisms are the same.

**Keywords:** Internet of things · LoRa · Reporting frequency · Data accuracy · Packet loss · PM2.5

## 1 Introduction

In the recent years, many cities utilize the environmental information obtained from small sensors to improve living experience. Small sensors collect data and forward them to the server via wireless technologies such as NB-IoT [1], LoRa [2], and SigFox [3]. After that, the server can analyze the data and make strategic decisions based on the analytical results. For instance, an intelligent ventilation system can dynamically control intake/extractor fans based on the amount of carbon dioxide emission sensed in a classroom. By improving the air quality, students can breathe fresh air which makes students doze off less and concentrate more in the class.

To develop a smarter campus, NCTU is deploying several IoT-based applications and devices to monitor temperature, particulate matter (PM), carbon dioxide emission, etc. For those devices deployed in hard-to-reach locations, replacing batteries for these devices is a big issue. One could prolong the life time of a device by letting the device reduce the number of communication (i.e., reduce the reporting frequency to the IoT server). The device then could enter the sleeping mode to save their energy [4,5].

© ICST Institute for Computer Sciences, Social Informatics and Telecommunications Engineering 2019
Published by Springer Nature Switzerland AG 2019. All Rights Reserved
J.-L. Chen et al. (Eds.): WiCON 2018, LNICST 264, pp. 193–202, 2019.
https://doi.org/10.1007/978-3-030-06158-6_20

Nevertheless, environmental data is time variant, where every trail of environment changes may be necessary for IoT server to conclude a significant discovery. It is unwise to trade all trails of changes for saving more energy. The questions are how many trails and which trails to be traded. Therefore, in this letter, two reporting mechanisms that extend the battery life of the IoT devices are investigated. The tradeoff between energy efficiency and accuracy of the collected data are discussed. To our best knowledge, most PM2.5 studies focus on forecasting the degree of air pollution, dealing with large scale data, or searching for the sources of air pollution which do not cover the issue stated above [6–9]. This letter compares the reporting mechanisms for the data accuracy and power saving. The main contributions of the letter are as follows: (a) we establish an IoT-based application on our campus including sensor device deployment, wireless system establishment, and IoT-based platform construction (front-end and back-end systems), (b) we continuously collect massive PM2.5 data which is gathered from Aug 2016 to present, (c) we observe the tradeoff between data accuracy and reporting frequency with various interesting finding, and (d) we improve the data accuracy and energy efficiency.

The letter is organized as follows: Sect. 2 presents two reporting mechanisms, and some investigations on data accuracy are given. Section 3 compares the performance of these two reporting mechanisms. Experimental results are provided. Finally, Sect. 4 concludes several interesting findings.

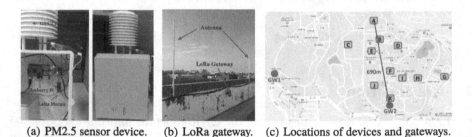

(a) PM2.5 sensor device.    (b) LoRa gateway.    (c) Locations of devices and gateways.

**Fig. 1.** The PM2.5 measurement system on the NCTU campus.

## 2    Reporting Mechanisms

In this section, two reporting mechanisms to collect the sensed data from the IoT devices are investigated: (1) *timer-based reporting*, and (2) *threshold-based reporting*. Here, we use PM2.5[1] concentration measurement deployed on the NCTU campus with 11 rooftop PM2.5 sensors as an example to evaluate our proposed reporting mechanisms [10]. The collection of PM2.5 concentration reported per minute since August 2016 is also used for cross validation [10]. Figure 1 shows eleven IoT devices and two IoT servers deployed on the campus. Every IoT

---

[1] PM2.5 is the suspended particulate matter smaller than 2.5 μm in diameter.

device is a PM2.5 sensor (PMS700) and a LoRa module (GL6509)[2]. The sensor is used to measures PM2.5 concentration and the LoRa module is used to transmits measurement results to the IoT server (see Fig. 1(a)). The IoT server is a LoRa outdoor 915 MHz gateway (WAPS-232N, see Fig. 1(b)) with two antennas where the receiver sensitivity can be down to −142 dBm and the RF TX power is 0.5 W (up to 27 dBm) [11].

**Table 1.** List of parameters

| | |
|---|---|
| $T$ | The obvervation time period |
| $\tau$ | The timer interval for timer-based reporting |
| $\epsilon$ | The threshold for threshold-based reporting |
| $v_i$ | The PM2.5 value measured at time $t_i$ |
| $v_I$ | The latest reported PM2.5 value measured by the IoT device before $t_i$ |
| $V$ | The set of reported PM2.5 values measured by the IoT device during the observation period $T$ |
| $V_\tau$ | The set of reported PM2.5 values measured per $\tau$ period |
| $V_\epsilon$ | The set of reported PM2.5 values where $|v_i - v_j| > \epsilon$ for $v_j \in V_\epsilon$ |
| $\|V\|$ | The number of reported PM2.5 values in $V$ |
| $\varepsilon_\tau$ | The expected error with timer interval $\tau$ |
| $\varepsilon_\epsilon$ | The expected error with threshold $\epsilon$ |
| $f_\tau$ | The reporting frequency with timer interval $\tau$ |
| $f_\epsilon$ | The reporting frequency with threshold $\epsilon$ |

In our study, the *reporting frequency* ($f$) and the *expected error* ($\varepsilon$) are used as the metrics to evaluate the energy efficiency and the accuracy of collected PM2.5 concentration, respectively. Their definitions are given as follows and are summarized in Table 1. An IoT device (a PM2.5 sensor) measures the PM2.5 values and reports them to the IoT server. Let $V$ be the set of PM2.5 values measured by the IoT device during an observation time period $T$, which are reported to the IoT server. Then the reporting frequency $f$ is defined as:

$$f = \frac{\|V\|}{T} \tag{1}$$

Let $v_i$ be the PM2.5 value at time $t_i$. Let $V(t_i) = \{v_j \in V | t_j \leq t_i\}$ and $t_I = \max\limits_{v_j \in V(t_i)} t_j$. Then $v_I$ is the PM2.5 value reported to the IoT server at the latest moment before $t_i$. In the measured system, we consider the PM2.5 value at $t_i$ as $v_I$. Therefore, the reporting accuracy at $t_i$ is determined by the measured error

---

[2] The maximum working power for PMS7003 is 100 mA × 5 V= 0.5 W at most. The RF power with 20dBm for GL6509 is 0.45 W. In other words, almost 50% of the device's energy is consumed by the LoRa transmission.

$\varepsilon(t_i)$ defined as $\varepsilon(t_i) = \frac{|v_i - v_I|}{|v_i|}$, and the reporting accuracy for $V$ is determined by the expected error $\varepsilon$ expressed as:

$$\varepsilon = \int_{t_i=0}^{T} \frac{\varepsilon(t_i)}{T} dt_i \qquad (2)$$

In the timer-based reporting, the IoT device periodically sends the measured PM2.5 values with the fixed intervals $\tau$. Let $V_\tau$ be the set of the PM2.5 values reported to the IoT server during $T$. Then from Eq. (1), the reporting frequency $f_\tau$ of the timer-based reporting mechanism with the interval $\tau$ is:

$$f_\tau = \frac{||V_\tau||}{T} = \frac{1}{\tau}$$

and the measured error $\varepsilon_\tau$ is the $\varepsilon$ value computed for $V_\tau$ using Eq. (2).

In the threshold-based reporting with the threshold $\epsilon$, the IoT device sends the PM2.5 value at $t_i$ to the IoT server if $|v_i - v_I|$ is larger than the threshold $\epsilon$ (i.e., $|v_i - v_I| > \epsilon$). The reporting frequency $f_\epsilon$ of the threshold-based reporting mechanism with the threshold $\epsilon$ is:

$$f_\epsilon = \frac{||V_\epsilon||}{T}$$

and the measured error $\varepsilon_\epsilon$ is the $\varepsilon$ value computed for $V_\epsilon$ using Eq. (2).

Figure 2 depicts the measured PM2.5 values at location 'A' from December 2016 to January 2017 where PM2.5 concentration was sampled every minute ($62\,days \times 24\,h/day \times 60\,min/hr = 89,280$ samples). That is, the unit for $t_i$ is *minute*. These sampled values $v_i$ will be utilized for both timer-based and threshold-based reporting mechanisms in the following sections[3].

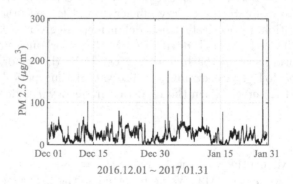

**Fig. 2.** Histogram of PM2.5 data at location 'A'.

---

[3] The observation period lasted 4 months with 174,240 sampled data ($121\,days \times 24\,h \times 60\,min$). Figure 2 illustrates partial results.

## 2.1   Timer-Based Reporting Mechanism

The timer-based reporting mechanism reports the measured data every moment when the timer $\tau$ is expired (Zero-Order Hold [12]). Figure 3(a) demonstrates that most expected errors $\varepsilon_\tau$ gradually ascend with the increase of $\tau$. A smaller $\tau$ expires sooner than a larger $\tau$ and causes a larger $\|V\|$, which in general makes the data reporting to the server more accurate but consumes more energy. What is interesting is that several **error reversals**[4] appear, e.g., when $\tau = 64$ (*mins*), $\tau = 88$ (*mins*), and $\tau = 106$ (*mins*) as shown in Fig. 3(a).

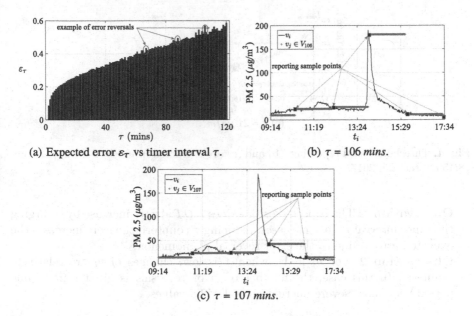

(a) Expected error $\varepsilon_\tau$ vs timer interval $\tau$.          (b) $\tau = 106$ *mins*.

(c) $\tau = 107$ *mins*.

**Fig. 3.** Timer-based reporting. (b) and (c) are extracted from Fig. 2 during 9:14 ∼ 17:34 on Dec. 29, 2016.

The error reversal phenomenon can be explained in Figs. 3(b), (c) by re-examining the $\tau$ configured as 106 (*mins*) and 107 (*mins*) extracted from *9:14 a.m.* to *5:34 p.m.* in the day of Dec. 29 of Fig. 2. When $\tau$ is set to 106 (*mins*) in Fig. 3(b), the reporting moment around 190 $\left(\frac{\mu g}{m^3}\right)$ resulting large $\varepsilon_{106}$ in the following 106 min. On the other hand, the sample points shown in Fig. 3(c) do not lead to large differences between $v_i$ and $v_I$ when $\tau$ is set to 107 (*mins*). Even though the process that the PM2.5 concentration reaches the highest value and then slowly goes down for almost 2 h (i.e., *13:24∼15:29*), it is a relatively high variation as far as large $\tau$ is concerned.

---

[4] *Error reversal* is defined as an incident where the reporting accuracy obtained by a smaller timer is worse than that by a larger timer.

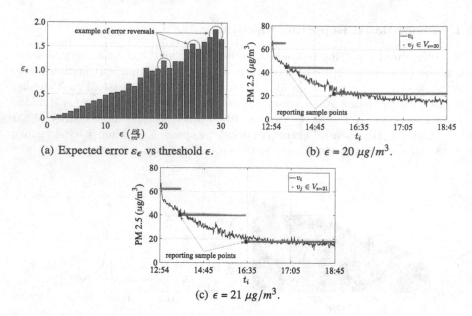

(a) Expected error $\varepsilon_\epsilon$ vs threshold $\epsilon$.

(b) $\epsilon = 20\ \mu g/m^3$.

(c) $\epsilon = 21\ \mu g/m^3$.

**Fig. 4.** Threshold-based reporting. (b) and (c) are extracted from Fig. 2 during 12:54 $\sim$ 18:45 on Jan. 25, 2017.

**Observation 1:** The expected error $\varepsilon$ does *NOT* always increase by enlarging the timer interval $\tau$. In some cases, reducing $\tau$ counterintuitively increases the expected error $\varepsilon$ due to the error reversal phenomenon.

**Observation 2:** For $v_j$ in $V$, when $f$ is low, changes of $v_i$ are relatively dramatic. In this case, the number of error reversals is greater in a time period with more severe fluctuation of PM2.5 values.

## 2.2    Threshold-Based Reporting Mechanism

In the threshold-based reporting, the PM2.5 sensor sends the data only on critical changes of data values. That is, when the difference between the latest reported data and the current measured data exceeds a certain threshold $\epsilon$. Figure 4(a) depicts the relation between the threshold $\epsilon$ and the expected error $\varepsilon$ where $\varepsilon$ is enlarged as the $\epsilon$ is augmented. Similarly, some threshold sizes, e.g., when $\epsilon = 20\ \left(\frac{\mu g}{m^3}\right)$, $\epsilon = 25\ \left(\frac{\mu g}{m^3}\right)$, $\epsilon = 29\ \left(\frac{\mu g}{m^3}\right)$, have larger $\varepsilon$ than their successors, i.e., $\epsilon = 21\ \left(\frac{\mu g}{m^3}\right)$, $\epsilon = 26\ \left(\frac{\mu g}{m^3}\right)$, and $\epsilon = 30\ \left(\frac{\mu g}{m^3}\right)$, respectively. The reason causing error reversals in the threshold-based reporting mechanism is the same as that in the timer-based reporting mechanism (see Figs. 4(b), 4(c)).

**Observation 3:** The expected error $\varepsilon_\epsilon$ does *NOT* always increase by enlarging the threshold $\epsilon$.

**Observation 4:** Error reversal phenomenon typically occurs when PM2.5 values instantly ascend/descend and then keep in similar values for a long time. For the reporting point of a relatively smaller $\tau$ or $\epsilon$ is located at the beginning of ascending/descending PM2.5 values. On the other hand, the reporting point of a larger $\tau$ or $\epsilon$ has a value closer to the upper/lower plateau.

## 3   Performance Discussion

In this section, we investigate the accuracy performance of the timer-based and threshold-based reporting mechanisms with and without considering packet loss.

### 3.1   Performance Without Packet Loss

Figure 5 demonstrates that when the expected errors of both reporting mechanisms are fixed at 0.5, the threshold-based reporting ('+' marker) outperforms the timer-based reporting ('□' marker) approximately by more than 37% in energy saving. This phenomenon is due to the fact that the threshold-based reporting mechanism only reports when a critical change occurs, whereas the timer-based reporting mechanism reports at every instant when the timer interval has expired even if there is no change between the previously reported data and the next. Additionally, the number of error reversals in the timer-based reporting mechanism is more than that in the threshold-based reporting mechanism, which is true even when $\tau$ is small. The reason is that the timer-based reporting mechanism cannot instantly react to the environment changes and thus cause to misuse previously reports severely.

### 3.2   Packet Loss Effects

To observe how packet loss affects both reporting mechanisms, an actual packet loss distribution is used. Table 2 shows the distribution of the number of consecutive packet loss which is acquired from extensive experiments by transmitting packets at specific moments and recording whether the packets were received or not [10]. The distribution is obtained by the measurement of LoRa packet transmission on NCTU campus (see Fig. 1). A uniform loss of packet is used for comparison. In other words, every time the measured data reported to the IoT server is lost uniformly or based on Table 2.

Figure 5 shows how packet loss affects both reporting mechanisms when uniform-loss and measured-loss distributions are applied in the processes of reporting. As we can see, the results for both the uniform-loss and the measured-loss distributions are about the same ('*' and '×' marks, or 'o' and '◇' markers). With packet loss in the process, one may instinctively think that the degradation of the threshold-based reporting mechanism will be more serious than that of the timer-based reporting mechanism because information of critical changes may be lost more easily. However, Fig. 5 demonstrates that the declined percentages in the timer-based and threshold-based reporting mechanisms are similar.

**Table 2.** Distribution of the number of consecutive packet losses

| # of consecutive packet losses | Frequency | Percentage | Cumulative |
|---|---|---|---|
| 1 | 18,660 | 84.85 | 84.85 |
| 2 | 2,596 | 11.80 | 96.65 |
| 3 | 496 | 2.26 | 98.91 |
| 4 | 123 | 0.56 | 99.47 |
| 5 | 30 | 0.14 | 99.61 |
| 6 | 22 | 0.10 | 99.71 |
| 7 | 18 | 0.08 | 99.79 |
| 8 | 8 | 0.04 | 99.82 |
| 9 | 7 | 0.03 | 99.85 |
| 10 | 4 | 0.02 | 99.87 |
| >10 | 28 | 0.13 | 100.00 |
| Total | 21,992 | 100.00 | |

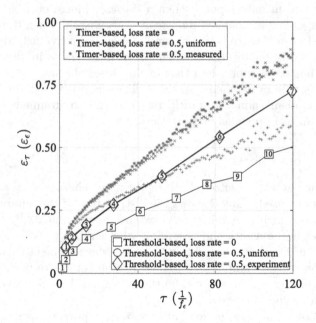

**Fig. 5.** Expected error $\varepsilon_\tau$ ($\varepsilon_\epsilon$) vs. reporting frequency $f_\tau$ ($f_\epsilon$). Note that, the value in a threshold-based marker represents $\epsilon$ under particular $f_\epsilon$.

In other words, the threshold-based reporting mechanism is still a better choice even when packets are lost in the communications, which is not trivial[5]. Specifically, the threshold-based reporting outperforms the timer-based reporting by more than 40% in energy saving when the expected errors of both reporting mechanisms are fixed to 0.5. Note that, the expected errors with the loss rate of 0.5 is approximately twice as greater as that with the loss rate of zero, which is a reasonable outcome.

**Observation 5:** The threshold-based reporting is a better choice than the timer-based reporting with or without packet loss.

**Observation 6:** Based on the PM2.5 data histograms, the basic strategy to select a $\tau$ or an $\epsilon$ depends on how much energy to save and how accurate it is required. That is, if $\varepsilon$ must be reduced from 0.5 to 0.25, $f$ could be increased from 1/120 to 1/40 by using the threshold-based reporting when there is no packet loss. Additionally, a particular $\tau$ or $\epsilon$ value that may incur error reversal should not be chosen.

**Observation 7:** Without from PM2.5 data histogram information, there are several ways to restrain error reversal: (1) using hybrid reporting method by combining the timer-based and threshold-based reporting mechanisms, i.e., reports data either when timer condition or threshold condition is met, (2) irregularly advancing/postponing some reporting points to alter their following reporting points, or (3) cross reporting with multiple settings of $\tau$ or $\epsilon$ (i.e., interleaved reporting: multiple conditions are used in turn). For example, if two thresholds, $\epsilon_1$ and $\epsilon_2$, are used, a PM2.5 value at $t_i$ will be reported when $|v_i - v_j| > \epsilon_1$ is met. The following PM2.5 value will be reported at $t_{i+x}$ if $|v_{i+x} - v_j| > \epsilon_2$. The reporting behavior will repeat the above two processes one-by-one over and over again [12].

## 4    Conclusion

In this letter, we investigated two reporting mechanisms to save the energy of IoT devices which are typically installed at hard-to-reach locations on NCTU campus. We discussed how much energy could be saved and how close the reported data to the time-variant environmental information could be. Several interesting findings are provided, including: (1) the threshold-based reporting mechanism is a better choice to report data, (2) reducing reporting frequency may not decrease the data accuracy, and (3) being irregular on reporting at some particular time helps restraining the occurrence of error reversals. In the future, we will apply the adaptive reporting mechanisms to reduce the error reversal phenomenon.

**Acknowledgment.** This work was supported in part by the Ministry of Science and Technology (MOST) under Grant 106-2221-E-009-006, Grant 106-2221-E-009-049-MY2 and Grant 107-2218-E-009-049, in part by Academia Sinica AS-105-TP-A07, Ministry

---

[5] Here, we only demonstrate the results where the packet loss probability is set to 0.5. The results with other packet loss probabilities are similar.

of Economic Affairs (MOEA) 106-EC-17-A-24-0619 and the Ministry of Education through the SPROUT Project Center for Open Intelligent Connectivity of National Chiao Tung University and Ministry of Education, Taiwan, R.O.C.

# References

1. 3GPP, Introduction of NB-IoT, TS 36.201 (2017)
2. LoRa Alliance. https://www.lora-alliance.org/lorawan-white-papers
3. Sigfox website. http://www.sigfox.com
4. Chang, C.-W., Chen, J.-C.: UM paging: unified M2M paging with optimal DRX cycle. IEEE Trans. Mobile Comput. **16**(3), 886–900 (2017)
5. Chang, C.-W., Chen, J.-C.: Adjustable extended discontinuous reception (eDRX) cycle for idle-state users in LTE-A. IEEE Commun. Lett. **20**(11), 2288–2291 (2016)
6. Liu, B., Yan, S., Li, J., Li, Y.: Forecasting PM2.5 concentration using spatio-temporal extreme learning machine. In: Proceedings of IEEE ICMLA, pp. 950–953 (2016)
7. Tang, M., Wu, X., Agrawal, P., Pongpaichet, S., Jain, R.: Integration of diverse data sources for spatial PM2.5 data interpolation. IEEE Trans. Multimedia **19**(2), 408–417 (2017)
8. Chang,J.-H., Tseng, C.-Y.: Analysis of correlation between secondary PM2.5 and factory pollution sources by using ANN and the correlation coefficient. IEEE Access **5**, 22812–22822 (2017)
9. Kumar, A., Kumar, A., Singh, A.: Energy efficient and low cost air quality sensor for smart buildings. In: Proceedings of IEEE CICT, pp. 1–4 (2017)
10. Reference withheld for double-blind review.
11. Gemtek IoT products web site. http://www.giotnetwork.com
12. Higgins, J.R.: Sampling theory in Fourier and signal analysis: foundations. Oxford Clarendon Press (1996)

# Container-Based Virtualization for Real-Time Data Streaming Processing on the Edge Computing Architecture

Endah Kristiani[1,2], Chao-Tung Yang[1]($\boxtimes$) (iD), Yuan-Ting Wang[3], Chin-Yin Huang[2](iD), and Po-Cheng Ko[1]

[1] Department of Computer Science, Tunghai University, Taichung 40704, Taiwan, ROC
endahkristi@gmail.com, ctyang@thu.edu.tw, pocheng0605@gmail.com
[2] Department of Industrial Engineering and Enterprise Information, Tunghai University, Taichung 40704, Taiwan, ROC
huangcy@thu.edu.tw
[3] Cloud Computing Laboratory, Chunghwa Telecom Laboratories, No. 99, Dianyan Rd. Yangmei, Taoyuan 326, Taiwan, ROC
yttom@cht.com.tw

**Abstract.** Container-based virtualization is one of the prominent technologies in the cloud computing. Containers virtualize at the operating system level which provides a lightweight operation than traditional virtualization on a hypervisor. The combination of the Internet of Things (IoT), edge computing and container-based virtualization is going to make system rapid, inexpensive, and more reliable. In this paper, we intend to implement a complete set of edge computing architectures based on containerization on an IoT environment. In this case, we implemented container-based virtualization which constructs Kubernetes Minion (Nodes) in the Docker container service independently for each service on the Edge side. We used humidity and temperature sensory data as our case study. We set up the Raspberry Pi on the Edge Gateway and Kubernetes minion on the Raspberry Pi to provide the service application, which contains Grafana, the open platform for analytics and monitoring. For short-term data storage, we use InfluxDB as a data store for large amounts of time-series data.

**Keywords:** Edge computing · Container-based virtualization · Kubernetes · Docker · Internet of Things (IoT)

## 1 Introduction

Internet of Things (IoT) industry has grown substantially. So that, it triggers an exponentially increasing amount of data which need to improve the data analysis process. Cloud computing is essential to the success of IoT, however pure cloud

J.-L. Chen et al. (Eds.): WiCON 2018, LNICST 264, pp. 203–211, 2019.
https://doi.org/10.1007/978-3-030-06158-6_21

computing itself not quite adequate for faster data analysis. The long distance of the network logic between the cloud and the end device might easily cause Network delay, thereby affecting the system can not respond promptly. In this case, the concept of edge computing [1, 2] meets the need for faster data analysis. Edge computing is a form of cloud computing, which pushes data processing out to the edge device to handle. This mechanism transports only the results of the data processing over networks. Therefore, it provides accurate results and consumes more lightweight network bandwidth than independent cloud computing. Additionally, we implemented Container-based virtualization which provides a lightweight operation than traditional virtualization.

In this paper, we integrated open source software to implement a complete set of edge computing architectures. Edge computing between IoT devices and the cloud establishes a relay station to process the data collected by the sensors and provide the most immediate preprocessing and response. We set up the Raspberry Pi on the Edge Gateway and Kubernetes minion on the Raspberry Pi to provide the service application, which contains Grafana [3], the open platform for analytics and monitoring. For short-term data storage, we use InfluxDB [4] as a data store for large amounts of time-series data.

In particular, our specific purpose is to deploy a complete set of cloud-edge computing architectures and IoT using container-based virtualization which constructs Kubernetes Minion (Nodes) in the Docker container service on the Edge side. In this case, we integrate Raspberry Pi 3+, DHT11 Humidity and Temperature Sensor, Grafana and InfluxDB in the Kubernetes and Docker environment.

The rest of the paper is organized as follows. Section 2 describes the background and related work. Section 3 presents the system architecture. Section 4 shows the experimental results. The last one, Sect. 5 provides a conclusion and the future work of this paper.

## 2    Background and Related Work

In this section, we provide several components that are approaching in this paper: Edge Computing, Docker, and Kubernetes.

### 2.1    Edge Computing

Edge computing is a method of optimizing cloud computing systems by performing data processing at the edge of the network, near the source of the data. IoT applications are ideally suited for edge computing architectures. Notably, in emerging IoT applications such as self-driving, drone, augmented reality (AR)/virtual reality (VR), and robotics. All of which are new applications that emphasize immediate of the image analysis and identification processing capabilities, low latency and high bandwidth requirements that need tens of microseconds or even milliseconds response time. In edge computing, the transfer of data to and from the cloud over the Internet can reach hundreds of milliseconds to respond time. Therefore these type of applications is very suitable to use the edge computing architecture.

## 2.2 Docker

Docker [5–8] is an open-source project that automates the deployment of applications inside software containers, by providing an additional layer of abstraction and automation of operating-system-level virtualization on Linux. Docker uses the resource isolation features of the Linux kernel such as cgroups and kernel namespaces, and a union-capable filesystem such as aufs and others to allow independent "containersto" run within a single Linux instance, avoiding the overhead of starting and maintaining virtual machines. The Linux kernel's support for namespaces mostly isolates an application's view of the operating environment, including process trees, network, user IDs and mounted file systems, while the kernel's cgroups provide resource limiting, including the CPU, memory, block I/O and network. Since version 0.9, Docker includes the libcontainer library as its way to directly use virtualization facilities provided by the Linux kernel, in addition to using abstracted virtualization interfaces via libvirt, LXC [9–11] (Linux Containers) and systemd-nspawn.

By using containers, resources can be isolated, services restricted, and processes provisioned to have an almost entirely private view of the operating system with their own process ID space, file system structure, and network interfaces. Multiple containers share the same kernel, but each container can be constrained to only use a defined amount of resources such as CPU, memory and I/O. Using Docker to create and manage containers may simplify the creation of highly distributed systems by allowing multiple applications, worker tasks, and other processes to run autonomously on a single physical machine or across multiple virtual machines. Docker enables the deployment of nodes to be performed as the resources become available or when more nodes are needed, allowing a platform as a service (PaaS)-style of deployment and scaling for systems like Apache Cassandra, MongoDB or Riak. Docker also simplifies the creation and operation of task or workload queues and other distributed systems. Docker architecture is different from virtual architecture.

## 2.3 Kubernetes

Kubernetes is particularly well-suited for microservices such architectures. Combining several containers into a single service, Kubernetes also provides an excellent service discovery mechanism for each service to communicate with one another. Most importantly K8S great programming can automatically expand services, and even for large-scale containers for rolling updates (Rolling update) and rollback (Rolling back/Undo), but also can integrate CI/CD and other DevOps tools, Absolutely allow users to manage an extensive system with the least effort [12].

## 2.4   Related Works

The Cisco introduced Fog Computing Systems as a new model to ease wireless data transfer to distributed devices in the Internet of Things (IoT) network paradigm. Cisco defines Fog Computing as a paradigm that extends Cloud computing and services to the edge of the network. Similar to Cloud, Fog provides data, compute, storage, and application services to end-users. The distinguishing Fog characteristics are its proximity to end-users, its dense geographical distribution, and its support for mobility. Services are hosted at the network edge or even end devices such as set-top-boxes or access points. By doing so, Fog reduces service latency, and improves QoS, resulting in superior user-experience. Fog Computing supports emerging Internet of Everything (IoE) applications that demand real-time/predictable latency (industrial automation, transportation, networks of sensors and actuators). Thanks to its wide geographical distribution the Fog paradigm is well positioned for a real-time big data and real-time analytics. Fog supports densely distributed data collection points, hence adding a fourth axis to the often mentioned Big Data dimensions (volume, variety, and velocity) [13].

China Venkanna Varma et al. [14] in 2016, studied the working of Docker networks, various factors of CPU context switch latency and how network IO throughput will be impacted with the number of live Docker containers. A Hadoop cluster environment built and executed benchmarks such as TestDFSIO-write and TestDFSIO-read against varying amount of the live containers. They observed that Hadoop throughput is not linear with increasing number of live container nodes sharing the same system CPU.

## 3   System Architecture

To develop the proposed solution by this paper, we needed the use of different types of software and hardware components. The used hardware was a Raspberry Pi 3 Model B+ with DHT11 temperature and humidity sensor. The details of hardware and software specification describe as following in Table 1: To get a general overview, Fig. 1 shows the scheme of the node architecture with all of the systems components. In the first step, we deploy the raspberry using kubernetes and docker with grafana installed and connected to the DHT11 sensor. Data captured by sensor then send to the InfluxDB using MQTT. Grafana uses a plugin to connect with InfluxDB in order to visualize the data in the graph and give the alert as our rule.

The overall device architecture is shown in Fig. 2, mainly using Arduino LoRa Shield module and DHT11 sensor as the overall sensing module and LoRa sensing

**Table 1.** Hardware and software specification

| Category | Item | Specification | Description |
|----------|------|---------------|-------------|
| *Hardware* | *Raspberry* | *OS* | Raspbian Jessie |
| | | *CPU* | 4 Cores, Broadcom BCM2837 64 bits |
| | | | ARMv8 Processor, 1.2 GHz |
| | | *Power* | 5V@2.4A(with, MicroUSB) |
| | | *Storage* | *microSD* |
| | | *Network* | Ethernet (RJ45) |
| | | *WiFi* | BCM43143 WiFi |
| | | *Bluetooth* | BCM43438 wireless LAN and |
| | | | Bluetooth Low Energy (BLE) on board |
| | *Sensor* | *DHT11* | Temperature and Humidity |
| *Software* | *Application* | *Grafana* | An open platform for analytics and monitoring |
| | *Database* | *InfluxDB* | A data store for large amounts of time series data |

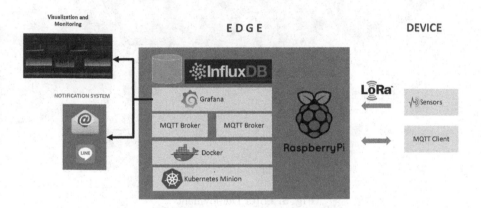

**Fig. 1.** The edge architecture

data collected by LoRa Nodes will be transmitted to LoRa Gateway through LoRa. In this process, LoRa offers the Low Power Wide Area Network (LPWAN) and the star-topology, and the LoRa Gateway is also connected to the miniature ramps made by the Raspberry Pi 3 for ultimate unified delivery to the data center(cloud).

## 4    Experimental Results

In this work, we build the system on campus with four LoRa nodes and a LoRa Gateway as shown in Fig. 3.

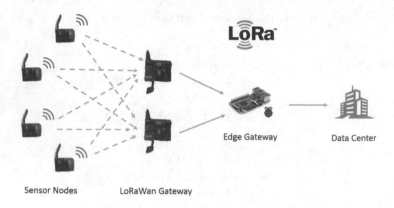

**Fig. 2.** The device architecture

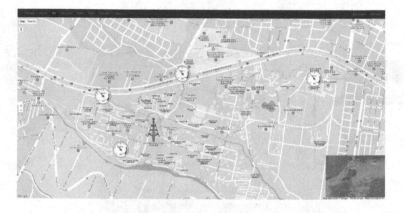

**Fig. 3.** LoRa Deployment

**Fig. 4.** Raspberry Pi integrated with DHT11

To implement an Edge Computing, first, we prepared Raspberry Pi integrated with DHT11 humidity and temperature sensor as shown in Fig. 4. Second, we set up docker container with Grafana and InfluxDB installed as shown in Figs. 5, 6 and 7.

**Fig. 5.** Docker container

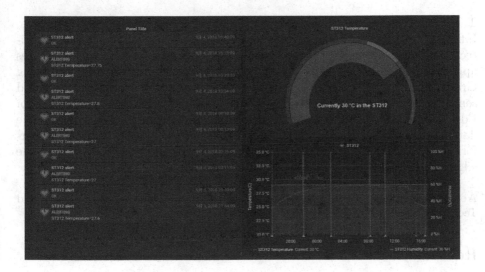

**Fig. 6.** Grafana dashboard

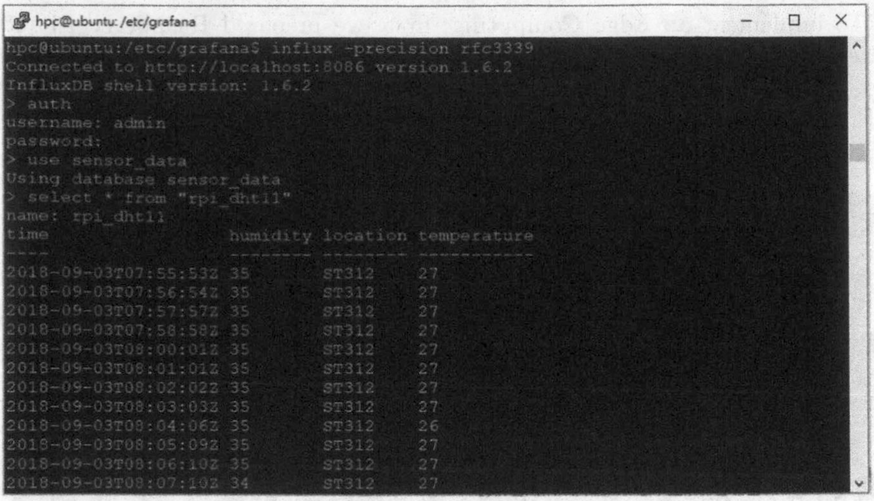

**Fig. 7.** InfluxDB

## 5    Conclusion

This paper integrates the technologies of Kubernetes, Docker, Grafana, InfluxDB, IoT, and LoRa to implement a complete set of edge computing architectures. From the experiment, we can prove that Edge Computing improves application performance such as analysis and monitoring system. By using Grafana and influxDB, we can monitor the movement of time-series data and send the alert based our rule automatically. In summary, the implementation of Edge Computing Architecture using container-based virtualization for real-time data streaming Processing provides significant improvement of application performance. By using this architecture, we can achieve lower latency levels on the edge, as opposed to a faraway cloud or data center.

**Acknowledgment.** This work was supported in part by the Ministry of Science and Technology, Taiwan R.O.C., under grants number 107-2221-E-029-008-.

## References

1. Varghese, B., Buyya, R.: Next generation cloud computing: new trends and research directions. Futur. Gener. Comput. Syst. **79**, 849–861 (2018)
2. Kristiani, E., Yang, C.-T., Wang, Y.T., Huang, C.-Y.: Implementation of an edge computing architecture using openstack and kubernetes. In: Kim, K.J., Baek, N. (eds.) ICISA 2018. LNEE, vol. 514, pp. 675–685. Springer, Singapore (2019). https://doi.org/10.1007/978-981-13-1056-0_66
3. Grafana (2018). https://grafana.com/
4. Influxdb (2018). https://www.influxdata.com/

5. Špaček, F., Sohlich, R., Dulk, T.: Docker as platform for assignments evaluation. Energy Procedia, 1665–1671 (2015)
6. Build, ship and run any app, anywhere (2015). https://www.docker.com/
7. Docker (software) (2015). http://en.wikipedia.org/wiki/Docker%28software%29
8. Liu, D., Zhao, L.: The research and implementation of cloud computing platform based on docker. In: 2014 11th International Computer Conference on Wavelet Active Media Technology and Information Processing (ICCWAMTIP), pp. 475–478 (2014)
9. Felter, W., Ferreira, A., Rajamony, R., Rubio, J.: An updated performance comparison of virtual machines and linux containers. In: 2015 IEEE International Symposium on Performance Analysis of Systems and Software (ISPASS), pp. 171–172 (2015)
10. Nakagawa, G., Oikawa, S.: Behavior-based memory resource management for container-based virtualization. In: Proceedings of 4th International Conference on Applied Computing and Information Technology, 3rd International Conference on Computational Science/Intelligence and Applied Informatics, 1st International Conference on Big Data, Cloud Computing, Data Science and Engineering, ACIT-CSII-BCD 2016, pp. 213–217 (2016)
11. Soltesz, S., Pötzl, H., Fiuczynski, M.E., Bavier, A., Peterson, L.: Container-based operating system virtualization: a scalable, high-performance alternative to hypervisors. In: Proceedings of the 2nd ACM SIGOPS/EuroSys European Conference on Computer Systems 2007, pp. 275–287 (2007)
12. Kubernetes (2017). https://kubernetes.io/
13. Ahmed, E., Rehmani, M.H.: Mobile edge computing: opportunities, solutions, and challenges (2017)
14. China Venkanna Varma, P., Kalyan Chakravarthy, K.V., Valli Kumari, V., Viswanadha Raju, S.: Analysis of network IO performance in hadoop cluster environments based on docker containers. In: Pant, M., Deep, K., Bansal, J.C., Nagar, A., Das, K.N. (eds.) Proceedings of Fifth International Conference on Soft Computing for Problem Solving. AISC, vol. 437, pp. 227–237. Springer, Singapore (2016). https://doi.org/10.1007/978-981-10-0451-3_22

# Location-Based Services

# An Efficient Mobile AR Navigation System Using Polygon Approximation Based Data Acquisition

Ching-Sheng Wang and Wei-Tsung Su[✉]

Department of Computer Science and Information Engineering, Aletheia University, New Taipei City, Taiwan
cswang@mail.au.edu.tw, suwt@au.edu.tw

**Abstract.** In recent years, most mobile navigation systems adopt augmented reality (AR) to provide location-aware and interactive multimedia contents for visitors' reference. Most AR navigation systems support only one target recognition and then only acquire corresponding contents from data servers for reducing storage and network costs. With the increase of multimedia navigation information, the performance of data acquisition for resource-constrained mobile devices must be improved for better user experience. In this paper, we propose not only the multi-target AR recognition mechanism but also the polygon approximation based data acquisition to improve performance of mobile AR navigation system by accelerating spatial data acquisition. In the proposed approach, the query efficiency and search precision can be well controlled according to the requirements of different applications.

**Keywords:** Augmented reality · Mobile navigation · *K*-means clustering Polygon approximation · Spatial data acquisition

## 1 Introduction

In recent years, most mobile navigation systems supports augmented reality (AR) for better user experience [1]. In AR display, users can seamlessly interact with location-aware multimedia contents. Nevertheless, there are still several challenges in supporting location-aware AR navigation system.

The first challenge is to recognize multiple targets in AR display at a time. Most AR navigation systems can identify exhibits by recognizing a special marker (e.g. QR code) within a close range [1–5]. On the other hand, several markerless AR navigation system can identify exhibits by directly recognizing images of exhibits [6–8]. However, the above AR recognition technologies can only recognize one target at a time. Therefore, in this paper, we proposed a mobile AR navigation system supporting multi-target recognition based on the *k*-means clustering algorithm [9], which is able to simultaneously recognize multiple targets from a long distance.

© ICST Institute for Computer Sciences, Social Informatics and Telecommunications Engineering 2019
Published by Springer Nature Switzerland AG 2019. All Rights Reserved
J.-L. Chen et al. (Eds.): WiCON 2018, LNICST 264, pp. 215–224, 2019.
https://doi.org/10.1007/978-3-030-06158-6_22

The second challenge is to improve the efficiency of multi-target recognition in resource-constrained mobile devices. Spatial data query can help to improve above multi-target AR recognition by reducing the search range from all target dataset to the targets near users. However, the distance between users and candidate targets cannot be calculated by simply using Eular distance or Haversine formula [10]. To accurately calculate the distance between two geolocations, WGS84 is widely accepted in many implementations [11]. Unfortunately, the complexity is too high to degrade the query efficiency accordingly while the number of target dataset increases [12]. Therefore, in this paper, the polygon approximation-based data acquisition [13, 14] is employed. Instead of a circle, an $n$-sided polygon is used as the use-specified search area to improve query efficiency with compromising some search precision.

The remainder of this paper is organized as follows. Section 2 introduces the system framework. Section 3 describes the proposed mobile AR navigation system supporting multi-target recognition and how the proposed polygon approximation-based data acquisition can improve the efficiency of multi-target recognition in resource-constrained mobile devices. Section 3 is system implementation and demonstration. Section 4 provides the performance evaluation of proposed polygon approximation-based spatial data query approach. Section 5 offers the conclusion of this paper.

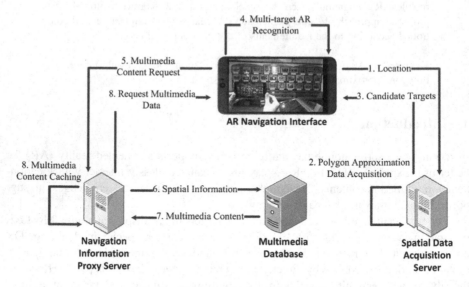

**Fig. 1.** Diagram of system framework.

## 2 System Overview

Figure 1 shows the framework of proposed system. When visitors recognize images through AR navigation interface on a mobile device, the location is first sent to spatial data acquisition server to obtain the candidate targets near visitors with using the proposed polygon approximation based data acquisition. With this information, AR navigation interface can efficiently perform multi-target AR recognition and then directly show the related navigation information of the recognized image targets. In the absence of multimedia content of user-specified targets, the system will request the navigation information proxy server to obtain the multimedia content from multimedia database. In order to improve the performance, the multimedia contents of other candidate targets can be pre-fetched at the same time.

With the use of multi-target AR recognition technology, this system completes feature detection and clustering of multiple image targets in advance, and then, uses a mobile device to shoot and recognize the photos displayed in the exhibition area in order to further display the corresponding 3D and multimedia navigation information. When the camera of a mobile device shoots image target with AR navigation information, the system will process the images into gray scale images, detect and recognize the image feature points and their distribution, and search the corresponding 3D and multimedia navigation information of individual images according to the recognition results of the clustering image targets, which will be further shown in the navigation interface. To improve the search efficiency, the proposed polygon approximation-based spatial data query is applied.

### 2.1 Multi-target AR Recognition

As shown in Fig. 2, the processing flow of multi-target AR recognition in this paper mainly includes 5 steps: (1) calculate the recognition rating and relative location of individual targets; (2) determine the representative target from the targets with high recognition rating; (3) calculate the distance between all the targets and the representative target, and complete preliminary clustering according to the k-means clustering algorithm; (4) optimize the preliminary clustering result into multi-target clustering images with a length-width ratio suitable for image recognition; (5) at the time of AR recognition, complete the image recognition of all the targets and AR navigation information displays via the optimized multi-target clustering result.

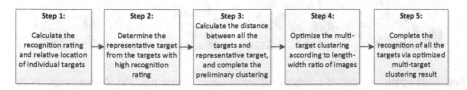

**Fig. 2.** Diagram of the processing flow of multi-target AR recognition.

The revised $k$-means clustering algorithm, as proposed in this paper for multi-target AR image clustering, is $\underset{S}{argmin} \sum_{i=1}^{k} \sum_{x \in S_i} ||x - \mu_i||^2$ where $S_i$ represents Cluster $i$; $\mu_i$ represents image targets with a rating of high recognition in $S_i$ cluster, which can be used as the representative target of Cluster $i$; $x$ refers to other image targets with low ratings of recognition, and is the affiliated target in Cluster $i$. The shortest distance between all the targets and representative targets is calculated to complete the preliminary clustering of all the images; finally, the preliminary clustering results are optimized into clustering images with a length-width ratio suitable for image recognition, which is used for AR image recognition.

**Fig. 3.** Diagram of the feature point analysis of image recognition. (a) The image with many feature points. (b) The image with few feature points.

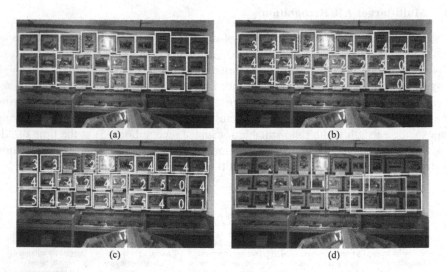

**Fig. 4.** Diagram of the test results of multi-target clustering. (a) Image segmentation. (b) Analysis of recognition rating. (c) Preliminary clustering results. (d) Final clustering results.

Regarding research into the recognition ratings of images, this paper applies Vuforia SDK to analyze the recognize features of all images, which are saved in the Unity package format, and used to recognize images; afterwards, the corresponding navigation information can be accessed in real time according to the records in the database. Figure 3 shows the preliminary test results of this paper: the symbol ("+") in the figure represents the feature points that can be used for image recognition; the more the ("+") symbols, the higher the recognition rating of this image as shown in Fig. 3a; otherwise, the fewer the ("+") symbols, the lower the recognition rating of this image, and in such a situation, it is difficult to complete image recognition as shown in Fig. 3b. Accordingly, the rating for the rating of recognition can be given, ranging from 1 star to 5 starts, as based on the quantity of feature points, in order to distinguish the level of difficulty regarding the rating of recognition. The recognition rating of images is positively correlated to the quantity of starts: 5 stars denote that the image is the easiest to be recognized, 4 stars denote that the image is the second easiest to be recognized, 1 star denotes that the image is extremely difficult to be recognized, and no starts denote that the image cannot be recognized.

The relevant tests are as shown in Fig. 4, among which, Fig. 4a is a diagram of individual image segmentation; while Fig. 4b shows the analysis of the recognition rating of individual images. According to the recognition rating of the images, this system applies the proposed multi-target clustering algorithm, chooses targets with higher recognition ratings as the representative targets, and then, calculates the distance between other targets and the representative targets; finally, preliminary clustering is completed on the principle of the shortest distance as shown in Fig. 4c. It can be found only from Fig. 4c that the shape of the preliminary clustering result is irregular, meaning its shape is inconsistent with the rectangle picture shot by the camera, which goes against image recognition. Preliminary testing found that the length-width ratio of most mobile phones is 3:2, thus, the best ratio of cluster image recognition should be 3 photos in width and 2 photos in height, namely 6 photos. Therefore, this paper further merges the preliminary clustering results into a cluster image with 6 photos in one group, where the length-width ratio is 3:2, in order to facilitate image recognition as shown in Fig. 4d.

## 2.2  Polygon Approximation-Based Data Acquisition

Users can select the number of $n$-sided polygon for approximating a circle search area according to their requirements. The users who demand high search precision can select a large $n$. However, the query efficiency will be degraded. On the contrary, the users who demand high search efficiency can select a small $n$. However, the query precision can be degraded.

In addition, users can also select to use (1) inner-type or (2) outer-type of polygon approximation as shown in Fig. 5. The $n$-sided polygon will be placed into the circle search area in inner-type polygon approximation. In outer-type polygon approximation, the circle search area will be placed into the $n$-side polygon. The different types of polygon approximation will incur different errors as shadow area in Fig. 5. Since the $n$-sided polygon will be placed into the search area in inner-type polygon approximation, the error is false negative that indicates some data in the search area may be excluded in the search results. On the contrary, outer-type approximation incurs false positive that indicate some data not in the search area may be included in the search results. In this paper, we use the case of $n = 4$ as an example because the query efficiency can be simple in a reasonable degradation of search precision [15].

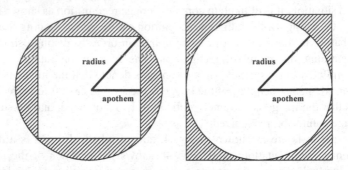

**Fig. 5.** Types of polygon approximation. (a) Inner-type. (b) Outer-type.

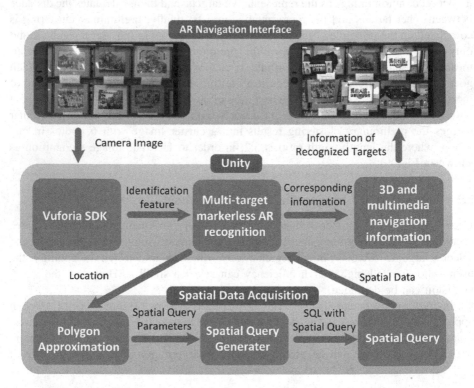

**Fig. 6.** The implementation flow of multi-target AR recognition and the display.

## 3  Implementation and Demonstration

Figure 6 shows the implementation flow of multi-target AR recognition and the display of this system. During system implementation, Unity is used to develop the user interface of mobile AR navigation system and integrate the functions of location awareness, network transmission, etc. First, Vuforia SDK is used to analyze the recognition feature of the image target to be saved in the Unity package format, which can be used to access the corresponding navigation information of individual image targets in real time according to the records in the database. In addition, during the period of real-time imaging, according to the distance and the angle between the images and the camera lens are used to show the corresponding 3D objects or multimedia information of individual image targets at the right location and angle; finally, they are combined with the real-time images, as captured by the camera, to be shown on the screen by mixing virtual and reality as shown in the results shown in the upper right of Fig. 6.

In order to improve the efficiency of multi-target recognition, the proposed spatial data acquisition is invoked in the step of multi-target AR recognition as shown in Fig. 6. In the step of polygon approximation, the coordinates of corners of $n$-sided polygon will be calculated. Then, a spatial query statement can be generated based on the coordinates of corners of $n$-sided polygon. Finally, the candidate targets can be obtained by submitting spatial query. Only the candidate targets will be searched in above multi-target AR recognition.

Figure 7 shows the test results of this system. As shown in Fig. 7a, b, this system can simultaneously detect and recognize multiple photos/targets on a large scale, and from a long distance, and accurately display the corresponding navigation information of individual targets. Moreover, users can click any AR target from all the interfaces to further acquire the navigation information related to this target. For instance, users can click the Tamsui Oxford College in the lower right corner of Fig. 7b and then view more navigation information, such as the navigation photo shown in Fig. 7c and navigation video shown in Fig. 7d.

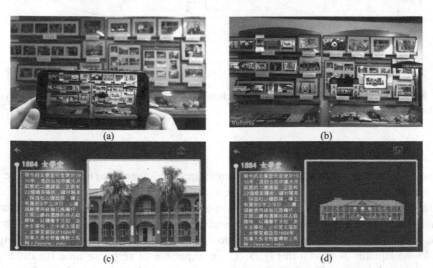

**Fig. 7.** Diagram of system on-site test results. (a) Usage scenario. (b) Screen capture of navigation interface. (c) Display navigation photo. (d) Display 3D model

## 4    Performance Evaluation

In this section, we will evaluate the proposed polygon approximation-based spatial data query approach in both numerical analysis and experimental investigation.

### 4.1    Numerical Analysis

In Fig. 5, radius of circle is denoted by $r$. The apothems of polygons in inner-type and outer-type polygon approximation are denoted by $a_i$ and $a_o$, respectively. First, the query performance will be the same for two types of polygon approximation because they both determine whether a geolocation is in a square. Then, to compare the search precision of two types of polygon approximation, we need to calculate the shadow areas in Fig. 5. For inner-type polygon approximation, the error as the shadow area in Fig. 8a can be calculated by $e_i = (\pi r^2 - 4a_i^2)$ where $a_i = r/\sqrt{2}$. Thus, $e_i = (\pi r^2 - 2r^2)$. On the other hand, for outer-type polygon approximation, the error as the shadow area in Fig. 8b can be calculated by $e_i = (\pi r^2 - 4a_i^2)$ where $a_o = r$. Thus, $e_o = (4r^2 - \pi r^2)$. The difference of $e_i$ and $e_o$ is then given by

$$e_i - e_o = (\pi r^2 - 2r^2) - (4r^2 - \pi r^2) = 2\pi r^2 - 6r^2 > 0$$

Thus, outer-type polygon approximation has better search precision than inner-type polygon approximation. The numerical analysis in case of $n = 4$ is shown in Fig. 8.

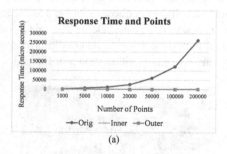

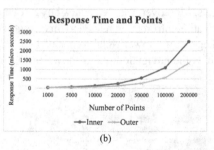

(a)    (b)

**Fig. 8.** Response time of different approaches. (a) Original, inner-type, and outer-type. (b) Inner-type and outer-type only.

### 4.2    Experimental Investigation

In the experiments, we will randomly deploy points in a square area that is the square of outer-type polygon approximation. The search center and search radius are set as the center and the apothem of this square, respectively. The original approach will calculate the distance between search center and each point based on WGS84. The inner-type and outer-type polygon approximation approaches will check if each point is inside the squares as shown in Fig. 5. The comparison of response time for different approaches is shown in Fig. 9. Because the complexity of distance calculation based on

WGS84, the original approach takes a long time to finish a request. In addition, we can see that outer-type polygon approximation outperforms inner-type polygon approximation because it requires a square root computation to find the four points of square of inner-type polygon approximation.

Although the inner-type and outer-type polygon approximation approaches can improve query efficiency, the search precision can be decreased. The search precision is defined as $1 - (P - P_{ori}/P_{ori})$ where $P_{ori}$ and $P$ are the number of points found by original approach and the number of points found by the polygon approximation approach, respectively. As shown in Fig. 9, the search precision of outer-type polygon approximation always outperforms inter-type polygon approximation no matter the square size is $100 \times 100$ or $10 \times 10$. However, the search precision will be lower if the search area is too small.

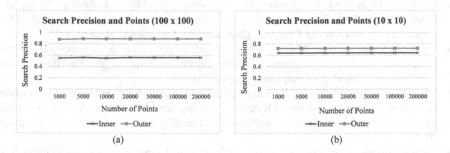

**Fig. 9.** Search precision of different approaches with square sizes: (a) $100 \times 100$ and (b) $10 \times 10$.

## 5 Conclusion

This paper presents a mobile AR navigation system that supports multi-target recognition and adopts polygon approximation based data acquisition to improve system performance. The proposed system can simultaneously recognize multi-target with the $k$-means clustering algorithm as proposed in this paper and then acquire and display the corresponding 3D and multimedia navigation information from data servers. For resource-constrained mobile devices, a polygon approximation based data acquisition is proposed to accelerate spatial data query. By selecting the number of sides of $n$-sided polygon and the types of polygon approximation, the users can control query efficiency and search precision according to application requirements. The experimental results show that the proposed polygon approximation approach can efficiently improve the query efficiency with compromising search precision. However, the search precision can be still near 90% in the case of that the sides of polygon is 4 and the outer-type polygon approximation is selected.

**Acknowledgment.** The authors would like to thank the Ministry of Science and Technology of the Republic of China, Taiwan for financially supporting this research under Contract No. MOST 107-2221-E-156-004 and MOST 107-2221-E-156-001-MY2. Besides, the author would like to acknowledge Shih-Han Chen and Shih-Hui Hung, for their assistance in making this system possible.

# References

1. Wang, H.S., Huang, C.J., Lin, C.H., Wu, J.W.: A study of using tangible augmented reality system to enhance the learning effects on museum artifacts. J. Educ. Media Librar. Sci. **50**(1), 135–167 (2012)
2. Chou, C.Y.: A study on the user interface of mobile augmented reality for the guide in a heritage building. Thesis for Master of Science Department of Industrial Design, Tatung University, Taiwan, July 2010
3. Lin, G.L.: The research on tour guidance associated with augmented reality, QR code and mobile device. Thesis for Master of Graduate School of Digital Life Technology, Kun Shan University, Taiwan, June 2013
4. Chen, C.Y., Chang, B.R., Huang, P.S.: Multimedia augmented reality information system for museum guidance. Personal Ubiquitous Comput. **18**(2), 315–322 (2014)
5. Wolff, A., Mulholland, P., Maguire, M., O'Donovan, D.: Mobile technology to support coherent story telling across freely explored outdoor artworks. In: Proceedings of the 11th Conference on Advances in Computer Entertainment Technology, November 2014
6. Yu, K.M., Chiu, J.C., Lee, M.G., Chi, S.S.: A mobile application for an ecological campus navigation system using augmented reality. In: Proceedings of the 8th International Conference on Ubi-Media Computing, August 2015
7. Ruta, M., Scioscia, F., Ieva, S., Filippis, D.D., Sciascio, E.D.: Indoor/outdoor mobile navigation via knowledge-based POI discovery in augmented reality. In: Proceedings of the International Conference on Web Intelligence and Intelligent Agent Technology, December 2015
8. Breuss-Schneeweis, P.: The speaking celt"-augmented reality avatars guide through a museum-case study. In: Proceedings of the ACM International Joint Conference on Pervasive and Ubiquitous Computing, September 2016
9. Wang, C.S., Hung, S.H., Chiang, D.J.: A markerless augmented reality mobile navigation system with multiple targets display function. In: Proceedings of 2017 IEEE International Conference on Applied System Innovation, Sapporo, Japan, May 2017
10. Wikipedia: Haversine formula. [Online]. https://en.wikipedia.org/wiki/Haversine_formula
11. Android Location API. [Online]. https://developer.android.com/reference/android/location/Location.html#distanceTo(android.location.Location)
12. Airas, M.: Measuring geodetic distance calculation performance. 12 Jan 2015. [Online]. http://eniramltd.github.io/devblog/2015/01/12/geodetic_calculations.html
13. Bhowmick, P., Bhattacharya, B.B.: Approximation of digital circles by regular polygons, Proceedings of Third international conference on Advances in Pattern Recognition, Bath, UK, 2005
14. Su, W.T., Wei, H.Y., Yeh, J.H., Chen, W.C.: An efficient approach based on polygon approximation to query spatial data on digital archiving system. In: Proceedings of 2017 IEEE International Conference on Applied System Innovation, Sapporo, Japan, May 2017
15. Ye, Y., Guangrui, F., Shiqi, Q.: An algorithm for judging points inside or outside a polygon. In: Proceedings of 2013 Seventh International Conference on Image and Graphics, Qingdao, China, 2013

# Location-Based Hotel Recommendation System

Chien-Liang Chen[1]([✉]), Ching-Sheng Wang[1], and Ding-Jung Chiang[2]

[1] Department of Computer Science and Information Engineering,
Aletheia University, New Taipei City, Taiwan
clchen@au.edu.tw
[2] Department of Digital Multimedia Design, Taipei Chengshih
University of Science and Technology, Taipei, Taiwan

**Abstract.** In recent years, the hotel industry in Taiwan has begun to flourish as the economy has grown. In order to attract more tourists to make changes in various services and facilities, the hotel's types have begun to make a difference. However, the content of the website is full of personal subjective or unilateral information, which is easy for tourists to lose in it or waste a lot of time cost. Therefore, we hope to provide more comprehensive hotel recommendations and use the traditional recommendation technology combined with location-based services to make recommendations. Different from the conventional recommendation, only comprehensive factors are considered. The study included three individual factors – service, price, facility to do a single rating and combined with the location of the tourist to make recommendations so that the recommendations can be closer to the needs of tourists. We selected 50 high-profile hotels, including five categories of mountain, sea, hot springs, theme parks, and resort hotels. Through the recommendation system, we recommend hotels that have not yet been lived by tourists, as a list of hotels to choose from it.

**Keywords:** Location-based services · Recommendation system

## 1 Introduction

With the carry out of the Taiwan government on the two days weekend, the domestic tourism trend has been gradually improved, and the hotel industry has been promoted. The choice of tourists in the hotel has been upgraded from the previous money-oriented to functional orientation, and the hotel has also improved from merely providing accommodation services to meeting the needs of tourists. Therefore, the hotel market began to divide into different tourist groups, and the hotel started to split into different design styles, plans, functions and so on. Besides, tourists themselves have different preferences for hotel choices. We believe that tourists will also affect the selection of the hotel because of their traits, personality, behavior and other factors. So how to provide tourists with a hotel that suits their preferences or needs is even more critical.

O'Mahony and Smyth [1] explored the hotel recommendation system and used TripAdvisor, an internationally renowned hotel recommendation website, as an example. The website can be selected based on the areas, prices, tourist's ratings,

© ICST Institute for Computer Sciences, Social Informatics and Telecommunications Engineering 2019
Published by Springer Nature Switzerland AG 2019. All Rights Reserved
J.-L. Chen et al. (Eds.): WiCON 2018, LNICST 264, pp. 225–234, 2019.
https://doi.org/10.1007/978-3-030-06158-6_23

equipment, brands, etc. or advanced selected, such as value, romantic, family, luxury, business, etc. We understand that the collaborative filtering system develops the operation mode of the website. The photos taken by a large number of tourists are used to improve the authenticity of the website, and the tourist's ratings and comments are provided to make hotel reviews and convert to a built-in score to rank. In order to provide more accurate information, it is necessary to widely classify various types of hotels, and offer more types of hotels to provide consumers with choices, such as providing services for childcare and babies, services for hot spring hotels, and the hotels close to the ocean which can provide services for offshore facilities, these are passengers who can attract special needs.

With the rapid development of the Internet and information technology, it continues to influence and change the way of competition. The tourism industry is far-reaching influence by e-commerce. With the increasing demand for tourism by domestic tourists, the information provided by the current tourism website is mainly based on the suit travel itinerary. The travel websites have begun to provide simple screening to query travel itineraries, allowing users to enter destinations, countries, dates, hotels, etc., but the recommendation results are limited to fixed models. It will not produce different results for different types of people. The result of low interactions makes the website platform still limited to the role of a provider of travel information, and it can't provide the appropriate itinerary by understanding the needs of tourists. Therefore, for users with different travel preferences, the system will gradually plan the travel itinerary according to their record description and interaction process, and select a complete travel itinerary, corresponding to the next trip plan.

The factors that Japanese tourists are willing to choose hot spring hotels are divided into three categories. The first is hygienic and clean hot spring facilities. The second is complete fire safety facilities, and the third is hotels provide a safe leisure environment and facilities. The quality of service, the willingness to revisit, and the willingness to recommend are essential differences in the characteristics of tourists. Visitors will also consider the setting of barrier-free facilities and the complete of fire-fighting equipment as a factor in choosing a hotel. It can be seen that tourists are not only required to improve the quality of accommodation but also become an overall improvement. If tourists can collect and filter the categories of hotels before the trip, they can reduce the conflicts with cultural and environmental factors. Therefore, if the hotel recommendation system can be reinforcement, the satisfaction of tourists and the willingness to revisit will be enhanced.

For domestic tourists, the use of employee advertisements as the brand representative is the best, but for foreign visitors, the brand representative is no different from the recommended advertising effect. Travelers may be attracted to the brand representative because of their own work experience, or because of the subjective impressions of the brand representative, such as image, type, personality, etc., to determine whether the sightseeing area matches their type. This means that if today's brand representative is a sunny and outgoing person, the fans who are also outdoor sports will score higher on the place where they endorse. On the contrary, foreigners are less affected by this because they do not understand Taiwan's famous people.

The domestic tourism market is booming, the demand for hotels and the quality of services are improved, and local international tourist hotels such as in Kaohsiung and

Hualien have been significantly affected by tourist accommodation demand. Some hotels can't keep up with the changes in the environment regarding hardware and software. Tourists will have cognitive gaps in use and affect tourist satisfaction. A good recommendation system with the popularity of the Internet is a must. The above studies have shown that whether it is a star hotel, a theme hotel, a cheap hotel, etc., the choice of hotel varies from person to person, we believe that different personality traits may affect the difference in tourists' selection of hotels. For example, the tourists with extroverted personality traits may have more sense of agreement for the theme-type hotels. Those who are more concerned about the quality of life may prefer star hotels with higher stability, while those who like early adopters may choose cheap hotels.

We believe that different tourists will have different opinions and distinct needs in the hotel selection. At this stage, hotel recommendation websites such as Agoda, TripAdvisor, Booking.com, etc., provide simple classification and filtering, such as price and environmental evaluation, traffic, etc. as a simple recommendation result. We believe that the recommended results are roughly the same, and sometimes it may not be enough to suggest a hotel that allows tourists to agree, or it may incur additional costs due to unwanted hotel facilities. Besides, the website is not very interactive with tourists, so the hotel website is considered to be a platform for providing hotel information, making it difficult to understand the needs of tourists and provide suitable hotels for them. We know that the personal characteristics of tourists will have different opinions on the choice of hotels, so we hope to recommend people who like to travel, advise them to some hotels as a pocket list. If they have more opportunities in the future, they can make choices based on the pocket list.

In today's highly competitive hotel industry, if you do not take into account the real needs of tourists, you can't satisfy tourists and create word of mouth. Hotel recommendation itself is a sophisticated service. How to analyze tourist preferences and hotel type matching is a good recommendation system must pay attention. Therefore, this study combines tourist location and collaborative filtering recommendation algorithm to explore the ratings of different types of hotels by different tourists and analyze the hotels that meet the individual tourists to make recommendations to achieve the purpose of hotel recommendation.

## 2  Related Work

The recommendation system is based on the user's personal needs and preferences, assisting in the process of searching for a significant amount of information [2]. It uses the knowledge of an expert or a large number of users to find what you need. It is also an application for personalization problems. It is widely used in smart network systems to remove spam and provide consumer filtered information quickly. We review many large e-commerce websites, all of which are systematic recommendation models.

The primary purpose of information filtering is to filter out the information you want so that users can access and use it in a natural way [3]. More and more Internet companies such as eBay, Amazon.com, Lotte, etc. use online recommendation systems for movies, music, books, web pages and other related products. The recommendation system will filter out the desired content when the consumer browses the comprehensive information according to the user's browsing preferences. If the system can accurately predict the consumer's choice for the purchased product, the transaction volume may be increased to achieve a win-win goal.

The recommendation system can be divided into three main categories depending on the recommended method of use: content-based filtering, collaborative filtering, and hybrid approach. The recommendation system has been widely used on the Internet to collect and store consumer preferences in an explicit or implicit manner and to identify products that meet their consumption habits quickly. Different recommendation systems focus on solving different recommendation problems. The scope includes system recommended applications, data acquisition methods, and recommended method innovations, etc. The following is a detailed introduction to approach recommendation system.

## 2.1   Content-Based Filtering

The content-based recommendation system is derived from the use of information. It works by collecting consumer habits, such as contents that have been browsed, and the attributes of the element, e.g., like keywords or idioms, to analyze user information. Each product has its attribute string, and the collection of products is a collection of attribute strings. It is built in the database value to represent the user's profile (user profile). Briefly, it is based on the attributes and content of the item to find related products in the database to make recommendations. For example, the consumer uses the recommended service for renting online movies. The content-based filtering system analyzes the types of related videos that the customer has previously rented, and then selects the videos with higher similarity to the users.

The recommendation system is based on the analysis of the content of the item when giving information, rather than the evaluation of the person's product. The recommendation system is based on the analysis of the content of the item when presenting information, instead of people's assessment of their products. It means that the product is recommended for the listed content traits, and it also gives users confidence in the recommendation system and perspectives on their own preferences. The content-based recommendation system calculates the consumer's preference for the product, and then passes the value to the prediction module to calculate the product that is of interest to him. Mooney and Roy [4] proposed a content-based book recommendation system, which uses Information extraction and machine learning to classify text and record the user's preference weight for each text, then use this preference to achieve the purpose of recommendation.

## 2.2   Collaborative Filtering

Collaborative recommendation operation is to use the group's point of view to recommending the item to the user. By recording and comparing the user's preference information about the product or service, the user divides into different clusters, and each cluster is a highly relevant user. In 1992, the first Tapestry system developed by Goldberg et al. [5], its concept was to be annotated by the user to read the electronic files. When other users query, it will filter out the data in the system according to the query conditions to make recommendations. For example, A and B are lovers of love stories. One day, A saw a love story and felt very good and left a positive comment. When B wants to read a love story one day, the system will give priority to recommending this book to him. Thus, it is increasing the possibility that B will read the novel, and this way has the opportunity to achieve the recommended effect.

Resnick et al. [6] proposes that collaborative filtering is based on the behavioral perspective of the surrounding or group, and seeks users with the same experience or opinions as the basis for personalized information. Dhillon [7] divides users into different clusters by recording and comparing data using product or service preferences, each of which is a more relevant user. Therefore, the collaborative recommendation system can effectively aggregate similar groups of attributes or preferences, and then provide samples to users in the same group as a reference to meet the basis of people usually refer to others before making decisions. The primary structure is as follows: First, use the product rating provided by the customer to establish the user usage situation, and then find a similar user group from the customer group, which can also be called the nearest neighbors. Therefore, the purchased product can be introduced to the target customer by other members of the same group.

Collaborative recommendation uses other users' experience in using the product to make a rating threshold. If the rating exceeds the system's setting conditions, it will be recommended to the user. However, if the number of samples that have not been evaluated or evaluated is too few, useful recommendations cannot be made, so this recommended method applies to popular products [4]. However, if it is a brand new product, it cannot be effectively recommended by using the collaborative recommendation method.

## 2.3  Hybrid Approach Recommendation

Hybrid approach recommendations, as the name implies, combine two or more selection mechanisms. Collaborative recommendations can't achieve accurate predictions, only recommendations for similar users' preferences, without reference to the common preferences of similar users and target users. Therefore, a hybrid recommendation technique is proposed, which uses collaborative filtering to find users with similar preferences, and then uses content-based guidance to analyze the common preferences of users and target users to recommend items that match their preferences.

Kim et al. [8] analyze the two main types of hybrids in today's technology – sequential combination and linear combination. The sequential combination, this type of recommendation system is mainly divided into two steps. Firstly, content filtering method first finds users with the same preferences or similar. Then, it makes predictions through collaborative filtering. Linear combination, the recommended system of this type is RAAP and Fab filtering systems, which can help consumers to classify different areas of information on the network, and then recommend the URLs of the website to interested users. Fab uses content-based filtering to replace the user's rating file, so the quality of the recommendation is entirely dependent on the content filtering technology. Besides, the hybrid recommendation system method can be divided into two categories as follows:

The first is to combine individual recommendation results, mainly to mix two or more recommendation methods. Ahmad Wasfi [9] has proposed the system Prof-builder, which uses a collaborative and content recommendation system to generate two different lists. Content-based is mainly for users to browse the website page, and recommend similar websites according to the content of the website and user preferences. The collaborative filtering method is to compare the path analysis of the browsing path of the neighboring user for the user to browse the website path and recommend the related website for the user. Besides, Claypool et al. [10] also proposed the Personal Tango system, which separates the content-oriented recommendation and the collaborative recommendation method, and the degree of recommendation is the two multiplied by individual weights.

The second is to combine the two recommended methods to produce a set of recommendation results, and Fab is a typical hybrid recommendation system proposed by Balabanović and Shoham [11]. It combines content-oriented and collaborative filtering in two different ways, recommending favorite articles for readers on the website, recording each reader's preferences in detail, and finding similar readers, and then recommending articles with collaborative filtering recommendation techniques to a reader, this method is more accurate than any single recommendation.

## 3 Methodology

In 2001, Sarwar et al. [12] proposed Item-Based Collaborative Filtering Algorithms. Item-Based Collaborative Filtering is used to estimate the similarity to be calculated by calculating the similarity between various items. It has an underlying assumption that items that generate user interest must be similar to items with higher ratings before. It first calculates the similarity between the items that have been evaluated and the items to be predicted and uses the similarity as the weight to weight the scores of the items that have been evaluated to obtain the expected value of the items to be measured. For example, to perform similarity calculations for item A and item B, first, it finds out the item A and item B have rated at the same time. Then, it works a similarity calculation on these combinations and uses user-based collaboration filter to do the operation.

The advantage of item-based collaborative filtering is that it does not need to consider the differences between users, nor does it need to use the user's historical data to perform user identification. For the items, the similarity between them is relatively stable, so the similarity calculation step with large workload can be completed offline, thus reducing the amount of online calculation and improving the recommendation efficiency, especially when the user is more than the item. There are more than 60 methods for calculating similarity and increasing. It commonly used and well-known methods include, Persons Correlation Coefficient, Cosine-based Similarity, Adjusted Cosine Similarity and Euclidean Distance, etc.

In this system, we first use the mobile device to obtain the location of the tourist and find the location of the nearby hotel, and then we use the item-based collaborative filtering method to conduct the recommendation analysis and finally recommend several nearby hotels to provide tourist choice. The system architecture diagram is shown in the figure. In the process of recommending analysis, we take into account the impact of tourists' habits on rating score, such as the rating score is too low or the rating score is too high. Therefore, the recommendation result may be inaccurate due to such a difference. Consequently, we use adjusted cosine similarities for analysis. We take into account the impact of tourist scoring habits, and for every tourist, it will be avoided by tourist evaluate score of each hotel subtracting the average tourist evaluate score of all hotels. The final result is the similarity between the two hotels, which will get between $-1$ and $1$. Using the user's average rating, adjust each user's rating tendency to get a more consistent similarity calculation result, the formula is as follows:

$$\text{sim}(i, j) = \frac{\sum_{u \in U}(R_{u,i} - \bar{R}_u)(R_{u,j} - \bar{R}_u)}{\sqrt{\sum_{u \in U}(R_{u,i} - \bar{R}_u)^2}\sqrt{\sum_{u \in U}(R_{u,j} - \bar{R}_u)^2}} \tag{1}$$

where $\text{sim}(i, j)$ represents the similarity between hotel $i$ and hotel $j$. $R_{u,i}$ represents the rating of tourist $u$ on hotel $i$. $R_{u,j}$ represents the rating of tourist $u$ on hotel $j$. $\bar{R}_u$ denotes the average rating given by tourists to all hotels. $U$ represents a set of tourists who have rated hotel $i$ and hotel $j$ (Table 1).

Table 1. The scores of rated hotels by all tourists.

|  | Hotel 1 | Hotel 2 | Hotel 3 | Hotel 4 | Hotel 5 | Hotel 6 |
|---|---|---|---|---|---|---|
| Tourist 1 | 1 | 5 | 1 | 2 | 2 | 4 |
| Tourist 2 | 3 | 3 | 0 | 3 | 2 | 4 |
| Tourist 3 | 3 | 0 | 2 | 0 | 2 | 2 |
| Tourist 4 | 2 | 5 | 2 | 0 | 0 | 2 |
| Tourist 5 | 0 | 3 | 0 | 0 | 0 | 5 |
| Tourist 6 | 0 | 3 | 1 | 5 | 1 | 4 |

In the following table, for example, if we want to predict the rating of the tourist 2 to the hotel 3, the similarity to the hotel 3 must be calculated for all the hotels, and the similarity calculations of the hotel 5 and the hotel 3 are as follows:

$$\bar{R}_u = (3 + 3 + 0 + 3 + 2 + 4)/5 = 3)$$

$$\text{sim}(\text{Hotel5}, \text{Hotel 3}) = \frac{[(2 - 3)(1 - 3) + (2 - 3)(2 - 3) + (1 - 3)(1 - 3)]}{\sqrt{(2 - 3)^2 + (2 - 3)^2 + (1 - 3)^2}\sqrt{(1 - 3)^2 + (2 - 3)^2 + (1 - 3)^2}}$$
$$\approx 0.953$$

After calculating the similarity between the hotels, the next is to make predictions for hotels that have not yet been scored, and the prediction method uses the weighted sum method to make predictions. The weighted sum is a weighted summation of the hotels that have been scored by the tourists. The obtained weight is the similarity between each hotel and the hotel $i$, and then the average sum of all similarities is calculated. The rating of tourist $u$ on hotel $i$ is as follows:

$$P_{u,i} = \frac{\sum_{j \in N}(S_{i,j} * R_{u,j})}{\sum_{j \in N}(|S_{i,j}|)} \tag{2}$$

where $N$ denotes a set of hotels with the highest similar degree to hotel $i$. $S_{i,j}$ denotes the similarity between hotel $i$ and hotel $j$. $R_{u,j}$ denotes the rating of tourist $u$ to hotel $j$.

Taking the example above just as an example, suppose we currently want to predict the rating of the tourist 2 to the hotel 3, it uses the similarity formula to calculate the hotel 1, and the hotel 5 is the most similar to the hotel 3, with similarities of 0.913 and 0.953 respectively. Therefore, the final prediction score $P_{u,i} = \frac{(0.913*3 + 0.953*2)}{(0.913 + 0.953)} \approx 2.5$, where $P_{u,i}$ represents the predicted tourist $u$'s rating score on hotel $i$.

## 4    Results

We use the questionnaire to collect data and analyze the tourists' overall satisfaction with the hotel and analyze and count the satisfaction. The results are shown in Figs. 1, 2 and 3. The data is built into a database and provided to the recommendation module. We use the mobile device to obtain the tourists' location and combined with the system's recommendation system. Finally, we can calculate the tourist's score for the hotel that has not yet been scored, and recommend the hotel with the higher predicted score to the tourist for reference.

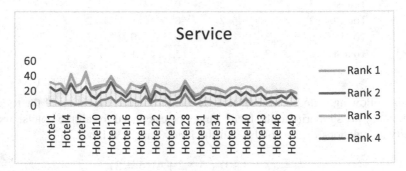

**Fig. 1.** The score of hotel in service

The system calculates the similarity between the hotel where the tourist has lived and the hotel that tourist has not lived. The similarity will be between −1 and 1. The closer the value is to 1, the more similar the two hotels are. Next, the tourist can enter the lowest similarity, which means to determine the similarity of the hotel you want to find. The system begins performing the calculation of the predicted values and displays the most appropriate results on the mobile device. When the value of the input similarity is too high, the system cannot successfully calculate the predicted recommendation score, and the value of the lowest similarity needs to be adjusted downward.

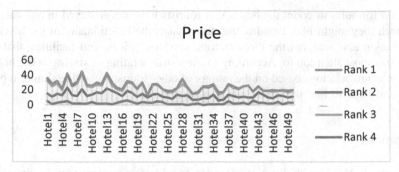

**Fig. 2.** The score of hotel in price

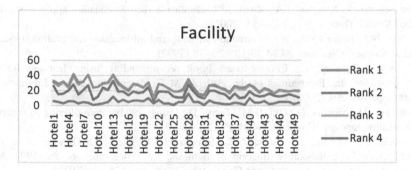

**Fig. 3.** The score of hotel in facility

Taking the Fig. 2 as an example, in the rating of Hotel 8, most passengers gave a score of three and four points, which is very similar to the rating of Hotel 5. Therefore, we take tourist A as an example. He has stayed at the hotel 5, and he has given a score of 4, but he has not stayed at the hotel 8. We predict that the score will be quite close. Consequently, in the system, the average score of each tourists' hotel is obtained, and then the lowest similarity is entered and brought into the system, and the predicted score is 4 points, which is similar to our predicted score. Hence, we believe that users will have similar ratings for hotels in close or similar ratings.

## 5 Conclusion

As the economy grows, tourists begin to pay attention to hotels. The hotel makes a more detailed distinction, and the hotel has started to make changes in various services or facilities, unlike the services that used to provide accommodation only. The Internet is the most direct source of information search for tourists, but fake messages often confuse tourists. Therefore, the recommendation system is more important, but the recommendation system now makes recommendations based on some simple factors. Therefore, this study proposes a hotel recommendation system based on user location and item-based collaborative filtering recommendation. It uses hotel similarity and prediction formulas to count the hotels that tourists have never stayed in and calculate how much they might like. Besides, this study takes the functionality of the hotel as a consideration and analyzes the three factors, services, prices, and facilities, that consumers pay most attention to. According to the tourist's rating of staying at the hotel, it makes recommendations based on the ratings of other tourists who like similar types of hotels, and hope to find the right hotel as a pocket list.

# References

1. O'Mahony, M.P., Smyth, B.: A classification-based review recommender. In: Bramer, M., Ellis, R., Petridis, M. (eds.), Research and Development in Intelligent Systems XXVI, pp. 49–62 (2010)
2. Ben Schafer, J., Konstan, J.A., Riedl, J.: E-commerce recommendation applications. Data Min. Knowl. Discov. **5**(1), 115–153 (2001)
3. Belkin, N.J., Bruce Croft, W.: Information filtering and information retrieval: two sides of the same coin? Commun. ACM **35**(12), 29–38 (1992)
4. Mooney, R.J., Roy, L.: Content-based book recommending using learning for text categorization. In: Proceedings of the Fifth ACM Conference on Digital Libraries, DL 2000, pp. 195–204 (2000)
5. Goldberg, D., Nichols, D., Oki, B.M., Terry, D.: Using collaborative filtering to weave an information tapestry. Commun. ACM **35**(12), 61–70 (1992)
6. Resnick, P., Iacovou, N., Suchak, M., Bergstrom, P., Riedl, J.: Grouplens: an open architecture for collaborative filtering of netnews. In: Proceedings of the 1994 ACM Conference on Computer Supported Cooperative Work, pp. 175–186 (1994)
7. Dhillon, N.: Achieving effective personalization and customization using collaborative filtering. http://home1.gte.net/dhillos/cf. October 1995
8. Kim, B.M., Li, Q., Park, C.S., Kim, S.G., Kim, J.Y.: A new approach for combining content-based and collaborative filters. J. Intell. Inf. Syst. **27**(1), 79–91 (2006)
9. Ahmad Wasfi, A.M.: Collecting user access patterns for building user profiles and collaborative filtering. In: Proceedings of the 4th International Conference on Intelligent User Interfaces, IUI 1999, pp. 57–64 (1999)
10. Claypool, M., Gokhale, A., Miranda, T., Murnikov, P., Netes, D., Sartin, M.: Combining content-based and collaborative filters in an online newspaper (1999)
11. Balabanović, M., Shoham, Y.: Fab: content-based, collaborative recommendation. Commun. ACM **40**(3), 66–72 (1997)
12. Sarwar, B., Karypis, G., Konstan, J., Riedl, J.: Item-based collaborative filtering recommendation algorithms. In: Proceedings of the 10th International Conference on World Wide Web, pp. 285–295 (2001)
13. Montaner, M., L´opez, B., De La Rosa, J.L.: A taxonomy of recommender agents on theinternet. Artif. Intell. Rev. **19**(4), 285–330 (2003)
14. Porter, M.E.: Strategy and the internet. Harv. Bus. Rev. **79**(164), 62–78 (2001)
15. Sarwar, B.M., Konstan, J.A., Borchers, A., Herlocker, J., Miller, B., Riedl, J.: Using filtering agents to improve prediction quality in the grouplens research collaborative filtering system. In: Proceedings of the 1998 ACM Conference on Computer Supported Cooperative Work, pp. 345–354 (1998)

# Developing a Beacon-Based Location System Using Bluetooth Low Energy Location Fingerprinting for Smart Home Device Management

Chih-Kun Ke[✉], Wang-Chi Ho, and Ke-Cheng Lu

Department of Information Management, National Taichung University
of Science and Technology, No. 129, Sec. 3, Sanmin Rd, North Dist, Taichung
40401, Taiwan R.O.C.
{ckk, s1310634003, s1110231051}@nutc.edu.tw

**Abstract.** This study explores BLE (Bluetooth Low Energy) Beacon indoor positioning for smart home power management. We propose a novel system framework using BLE Beacon to detect the user location and conduct power management in the home through a mobile device application. Due to the BLE Beacon may produce the multipath effect, this study uses the positioning algorithm and hardware configuration to reduce the error rate. Location fingerprint positioning algorithm and filter modification are used to establish a positioning method for facilitating deployment and saving computing resources. The experiments include observing the RSSI (Received Signal Strength Indicators) and selecting the filters; discussing the relationship between the characteristics of the BLE Beacon signal accuracy and the number of the BLE Beacon deployed in space; the BLE Beacon multilateration positioning combined with the In-Snergy intelligent energy management system for smart home power management. The contribution is to allow users to enjoy smart home services based on the location using a mobile device application.

**Keywords:** Bluetooth low energy beacon · Smart home · Multipath effect · Fingerprint location algorithm · Multilateration positioning

## 1 Introduction

In recent years, information and communication technology has been increasingly advanced. In order to achieve a more convenient living environment, people began to pursue the ability to make objects intelligent and transmit information, resulting in the IoT (Internet of Thing) concept [1–3]. With the maturity of cloud computing and IoT technology, smart homes have become an important trend in the future [4]. The smart home is an applied case of the concept of IoT to control the appliances in the home via the WSNs (Wireless Sensor Networks) anytime and anywhere, and cloud computing facilitates users to make the home appliances more intelligent to obtain convenient services [4, 5]. In order to detect a human position, people invented satellites to provide GPS (Global Positioning System) positioning. However, as the scope of people

J.-L. Chen et al. (Eds.): WiCON 2018, LNICST 264, pp. 235–244, 2019.
https://doi.org/10.1007/978-3-030-06158-6_24

activities is no longer limited to the unshielded surface on the earth, GPS cannot provide accurate positioning services if people stay in the indoor space or go cross the building. How to detect the location of the people in the indoor space will become an important research topic. Due to the GPS positioning is inappropriate using in the indoor environment, the demand for indoor positioning is generated. Among the indoor positioning technologies [6], for example, ultrasonic, infrared ray, Wi-Fi, RFID (Radio Frequency Identification Device), UWB (Ultra Wideband), and Bluetooth, BLE (Bluetooth low energy) Beacon has micro-positioning and seamless integration. Its features such as mode, power saving, and low cost will be an applied technology worth exploring in indoor positioning [6–8].

However, BLE Beacon technology has not been popularized for indoor positioning because its frequency is based on 2.4 GHz radio band, which is prone to multipath effects and causes errors in positioning [1, 6, 8–13]. In addition, the traditional smart home deploys various sensors, the detection may be inaccurate when sensing. For example, an infrared sensor is used to identify a user's position while the user stays in indoors. However, if the sensor does not detect the movement of the human body for a long time, it performs an automatic configuration process, such as turning off the home appliance power or locking the door which may cause big trouble. The innovation and popularization of mobile device facilitate people obtaining useful messages and performing convenient business operations in a very short time. The mobile devices are almost indispensable auxiliary tools of human life. Therefore, in response to the design of the emerging smart home application, the Bluetooth function built into the mobile device and the BLE Beacon can be used for multilateration positioning, and through various standards of the positioning algorithms [6], for example, the RSSI (Received Signal Strength Indicator), CSI (Channel State Information), fingerprinting/scene analysis, AoA (Angle of Arrival), ToA (Time of Arrival), TDoA (Time Difference of Arrival), RToF (Return Time of Flight), and PoA (Phase of Arrival) of the received signal, to enhance the accuracy of positioning. Then, according to the positioning, the user can remotely manual control the smart home appliance in the room. In addition to the manual remote control, the smart home application automatically turns on the power of the smart home in the room when entering the room. Oppositely, when the user leaves a room for a period of time, the smart home application automatically turns off the appliance to shut down the power to achieve effective power control. It makes people lives becoming more intelligent.

This study explores the BLE Beacon indoor positioning and proposes a novel system framework using BLE Beacon to detect the user location and conduct smart home power management by a mobile device application [14]. Location fingerprint positioning algorithm and filter modification are used to establish a positioning method for facilitating deployment and saving computing resources. The proposed system includes the BLE Beacon positioning system, smart home management server, knowledgebase, mobile device application, smart home gateway, and cloud smart socket for remote control. Through the BLE Beacon-based positioning system combined with the smart home management server, the user location is estimated to provide a friendly and adaptable smart home appliance power control function via smart home gateway and cloud smart socket. Users can use a mobile device application (App) to mutually or automatically control the appliance power anytime, anywhere. The system operation data is stored in a knowledgebase. Therefore, the contribution of this work is to use BLE Beacon multilateration positioning to perform the smart home power management of achieving a user-oriented smart home. The IoT technology solves the problems encountered in human life so that users can enjoy the appropriate smart home services.

The remainder of this paper is organized as follows. Section 2 presents the novel system framework using BLE Beacon to detect the user's location and conduct power management in the home through a mobile device application. Section 3 introduces the positioning algorithm based on the location fingerprinting. The experiments follow in Sect. 4. Section 5 has the relevant evaluation and discussion. Finally, Sect. 6 presents our conclusions.

## 2  The Proposed System Framework for Smart Home Power Management

This section introduces the BLE beacon-based location system using location fingerprint positioning for smart home power management, including the BLE Beacon positioning system, smart home management server, knowledgebase, mobile device application and In-Snergy intelligent management system [15] for remote control. Based on the indoor positioning to provide smart services to users. Figure 1. shows the proposed system framework workflow, including 5 steps are illustrated as follows.

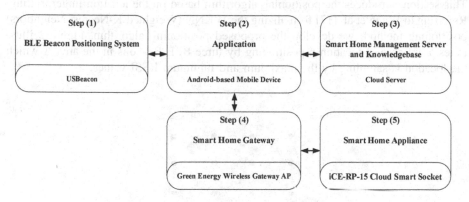

**Fig. 1.**  The system framework workflow

Step (1)  BLE Beacons [16] are installed at some fixed positions to establish a coordinate system. The sampling distribution map of BLE Beacons is established and stored in the knowledgebase. BLE Beacons broadcast signals to the Android-based mobile device's App.

Step (2)  The Android-based mobile device's App receives the signals, transmits the RSSI values of BLE Beacons and its own location data to the smart home management server, and gives related control instructions.

Step (3) The smart home management server analyses these data and instructions by signal intensity attenuation positioning, triangle positioning and location fingerprint positing algorithm, estimates the mobile device's location, and determines which appliance is being chosen. Then, the server sends data and instructions via the App to the smart home gateway [15]. These data and instructions contain the information of the appliances that need to be controlled and the information of the specific cloud smart socket [15].

Step (4) The smart home gateway analyzes the instructions, confirms the appliance number and sends instructions to the specific appliance.

Step (5) Finally, the chosen appliance is operated under the App control instructions. The control instruction is divided into the active service and passive service. The active service is smart appliance that do not require users to turn on/off. In other words, the smart appliance triggered by the control instructions will automatically turn on/off in the room. The passive service is the appliance that need users to turn on/off, such as fans, TVs, lamps, and air-conditioners, etc. Our proposed system facilitates users to enjoy the appropriate smart home services.

# 3   Positioning Algorithm Based on the Location Fingerprinting

This section introduces the positioning algorithm based on the location fingerprinting. Referring to Wang et al. [17] formalizing the WKNN (Weighted K-Nearest Neighbors) positioning method, we develop the proposed positioning algorithm. Figure 2 illustrates a use case of location p positioning by three BLE Beacons in the area A which the location is sampling by the maximum and minimum RSSI values.

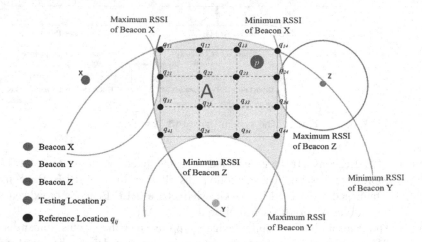

**Fig. 2.** The positioning diagram

Based on the Eq. (1), let $R_p$ denotes the RSSI data collected at a testing location $p$ over a period of time, is shown as the Eq. (2).

$$RSSI = -10nlog_{10}(d) + A \tag{1}$$

$$R_p = \begin{bmatrix} \alpha_1^p & \cdots & \alpha_n^p \end{bmatrix} = \begin{bmatrix} rssi_{11}^p & \cdots & rssi_{1n}^p \\ \vdots & \ddots & \vdots \\ rssi_{m1}^p & \cdots & rssi_{mn}^p \end{bmatrix} \tag{2}$$

where $rssi_{ij}^p$ is the RSSI value received at a testing location $p$ from the $j$th BLE Beacon at the $i$th sampling time, $1 \le i \le m$, $1 \le j \le n$, $m$ is the number of sampling time, $n$ is the number of BLE Beacons. The RSSI value in the $i$th row of $R_p$ are collected from the different Beacons concurrently. The RSSI value in the $j$th column of $R_p$ are received from the same Beacon at different time. The $\bar{\alpha}_j^p$ is the mean vector (using mean filter mentioned in Sect. 4) of the $j$th column of $R_p$, is shown as the Eq. (3).

$$\bar{R}_p = \begin{bmatrix} \bar{\alpha}_1^p & \cdots & \bar{\alpha}_n^p \end{bmatrix} \tag{3}$$

In the same way, the RSSI data collected at a reference location $q$ over a period time are represented as the Eq. (4), and the Eq. (5) shows the mean vector at a reference location $q$.

$$R_q = \begin{bmatrix} \alpha_1^q & \cdots & \alpha_n^q \end{bmatrix} = \begin{bmatrix} rssi_{11}^q & \cdots & rssi_{1n}^q \\ \vdots & \ddots & \vdots \\ rssi_{m1}^q & \cdots & rssi_{mn}^q \end{bmatrix} \tag{4}$$

$$\bar{R}_q = \begin{bmatrix} \bar{\alpha}_1^q & \cdots & \bar{\alpha}_n^q \end{bmatrix} \tag{5}$$

Thus, the Euclidean distance $d_q$ is estimated between the testing location $p$ and the reference location $q$, is shown as the Eq. (6).

$$d_q = \frac{1}{n} \left( \sum_{j=1}^{n} \left| \bar{\alpha}_j^p - \bar{\alpha}_j^q \right|^2 \right)^{\frac{1}{2}} \tag{6}$$

The final location is estimated by the Eq. (7).

$$C = \frac{\sum_{q=1}^{K} \frac{C_q}{d_q + \varepsilon}}{\sum_{q=1}^{K} \frac{1}{d_q + \varepsilon}} \tag{7}$$

where $C_q$ is the coordinate of the $q$th reference location among $K$ reference locations, $\varepsilon$ is a number used to avoid division by zero.

# 4    Experiments

This section explores the RSSI characteristics of BLE Beacon and performs the experiments on BLE Beacon multilateration positioning. In BLE specification [18], the GATT (Generic ATTribute protocol) is defined to operate on the upper layers of the BLE stack. In order to monitor the RSSI of BLE Beacon, we developed a mobile device App using Google Android public API Bluetooth GATT [19]. The App can directly observe the packet sent by BLE Beacon, and read the BLE Beacon identification, physical address, and receive it within 1 s. Besides, the relevant information includes the signal strength, average signal strength, TX power value and the derived distance. So that we can enforce the location fingerprint positioning sampling, collect the maximum and minimum RSSI values of the BLE Beacon within the location range and store data in the knowledgebase. According to the room information and the instant receipt of the BLE Beacon signal, the smart home management system has ability to determine the user location. The smart home management system carried out a series of tasks to analyze the characteristics and positioning methods of BLE Beacon. Then it uses the positioning algorithm to estimate the location of the room and transmit the data and control instructions via WebAPI to the smart home gateway. At last, the chosen appliance operates under the mobile device App control instructions. It is expected to find the best deployment for the BLE Beacon in a smart home and use the positioning algorithms to reduce the error rate. The analysis tasks are illustrated in follows.

- **Observation of RSSI signals and selection of the filters**: The purpose of using the filter is to handle the error rate. Since the multipath effect problem of BLE Beacon highlights the importance of the filter, we explore the difference between the mean filter and the median filter. The mean filter is used to execute the experiments. Each experimental location of a BLE Beacon is defined as the reference location which is used in the proposed positioning algorithm mentioned in Sect. 3. Besides, the measured maximum, minimum, and mean RSSI of BLE Beacon signal values are used for location positioning.
- **Explore the characteristics of BLE Beacon**: The deployment of BLE Beacon in indoor positioning has a great influence on the positioning accuracy. We conducted a series of experiments to understand the characteristics of BLE Beacon. The signal transmitted by the USBeacon using the chip-type Bluetooth antenna is directional. When deploying the BLE Beacon, it shall avoid getting the wavy signal to prevent the influence of positioning. In addition, it is recommended to deploy the BLE Beacon in the corner of the area.
- **Single space and multiple spaces positioning experiment**: The single space positioning experiment may require several BLE Beacons deployed in a space of 1.5 m × 1.5 m to coordinate an experimental space. The positioning by single BLE Beacon is not the good solution and the range of error rate is large. Two BLE Beacons deployment can reduce the positioning error rate. It is recommended to coordinate a rectangular space by deploying more than three BLE Beacons. A multiple spaces positioning experiment is performed using three BLE Beacons to coordinate four spaces, including the Room 1, Room 2, Room 3, and Bathroom 1, are shown in Fig. 3. The experiment results of 10 test locations show that the

overlap area produced by the proposed positioning method. The suggested solution of this status is to deploy the BLE Beacon in the overlap area. Positioning with multiple BLE Beacons can increase the uniqueness of the positioning area and reduce the occurrence of errors.

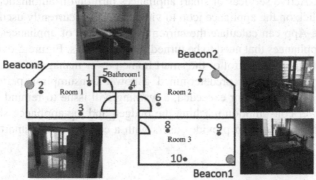

| | Beacon 1 | | Beacon 2 | | Beacon 3 | |
|---|---|---|---|---|---|---|
| | max | min | max | min | max | min |
| Room 1 | 70.8333 dBm | -91 dBm | -77 dBm | -91 dBm | -57 dBm | -80 dBm |
| Bathroom 1 | -75.2 dBm | -89.5 dBm | -61 dBm | -83.75 dBm | -69 dBm | -92 dBm |
| Room 2 | -61.333 dBm | -85.5 dBm | -58.25 dBm | -86.667 dBm | -77 dBm | -95 dBm |
| Room 3 | -44.5 dBm | -71 dBm | -65 dBm | -88.5 dBm | -83 dBm | -99 dBm |

| Testing Location | Area | Beacon 1 | Beacon 2 | Beacon 3 |
|---|---|---|---|---|
| 1 | Room 1 | -86.25 dBm | -84 dBm | -74.5 dBm |
| 2 | Room 1 | -87.33 dBm | -86.75 dBm | -66.4 dBm |
| 3 | Room 1 | -87.5 dBm | -89 dBm | -61 dBm |
| 4 | Bathroom 1 | -83 dBm | -75 dBm | -76 dBm |
| 5 | Room 1 / Bathroom 1 | -88.5 dBm | -78.6 dBm | -74 dBm |
| 6 | Room 2 / Bathroom 1 | -77 dBm | -70.833 dBm | -88.75 dBm |
| 7 | Room 2 | -72.25 dBm | -70.6667 dBm | -94.6667 dBm |
| 8 | Room 3 | -51.4444 dBm | -85.75 dBm | -96.667 dBm |
| 9 | Room 2 / Room 3 | -64 dBm | -71.6667 dBm | -93.75 dBm |
| 10 | Room 3 | -54.4289 dBm | -71.6667 dBm | -95 dBm |
| | | The measured unit of RSSI is decibel-milliwatts (dBm) | | |

**Fig. 3.** Multiple space positioning experiment [14]

- **Smart home power management via mobile device App**: The PHP (Hypertext Preprocessor) combined with In-Snergy WebAPI to implement the proposed system in order to communicate with In-Snergy smart green energy management system. Besides, a mobile device application (App) is developed in an Android platform to facilitate user to manage the appliance power in a smart home. Users customizes and deploys the appliances in App. By integrating the App and BLE Beacon positioning system with the In-Snergy smart green energy management system, the App provides the function of controlling the appliance via smart home gateway and cloud smart socket. After the user is positioned via the BLE Beacon, the In-Snergy Smart Green Management System remotely controls the state of operation of the appliances. Active services of smart appliances turn on/off automatically for users. User can click on the appliance icon to view the details currently used, as shown in Fig. 4. The App can calculate the current power usage of appliances. Passive services are appliances that need to be turned on/off by users. Figure 5 demonstrates an experiment on a fan control of the smart home power management. Users can also set the threshold of the predetermined a power consumption period. Once the threshold is approached or exceeded, a warning will issue to remind users that the current power consumption reaching the budget, and the appliance shall be turned off. The proposed system provides users with a context-aware smart home power management.

**Fig. 4.** Mobile device App shows the details of currently used appliance

**Fig. 5.** An experiment on a fan of smart home power management

## 5    Discussion and Evaluation

BLE Beacon technology has become popular [8]. Chen et al. [7] presents that the BLE beacons have already been deployed in retail industry, showing the proximity of items on the customers' phones and thus creating a more engaging shopping experience. In smart life environment, Nath et al. [3] proposed a voice based location detection system which can be integrated in a smart home environment. The system is suitable for large scale application where user may need to keep track of multiple patients. The contribution is to reduce the burden of learning curve of new technologies on family and caregivers. Liu et al. [5] designed an indoor control system to achieve equipment remote control by using low-energy Bluetooth (BLE) beacon and Internet of Things (IoT) technology. The smart home control system has been implemented by hardware, and precision and stability tests have been conducted, which proved the practicability and good user experience of this solution. Xiong et al. [20] implemented a distinctive system based on indoor location and attitude estimation. They proposed the indoor location algorithm combining image pattern recognition with fingerprint matching. Users can choose the appliances that he wants and control them by touching the screen of the mobile device while the mobile device is pointing to the appliance. This study explores the BLE Beacon for indoor positioning. Through a series of experiments, we realized the characteristics of the chip-type BLE Beacon and the rules for deploying BLE Beacon. Besides, we found that the mobile device cannot receive the BLE Beacon signal when the Wi-Fi access point is turned on. But the mobile device does not be interference when using Wi-Fi to access the Internet. The recommendation is not to open Wi-Fi sharing when using BLE Beacon positioning. According to the experiment results, it is found that the use of the positioning method for indoor positioning is feasible, but this is based on the deployment of sufficient BLE Beacon. The experiment results also present that single BLE Beacon can be deployed in a unit space to maintain the most basic accuracy of positioning. The more BLE Beacons are deployed, the higher the accuracy of spatial positioning.

## 6   Conclusion

This study proposed a novel system to detect the user indoor location using the mobile device and BLE Beacon Multilateration positioning. An Application (App) is developed to facilitate user to manage the appliance power in a smart home. The proposed system gives users a smart home experience, making home life more comfortable and convenient. Based on the BLE Beacon positioning, the user location is analyzed to get the corresponding power management service. In addition, the system allows the user to realize the power usage in the home and how to achieve power saving optimization. The contribution of this work is to make the home smarter, and its applied field is not limited to smart home. The proposed system can be applied to various situations in the living environment, such as shopping malls, exhibition halls, amusement parks, and facilities, etc., to achieve the benefits of reducing the cost. Future work can improve the system towards integrating artificial intelligence or machine learning with positioning to achieve the best benefits.

**Acknowledgement.** This research was supported in part by the Ministry of Science and Technology, R.O.C. with a MOST grant 107-2221-E-025-005.

## References

1. Huh, J.H., Seo, K.: An indoor location-based control system using Bluetooth beacons for IoT systems. Sensors **17**(12), 2917, 1–22 (2017). https://doi.org/10.3390/s17122917
2. Jeon, K.E., She, J., Soonsawad, P., Ng, P.C.: BLE beacons for internet of things applications: survey, challenges, and opportunities. IEEE Internet Things J. **5**(2), 811–828 (2018). https://doi.org/10.1109/JIOT.2017.2788449

3. Nath, R.K., Bajpai, R., Thapliyal, H.: IoT based indoor location detection system for smart home environment. In: Proceedings of the 2018 IEEE International Conference on Consumer Electronics (ICCE), Las Vegas, NV, 12–14 January 2018, pp. 1–3. https://doi.org/10.1109/icce.2018.8326225

4. Alelaiwi, A., Hassan, M.M., Bhuiyan, M.Z.A.: A secure and dependable connected smart home system for elderly. In: Proceedings of the IEEE International Conference on Dependable, Autonomic and Secure Computing, 15th International Conference on Pervasive Intelligence & Computing and 3rd International Conference on Big Data Intelligence and Computing and Cyber Science and Technology Congress (DASC/PiCom/DataCom/CyberSciTech), Orlando, FL, USA, 6–10 November 2017, pp. 722–727

5. Liu, Q.H., Yang, X.S., Deng, L.Z.: An IBeacon-based location system for smart home control. Sensors 18(6), 1897, 1 13 (2018). https://doi.org/10.3390/s18061897

6. Zafari, F., Gkelias, A., Leung, K.K.: A survey of indoor localization systems and technologies. CoRR abs/1709.01015 (2017)

7. Chen, D.Y., Shin, K.G., Jiang, Y.R., Kim, K.H.: Locating and tracking BLE beacons with Smartphones. In Proceedings of the 13th International Conference on emerging Networking EXperiments and Technologies (CoNEXT 2017), pp. 263–275 (2017). https://doi.org/10.1145/3143361.3143385

8. Betzing, J.H.: Beacon-based customer tracking across the high street: perspectives for location-based smart services in retail. In: Proceedings of the 24th Americas Conference on Information Systems, New Orleans, LA, US (2018)

9. Faragher, R., Harle, R.: Location fingerprinting with bluetooth low energy Beacons. IEEE J. Sel. Areas Commun. 33(11), 2418–2428 (2015). https://doi.org/10.1109/JSAC.2015.2430281

10. Daniş, F.S., Cemgil, A.T.: Model-based localization and tracking using bluetooth low-energy Beacons. Sensors 17 (11), 2484, 1–23 (2017). https://doi.org/10.3390/s17112484

11. de Blasio, G., Quesada-Arencibia, A., García, C.R., Molina-Gil, J.M., Caballero-Gil, C.: Study on an indoor positioning system for harsh environments based on Wi-Fi and bluetooth low energy. Sensors 17(6), 1299, 1–28 (2017). https://doi.org/10.3390/s17061299

12. Pu, Y.C., You, P.C.: Indoor positioning system based on BLE location fingerprinting with classification approach. Appl. Math. Model. 62, 654–663 (2018). https://doi.org/10.1016/j.apm.2018.06.031

13. Longo, A., et al.: Localization and monitoring system based on BLE fingerprint method. WAIAH@AI*IA (2017)

14. Ke, C.K., Lu, C.C., Kuo, T.W.: Smart home power control via mobile device based on BLE Beacon multi-point positioning. In: Proceedings of the 24th TANET 2018, Taoyuan, Taiwan (R.O.C.) (2018)

15. iFamily (2014). https://www.insnergy.com/#!ifamilyMain

16. THLight (2018). http://www.thlight.com/home/index

17. Wang, Q., Sun, R., Zhang, X.D., Sun, Y.R., Lu, X.J.: Bluetooth positioning based on weighted K-nearest neighbors and adaptive bandwidth mean shift. Int. J. Distrib. Sens. Netw. 13(5), 1–8 (2017). https://doi.org/10.1177/1550147717706681

18. Sig, B.: Bluetooth Specification Version 4.0 (2010). http://www.bluetooth.org

19. Public API for the Bluetooth GATT (2018). https://developer.android.com/reference/android/bluetooth/BluetoothGatt

20. Xiong, M., Wu, Y., Ding, Y., Mao, X., Fang, Z., Huang, H.: A smart home control system based on indoor location and attitude estimation. In: Proceedings of the International Conference on Computer, Information and Telecommunication Systems (CITS), Kunming, China, 6–8 July 2016; pp. 1–5

# Financial Applications

# Applying Information Quantity Analysis to Sold Price of Real Estate

Huan-Siang Luo[1(⊠)] and Kou-Hsiu Tesng[2]

[1] Department of Civil Engineering, College of Architecture and DesignChung Hua University, 707, Sec. 2, WuFu Rd, Hsinchu 30012, Taiwan
j2006ms660822@yahoo.com.tw
[2] Department of Law, Hsuan University, No.48, Hsuan Chuang Rd, Hsinchu City 30012, Taiwan
hcusec@hcu.edu.tw

**Abstract.** The register of real estate sold price can successfully inhibit investors from speculating illegally on the real estate market. Due to the advantages of conference and confidentiality of traditional questionnaires, the purpose of this study aims to investigate and compare the various factors that influence the sold price of real estate by means of Fuzzy Delphi Method. In addition, various professionals, including real estate marketers, university professors and relevant government officials, take part in the questionnaire for our analysis.

**Keywords:** Realestate deal · Register of sold price · Fuzzy Delphi Method

## 1 Introduction

The current study is aimed to investigate and analyze the various factors that influence the sold price of real estate by means of Fuzzy Delphi Method and in-depth interviews. In Taiwan, the real estate trade used to be off-the-books deal, which caused problematic tradings. Now, it is necessary to register and to announce the sold price when a deal of real estate is done. We will conclude and analyze the various factors by reviewing relevant literature, by employing Fuzzy Delphi Method, and by in-depth interviews with real estate representatives, professors and government officials. The findings will be of great significance to future research relevant to the trading of real estate and to the development and implementation of certain government laws and policies on real estate.

## 2 Literature Review

According to the Civil law, number sixty-six, in Taiwan, the definition of real estate: The meaning of real estate refers to the land itself and the constructions built on the specific territory. According to the Law of real estate agency management, the definition of real estate means the land itself and the constructions built on the specific territory, houses, and other transferable rights. Furthermore, according to the stock exchange law on real estate, number 4, item 1, the definition of real estate refers to land, remodeled buildings, roads, bridges, tunnels, railway, piers, parking lots and any constructions that

J.-L. Chen et al. (Eds.): WiCON 2018, LNICST 264, pp. 247–253, 2019.
https://doi.org/10.1007/978-3-030-06158-6_25

are of value, and facilities that are set up on the land, but the buildings, facilities, and constructions become valueless if taken away from the land. In addition, the value of the land, that of the facilities, and that of the constructions become depreciated because of the deprivation of the land. Thus, these are what the real estate means.

# 3 Methodology

## 3.1 Setting up the Factors and Criteria

The objective of this study is to investigate and compare the various factors that affect the register of real estate sold price by means of Fuzzy Delphi Method. To maintain the authenticity of the current study and to keep its originality of the multi-criteria decision making, we invited real estate marketers, university professors, government officials, and experts to talk at interviews and to take part in our questionnaire. After collecting and analyzing these relevant factors, we used Fuzzy Delphi Method for quantification and description.

## 3.2 Fuzzy Delphi Method

Fuzzy Delphi Method was proposed by Ishikawa et al. [1, 2], and it was derived from the traditional Delphi technique and fuzzy set theory. Delphi method can direct measure perception of service, performance service quality measurement [3]. Noorderhaben indicated that applying the Fuzzy Delphi Method to group decision can solve the fuzziness of common understanding of expert opinions [4]. As for the selection of fuzzy membership functions, previous research was usually based on triangular fuzzy number, trapezoidal fuzzy number and Gaussian fuzzy number. This study applied the Two Triangle Fuzzy Numbers method and the Gray statistics method theory to solving the group decision [5]. This research applied FDM for the screening of alternate factors. The fuzziness of common understanding of experts could be solved by using the fuzzy theory and could be evaluated on a more flexible scale. The efficiency and quality of questionnaires could be improved. Thus, more objective evaluation factors could be screened through the statistical results. The scores we got will fall on a continuum between the smallest value and the largest value. The latter is called the most optimistic value whereas the former is called the most conservative value.

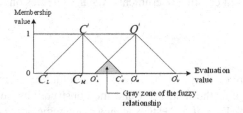

Two Triangle Fuzzy Numbers Method                    Source : Zheng Changbin, 2001

**Table 1.** Scores obtained by screen results of evaluation under the "Function" dimension

| Evaluation item | Conservative value | | Optimistic value | | Single value | | Geeometric mean | | | Verification value | | | Expert consensus |
|---|---|---|---|---|---|---|---|---|---|---|---|---|---|
| | Min | Max | Min | Max | Min | Max | $C^i$ | $O^i$ | $a^i$ | $M^i$ | $Z^i$ | $M^i \cdot Z^i$ | $G^i$ |
| Leasing | 5 | 8 | 9 | 10 | 5 | 10 | 6.70 | 9.32 | 8.03 | 2.62 | −1.00 | 3.62 | 8.01 |
| Residence | 3 | 9 | 8 | 10 | 6 | 10 | 6.10 | 9.38 | 7.59 | 3.28 | 1.00 | 2.28 | 8.32 |
| Shop | 3 | 8 | 8 | 10 | 6 | 10 | 6.21 | 9.10 | 7.79 | 2.89 | 0.00 | 2.89 | 7.66 |
| Investment | 5 | 8 | 8 | 10 | 7 | 9 | 6.21 | 8.65 | 7.7 | 2.44 | 0.00 | 2.44 | 7.43 |

**Table 2.** Scores obtained by screen results of evaluation under the "Management" dimension

| Evaluation item | Conservative value | | Optimistic value | | Single value | | Geometric mean | | | Verification value | | | Expert consensus |
|---|---|---|---|---|---|---|---|---|---|---|---|---|---|
| | Min | Max | Min | Max | Min | Max | $C^i$ | $O^i$ | $a^i$ | $M^i$ | $Z^i$ | $M^i$-$Z^i$ | $G^i$ |
| Public | 4 | 10 | 7 | 10 | 6 | 10 | 6.30 | 8.41 | 7.53 | 2.11 | 3.00 | −0.89 | 7.83 |
| Private | 6 | 10 | 7 | 10 | 6 | 9 | 8.82 | 8.42 | 7.22 | −0.40 | 3.00 | −3.40 | 8.64 |

**Table 3.** Scores obtained by screen results of evaluation under the "Content" dimension

| Evaluation item | Conservative value | | Optimistic value | | Single value | | Geometric mean | | | | Verification value | | | Expert consensus |
|---|---|---|---|---|---|---|---|---|---|---|---|---|---|---|
| | Min | Max | Min | Max | Min | Max | $C^i$ | $O^i$ | $a^i$ | $M^i$ | $Z^i$ | $M^i$-$Z^i$ | $G^i$ |
| Size of building | 5 | 8 | 9 | 10 | 5 | 10 | 6.64 | 9.32 | 8.03 | 2.68 | −1.00 | 3.68 | 7.98 |
| Price of building | 5 | 9 | 9 | 10 | 6 | 10 | 7.51 | 9.59 | 7.65 | 2.08 | 0.00 | 2.08 | 8.55 |
| Location of building | 3 | 8 | 8 | 10 | 6 | 10 | 6.21 | 9.38 | 7.79 | 3.17 | 0.00 | 3.17 | 7.80 |
| Age of building | 5 | 8 | 6 | 10 | 7 | 9 | 6.21 | 8.35 | 7.7 | 2.14 | 2.00 | 0.14 | 7.14 |

**Table 4.** Scores obtained by screen results of evaluation under the "Category" dimension

| Evaluation item | Conservative value | | Optimistic value | | Single value | | Geometric mean | | | Verification value | | | Expert consensus |
|---|---|---|---|---|---|---|---|---|---|---|---|---|---|
| | Min | Max | Min | Max | Min | Max | $C^i$ | $O^i$ | $a^i$ | $M^i$ | $Z^i$ | $M^i$-$Z^i$ | $G^i$ |
| Land | 4 | 10 | 8 | 10 | 5 | 9 | 6.01 | 9.10 | 7.53 | 3.09 | 2.00 | 1.09 | 8.43 |
| Building | 5 | 9 | 8 | 10 | 7 | 9 | 6.51 | 9.18 | 8.05 | 2.67 | 1.00 | 1.67 | 8.32 |
| Studio apartment condo | 4 | 10 | 6 | 10 | 5 | 9 | 7.73 | 8.40 | 7.07 | 0.67 | 4.00 | -3.33 | 8.06 |
| Townhouse | 6 | 9 | 8 | 10 | 7 | 9 | 8.08 | 9.24 | 7.97 | 1.16 | 1.00 | 0.16 | 8.57 |
| Shop | 4 | 10 | 7 | 10 | 5 | 9 | 8.49 | 8.55 | 7.25 | 0.06 | 3.00 | -2.94 | 8.52 |
| Commercial business buildings | 3 | 10 | 7 | 10 | 5 | 10 | 6.06 | 9.02 | 7.98 | 2.96 | 3.00 | -0.04 | 7.81 |
| Factory office | 4 | 10 | 6 | 10 | 5 | 10 | 6.18 | 8.85 | 7.72 | 2.67 | 4.00 | -1.33 | 7.71 |
| Barn storage | 3 | 9 | 7 | 10 | 6 | 10 | 5.78 | 8.61 | 7.70 | 2.83 | 2.00 | 0.83 | 7.67 |

*Source* This study

## 4   Questionnaire

Based on the previous studies related on the register of real estate sold price, before the designing of our questionnaire, we also take into the consideration the criteria, the appropriateness, the feasibility and legislation of the register system. We divided the questionnaire into four primary themes or categories. They are functions of real estate, managements of real estate, contents of real estate, and types of real estate, each focusing on the specific areas in which experts might consider register of real estate sold price distinctively from government officials.

## 5   Data Analysis and Results

The focus of this study targets to investigate and compare the various factors that influence the sold price of real estate by means of Fuzzy Delphi Method. Due to the special knowledge in real estate occupation, various professionals, including real estate marketers, university professors and relevant government officials, take part in the questionnaire for our analysis. Next, the analysis of our questionnaire is as following (Tables 1, 2, 3 and 4).

## 6   Conclusion

The purpose of this study is to investigate and compare the various factors that influence the sold price of real estate. Based on the previous analyses, the findings revealed that the factors of "residence", "privacy", "townhouse", and "reasonable price" are the most significant factors stimulating the register of real estate sold price. This finding is of major importance to the lawmaking and policy making with regards to the real estate, which requires long-term observation and flexible evaluation.

## References

1. Ishikawa, A., Amagasa, M., Shiga, T., Tomizawa, G., Tatsuta, R., Mieno, H.: The max-min Delphi method and fuzzy Delphi method via fuzzy integration. Fuzzy Sets Syst. **55**, 241–253 (1993)
2. Shiau, T.-A., Liu, J.-S.: Developing an indicator system for local governments to evaluate transport sustainability strategies. Ecol. Indic. **34**, 361–371, Nov (2013)

# Factors Influencing Online Group Buying in Taiwan: An Empirical Study Based on the TPB Framework

Chih-Ching Hung[1], Nai-Chang Cheng[2], Shang-En Yu[3]([⊠]),
and Hong-Tsu Young[1]

[1] Department of Mechanical Engineering, National Taiwan University,
Taiwan, China
{d96522004, hyoung}@ntu.edu.tw
[2] Tainan Human Resources Association, Taiwan, China
chengnaichang@gmail.com
[3] Department of Tourism, Ming Chuan University, Taiwan, China
yushine@mail.mcu.edu.tw

**Abstract.** The motivation behind this paper is to give a clarification of elements impacting on the web aggregate purchasing of Taiwanese adopter of online gathering purchasing, which can help the professionals of Taiwan to grow better market techniques. An observational review was utilized to test the speculations. A structural equation modeling (SEM) is proposed to survey the connections of the exploration show. Finding – The discoveries in this paper demonstrate that the emotional standards and state of mind toward online gathering purchasing are critical factors in anticipating the buyer goal of purchasing together in Taiwan. Additionally, the apparent trust and helpfulness are huge to enhance the state of mind. Down to earth suggestions – The outcomes in the paper encourage to comprehend what empowers and hinders the buy aim of adopters of online music in Taiwan. The estimation of this paper is to build up a hypothetical model consolidating an expansion of trust and TAM model with TPB to explore the buy conduct of OGB in Taiwan. The consequences of this investigation help OGB specialists of Taiwan and other Asian countries culture like Taiwan to make a win plan of action.

**Keywords:** Online group buying · Theory of planned behavior
Theory of planned behavior

## 1 Introduction

Gathering purchasing is the point at which a thing must be purchased in a base amount or dollar sum, and a few people consent to approach the seller so as to get rebates. The customers advantage by paying less, and the business benefits by offering numerous things without a moment's delay (Kauffman and Wang 2002). Because of the clients pick aggregate acquisition to get bring down costs and to upgrade haggling power, assemble purchasing conduct has moved toward becoming amazingly popular. (Umit Kucuk and Krishnamurthy 2007). Gathering purchasing additionally is a shopping

J.-L. Chen et al. (Eds.): WiCON 2018, LNICST 264, pp. 254–262, 2019.
https://doi.org/10.1007/978-3-030-06158-6_26

methodology beginning in social orders with predominately Chinese societies, and the wonder has been best in China, where purchasers have utilized the intensity of this approach. The ascent of the Web has caused a fast increment in online gathering purchasing (OGB) populace. Unique in relation to customary gathering guying, OGB individuals are associated over Web, and a large portion of them are outsiders. It is currently to a great degree prevalent, with one surely understood gathering purchasing site's income hopping from NT$13 million 2008 August to NT$27 million toward the finish of 2008, and a normal of in excess of 700 new gatherings being set up every day. These figures show that an ever increasing number of individuals are utilizing the Web in imaginative approaches to set aside extra cash. By utilizing OGB, it is anything but difficult to discover more individuals in a brief timeframe to share cargo costs and to purchase in mass in order to bring down costs. It is additionally less demanding to get greater rebates when more individuals partake in a gathering buy. Moreover, online gathering purchasers will typically take the suggestions, alerts and remarks that show up on related social association into thought before making a buy. Such social cooperations therefore work as the primary wellspring of emotional standards in this procedure, since they will impact web based shopping choices. Along these lines, as the focal point of this examination is OGB, the possibility of the abstract standards should think about (Grabner-Kraeuter 2002; Hsu and Lu 2004; Yu et al. 2005). Likewise, the idea of self-viability is utilized as seen conduct control (Ajzen 2002; Hsu et al. 2007), which implies the impression of the straightforwardness or trouble of the OGB conduct. The reason for this examination is to all the more likely comprehend the inspirations driving a client's choice to buy through OGB site. We start with the TPB hypothetical viewpoints for researching client buy inspiration, as this should empower a more far reaching examination of acknowledgment of OGB. We at that point introduce the examination strategy and discoveries. At last, we finish up the paper with an exchange on the ramifications of our investigation for hypothesis and work on, bringing up constraints and zones for future research in the mean time.

## 2    Literature Review

### 2.1    Theory Used in Online Behavior Related Studies

Online group buying (OGB) is considered as an uncommon kind of procurement conduct, and has turned out to be more prominent in Taiwan as of late. The choice to attempt aggregate purchasing could be impacted by the potential forerunners, for example, individual and social elements. The theory of planned behavior (TPB) and technology acceptance model (TAM) are generally used to talk about the impacts of these forerunners on conduct. Notwithstanding, a reconciliation of these two methodologies would permit a more extensive comprehension of gathering purchasing conduct. Figure 1 illustrates the research model. The research model was constructed in light of the TPB and TAM. This model breaks down the state of mind segment into apparent value, saw usability and trust. In mix, state of mind toward the conduct, emotional standards, and saw social control prompt the arrangement of a social intention (Ajzen and Fishbein 2005). Every one of the builds in this examination demonstrate and the hypotheses are point by point in Fig. 1.

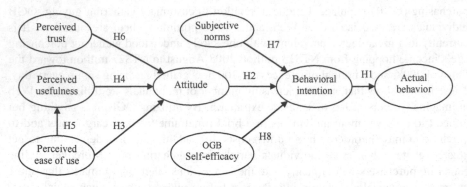

**Fig. 1** Research model

## 2.2 Theory of Planned Behavior (TPB)

The TPB is a theory about the connection amongst states of mind and conduct, and is a standout amongst the most prescient influence speculations. It has been connected to investigations of the relations among convictions, demeanors, goals and practices in different fields.

According to the TPB, if individuals assess the recommended conduct as positive (state of mind), and in the event that they think their huge others needed them to play out the conduct (emotional standards), this outcomes in a higher expectation (motivation), and they will probably participate in such conduct. Numerous investigations affirm that demeanors effectsly affect expectation, and in this way on behavior (Ajzen and Fishbein 1975; Vijayasarathy 2004). Therefore, this study proposes the following hypotheses:

*H1.*    Intention toward OGB has a positive effect on OGB behavior.
*H2.*    Attitude toward OGB has a positive effect on OGB intention.

## 2.3 Technology Acceptance Model (TAM)

The TAM is a data frameworks theory that models how clients come to acknowledge and utilize an innovation. The model proposes that when clients are given another innovation, various variables impact their choice about how and when they will utilize it. TAM declares that states of mind toward new innovation are controlled by seen handiness (PU) and saw usability (PEOU) (Davis 1989). In this examination, PU is characterized as "how much a man trusts that utilizing a specific framework would upgrade a man conduct expectation". Conversely, PEOU is characterized as "how much a man trusts that utilizing a specific framework would be free from exertion In the theory of TAM, PU and PEOU shape the state of mind toward expectation. Also, the PEOU of the site is decidedly identified with PU of the site. This paper thus proposes the following hypotheses:

*H3.*    Perceived usefulness (PU) has a positive effect on attitude towards OGB.
*H4.*    Perceived ease of use (PEOU) has a positive effect on attitude towards OGB.
*H5.*    Perceived ease of use (PEOU) has a positive effect on perceived usefulness (PU).

## 2.4    Perceived Trust

Ongoing investigations have incorporated the build of "trust" in the stretched out TAM to investigate customer acknowledgment of Web services (Gefen et al. 2003; Wu and Chen 2005). Seen trust has been viewed as a sort of disposition to expand the eagerness to utilize online shops or administrations.

*H6.*    Perceived trust has a positive effect on attitude towards OGB.

## 2.5    Subjective Norms

Abstract standards is characterized as "a person's impression of social standardizing weights, or pertinent others' convictions that he or she should perform such behavior (Ajzen 1991). Taiwan's soonest type of OGB can be followed back to Announcement Board Frameworks (BBS) in colleges in the mid-1990s. Since those early days, and with the fast spread of the Web, VC organized around customer interests have developed fundamentally, and could reshape the manner in which purchasers and merchants direct electronic business, where individuals are as prone to be offended as they are to be enlightened (Hsu and Lu 2007; Williams and Cothrel 2000). These VC can be viewed as the real wellspring of abstract standards, since they unmistakably influence OGB expectation. This study thus proposes subjective norms have an influence on intention:

*H7.*    Subjective norms have a positive effect on OGB behavioral intentions.

## 2.6    OGB Self-efficacy

Self-viability assumes a critical part in impacting singular inspiration and conduct is the same as saw social control in the TPB demonstrate (Bandura 1982, 1986; Fishbein and Cappella 2006; Igbaria and Iivari 1995). Individuals who have high self-viability will probably perform related social expectation than those with low self-adequacy. Self-adequacy is consequently expected to encourage the shaping of social goals. OGB self-viability portrays clients' self-appraisals of their capacities to utilize an OGB site framework. In addition, it could foresee client impression of conduct control towards site administrations. Accordingly, we hypothesize:

*H8.*    OGB self-efficacy has a positive effect on OGB behavioral intention.

# 3  Research Methodology

## 3.1  Measurement

Measures were picked from approved surveys utilized in earlier research when conceivable. Seen value and saw convenience were estimated utilizing things got from Davis (Davis 1989). Abstract standards, state of mind and aim were estimated utilizing things in light of Fishbein (Ajzen and Fishbein 1975). Seen trust was estimated utilizing things in light of Suh (Suh and Han 2002, 2003). At long last, OGB self-adequacy was estimated utilizing things from Compeau (Compeau and Higgins 1995).

In this examination, things used to operationalize the develops incorporated into each researched display were predominantly adjusted from past investigations for use in the internet shopping setting. This examination estimated eight develops: OGB conduct, aim, state of mind, saw value, and saw convenience, saw trust, abstract standards and OGB self-viability. Different things were utilized to quantify all builds, and all things were estimated utilizing a seven-point Likert scale (going from 1 = emphatically deviate, to 7 = firmly concur). Terms, for example, "likely", "satisfactory", and "required" were utilized to survey clients' expectations. Genuine conduct was estimated utilizing two things from shopping recurrence and amount.

## 3.2  Sampling and Data Collection

This investigation centers around OGB clients in Taiwan. We for the most part embrace online field studies since they have a few favorable circumstances over conventional paper-based mail-in-surveys (Tan and Teo 2000). In particular, they are less expensive to direct, inspire quicker reactions and are geologically unhindered. Also, such studies have been broadly utilized lately, and Web specialists are coming to acknowledge online research (Wright 2005).

# 4  Result and Analyses

## 4.1  Statistical Analyses

This investigation tried the proposed demonstrate utilizing SEM, a ground-breaking second-age multivariate procedure for dissecting causal models including an estimation of the accompanying two segments: the estimation and the basic models (Hair et al. 2006; Joreskog and Sorbom 1997; Maruyama 1997). In our examination, the product Amos 8 was utilized so as to survey the estimation and the basic models, with the previous tried before the last mentioned. The estimation show determines how speculative builds are estimated as far as the watched factors, (for example, self-viability, goal and conduct). Besides, the basic model determines the causal connections among the inert variables(Anderson and Gerbing 1988).

## 4.2    Tests of the Structural Model

We examined the structural equation model by testing the hypothesized relationships among various constructs, as shown in Fig. 2

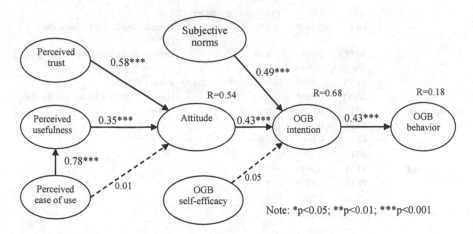

**Fig. 2** Results of SEM analysis

The results support the influence of OGB intention on behavior ($\beta = 0.43$, $p < 0.001$), supporting H1. The hypothesized paths from attitude toward OGB is significant in the prediction of OGB intention ($\beta = 0.43$, $p < 0.001$), supporting H2. Consistent with our expectations, the perceived ease-of-use (PEOU) was positively related to the perceived usefulness (PU) ($\beta = 0.8$; $p < 0.001$). The other path coefficients of PU to attitude toward OGB was statistically positively significant ($\beta = 0.35$; $p < 0.001$), but was insignificant ($\beta = 0.01$; $p > 0.05$). The path from PEOU cannot explain observed variance in attitude. Therefore, Hypotheses 3 and 4 are supported. The hypothesized paths from trust is significant in the prediction of OGB ($\beta = 0.58$, $p < 0.001$), supporting H5. The effect of subjective norms on behavioral intention was also significant ($\beta = 0.49$; $p < 0.001$), supporting H6. More specifically, subjective norms and attitude explain 70% of the variance in OGB intention. For the last hypothesis, we examined the personal factor of perceived behavioral control with self-efficacy, and the results did not support H7 ($\beta = 0.05$; $p > 0.05$).

Table 1 shows the SEM analysis has a good fit, as seen from the goodness of fit indices (GFI = 0.842; AGFI = 0.808; CFI = 0.935; RMSEA = 0.072), and the chi-square index is significant ($\chi^2 = 865.372$; d.f. = 308; $\chi^2$/d.f. = 2.81). The results indicate that the research model exhibited a satisfactory overall fit to the collected data and was capable of providing a reasonable explanation of users' acceptance of OGB.

**Table 1.** Overall fit indices of the CFA model

| Fit index | | Scores | Recommended cut-off value | Reference |
|---|---|---|---|---|
| Absolute fit measures | $\chi^2$ | 566.759 | Near to degree of freedom | |
| | d.f. | 218 | The higher, the better | |
| | GFI | 0.886* | $\geq 0.80$ | Etezadi-Amoli and Farhoomand (1996) |
| | RMR | 0.088 | $\leq 0.05$ | Browne and Cudeck (1992) |
| | RMSEA | 0.068* | $\leq 0.08$ | |
| | ECVI | 1.956* | Between 1.766 ∼ 2.169 | Kline (2004) |
| | AGFI | 0.843* | $\geq 0.9$ | Hayduk (1989), Ullman and Bentler (2004) |
| Incremental fit measures | NFI | 0.922** | $\geq 0.9$ | |
| | TLI | 0.942** | $\geq 0.9$ | |
| | CFI | 0.950** | $\geq 0.9$ | |
| | RFI | 0.950** | $\geq 0.9$ | |
| Parsimonious fit measures | PNFI | 0.794** | >0.5 | |
| | PCFI | 0.819** | >0.5 | |
| | $\chi^2$/d.f. | 2.600** | Between 1 ∼ 3 | |

Acceptability: ** (acceptable), * (marginal).

## 5  Discussion

This examination looks at OGB in view of TAM factors that were hypothetically legitimized to impact apparent convenience and saw usability, and an exploration model to research innovation acknowledgment was created and experimentally analyzed, utilizing reactions from 348 clients of an OGB site. This examination uncovers OGB conduct goal can be anticipated by the proposed demonstrate (R2 = 68%). Seen trust has an effect on OGB demeanor. The aim to utilize OGB is chiefly emphatically impacted by abstract standards and state of mind toward site (bolstered by the greater part of the individual ways hypothesized by TPB), yet it isn't altogether affected by the apparent conduct control (OGB self-viability) as to OGB goal. At the end of the day, self-viability (trust in site capacities) isn't a determinant of utilization expectation. Numerous clients are sure to utilize sites for shopping since they officially connected with numerous exchanges previously all in all online stores. The "apparent value" was found to have solid impact on their social aims to utilize. Further, saw trust is likewise a predecessor of the state of mind toward OGB, and this, thus, impacts the OGB aim.

## 6  Conclusion and Implications

This investigation gives a hypothetical comprehension of the variables adding to OGB conduct. This examination gives a convincing hypothetical structure to directing an observational examination for this line of research, and future works can stretch out this to all the more likely explore web based shopping. For training this examination likewise gives some experimental recommendations to OGB conduct. To start with, originators ought to enhance the ease of use of online gathering shopping frameworks, making them both simpler to utilize and more available. Second, with a specific end goal to expand the impact of emotional standards on clients, we prescribe that site specialists should fabricate trust and input systems into their destinations. What's more, VCs should center around uniting individuals to associate through visit rooms and gatherings, where they can share individual data and thoughts regarding different online gathering shopping points.

# References

Ajzen, I.: The theory of planned behavior. Organ. Behav. Hum. Decis. Process. **50**(2), 179–211 (1991)

Ajzen, I.: Perceived behavioral control, self-efficacy, locus of control, and the theory of planned behavior. J. Appl. Soc. Psychol. **32**(4), 665–683 (2002)

Ajzen, I., Fishbein, M.: Belief, Attitude, Intention, and Behavior: An Introduction to Theory and Research. Addison-Wesley, MA (1975)

Ajzen, I., Fishbein, M.: The influence of attitudes on behavior. The Handbook of Attitudes, vol. 173, pp. 221 (2005)

Anderson, J.C., Gerbing, D.W.: Structural equation modeling in practice: a review and recommended two-step approach. Psychol. Bull. **103**(3), 411–423 (1988)

Bagozzi, R.P., Yi, Y.: On the evaluation of structural equation models. J. Acad. Mark. Sci. **16**(1), 74–94 (1988)

Bandura, A.: Self-efficacy mechanism in human agency. Am. Psychol. **37**(2), 122–147 (1982)

Bandura, A.: Social Foundations of Thought and Action: A Social Cognitive Theory. Prentice-Hall, Englewood Cliffs, N.J. (1986)

Chu, C.W., Lu, H.P.: Factors influencing online music purchase intention in Taiwan. Internet Res. **17**(2), 139–155 (2007)

Compeau, D., Higgins, C.A.: Computer self-efficacy: development of a measure and initial test. MIS Q. **19**(2), 189–211 (1995)

Davis, F.: Perceived usefulness, perceived ease of use, and user acceptance of information technology. MIS Q. **13**(3), 319–340 (1989)

Fishbein, M., Cappella, J.N.: The role of theory in developing effective health communications. J. Commun. **56**(1), 1–17 (2006)

Fornell, C., Larcker, D.F.: Evaluating structural equation models with unobservable variables and measurement error. J. Mark. Res. **18**(1), 39–50 (1981)

Gefen, D., Karahanna, E., Straub, D.W.: Trust and TAM in online shopping: an integrated model. MIS Q. **27**(1), 51–90 (2003)

Grabner-Kraeuter, S.: The role of consumers' trust in online-shopping. J. Bus. Ethics **39**(1), 43–50 (2002)

Hair, J.F., Black, W.C., Babin, B.J., Anderson, R.E. (2006). Multivariate data analysis: prentice hall

Hsu, C.L., Lu, H.P.: Why do people play on-line games? An extended TAM with social influences and flow experience. Inf. Manag. **41**(7), 853–868 (2004)

Hsu, C.L., Lu, H.P.: Consumer behavior in online game communities: a motivational factor perspective. Comput. Hum. Behav. **23**(3), 1642–1659 (2007)

Hsu, M.H., Ju, T.L., Yen, C.H., Chang, C.M.: Knowledge sharing behavior in virtual communities: the relationship between trust, self-efficacy, and outcome expectations. Int. J. Hum Comput Stud. **65**(2), 153–169 (2007)

Igbaria, M., Iivari, J.: The effects of self-efficacy on computer usage. Omega **23**(6), 587–605 (1995)

Joreskog, K., Sorbom, D.: LISREL 8: User's Reference Guide. Scientific Software, Lincolnwood, IL (1997)

Kauffman, R.J., Wang, B.: Bid Together, Buy Together: On the Efficacy of Group-Buying Business Models in Internet-Based Selling. CRC, FL (2002)

Maruyama, G.: Basics of Structural Equation Modeling. Sage Publications, Thousand Oaks (1997)

Pikkarainen, T., Pikkarainen, K., Karjaluoto, H., Pahnila, S.: Consumer acceptance of online banking: an extension of the technology acceptance model. Internet Res. **14**(3), 224–235 (2004)

Shih, Y., Fang, K.: The use of a decomposed theory of planned behavior to study Internet banking in Taiwan. Internet Res. **14**(3), 213–223 (2004)

Suh, B., Han, I.: Effect of trust on customer acceptance of Internet banking. Electron. Commer. Res. Appl. **1**(3–4), 247–263 (2002)

Suh, B., Han, I.: The impact of customer trust and perception of security control on the acceptance of electronic commerce. Int. J. Electron. Commer. **7**(3), 135–161 (2003)

Tan, M., Teo, T. (2000). Factors influencing the adoption of Internet banking. J. AIS, 1(1es)

Umit Kucuk, S., Krishnamurthy, S.: An analysis of consumer power on the internet. Technovation **27**(1–2), 47–56 (2007)

Vijayasarathy, L.: Predicting consumer intentions to use on-line shopping: the case for an augmented technology acceptance model. Inf. Manag. **41**(6), 747–762 (2004)

Williams, R.L., Cothrel, J. (2000). Four smart ways to run online communities. Sloan Manag. Rev. 81–91

Wright, K.B.: Researching Internet-based populations: advantages and disadvantages of online survey research, online questionnaire authoring software packages, and web survey services. J. Comput. Mediat. Commun. **10**(3), 11 (2005)

Wu, I.L., Chen, J.L.: An extension of trust and TAM model with TPB in the initial adoption of on-line tax: an empirical study. Int. J. Hum Comput. Stud. **62**(6), 784–808 (2005)

Yu, J., Ha, I., Choi, M., Rho, J.: Extending the TAM for a t-commerce. Inf. Manag. **42**(7), 965–976 (2005)

# Empirical Analysis on Price-volume Relation in the Stock Market of Shanghai and Shenzhen

Shih Yung Wei[1], Xiu-Wen Ye[2($\boxtimes$)], Cheng-Yong Liu[3],
Kuo-Chu Yang[4], and Chih-Chun Hou[2]

[1] Business School of Yulin Normal University, Yulin, China
[2] Yulin Normal University, Yulin, China
{2315405512,992965723}@qq.com
[3] Beijing Institute of Technology, Zhuhai 519088, P.R. China
[4] Department of Life-and-Death Studies, Nanhua University,
Taiwan, Republic of China

**Abstract.** In this paper, the Granger causality test is used to explore the price-volume relation of the Shenzhen Stock Exchange and the Shanghai Stock Exchange and the spillover effect during the consolidation and the bull market. The research results show that price occurs after trading volume regardless of the consolidation period or the period of entering bull market, and spillover effect is not significant during consolidation. After the stock exchanges entered the bull market the spillover effect is rather significant because the causality existed between the Shenzhen Stock Exchange and the Shanghai Stock Exchange due to stock index change.

**Keywords:** Price-volume relation · Spillover effect · Causality

## 1 Introduction

The information transfer stock market is always the concerns of financial and economic experts such as spillover effect between the markets and price-volume relationship. The relevant research topics are discussed every year but the conclusions are different. How is the spillover effect between the markets generated? Wei et al. (2011) noted that the effect spillover of the stock exchanges is not necessarily dominated by a stock exchange, and the situation may change with market and time.

In addition, scholars have different opinions on the price-volume relation: Does the price occur before volume? Does the volume occur before the price? Does the price and trading volume occur at the same time? Wei et al. (2014) indicated that the price-volume relation may change with the market and time.

The Chinese stock exchanges started to enter bull market after the second half of 2014, and had been in the consolidation period before the period. Thus, the two periods of 2014 are just the research time. This paper intends to study the price-volume relation between the two stock exchanges and explore information transfer between the two stock exchanges during the periods of consolidation and bull market.

This paper is divided into five parts. The first part presents introduction, which discusses the research motivations, and the second part reviews the past literature,

J.-L. Chen et al. (Eds.): WiCON 2018, LNICST 264, pp. 263–276, 2019.
https://doi.org/10.1007/978-3-030-06158-6_27

which discusses the price-volume relation and the spillover effect. The third part introduces the research data and methods. The main research method in this paper is to test the research data through Granger causality test. The research data included 2014 market indexes and trading volume of the Shenzhen Stock Exchange and the Shanghai Stock Exchange. The fourth part is empirical analysis, which mainly includes the empirical result report. The final part is conclusion. The conclusions and the suggestions are made based on the research results.

## 2 Literature Review

The research theme is divided into two parts: the first is price-volume relation in the Shenzhen Stock Exchange and the Shanghai Stock Exchange and the rolling stock relationship between the two stock exchanges. The relevant two literatures are introduced as follows.

### 2.1 Price-volume Relation

The empirical research on the price-volume relation can be traced back to the empirical research by Osborne (1959) and found that the stock price change is directly proportional to square root of the trading frequency. However, the research theme is to discuss relation between the stock price change and trading frequency not directly discuss the relation between the stock price and the trading volume. However, the conclusions caused many discussions on price-volume relation. The previous studies mainly discussed the relation between the price and trading volume in the same period. After the middle 1980s, the attention was paid to the causality between price and volume. These studies related to the price-volume relation of the same period found that positive relation between the price and the trading volume, such as Granger and Morgenstern (1963), Godfrey et al. (1964), Ying (1966), Crouch (1970), Clark (1973), Epps and Epps (1976), Epps (1975), Wood et al. (1985), Harris (1987), Karpoff (1987), Jain and Joh (1988), Bessembinder and Seguin (1992), Basci et al. (1996), Bessembinder et al. (1996), Cooper (1999).

However, whether the positive relation between price and volume implies that either price or trading volume can be used to estimate the other initiated another wave of studies on causality between price and volume. These studies mainly analyzed the leading and lag relation of the trading volume with the price (vice versa) to explore whether causality exists between price and trading volume such as Jaffe and Westerfield (1985), Harris (1987), Smirlock and Starks (1985), Eun and Shim (1989), Hamao et al. (1990), Jarrow (1992), Fendenia and Grammatikos (1992), Campbell and Hentschel (1992), Hiemstra and Jones (1994), Theodossiou and Unro (1995), Chiang and Chiang (1996), Brennan et al. (1998), Kumar et al. (1998), Martens and Poon (2001), Wang and Cheng (2004), Baker and Stein (2004), Leigh et al. (2004), Mazouz (2004), How et al. (2005), Cheuk et al. (2006), Gebka et al. (2006). Among the studies, some indicated the price occurs after trading volume, some indicated trading volume occurs after price, some indicated two-way feedback between the price and the trading volume, some suggested some market microstructure, behavioral finance and spillover effect, or some applied the event studies to discuss the price-volume relationship. The empirical research results have difference and the price-volume relationship between the stock markets have been widely supported.

## 2.2 Market Transfer Effect

The scholars always concern the empirical studies on correlation between the stock markets in various countries. Eun and Shim (1989) explored the correlation between the stock markets in the main countries from 1979 to 1985 and found the US stock markets are the main leading indexes. Hamao et al. (1990) studied the correlation between the US, the UK and Japan during January to October 1987. They found that the influence results: the US → Japan → the UK → Japan. The US Congress questioned the impact on UK stock markets. However, Karolyi and Stulz (1996) found that the US, Japan, the UK, Canada, and Germany correlate each other, and not only the US has the leading effect. Cheung and Mak (1992) studied the spillover effect of the main stock markets in Asian and found that Japanese stock markets have leading effect on Hong Kong, Singapore and Thailand stock markets. Roca et al. (1998) explored the stock market in Southeast Asia, found a bi-directional relation between Taiwan and the Philippines, and Singapore has leading indexes in Southeast Asia.

Especially after the financial crisis, the studies found correlation between stock markets in different regions was significant. For example, Lin et al. (1994) discussed impact of the global stock market crash in 1987 period and found that the US stock market has spillover effect on the Japanese stock market. Forbes and Rigobon (2002) studied the relation between the stock markets in various countries after the 1997 Asian Financial Crisis, and found correlation exist between Hong Kong and other countries. King and Wadhwani (1990) and Khalid and Kawai (2003) also obtained the same result.

## 3 Research Data and Research Method

The price-volume relation in the Shenzhen Stock Exchange and Shanghai Stock Exchange was discussed in this paper. The research data and the research method are introduced in two parts. The first part introduces source of the research data and the research period, and the second part is the research method. This paper is focused on the price-volume relation and the second part discusses the research methods. The paper focuses on the relationship between price and volume, and the main research methods include Unit Root Test and Granger causality test.

### 3.1 Research Data

This paper y discusses the price-volume relation and the spillover effect in the Shenzhen Stock Exchange and Shanghai Stock Exchange during the period of 2014/1/1–2014/12/31. The data were sourced from the Taiwan Economic Journal Database (TEJ).

The Fig. 1 shows the rise was up to 50% after the Chinese exchange markets enter the bull market in the second half of 2014. Thus, this study intended to analyze the bear market and bull market in China.

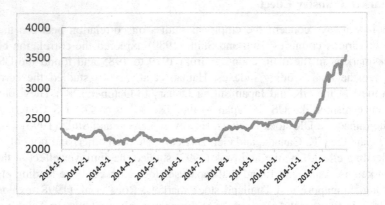

**Fig. 1.** Trend chart of HS 300 price index in 2014

Figures 2 and 3 show Shenzhen Stock Exchange and Shanghai Stock Exchange entered a bull market in the second half of 2014, and the rise exceeded 50%.

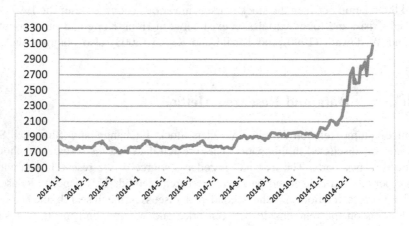

**Fig. 2.** Trend chart of Shanghai Composite Index in 2014

As shown in Figs. 4 and 5, the daily trading volume of Shenzhen Stock Exchange and Shanghai Stock Exchange increased in the second half of the year and the growth was very especially significant in Shanghai Stock Exchange.

Based on the previous research experience, the index and trading volume may have unit root, and thus it is necessary to conduct the first-order difference for the two data series. This study intended to use return rate for discussion. The calculated return rate is

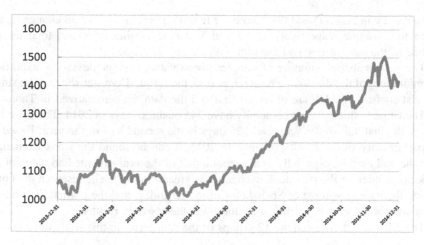

**Fig. 3** Trend chart of Shenzhen Composite Index in 2014

natural logarithm of the closing index of the t day divided by the closing index of the t-1 day. The change rate of the trading volume is the natural logarithm of the total trading volume of the t day divided by the total trading volume of the t-1 day. The return rate and the change rate are calculated as follows:

$$r_t = \left[ \ln\left( \frac{I_t}{I_{t-1}} \right) \right] \times 100 \tag{1}$$

$$v_t = \left[ \ln\left( \frac{V_t}{V_{t-1}} \right) \right] \times 100 \tag{2}$$

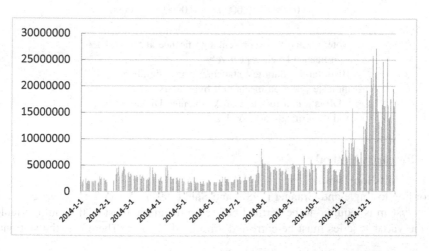

**Fig. 4.** Daily trading volume trend of Shanghai Composite Index in 2014

where r and v in Eqs. (1) and (2) denote the return rate on the index and change rate of the trading volume respectively, and I and V denote closing price and total trading volume of the current day and the total volume and t is time.

The basic statistics (number of samples, mean value, average deviation, maximum and minimum) of the data of the research period, the Jarque-Bera statistic and the single root test statistic of ADF are observed first and the data are summarized in Table 1.

The China's stock exchanges totally have 245 business days in 2014. There are 119 days in the first half of the year, and 126 days in the second half of the year. Based on the performance of the stock exchange in 2015, it can be found the stock exchanges enter the bull market, especially in the second half of the year (the median value of the stock price index of the two stock exchanges is greater than 0). The research data only include the trading volume of Shenzhen Composite Index, and the normal distribution is not significant. However, this does not affect the research results.

The ADF results showed the 12 groups of the data series in this study have no unit root.

**Table 1.** Descriptive statistics

| Period | Price | Volume | Price | Volume |
|---|---|---|---|---|
| Number | 245 | 245 | 245 | 245 |
| Mean | 0.2067 | 0.7423 | 0.1189 | 0.3078 |
| Max. | 5.3506 | 84.8025 | 3.4415 | 46.2 |
| Min. | −7.3843 | −63.5145 | −4.409 | −46.3731 |
| σ | 1.3751 | 23.1277 | 1.2099 | 15.0167 |
| JB | 293.377 | 19.1411 | 45.1502 | 2.9622 |
| | 0.0000 | 0.0000 | 0.0000 | −0.2300 |
| | *** | *** | *** | |
| ADF | −7.0225 | −21.3116 | −15.1496 | −18.8775 |
| | 0.0000 | 0.0000 | 0.0000 | 0.0000 |
| | *** | *** | *** | *** |

Note: ** and ***Represent significance at 5% and 1% significance level respectively
JB is Jarque-Bera test statistics which significantly indicate rejection meets null hypothesis
ADF is a unit root test of Augmented Dickey-Fuller, and the critical value of 1% is −3.44

## 3.2    Research Method

### 3.2.1    Unit Root Test

According to Engle and Granger (1987) and Said (1991), the stationary variable series in the system is required to be verified before co-integration test of the multivariables, and the variable series must be corrected through difference. Therefore, the stationary

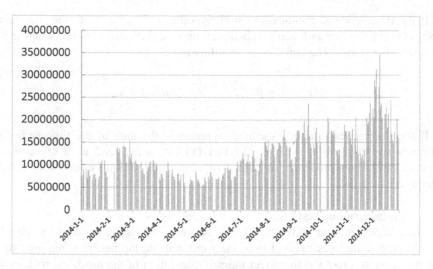

**Fig. 5.** Daily trading volume trend of 2014 Shenzhen Composite Index

distribution of the time series must be identified through the single root test. Also, the order of integration of the time series can be identified through unit root test.

According to the time-series literature by Pagan and Wickens (1989), it can be found that the unit root test includes Dickey-Fuller (DF), Augmented Dickey-Fuller (ADF) and Phillips & Perron (PP). ADF is stronger and more stable than DF. ADF and PP can solve white noise problem caused by the moving average term. The Schwert (1987) pointed out that ADF is better than PP. Thus, ADF is used to test stability of the time series in this paper.

In ADF, the regression analysis is conducted for the series lagging one period and the first-order differential lag term after the first-order difference of the non-stationary data series. First, the time tendency is not considered, and the regression equation is applied:

$$\Delta Y_t = \beta + \beta_1 Y_{t-1} + \sum_{k=1}^{n} \gamma_k \Delta T_{t-k} + \varepsilon_t \tag{3}$$

In Eq. (4), $\varepsilon_t$ is white noise process, and the appropriate lag period n is selected to make white noise uncorrelated between error terms. From Eq. (3), $\beta_1 = 0$ if $Y_t$ is not stationary, and $\beta_1 \neq 0$ if $Y_t$ is stationary. Thus, the statistical test is assumed to be

$H_0$    $\beta_1 = 0$ (when $Y_t$ data series has unit root, it is non-stationary time series)
$H_1$    $\beta_1 \neq 0$ (when $Y_t$ data series has no unit root, it is stationary time series).

If the time series $Y_t$ cannot reject null hypothesis $H_0$ after ADF, the data series needs further difference and then is substituted into the ADF model to test whether it is stationary time series. The equation is as follows:

$$\Delta dY_t = \beta + \beta_1 Y_{t-1} + \sum_{k=1}^{n} \gamma_k \Delta dT_{t-k} + \varepsilon_t \tag{4}$$

If the time series $Y_t$ rejects the null hypothesis, the data of the time series are stationary and conform to ARMA. ($Y_t$) is I (1) data series, and most of economic variables often show properties of I (1). I (d) shows the stationary state after d-order difference of the data.

### 3.2.2    Co-integration Test

The most important issue of the time series research is to select the most suitable lag periods. According to Schwert (1987), the most suitable lag period is required to be determined in unit root test to correct the self-correlation of the residuals, making the residual terms exhibit white noise process. If the lag period is too long, the model may have over-parameterization. The estimated results have no efficiency. In contrast, the selected lag period is too short, deviation may occur due to Parsimonious Parameterization. The above two situations may affect the model analysis and operation and further affect results evaluation. Thus, selection of lag periods should be careful in the economic quantitative analysis. In view of this, the optimum lag period should be generally selected by using Akaike Information Criterion (AIC). Thus, this study selected the optimum lag period based on AIC.

The general linear co-integration test method has two types: one is to use stationary characteristics of the residuals with long term equilibrium relationship to determine whether linear co-integration relationship exists between time series. The second method, as proposed by Johansen (1988), is to use maximum likelihood estimate to estimate the co-integration relationship between variables and identify the number of co-integrating vectors. This study uses the Johansen's maximum likelihood estimate to test the co-integration relation between the variables.

### 3.2.3    Granger Causality Test

Granger (1969) defined the causality between the two time series through predictive ability of the variables. According to the definition of Granger causality, another series is added by using different information sets, and the causality test is based on whether it can reduce estimate error. Granger causality refers to a statistical causality, and more accurately is called and leading and lag relation.

The two sequences X and Y are supposed. Besides X past data, if Y past data are used for estimate using X, the estimate will be more accurate. Thus, Y causes X; in contrast, if X past data are used for estimate using Y, Y estimate error can be reduced, and thus X causes Y. If the two situations occur at the same time, X and Y have feedback relationship,

Granger not only defined causality in the literature but also developed one pair of variable regression equations:

$$y_t = \alpha_0 + \alpha_1 y_{t-1} + \cdots + \alpha_1 y_{t-n} + \beta_1 x_{t-1} + \cdots + \beta_1 x_{t-n} \tag{5}$$

$$x_t = \alpha_0 + \alpha_1 x_{t-1} + \cdots + \alpha_1 x_{t-n} + \beta_1 y_{t-1} + \cdots + \beta_1 y_{t-n} \tag{6}$$

However, this regression equation has a small deficiency, which assumes that contemporaneous relation exists between X and Y in the same period. This means addition of Y (X) information in the same period is helpful for the X (Y) estimate. In this case, the test results only have three types of causality defined by Granger, i.e. independence between x and y, causality between x and y and feedback between x and y. For all the data pairs (x, y), the tested F value is Wald statistics, and the joint hypothesis is: $\beta_1 = \beta_2 = \cdots = \beta_t = 0$. In Eq. (5), the null hypothesis is x does not Granger-cause y. In Eq. (6), the null hypothesis is y does not Granger-cause x.

# 4   Empirical Analysis

## 4.1   Selection of Lag Period

The lag period is tested by AIC in Table 2. Thus, the 5th period has the minimum (3.4650) throughout 2015. Next, this study conducts co-integration analysis and uses AR (5) for the causality test. The earlier and later periods of 2015 adopt AR (1) and AR (6), and the minimum value is 2.7251 and 3.8109.

**Table 2.** AIC scale

| AR(1) | AR(2) | AR(3) | AR(4) | AR(5) | AR(6) |
|---|---|---|---|---|---|
| 3.4774 | 3.4907 | 3.5047 | 3.5056 | **3.465** | 3.4907 |

Note: the boldface represents minimum

## 4.2   Co-integration Test

Next, the Johansen co-integration test is conducted to test whether co-integration relationship exists between the four time series price and volume of Shenzhen Stock Exchange and Shanghai Stock Exchange. From Likelihood Ratio in Table 3, LR1 value is 223.7058 which is greater than the critical value 54.46 of 1%. Thus, the null hypothesis is rejected. This means at least one co-integrated variable exists. It can be deduced that co-integration exists between price and trading volume of the Shenzhen Stock Exchange and Shanghai Stock Exchange in 2015.

**Table 3.** Co-integration test of price-volume relationship of Shenzheng Stock Exchange and Shanghai Stock Exchange in 2014

| Eigen value | Likelihood ratio | Critical value | | Ho |
|---|---|---|---|---|
| | | 5% | 1% | |
| λ1 | LR1 | C1 | | 0 < R |
| λ2 | LR2 | C2 | | 1 < R |
| λ3 | LR3 | C3 | | 2 < R |
| 0.3137 | 223.7058*** | 47.21 | 54.46 | |
| 0.2506 | 133.7384*** | 29.68 | 35.65 | |
| 0.1564 | 64.78588*** | 15.41 | 20.04 | |

Note: ***Represents significance level of 5%
λ1 represents eigenvalue of the first vector
LR1 represents probability-likelihood of the first vector
C1 represents tested critical value of the first vector
R represents number of co-integrated vectors existed

### 4.3  Causality Test

Through the Granger causality test, it has been found that the price occurs before trading volume in Shenzhen Stock Exchange and Shanghai Stock Exchange (Table 4). Furthermore, the Shenzhen Index also has spillover effect on Shanghai Index and trading volume.

**Table 4.** Test results of the relation between price and trading volume in the Shenzhen Stock Exchange and Shanghai Stock Exchange throughout 2014

| Result/Cause | F-Statistic | |
|---|---|---|
| Shanghai Exchange Volume → Shanghai Composite Index | 0.7280 | No |
| Shanghai Composite Index → Shanghai Exchange Volume | 7.0521*** | Yes |
| Shenzhen Composite Index → Shanghai Composite Index | 1.9317* | Yes |
| Shanghai Composite Index → Shenzhen Composite Index | 1.2412 | No |
| Shenzhen Exchange Volume → Shanghai Composite Index | 1.2625 | No |
| Shanghai Composite Index → Shenzhen Exchange Volume | 6.1390*** | Yes |
| Shenzhen Composite Index → Shanghai Composite Index | 8.2358 | No |
| Shanghai Exchange Volume → Shanghai Composite Index | 0.6524 | No |
| Shenzhen Exchange Volume → Shenzhen Exchange Volume | 1.7630 | No |
| Shanghai Exchange Volume → Shenzhen Exchange Volume | 0.5503 | No |
| Shenzhen Exchange Volume → Shenzhen Composite Index | 0.7079 | No |
| Shenzhen Composite Index → Shenzhen Exchange Volume | 24.9110*** | Yes |

Note: ***Represents the null hypothesis is rejected when the significance level is 1%
**Represents the null hypothesis is rejected when the significance level is 5%
*Represents the null hypotheses is rejected when the significance level is 10%

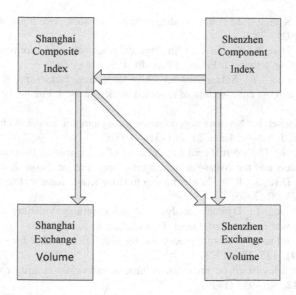

## 5 Conclusion

In this paper, the Granger causality is used to discuss the price-volume relationship between the Shenzhen Exchange Stock and the Shanghai Exchange Stock and the spillover effect. The findings are consistent with the research by Wei et al. (2011). Wei et al. (2014) indicated the market information changes. All the rules may change with time and place.

For Shenzhen Stock Exchange and Shanghai Stock Exchange, the price occurred before trading volume in any period. The spillover effect did not occur during the consolidation. However, the high stock market mobility means the markets enter the bull market. The spillover effect was very significant. The two markets are correlated and affect each other.

It can be found that the trading volume of the stock e may be affected by different markets. The stock price of the Shanghai Stock Exchange may affect the trading volume of Shenzhen Stock Exchange, and the Shenzhen Stock Exchange may have spillover effect on the Shanghai Stock Exchange. Thus, the government implements the Shanghai-Hong Kong Stock Connect. The stock exchanges has leading index.

The consolidation occurred in the first half of 2014, and the stock exchanges entered the bull market in the second half of 2014. However, it is pitiful that this study did not explore the bear market. The future research can fill in the gap.

## References

Baker, M., Stein, J.C.: Market liquidity as a sentiment indicator. J. Financ. Mark. **7**, 271–299 (2004)

Basci, E., Ozyidirim, S., Aydogan, K.: A note on price-volume dynamics in an emerging stock market. J. Bank. Financ. **20**, 389–400 (1996)

Bessembinder, H., Seguin, P.J.: Futures-trading activity and stock price volatility. J. Financ. **47**, 2015–2134 (1992)

Bessembinder, H., Chan, K., Seguin, P.J.: An empirical examination of information, difference of option, and trading activity. J. Financ. Econ. **40**, 105–134 (1996)

Brennan, M., Chordia, T., Subrahmanyam, A.: Alternative factor specifications, security characteristics, and the cross-section of expected stock returns. J. Financ. Econ. **49**, 345–373 (1998)

Campbell, J., Hentschel, L.: No news is good news: an asymmetric model of changing volatility in stock returns. J. Financ. Econ. **31**, 281–318 (1992)

Cheung, Y., Mak, S.: The international transmission of stock market fluctuation between the developed markets and the Asian-Pacific markets. Appl. Financ. Econ. **2**, 43–47 (1992)

Cheuk, M.Y., Fan, D.K., So, R.W.: Insider trading in Hong Kong: some stylized facts. Pac-Basin Finance J **14**, 73–90 (2006)

Chiang, T.C., Chiang, J.: Dynamic analysis of stock returns volatility in an integrated international capital market. Rev. Quant. Financ. Acc. **6**, 5–17 (1996)

Clark, P.K.: A subordinated stochastic process model with finite variance for speculative prices. Econometrica **41**, 135–155 (1973)

Cooper, M.: Filter rules based on price and volume in individual security overreaction. Rev. Financ. Stud. **12**, 901–935 (1999)

Crouch, R.L.: A nonlinear test of the random-walk hypothesis. Am. Econ. Rev. **60**, 199–202 (1970)

Engle, R.F., Granger, C.W.: Co-integration and error correction: representation, estimation and testing. Econometrica **55**, 251–276 (1987)

Epps, T.W., Epps, M.L.: The stochastic dependence of security price changes and transaction volumes: implications for the mixture of distributions hypothesis. Econometrica **44**, 305–321 (1976)

Epps, T.W.: Security price changes and transaction volumes: theory and evidence. Am. Econ. Rev. **65**, 586–597 (1975)

Eun, C., Shim, S.: International transmission of stock market movements. J. Financ. Quant. Anal. **24**, 241–256 (1989)

Fendenia, M., Grammatikos, T.: Options trading and the bid–ask spread of the underlying stocks. J. Bus. **65**, 335–351 (1992)

Forbes, K., Rigobon, R.: No contagion, only interdependence: measuring stock market comovements. J. Financ. **5**, 2223–2261 (2002)

Gebka, B., Henke, H., Bohl, M.T.: Institutional trading and stock return autocorrelation: empirical evidence on polish pension fund investors' behavior. Glob. Financ. J. **16**, 233–244 (2006)

Godfrey, M.D., Granger, C., Morgenstern, W.: The random walk hypothesis of stock market behavior. Kyklos **17**, 1–30 (1964)

Granger, C.: Investigating causal relations by econometric models and cross-spectral methods. Econometrica **37**, 422–438 (1969)

Granger, C., Morgenstern, W.: Spectral analysis of New York stock market prices. Kyklos **16**, 1–27 (1963)

Hamao, Y., Masulis, R.W., Ng, V.: Correlations in price changes and volatility across international stock markets. Rev. Financ. Stud. **3**, 281–307 (1990)

Harris, L.: Transaction data tests of the mixture of distributions hypothesis. J. Financ. Quant. Anal. **22**, 127–139 (1987)

Hiemstra, C., Jones, J.D.: Testing for linear and nonlinear granger causality in the stock price-volume relation. J. Financ. **49**, 1639–1664 (1994)

How, J.C.Y., Verhoeven, P., Huang, C.X.: Information asymmetry surrounding earnings and dividend announcements: an intra-day analysis. Math. Comput. Simul. **68**, 463–473 (2005)

Jaffe, J., Westerfield, R.: The weekend effect in common stock returns: the international evidence. J. Financ. **40**, 433–454 (1985)

Jain, P., Joh, G.: The dependence between hourly prices and trading volume. J. Financ. Quant. Anal. **23**, 269–284 (1988)

Jarrow, R.: Market manipulation, bubbles, corners and short squeezes. J. Financ. Quant. Anal. **27**, 311–336 (1992)

Johansen, S.: Statistical analysis of co-integration vector. J. Econ. Dyn. Control. **12**, 231–254 (1988)

Karolyi, G.A., Stulz, R.M.: Why do markets move together? An investigation of U.S.-Japan stock return comovements. J. Financ. **51**, 951–986 (1996)

Karpoff, J.M.: The relation between price changes and trading volume: a survey. J. Financ. Quant. Anal. **22**, 109–126 (1987)

Khalid, A.M., Kawai, M.: Was financial market contagion the source of economic crisis in Asia? Evidence using a multivariate VAR Model. J. Asian Econ. **14**, 131–156 (2003)

King, M., Wadhwani, S.: Transmission of volatility between stock market. Rev. Financ. Stud. **3**, 5–33 (1990)

Kumar, R., Sarin, A., Shastri, K.: The impact of options trading on the market quality of the underlying securities: an empirical analysis. J. Financ. **53**, 717–732 (1998)

Leigh, W., Modani, N., Hightower, R.: A computational implementation of stock charting: abrupt volume increase as signal for movement in New York stock exchange composite index. Decis. Support. Syst. **37**, 515–530 (2004)

Lin, W., Engle, R., Ito, T.: Do bulls and bears move across borders? International transmission of stock returns and volatility. Rev. Financ. Stud. **7**, 507–538 (1994)

Martens, M., Poon, S.H.: Returns synchronization and daily Correlation dynamics between international stock markets. J. Bank. Financ. **25**, 1805–1827 (2001)

Mazouz, K.: The effect of CBOE option listing on the volatility of NYSE traded stocks: a time-varying variance approach. J. Empir. Financ. **11**, 695–708 (2004)

Osborne, M.F.M.: Brownian motion in the stock market. Oper. Res. **7**, 145–173 (1959)

Pagan, A.R., Wickens, M.R.: A Survey of recent econometric methods. Econ. J. **99**, 962–1025 (1989)

Roca, E., Selvanathan, E., Shepherd, W.: Are the ASEAN equity markets interdependent? ASEAN Econ. Bull. **15**, 109–121 (1998)

Said, S.E.: Unit-roots test for time-series data with a linear time trend. J. Econ. **47**, 285–303 (1991)

Schwert, G.W.: Effect of model specification on tests for unit roots in macroeconomic data. J. Monet. Econ. **20**, 73–103 (1987)

Smirlock, M., Starks, L.: A further examination of stock price changes and transactions volume. J. Financ. Res. **8**, 217–225 (1985)

Wei, S.-Y., Lin, S.-H., Chen, J.-T., Wang, H.-B., You, C.-F.: An empirical study on price-volume relationship of firm size indices using the DCC-Garch model. Int. J. Econ., Commer. Manag. **2**(4), 1–8 (2014)

Weim S.-Y., Hong, W.-C., Wang, K.: Firm Size Transmission Effect and Price-volume Relationship analysis during financial tsunami periods. Int. J. Appl. Evol. Comput. **3**(3), 59–79 (2011)

Theodossiou, P., Unro L: Relationship between volatility and expected returns across international stock markets. J. Bus. Financ. Account. **22**, 289–300 (1995)

Wang, C.Y., Cheng, N.S.: Extreme volumes and expected stock returns: evidence from China's stock market. Pac. Basin Financ. J. **12**, 577–597 (2004)

Wood, R.A., Mcinish, T.H., Ord, J.K.: An investigation of transactions data for NYSE stocks. J. Financ. **60**, 723–739 (1985)

Ying, C.C.: Stock market prices and volumes of sales. Econometrica **34**, 676–685 (1966)

# Heterogeneous Goods, Strategic Investment, and First Mover Advantages: Real Options Theory and Empirical Study

Shih Yung Wei[1], Xiu-Wen Ye[2(✉)], Cheng-yong Liu[3], and Chih-Chun Hou[2]

[1] Business School of Yulin Normal University, Yulin, China
[2] Yulin Normal University, Yulin, China
2315405512@qq.com
[3] Beijing Institute of Technology, Zhuha 519088, P.R. China

**Abstract.** This study uses Real Options Analysis to receive information regarding market uncertainty. Traditional studies assume that the market is perfectly competitive and homogeneous. However, the automobile market is imperfectly competitive and its goods are heterogeneous. Automobile firms may obtain first mover advantages through irreversible investment when the market is imperfectly competitive. First mover advantages can be regarded as barriers to entry because followers cannot earn profits by entering the market and raising market share. Moreover, traditional surveys exploited the Generalized Autoregressive Conditional Heteroskedasticity (GARCH) model to estimate the uncertainty (volatility). In this study, the Kalman Filter is adopted for replacing the GARCH model to improve the weaknesses in the traditional estimation method. In this study, the significant level is 0.05, and the adjusted R2 of Toyota and Honda are 0.87 and 0.58.

**Keywords:** Real options theory · First mover advantage · Strategic investment Kalman Filter

## 1 Introduction

It is widely seen the differentiation in society, but what it means in the strategic management? For example, the electric vehicle business can be regarded as the leading industry of the future. We argue that they can be a disruptive innovation toward the automobile industry. This occurrence is similar to how digital cameras affected traditional cameras. For example, a Chinese manufacturer of automobiles and rechargeable batteries, BYD Co. Ltd., is regarded as a high potential automobile manufacturer in the automobile industry. The investment guru Warren E. Buffett has also invested in BYD Co. Ltd. because of their electric vehicle and rechargeable battery technologies.

Electric vehicles and lithium batteries are complementary technologies. Moreover, lithium battery technology is a key component of developing electric vehicles. The optimism regarding the future of the electric vehicle market has prompted most manufacturers in the automobile industry to actively invest in lithium battery R&D. In

J.-L. Chen et al. (Eds.): WiCON 2018, LNICST 264, pp. 277–294, 2019.
https://doi.org/10.1007/978-3-030-06158-6_28

Taiwan, most firms involved in the R&D of lithium battery focus on its material component and their targeted use is in power tools and electric vehicles.

When a firm is deciding on an investment plan, the characteristics of goods are classified as either substitute or complementary goods. For example, EPSON printers require the use their brand of ink cartridges, and APPLE MacBooks require the use of a Macintosh operating system. The electric vehicle market is a high potential market in the future, and electric vehicles and lithium batteries are complementary; thus, manufacturers in the automobile industry are more willing to enter the lithium battery industry. This paper examines the appropriate timing for entering the lithium battery industry to advise automobile manufacturers when they decide to invest.

Traditional methods involve exploiting the Net Present Value (NPV) to evaluate the benefits of entering a market. This method neglects the uncertainty of a market. Because the market is unpredictable, considering the uncertainty is appropriate and may raise the positive value of real options. Moreover, the traditional NPV method overlooks the irreversibility of an investment. These key elements may misestimate the value of an investment.

Several scholars suggested that the real value of an investment involves NPV and the investment's opportunity costs (McDonald and Siegel 1986; Dixit and Pindyck 1994). Moreover, delaying a project in an uncertain market is better than completing a project immediately (Kogut and Kulatilaka 1994; O'Brien et al. 2003; Alessandri et al. 2012). Delaying a project in uncertain markets and during irreversible decision-making situations may lead to positive values in delay options. Firms may delay until new information is released and only then decide to use them (McDonald and Siegel 1986; Dixit and Pindyck 1994; McGrath 1999; Bo et al. 2006; Michailidis 2006). Therefore, the value of deferral options can be regarded as a value of waiting. This characteristic of flexible decision-making is important for management and investment, but is neglected in the traditional NPV method. This study adopts the Real Options Approach (ROA) method that considers the uncertainty, irreversibility, and flexibility characteristics of a project plan to alleviate the shortcomings of the NPV method. For example, Kulatilaka and Perotti (1998) emphasized the value of a strategy under uncertainty in an imperfectly competitive market and exploited growth options to invest strategically. Tong and Reuer (2007) identified the importance of ROA for strategic management: First, ROA requires research to revisit the received wisdom, and offers unique predictions, on firms' decisions for many types of strategic decisions. Second, ROA uniquely posits an asymmetric payoff structure for investments with embedded options by suggesting that real options enable firms to reduce downside risk while accessing upside opportunities. Third, ROA sheds new light on firms' resource allocation processes by informing strategic decision making.

Cottrell and Sick (2001) argued that a pioneer may obtain a first mover advantage that can preclude followers from divvying market shares. Moreover, the irreversible investment of a firm may lead to the benefits of a first mover advantage when the market is imperfectly competitive; that is, the first mover advantage may cause barriers to entry, which may hinder followers from obtaining profits. Although the pioneer advantage may raise monopoly power, several scholars have indicated the presence of advantages for followers. For example, followers may reap benefits from the free-rider effect; that is, followers can save in R&D costs by modeling a pioneer's products

(Schnaars 1994). Moreover, followers can efficiently enter the market by learning from the experiences of a pioneer (Cottrell and Sick 2002). Several empirical studies showed that followers obtain better profits compared to the pioneer in the computer market, motorcycle industry, and electric generator market (Cottrell and Sick 2001).

Cottrell and Sick (2002) further argued that the first mover possesses advantages such as leading technologies and learning curve benefits. Lieberman and Montgomery (Leiberman and Montgomery 1998) indicated that the pioneer may have priority in choosing its suppliers. These pioneer advantages of firms may directly affect costs. Therefore, first mover advantages are important for firms to obtain profits. Whether the first mover advantage affects the profits of automobile firms that desire entering the lithium battery market is important.

Several empirical studies such as the O'Brien et al. (2003) study have traditionally exploited the Generalized Autoregressive Conditional Heteroskedasticit (GARCH) method to estimate volatility (uncertainty). However, the GARCH model cannot effectively estimate volatility. Therefore, Sommacampagna and Sick (2004) used the Kalman Filter to examine the volatility of the ratio of well drilling. Moreover, Welch and Bishop (2006) indicated that the Kalman Filter can effectively estimate uncertainty. This study implements the Kalman Filter to accurately estimate the uncertainty.

Generally, the assumption that a market is perfectly competitive simplifies the issue for discussion. However, the realization of a perfectly competitive market is difficult in practice; thus, this paper assumes that an automobile market is imperfectly competitive.

This study is organized as follows: Sect. 2 shows the theoretical model and propositions, Sect. 3 establishes the research method, Sect. 4 provides an analysis of empirical results, and Sect. 5 is the Conclusion with a discussion of future studies.

## 2 Theoretical Model

The equilibrium output of the Cournot-Nash model and the values of a firm.

This study assumes that only two firms (firm 1 and 2) exist, which sell heterogeneous goods (Goods 1 and 2) in the automobile market. The inverse demand curves are as follows[1]:

$$p_{11} = \theta_0 - a(q_{11} + q_{21}) - b(q_{12} + q_{22}) \tag{1}$$

$$p_{21} = \theta_0 - a(q_{11} + q_{21}) - b(q_{12} + q_{22}) \tag{2}$$

$$p_{12} = \theta_0 - a(q_{12} + q_{22}) - b(q_{11} + q_{21}) \tag{3}$$

$$p_{22} = \theta_0 - a(q_{12} + q_{22}) - b(q_{11} + q_{21}) \tag{4}$$

where i = 1, and i = 2 represents firm 1 and 2; j = 1, and j = 2 represents goods 1 (battery) and 2 (vehicle); $p_{i,j}$ and $q_{i,j}$ are prices and quantities; $a$ represents a vertical

---

[1] We followed Vives (1984) model setting.

differentiation of substitution and follows the law of demand; $b$ represents the level of the differentiation between Goods 1 and 2; $0 < b < 1$ represents two substitute goods; $b < 0$ represents two complementary goods.

Furthermore, this study assumes that $\theta_0$ is the initial quantity of market demand and follows the Geometric Brown Motion (GBM):

$$\frac{d\theta_0}{\theta_0} = \alpha \, dt + \sigma \, dz \tag{5}$$

where $\alpha$ and $\sigma$ are instantaneous drift and standard deviation, respectively; $dz$ is the incremental Wiener process.

Moreover, this study assumes that there is no variable cost. Therefore, under the Cournot competition of Stage 2 at time t, the maximum profits of the firm $i$ are the following:

$$\text{Max } \pi_i(q_{i,2}, q_{j,2}, \theta) = (\theta_0 - aq_{i,2} - bq_{j,2})q_{i,2}, i \neq j \tag{6}$$

Let $V_i$ represent gross project value and the $NPV_i$ can be calculated as follows:

$$V_i = E\left[\int_0^\infty e^{-rt} \cdot \pi_i(\theta)dt\right] = \frac{\pi_i}{n \cdot \delta} \tag{7}$$

and

$$NPV_i = V_i - I \tag{8}$$

where $\pi_i$ represents the cumulative profit flow at time $t$, n is defined by the type of market competition, and $\delta = \sigma^2 + 2\alpha - r$ represents the constant equilibrium and risk-adjusted discount rate.

Under the Cournot-Nash competition, the reaction functions of these two equations are as follows:

$$R_i(q_{j2}) = \frac{\theta_0 - bq_{j2}}{2b} \tag{9a}$$

and

$$R_j(q_{i2}) = \frac{\theta_0 - bq_{i2}}{2b} \tag{9b}$$

The Cournot-Nash equilibrium is

$$q*_{1c} = q*_{2c} = \frac{\theta_0}{2a + b} \tag{10}$$

Therefore, under the condition of the duopoly market, the profit of firm $i$ is

$$\pi_{ic} = \frac{a\theta_0^2}{(2a+b)^2}, \ i = 1, 2 \tag{11}$$

Equation (11) indicates that the two goods are complementary goods when $b < 0$, and the two goods are substitute goods when $0 < b < 1$. Furthermore, the profits of the two firms can be affected by the duopoly market when the two goods are substitute goods. Moreover, under the Cournet-Nash equilibrium, the gross value of the project is

$$V_{ic} = \frac{a\theta_0^2}{\delta'(2a+b)^2}, \ i = 1, 2 \tag{12}$$

However, under a monopoly, the gross project value is

$$V_{1m} = \frac{\theta_0^2}{4a\delta'} \tag{13}$$

From Eqs. (12) and (13), the results are similar to the outcomes of the Cournot-Nash equilibrium and monopoly. When $a$ decreases, the $\theta_0$ and project value increases.

Competitors are a main consideration for firms that want to enter a market. When a pioneer enters into a new market, a monopoly may result and all the excess profits in the new market may be obtained. However, excess market profits may attract followers.

Following is the situation that occurs when followers enter a market, divvying the market share when a first mover possesses a monopoly.

## 2.1 The Strategy of Followers

Presuming that $\theta_0$ follows the Geometric Brown Motion (GBM),

$$\frac{d\theta_0}{\theta_0} = \alpha \, dt + \sigma \, dz$$

By using Ito's Lemma, the value of the investment can be expressed as

$$dV = \left( \alpha\theta_0 V' + \frac{1}{2}\sigma^2\theta_0^2 V'' + V_t \right)\vec{d}t + \sigma\theta_0 \vec{V}dz \tag{14}$$

The McDonald and Siegel (1986) study indicated that projects are valuable until exercised. Therefore, the present value can be a downward or return to zero. However, maturity is infinite; thus, the value of a project is unrelated to time maturity; thus, $V_t = 0$.

Let $V' = \partial V/\partial\theta_0$, $V'' = \partial^2 V/\partial\theta_0^2$, $V_t = \partial V/\partial t$, and the Bellman equation is followed; thus, Eq. (14) can be expressed as follows:

$$\alpha\theta_0 V' + \frac{1}{2}\sigma^2\theta_0^2 V'' + V_t - rV + \left[\frac{a\theta_0^2}{(2a+b)^2}\right] = 0 \qquad (15)$$

Thereafter, the value of the project $V_{ic}$ is

$$V_j(\theta) = A_{ic}\theta_0^{\beta_1} + B_{ic}\theta_0^{\beta_2} + \left[\frac{a\theta_0^2}{(2a+b)^2}\right]\frac{1}{\delta'} \qquad (16)$$

where $A_{ic}$ and $B_{ic}$ are endogenous constants, and $\beta_1$ and $\beta_2$ follow the quadratic form:

$$\frac{1}{2}\sigma^2\beta(\beta-1) + \alpha\beta - \gamma = 0$$

Moreover, $\beta_2$ should be greater than 0 to avoid the Bubble solution; thus, $\beta_{ic}$ is equal to 0. The solutions of $\beta_1$ and $\beta_2$ are the following:

$$\beta_1 = \frac{1}{2} - \frac{\alpha}{\sigma^2} + \sqrt{\left(\frac{\alpha}{\sigma^2} - \frac{1}{2}\right)^2 + \frac{2r}{\sigma^2}} > 0 \ (>0) \qquad (17a)$$

$$\beta_2 = \frac{1}{2} - \frac{\alpha}{\sigma^2} + \sqrt{\left(\frac{\alpha}{\sigma^2} - \frac{1}{2}\right)^2 + \frac{2r}{\sigma^2}}(<0) \qquad (17b)$$

Assuming that the followers suffer the same barrier to entry, the firm with the monopoly may maintain the sale quantity of their product. Furthermore, Eq. (16) shows the project value of firm $j$ after firm $i$ entered the market. When $A_{ic}$ and $B_{ic}$ are equal to 0 for firm $j$, the project value of the followers in the duopoly are as follows:

$$V_j(\theta_0) = \left[\frac{a\theta_0^2}{(2a+b)^2}\right]\frac{1}{\delta'} \qquad (18)$$

The NPV of the project exercised by firm $j$ is

$$NPV_j(\theta_0) = V_j(\theta_0) - I \qquad (19)$$

where $I$ represents the fixed cost of the project.

Moreover, let $\theta_i$ be the market demand of followers. When $\theta_i \geq \theta$, the NPV of the implemented project is

$$NPV_j(\theta_i; \theta) = E_\theta\{[V_j(\theta_i) - I]e^{-rt}\} \qquad (20)$$

where $E_{\theta_0}$ is the risk-neutral expectation operator.

$$T \equiv T(\theta_j; \theta_0) = inf(t \geq 0 : \theta \geq 0, \theta_0 = \theta)$$

then

$$E_{\theta_0}[e^{-rt}] = \left(\frac{\theta_0}{\theta_j}\right)^{\beta_1}$$

When $\theta_i^* \geq \theta_0$, firm $j$ (follower) implements the option to gain NPV.

$$NPV_i(\theta_i; \theta_0) = \left[\frac{a\theta_i^2}{(2a+b)^2} \cdot \frac{1}{\delta'} - I\right] \times (\theta/\theta_0)^{\beta_1} \tag{21}$$

The best choice for firm j is to implement its option when $\theta_i > \theta$. Therefore, under the condition of maximum profit and $\theta_i > \theta$, the optimal threshold is

$$\theta_j^* = \frac{\beta_1}{\beta_1 - 2} \cdot \frac{(2a+b)^2}{a\theta_0^2} \cdot \delta' \cdot I \tag{22}$$

where $\delta' = \sigma^2 + 2\alpha - r$.

Proposition 1: $\frac{\partial \theta_j^*}{\partial a} > 0$

The parameter "a" represents the degree of substitution between two goods. The barrier to entry increases as the degree of substitution between two goods increases. High substitution indicates that two goods possess low differentiation. Followers are insignificantly advantaged because of a high substitution degree (or low differentiation); that is, followers need to invest more resources into producing goods to earn profits. When the pioneer's high quality product attracts consumers, followers need to produce higher quality products to compete with the pioneer; thus, the threshold value of entering the market rises.

Proposition 2: $\frac{\partial \theta_j^*}{\partial b} > 0$

The parameter "b" represents the substitution between two goods. A higher degree of substitution (b > 0) indicates a higher threshold of market entry. Conversely, a lower degree of substitution (b < 0) indicates a lower threshold of market entry. When products produced by two firms are complementary, the pioneer may benefit from the entry of followers, which attracts more consumers into the market. Moreover, the degree of complement between two goods indicates that two goods are differential; thus, the threshold of market entry may decrease.

Proposition 3: $\frac{\partial \theta_j^*}{\partial \delta'} > 0$

The threshold of market entry decreases with a lower cost of capital, which may reduce risk. Therefore, the risk-adjusted interest rate may lower the threshold of market entry.

Proposition 4: $\frac{\partial \theta_j^*}{\partial I} > 0$

The threshold of market entry increases with the level of investment. Firms consider their capacity when planning to enter a market. Therefore, a high investment cost increases the threshold of market entry.

**Proposition 5:** $\frac{\partial \theta_j^*}{\partial \sigma} > 0$

The uncertainty in a market increases the risk-adjusted interest rate. Therefore, the threshold of market entry increases when the market is uncertain.

### 2.2    Market Entry Strategy of Pioneer

A pioneer can earn profits associated with the monopoly until followers enter the market. The value of the pioneer $V_i$ must satisfy the following quadratic differential equation:

$$\frac{1}{2}\sigma^2 \theta_0^2 V_i''(\theta) + V_t + \alpha \theta V_i'(\theta) - rV_i + \left(\frac{\theta_0^2}{4a}\right) = 0 \tag{23}$$

where $V' = \partial V/\partial \theta_0$, $V'' = \partial^2 V/\partial \theta_0^2$, $V_t = \partial V/\partial t$, and $V_t = 0$.

Thereafter, the function of the pioneer's investment value of can be expressed as the following:

$$V_i(\theta) = A_1 \theta_0^{\beta_1} + A_2 \theta_0^{\beta_2} + \left[\frac{\theta_0^2}{4a}\right] \cdot \frac{1}{\delta'} \tag{24}$$

When potential competitors abandon the market ($A_2$), Eq. (24) results in 0. The function of the pioneer's investment value can be revised to the following:

$$V_L(\theta) = A_1 \theta_0^{\beta_1} + \left[\frac{\theta_0^2}{4a}\right] \cdot \frac{1}{\delta'} \tag{25}$$

Followers enter the market at time t. The market structure transforms the monopoly into an oligopoly. Thereafter, the investment value of the pioneer becomes equal to the outcome of the Cournot-Nash model. Moreover, the value-matching condition indicates that the value of the option becomes equal to the value of investment:

$$V_i\left(\theta_j^*\right) = V_0\left(\theta_j^*\right) \tag{26}$$

Thereafter, the solution of $A_1$ is obtained to combine Eqs. (25) and (26):

$$A_1 = \frac{1}{\delta'}\left[\frac{\theta_0^{2-\beta_1}(4a+b)(-b)}{(2a+b)^2-4a}\right] \tag{27}$$

The NPV of the pioneer's implementation of the option to invest in the project plan is as follows"

$$NPV_i(\theta_i; \theta_0) = \left[A_1\theta_i^{\beta_1} + \frac{\theta^2}{4a}\frac{1}{\delta'} - I\right]\left(\frac{\theta}{\theta_i}\right)^{\beta_1} \tag{28}$$

Moreover, the pioneer (firm $i$) may choose to enter the market by the threshold of market entry:

$$\theta_i^* = \left(\frac{\beta_1}{\beta_1 - 2}\right)\left(\frac{4a\delta'I}{\theta_0^2}\right)$$

Thereafter, the thresholds of the two firms are indicated as follows.
Pioneer:

$$\theta_i^* = \left(\frac{\beta_1}{\beta_1 - 2}\right)\left(\frac{\delta'I}{\theta_0^2}\right)(4a)$$

Followers:

$$\theta_j^* = \left(\frac{\beta_1}{\beta_1 - 2}\right)\left(\frac{\delta'I}{\theta_0^2}\right)\left[\frac{(2a+b)^2}{a}\right]$$

The equation $4b + \frac{b^2}{a}$ can be obtained by the difference between the pioneer and follower. The two goods are substitutable because $0 < a < 1$ and $b > 0$; that is, the follower's threshold is higher than the pioneer's. Conversely, the two goods are complementary if $0 < a < 1$ and $b < 0$; thus, the follower's threshold is lower than the pioneer's. Moreover, the pioneer cannot obtain the first mover advantage when the two goods are complementary.

## 2.3    An Interim Summary

Firms will decide to enter a market based on the thresholds at different time points. First, there is no firm in the market because firms are waiting to invest. Thereafter, the pioneer enters the market when the pioneer reaches the threshold; that is, the first mover may obtain several benefits by entering the market. The market is a monopoly at this stage. Thereafter, the follower enters the market because it reaches the threshold; thus, the market structure transforms from a monopoly into an oligopoly.

# 3    Empirical Research

This study uses the stock prices of the two firms Toyota and Honda to evaluate the value of deferral options that automobile firms can use to invest in the battery market. Toyota is the pioneer and Honda is the follower in this study.

## 3.1    Research Design

The purpose of this paper is to examine whether the degree of market uncertainty and complement of the electric car and battery affects the stock prices of automobile firms. Thereafter, Toyota's stock price and Honda's stock price are analyzed using the regression model, whereby the stock prices are dependent variables and the market uncertainty and complement of goods are explanatory variables.

During the decision-making process of the investment, the market uncertainty and complement of goods may influence the value of the project. Therefore, the factors of uncertainty and complement are considered in this study.

First, the inverse demand function estimates the degree of complement. Thereafter, the uncertainty of the market is calculated with the Kalman Filter. This study uses the regression model to consider the previously indicated factors and estimate the influence between the two stock prices and two factors. Moreover, the dummy variable $D_t$ is equal to 1 when the uncertainty is higher than the threshold. Conversely, the dummy variable is equal to 0.

## 3.2    Empirical Model

The regression function of the pioneer (Toyota) is

$$S_{Lt} = \gamma_0 + b_{Lt} + \gamma_1 D_{Lt}\theta_L{}^* + \gamma_2\sigma_{Lt}^2 + \gamma_3 IR_t + + \varepsilon_{Lt}, \quad \varepsilon_{Lt} \overset{iid}{\sim} N(0, \sigma_L^2) \tag{29}$$

The regression function of the follower (Honda) is

$$S_{Ft} = \beta_0 + b_{Ft} + \beta_1 D_{Ft}\theta_F{}^* + \beta_2\sigma_{Ft}^2 + \beta_3 IR_t + \varepsilon_{Ft}, \quad \varepsilon_{Ft} \overset{iid}{\sim} N(0, \sigma_F) \tag{30}$$

where $S_{Lt}$ and $S_{Ft}$ are the stock prices of Toyota and Honda; $b$ is the complementary of goods; $D_t$ is the dummy variable; $\sigma_{Lt}^2$ and $\sigma_{Ft}^2$ are the volatilities of these two firms' profits; $\theta_{Lt}$ and $\theta_{Ft}$ are the variables of thresholds; $IR_t$ is the interest rate; and $\varepsilon_t$ is the error term.

## 3.3    Calculation of the Degree of Complement

The inverse demand functions of Toyota and Honda can derive the following functions:

$$CP_{Lt} = a_1 + a_2 \cdot CS_{Lt} + a_3 \cdot BS_{Lt} + a_4 \cdot BS_{Ft} + \varepsilon_{Lt}, \quad \varepsilon_{Lt} \overset{iid}{\sim} N(0, \sigma_L^2) \tag{31}$$

$$CP_{Ft} = b_1 + b_2 \cdot CS_{Ft} + b_3 \cdot BS_{Ft} + b_4 \cdot BS_{Lt} + \varepsilon_{Lt}, \quad \varepsilon_{Ft} \overset{iid}{\sim} N(0, \sigma_F^2) \tag{32}$$

where $CP$ is the price of automobile vehicle[2]; $CS$ is the car quantity (Toyota and Honda); $BS$ is the battery quantity; a1 and b1 are constants; a2 and b2 are the

---

[2] In this study, prices of cars are the standard cars of 2000 c.c. in automobile market.

coefficients of vehicle quantity; a3 and b3 are the coefficients of battery quantity; and a4 and b4 are the effects between own vehicle and competition's battery.

Moreover, the law of demand indicates that $a_2$ and $b_2$ are negative; that is, the quantities of demand decrease when the price increases. Furthermore, $a3$ and $b3$ are negative, which indicates that the electric cars and battery are complementary goods. When the price of a car increases, the quantity of demand decreases; thus, the demand of batteries decrease because of the relationship to complementary goods. The car's price and the battery's price are negative.

## 3.4  Estimation of Volatility

This study uses the Kalman Filter to estimate the volatility of firms' profits. The Kalman Filter includes the State equation and Observation equation, which are the dynamic model and recursive processes for estimating volatility.

The following are the advantages of using the Kalman Filter: 1) the Kalman Filter provides a recursive process to estimate the state of the past, present, and future, 2) the model can estimate the state of the past, present, and future under uncertainty, and 3) the optimal value of estimation can be identified by providing a sample.

## 3.5  Choice of Control Variable

Four aspects that can influence stock price are examined: the viewpoints of macroeconomics, industry, corporate, and others that were implemented in past surveys. First, the macroeconomic variables include the income, inflation rate, interest rate, money supply, exchange rate, and commodity price. Second, the industrial variables include the seasonal factor, market concentration rate, degree of competition, and technological innovation. Third, the corporate variables include the change of management, decision-maker, earning, risk premiums, and dividend. Finally, several other variables are included such as corporate behavior, psychology, non-fundamental elements, and lag (Culter et al. 1989; Lee 1998; Olsen 1998; Madsen and Davis 2006). The interest rate is implemented as a control variable in this study.

# 4  Empirical Results

## 4.1  Sample Collection

This work includes the sales quantities by Toyota and Honda, quantities of Japanese batteries, price of Japanese automobile vehicles, sales figures of Toyota and Honda, and Japanese interest rates. The sample period is from Q2 2004 to Q4 2007. These samples are figures were collected from the financial reports of Toyota and Honda, Japan Automobile Manufacturers Association (JAMA), Battery Association of Japan (BAJ), and Bank of Japan (BOJ).

## 4.2    Descriptive Statistics

### 4.2.1    Estimation of Substitution and Variance

1. Price of automobile vehicle (CP)

This study uses Japan's 2000 c.c. vehicle to represent the prices of Toyota and Japan, because the electric vehicle and hybrid vehicle possess a high price level. In this study, the mean of the price index of an automobile vehicle is 99.4 and the maximum is 100.1.

2. Quantities of automobile vehicle (CS)

The quantities of sales are collected by Toyota and Honda. Our JAMA-based samples are the sales quantities of Toyota's and Honda's 2000 c.c. vehicles. In Japan, the mean of sales quantities by Toyota are 127,996, the maximum is 157,790 (2006 Q1), and the minimum is 127,996 (Q2 2007). Conversely, the mean of the sales quantities by Honda are 35,968, the maximum is 62,325 (Q2 2004), and the minimum is 25,980 (Q3 2007).

The theoretical expectation is that the sales quantities of Toyota and Honda are negative toward the index of car price; that is, the law of demand is satisfied.

3. Quantities of battery (BS)

The samples were collected by the BAJ. The mean of the battery is 6472 and the maximum is 7610. The theoretical expectation is that the quantities of battery sales and quantities of car sales are positive; that is, batteries and vehicles are substitute goods.

4. Sales of firms (SV)

The information regarding Toyota's sales was revealed in the quarter after 2008 because of Japan's accounting principles. Data before 2008 are available in annual or half-year figures. For collecting the data before 2008 for this study, the quantity of car sales is used to estimate Toyota's sales by ratio, which shows the relationship between Toyota's sales and the quantity of national car sales in the Japanese automobile market. Furthermore, the Kalman Filter is used to estimate the variance in sales of Toyota and Honda. The results indicate that the mean return of Toyota is 4% and the maximum return of Toyota is 5%. Conversely, the mean return of Honda is 11% and the maximum return of Honda is 13%.

Regression function: effect between stock price

5. Stock price $(S_t)$

This study examines the stock prices of Toyota and Honda from the Tokyo Stock Exchange, which are code 7203 and code 7237. The average stock price of Toyota is 5692 Japanese Yen and the maximum stock price is 7840 Japanese Yen during our sample period. Conversely, the average stock price of Honda is 5017 Japanese Yen and the maximum stock price is 6950 Japanese Yen during our sample period.

In this empirical study, the stock prices represent the value of deferral options. If the firm undergoes a budget constraint, this indicates that the firm forgoes the right to delay its option. However, traditional wisdoms regarding uncertain markets suggest that firms delay their option until new information is received. The increase in stock price reflects the potential growth of a firm that investors believe in. Furthermore, the value of the deferral option may increase when a market becomes more uncertain; that is, the time value of a project represents the potentially positive value of new information that investors are waiting for.

## 6. Complementary ($a$)

The complementary ($a$) may be derived using the inverse demand function. A theoretical expectation is that the relationship between complements and stock price are positive. In this study, because the electric car and battery are complementary, firms may expand their product lines by producing cars, electric cars, hybrid cars, and batteries. This widening of product lines of one firm may increase its stock price.

Moreover, when the degree of complement increases, the pioneer obtains advantages from combining complementary goods. These advantages increase the threshold of entering the market for followers.

## 7. Variance ($\sigma^2$)

The variance is calculated using the sales data and represent the market uncertainty. Regarding deferral options, a positive relationship is present with the stock price and investing uncertainty. In an uncertain market, this may increase the potential benefits for investors. Moreover, the value of waiting may be beneficial with the increase in uncertainty, which may be reflected in stock prices.

## 8. Threshold ($M_{it}$)

The $\eta_L$ and $\eta_F$ are the impact of the threshold on stock price when dummy variables are equal to 1. These are positive values that are consistent with the results and the comparative static analysis theory. A higher threshold represents a high difficulty for followers in entering the market and a better performance of stock price for the pioneer. Bo et al. (2006) suggested that the threshold must be greater than 1 to consider the market uncertainty. This factor may exist in the value of deferral options.

## 9. Interest rate (IR)

The data regarding interest rates were collected from the benchmark interest rate of the BOJ. The average interest rate is 0.21% and the maximum interest rate is 0.5%. Economic theories indicate that the relationship between the interest rate and stock price is negative.

### 4.3    Analysis of Empirical Results

#### 4.3.1    Result of Complementary

This study estimates the complement of regression for Eqs. (31) and (32) by using the rolling window method: the coefficient of car sale and battery; $a_2$ and $a_3$, respectively. The results indicate that the relationship between the car sales quantity and car price are influenced by the law of demand ($a_2 < 0$). Moreover, $a_3$ is insignificant, and the results indicate that the complement of goods does not influence the car price. Furthermore, car price affects the battery sales quantity.

#### 4.3.2    Estimation of Volatility

After transferring the profits of Toyota and Honda toward the ratio of profit, the Kalman Filter approach is implemented to estimate the volatility. Thereafter, a series of volatility are obtained by using the rolling window method.

#### 4.3.3    Analysis of Regression Model of Stock Price

$$S_{Lt} = \gamma_0 b_{Lt} + \gamma_1 D_{Lt}\theta_L{}^* + \gamma_2 \sigma_{Lt}^2 + \gamma_3 IR_t + + \varepsilon_{Lt}, \quad \varepsilon_{Lt} \overset{iid}{\sim} N\left(0, \sigma_L^2\right) \tag{33}$$

$$S_{Ft} = \beta_0 b_{Ft} + \beta_1 D_{Ft}\theta_F{}^* + \beta_2 \sigma_{Ft}^2 + \beta_3 IR_t + \varepsilon_{Ft}, \quad \varepsilon_{Ft} \overset{iid}{\sim} N(0, \sigma_F) \tag{34}$$

Integrating the complementary, uncertainty, threshold, and control variable into Eqs. (33) and (34), the degree of influence is calculated between every variable and stock price.

The results indicate that market uncertainty does not affect the stock prices of Toyota and Honda. Moreover, the estimated results regarding the complement degree indicate that they significantly affected Toyota's stock price. Conversely, Honda's stock price was not affected by the complement degree between the electric car and lithium battery. The estimation of the threshold of market entry indicated that it did not influence the stock prices of Toyota and Honda. Furthermore, the results regarding interest rates indicated that they may have negatively influenced the stock prices of both Toyota and Honda. These results are in accordance with investment theories. In this study, the significant level is 0.05, and the adjusted R2 of Toyota and Honda are 0.87 and 0.58, respectively (Table 1).

These results indicate that the pioneer cannot profit from market uncertainty; thus, the existence of first mover advantages for the pioneer (Toyota) is determined in the following section.

#### 4.3.4    First Mover Advantages

According to Gal-Or (1985), compared to stock price of Honda, Toyota's stock price has a relatively weak performance from Q1 1999 to Q4 2005. The booming electric car market prompts the positive performance in Toyota' stock price. Moreover, Toyota's stock price surpassed Honda's in 2006 (Fig. 1).

**Table 1.** Results of regression model of the Toyota's and Honda's stock price

| RHS variables | Coefficient (Toyota) | Coefficient (Honda) |
|---|---|---|
| $C$ | 8.912*** | 8.19 |
| $\sigma^2$ | −2.151 | 4.48 |
| IR | 1.238*** | −0.66** |
| compl | −2783.95*** | 301.86 |
| Dummy threshold | 0.02 | −0.03 |
| Adjusted $R^2$ | 0.87 | 0.58 |
| Prob(F) | 0.000001 | 0.003 |

Note: **$\alpha = 0.1$; ***$\alpha = 0.05$; Sample period: Q4 2004–Q4 2007; Dependent variable: stock price

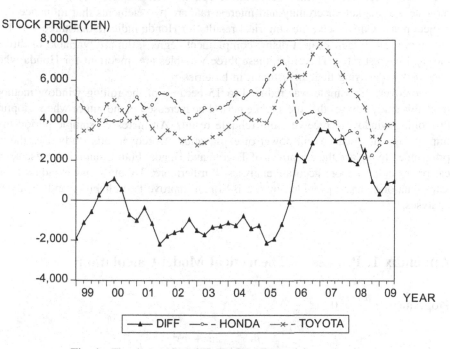

**Fig. 1.** The time series of Toyota's and Honda's stock price

Moreover, Table 2 shows that the t value is significant under the 95% confident level; that is, Toyota obtained first mover advantages through the R&D of lithium batteries, which are reflected in the firm's stock price.

**Table 2.** T test of stock price

| | Toyota | Honda |
|---|---|---|
| Mean | 4447.25 | 4440.59 |
| Variance | 1851662.551 | 1122319.793 |
| Number of observation | 43 | 43 |
| t test | 0.025070498 | |

## 5   Conclusion and Suggestion

This study examines the relationship between electric cars and lithium batteries, and their influences on the profits of electric car firms that enter into the lithium battery market. The empirical results indicate that Toyota's complementary goods are insignificant. Conversely, Honda's complementary goods are significant. Therefore, discussing the complementary nature between traditional automobiles and batteries is important. The managerial implication is that as complementary companies increase and produce goods, the demand and profits of industry rise, also.

From strategic perspective, we ought to encourage that firms produce complementary goods rather than substitute them under competition. Furthermore, this study used stock prices as the values of deferral options. The empirical results for Toyota indicate that market uncertainty and interest rate are two elements that influence their project plans. Conversely, the empirical results for Honda indicate that three variables are significant to their project plans: complement degrees, dummy variable of threshold, and interest rates. Therefore, these three variables are important for Honda when considering deferring their investment in batteries.

Moreover, the sample was reduced to 15 because of the rolling window method; thus, this study advises that the sample period be increased in the future when adopting the rolling window to receive more reliable results. An increased sample period may improve the significance and power of explanation. Moreover, this study uses the car price index to replace the car prices of Toyota and Honda. Future studies can use actual car prices employ more accurate analyses. Furthermore, Toyota's and Honda's actual sales data of batteries provided by the BAJ can improve the reliability and reality for analyses.

## Appendix 1: Process of Theoretical Model Calculation

Proposition 1: $\frac{\partial \theta_j^*}{\partial a} > 0$

$$\theta_{ic}^* = \frac{\beta_1}{\beta_1 - 2} \cdot \frac{(2a + b)^2}{a \cdot \theta^2} \cdot \delta^{'} I$$

Let

$$\frac{\partial \theta_j^*}{\partial a} = B \cdot \delta^{'} \cdot I \cdot 2(2a+b)(2)(a^{-1}\theta^{-2}) + B \cdot \delta^{'} \cdot I \cdot (2a+b)^2(-1)(a^{-2}\theta^{-2})$$

$$= B \cdot \delta^{'} \cdot I \cdot (a^{-1}\theta^{-2})\left[4(2a+b) + (-1)(2a+b)^2 \cdot a^{-1}\right]$$

$$= \left(\frac{B \cdot \delta^{'} \cdot I}{a\theta^2}\right) \cdot \left[4 - \frac{(2a+b)^2}{a}\right] > 0$$

# Appendix 2: Process of Kalman Filter Estimation

The dynamic model is used in the Kalman Filter to estimate uncertainty. The recursive processes comprise the following steps. The State equation is the dynamic process and the Observation equation is used to calculate the solution.
    State equation:

$$\xi_{t+1} = F\xi_t + v_{t+1} \tag{A.1}$$

Observation equation:

$$y_t = A'x_t + H'\xi_t + w_t \tag{A.2}$$

where A', H', and F are known; $x_t$ is an exogenous variable, $\xi_t$ is the variable of the impact of behavior. In the dynamic process, $\xi_t$ is given as a starting value. The value of $y_t$ can be calculated by implementing these variables and starting value.
    Thereafter, the systematic matrix is exploited to consider the uncertainty factor Q:

$$E\left(v_t, v_t'\right) = \begin{cases} Q, t = \tau \\ 0 \end{cases}$$

$$E\left(\omega_t, \omega_t'\right) = \begin{cases} R, t = \tau \\ 0 \end{cases}$$

where $Q$ and $R$ are the $(r \times r)$ and $(n \times n)$ matrix. Covariance is present when $t = \tau$. Moreover, if $t \neq \tau$, the co-variances are 0.
    The calculation steps of the Kalman Filter are the following: 1) implementing the recursive process; 2) calculating the $y_t$; and 3) renewing the value. The recursive process involves providing the starting value of $\xi_1$ and using $\xi_1$ in the Observation equation to obtain $y_t$, and using the $\xi_1$ in the State equation to obtain $\xi_2$.
    The Kalman Filter is used to calculate estimates. The Kalman Filter obtains the value of estimates and the uncertainty of estimates with the original value, and can be used to calculate the weight average expected value.

# References

Alessandri, T.M., Tong, T.W., Reuer, J.: Firm heterogeneity in growth option value: The role of managerial incentives. Strateg. Manag. J. **33**, 1557–1566 (2012)

Bo, H., Jacobs, J., Sterken, E.: A threshold uncertainty investment model for the Netherlands. J. Financ. Econ. **16**, 665–673 (2006)

Cottrell, T., Sick, G.: First-mover (Dis) advantage and real options. J. Appl. Corp. Financ. **14**(2), 41–51 (2001)

Cottrell, T., Sick, G.: Real options and follower strategies: the loss of real option value to first-mover advantage. Eng. Econ. **47**(3), 232–263 (2002)

Culter, D.M., Poterba, J.M., Summers, L.H.: What moves stock prices? J. Portf. Manag. **15**, 4–12 (1989)

Dixit, A.K., Pindyck, R.S.: Investment Under Uncertainty. Princeton University Press: Princeton, N.J. (1994)

Kogut, B., Kulatilaka, N.: Option thinking and platform investments: investing in opportunity. Calif. Manag. Rev. **36**(2), 52–71 (1994)

Kulatilaka, N., Perotti, E.C.: Strategic growth options. Manage. Sci. **44**, 1021–1031 (1998)

Lee, B.S.: Permanent, temporary, and non-fundamental components of stock prices. J. Financ. Quant. Anal. **33**, 1–32 (1998)

Leiberman, M., Montgomery, B.: First mover advantages. Strateg. Manag. J. **9**, 1–58 (1998)

Madsen, J.B., Davis, E.P.: Equity prices, productivity growth, and the new economy. Econ. J. **116**, 791–811 (2006)

McDonald, R.L., Siegel, D.R.: The value of waiting to invest. Q. J. Econ. **101**, 707–727 (1986)

McGrath, R.G.: Falling forward: real options reasoning and entrepreneurial failure. Acad. Manag. Rev. **24**(1), 13–30 (1999)

Michailidis, A.: Managing tourism investment opportunities under uncertainty: a real options approach. Int. J. Tour. Res. **8**(5), 381–390 (2006)

O'Brien, J.P., Folta, T.B., Johnson, D.R.: A real options perspective on entrepreneurial entry in the face of uncertainty. Manag. Decis. Econ. **24**(8), 515–533 (2003)

Olsen, R.A.: Behavioral finance and its implications for stock-price volatility. Financ. Anal. J. **54**, 10–18 (1998)

Schnaars, S.P.: Management Imitation Strategies: How Later Entrants Seize Markets from Pioneers. The Free Press, New York (1994)

Sommacampagna, C., Sick, G.: Estimation of Volatility of Cross Sectional Data: A Kalman Filter Approach. Working paper. University of Verona (2004)

Tong, W.T., Reuer, J.: Real options in strategic management. Adv. Strat. Manag. **24**, 3–28 (2007)

Welch, G., Bishop, G.: An Introduction to the Kalman Filter. Working paper. University of North Carolina at Chapel Hill (2006)

Vives, X.: Duopoly information equilibrium: cournot and bertrand. J. Econ. Theory **34**(1), 71–94 (1984)

# Analysis on Excess Return and Risk of Individual Stock—The Case Study of China

Cheng-Yong Liu[1], Shih-Yung Wei[2(✉)], and Xiu-Wen Ye[3]

[1] Beijing Institute of Technology, Zhuhai 519088, Guangdong
People's Republic of China
liucy13@126.com
[2] Business School, Yulin Normal University,
Guangxi, People's Republic of China
[3] Yulin Normal University, Guangxi, People's Republic of China

**Abstract.** This paper discusses the excess return, January effect and condition of risk premium of individual stock in Shenzhen and Shanghai stock markets, combined with size effect and status of industry sectors. The results indicate that 103 listed companies in China have significant excess return, including up to 45.45% of these listed companies belongs to the financial industry. The risk of financial industry, however, is larger than that of the market. In other industry sectors, there exists relatively higher occurring of January excess return in hotel industry, food and beverage industry, transportation, warehousing and post services. This may be associated with the Chinese New Year Festival.

**Keywords:** Abnormal return · Capital asset pricing model (CAPM)
Risk premium

## 1 Introduction

The concept of excess return was proposed by Fama et al. (1969), who suggested that events may contain hidden information and the fluctuation of stock price before or after a particular event can be used to test whether the market is swiftly and fully reflecting the information in the price. If the price fully reflects the information behind an event, then the market has price efficiency; thus, investors cannot obtain excess return from the release of new information.

The fluctuation of stock price not only reflects economic changes and business operation, but investors' psychological factors as well. Traditional financial theories in the past almost never took decision-making process into consideration. Behavioral finance, however, put more emphasis on human influence. According to behavioral finance, these factors include individual preferences, emotions and perception, relatively reducing the impact brought by the economy and corporate operation. Since Tversky et al. (1979) proposed the prospect theory, behavioral finance has become the new trend for market vision study.

As mentioned above, excess return thus becomes one of research topics in financing. The study of excess return is widely applied to the analysis of stock market. The most frequently applied situation of excess return is January effect, which means

J.-L. Chen et al. (Eds.): WiCON 2018, LNICST 264, pp. 295–306, 2019.
https://doi.org/10.1007/978-3-030-06158-6_29

that excess return occurs in almost every January. Wachtel (1942) was the first to study January effect. He pointed out that New York stock market has excess return and transaction volumes in January. Besides the January effect, from 1953 to 1977, French (1980) found that Standard & Poor's Indexes has weekend effect. The result showed that the return rate on Monday is significantly lower than that of the last day of the last week. Moreover, Ariel (1990) found that the return rate at the beginning and end of each month is much higher than that of other time period.

The test of excess return is often measured by CAPM (Capital Asset Price Model, Sharpe 1964; Lintner 1965). As the return of individual stocks in CAPM and risk coefficient have a linear relationship, and based on this, Sharpe (1964) developed a singular index model. Fama (1969) was the first to use this model to analyze the impact of stock split on stock price. Mackinlay (1997) also contended that the market model analysis was more accurate than constant average return model.

This study is divided into for parts. The first part is the introduction and literature review on excess return. The second part describes the methodology, including the research method of this study, as well as the origin and description of data. The third part discusses the empirical analysis, including the analysis of excess return, risk return, and company scales and industry sectors. The last part is the conclusion of this study.

## 2  Methodology

### 2.1  CAPM and Excess Return Version of the CAPM

This paper discusses the excess return of individual stock of China using the most basic financial theory, capital asset pricing model (CAPM). CAPM was developed by American financial experts Sharpe (1964), Lintner (1965), and Mossin (1966) in the 1960s. The aim is to help investors decide the price of capital asset. The securities require the linear relationship between rate of return and market risk (systematic risk) in case of market equilibrium. Market risk coefficient is measured by $\beta$ value. Capital asset refers to marketable securities like stocks and bonds, representing the reclaim right of return resulted from real asset. The model is as follows:

$$E(Ri) - Rf = \beta i \ [E(Rm) - Rf] \tag{1}$$

where:

Ri       Represents the return rate of individual asset (like individual stock)
E (Ri)   Represents the expected return rate of individual asset
Rm       Represents market (e.g.: indexes) return rate
Rf       Represents risk-free return rate

On the other hand, market model is the most commonly used method to test excess return by financial researchers. The dependent variable in this study is the return of individual stock of China minus risk-free interest rate, while the independent variable is the return of Shenzhen and Shanghai 300 index minus risk-free interest rate.

By referring to MacKinlay (1997)'s model, the above dependent variables and independent variables are conducted with linear regression for time series. The linear regression model of this study is as follows:

$$E(Ri) - Rf = \alpha i + \beta i \ [E(Rm) - Rf] \tag{2}$$

To be more specific, the model mentioned above is called excess return version of the CAPM. In the equation, $\alpha$ means the condition of excess return. If it is significant, it means the existence of excess return in the subject, on the contrary, there is no excess return. The other parameter $\beta$ in the format reflects the sensitivity of individual stock to the market (or the tape), which is also the correlation between individual stock and the tape, and also the risk profile for individual stock. $\beta = 1$ means that the risk return rate of this single asset and the average risk return of market portfolio change in the equal ratio. The risk of this singular asset is consistent with market investment portfolio risk. $\beta > 1$ means that the risk return rate of this singular asset is higher than the average risk return of market portfolio, so the risk of this singular asset is larger than that of the overall market investment portfolio. $\beta < 1$ means that the risk return rate of this singular asset is smaller than that of the average risk return of market portfolio. The risk of this singular asset is smaller than that of overall market investment portfolio.

## 2.2  Data Collection

Based on the analytical method, the research data in this study include 3 indicators. The first one is market index. This paper adopts Shanghai and Shenzhen 300 index aimed at Chinese market index. Shenzhen and Shanghai 300 index is jointly issued by Shanghai and Shenzhen stock exchange on April 8, 2005. Thus, the research period of this study is from April 2005 to December 2014. The second index is risk-free interest rate. Generally, risk-free interest rate is substituted by treasury security rate. The shortest period of Chinese treasury security is one year. The calculation in this study adopted the deposit interest rate to substitute risk-free interest rate. The third index is individual stock price, which is the main data of this study. From May 2005 to December 2014, there are altogether 1171 listed companies, which are all residual companies whose transactions have not been suspended for over 1 month.

According to China Securities Regulatory Commission (CSRS), the industries of the 1171 listed companies are classified as shown in Table 1. As seen, most of Chinese

Table 1. Statistical table for the industry sectors of Chinese listed companies.

| Industry sectors | Number |
| --- | --- |
| Agriculture, forestry, herding, fishing industry | 20 |
| Mining industry | 38 |
| Manufacturing industry | 658 |
| Electricity, heat, gas and water | 65 |
| Agriculture | 22 |

listed companies are in the manufacturing industry, totally 658 companies, followed by wholesale and retail industry and real estate industry, which is 109 and 102 respectively.

Shenzhen and Shanghai 300 index and the deposit interest rate for Chinese market indicators are showed in Figs. 1 and 2.

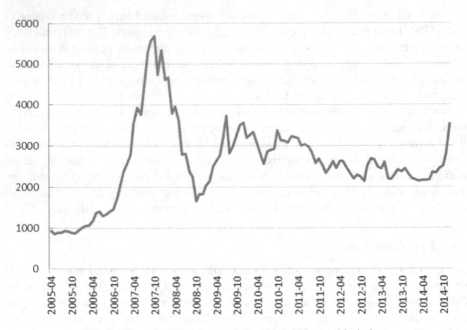

**Fig. 1.** Chart for Shenzhen and Shanghai 300 monthly index.

As shown in Fig. 1, the Chinese stock market set the record in the October of 2007, followed by the global financial tsunami. The stock market came into a bear market. In October 2008, the Lehman Brothers went broke, the stock market declined to the lowest point of the wave band. However, due to the great internal demand, Chinese stock market gradually began rising again. After 2009, the whole stock market went through a period of consolidation. In July 2006, the overall stock market became busy again. Therefore, Chinese stock market is divided into 5 periods in this study, namely, July, 2006–October, 2007, bull market (before the global financial tsunami), November, 2007–October, 2008, bear market (after the global financial tsunami), November, 2008–July, 2009 bull market in the second stage (after the European debt crisis), August, 2009–June, 2014, consolidation period(consolidation of the stock market), July, 2014–November, 2014, bull market in the third stage(after the restriction policy on housing).

Figure 2 shows the deposit interest rate in China, gradually making down-regulation after the global financial tsunami. After the European debt crisis in 2010, it was gradually up-regulated again. Its scope, however, has been remained between 1.71% and 3.33%.

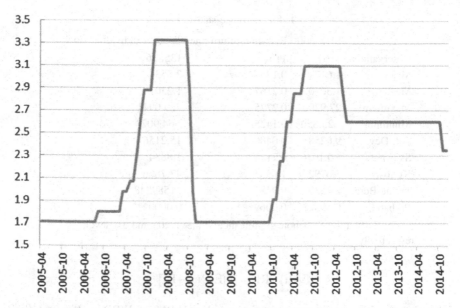

**Fig. 2.** Chart of deposit interest rate in China.

Descriptive Statistics of Variables

The measurement of return rate in this study is calculated in this way: the close index on the t-th day minus the daily close index on the t-1 day, divided by the daily close index on the t-1 day and multiplying by 100. The equation is as follows:

$$r_{i,t} = \left[\left(\frac{I_{i,t} - I_{i,t-1}}{I_{i,t-1}}\right)\right] \times 100$$

Basic statistics of variables of various studies are showed in Table 2. Jarque-Bera verified that the 3 groups of research data show normal distribution. Therefore, it is reasonable for this study to use general regression CAPM model to analyze excess return. The maximum monthly return rate of individual stock is 729.0941 in terms of the analysis of basic statistics. It occurs when transactions fill up four months after it is closed. Shenzhen and Shanghai 300 average value and individual stock general average value is 1.6171 and 2.5534 respectively, showing that the return of Chinese stock market is positive in the long run.

## 3 Empirical Result

The empirical analysis of this study is divided into two parts. The first part is to directly test the condition of excess return, analyze the condition of risk return rate of individual stock, and further analyze the effect of industry sectors and company scales. The second part is to analyze January effect.

The most basic theory—capital asset pricing model (CAPM)

**Table 2.** Basic statistics.

|  | SHZ 300 | Risk-free return rate | Total of individual stock |
|---|---|---|---|
| Observations | 116 | 116 | 135836 |
| Mean | 1.6171 | 0.1956 | 2.5534 |
| Median | 1.3070 | 0.2167 | 1.2307 |
| Maximum | 27.9290 | 0.2775 | 729.0941 |
| Minimum | −25.8505 | 0.1425 | −64.9024 |
| Std. Dev. | 9.6258 | 0.0480 | 15.2156 |
| Skewness | −0.1076 | 0.2178 | 1.8834 |
| Kurtosis | 3.6792 | 1.6331 | 47.7866 |
| Jarque-Bera | 2.4539 | 9.9486 | 11589248 |
| Probability | 0.0932* | 0.0069*** | 0.0000*** |

Notes: *, ** and ***Denote significance at the .1, .05 and .01 level, respectively.

$$E(Ri)-Rf = \beta i[E(Rm)-Rf]$$

Combined with excess return version of the CAPM of $E(Ri) - Rf = \alpha + \beta i$ [E (Rm) − Rf] CAPM by Campbell, Lo and MacKinlay (1997), this paper analyzes that from May 2005 to December 2014 in Shanghai and Shenzhen stock market of China there are altogether 1171 residual companies whose transactions have not been suspended for over 1 month. There are 103 companies having the excess return ($\alpha = 0.1$, significant level). The excess return information of these 103 companies is enclosed in Tables 3 and 4. As the company number is huge, those with insignificant level are not listed.

As shown in Table 3, the excess return of 4 companies in this research is significant. The monthly excess return is high, which is 2.15%(000651), 2.70%(000826), 4.00%(600340) and 3.37%(600570) respectively. The significance degree is shown in Table 5.

**Table 3.** The significance of abnormal return-1

| Code | α | Prob. | β | P | Code | α | Prob. | β | P |
|---|---|---|---|---|---|---|---|---|---|
| 000028 | 2.2705 | (0.0494)** | 0.5160 | (0.0000)*** | 600111 | 2.8483 | (0.0255)** | 1.2743 | (0.0000)*** |
| 000049 | 2.3938 | (0.0955)* | 0.3824 | (0.0104)*** | 600118 | 2.4154 | (0.0365)** | 0.9702 | (0.0000)*** |
| 000157 | 1.8361 | (0.0615)* | 1.2436 | (0.0000)*** | 600139 | 2.2393 | (0.0941)* | 1.0256 | (0.0000)*** |
| 000417 | 1.7567 | (0.0760)* | 0.7905 | (0.0000)*** | 600199 | 1.9630 | (0.0645)* | 0.8834 | (0.0000)*** |
| 000516 | 1.9763 | (0.0731)* | 0.8105 | (0.0000)*** | 600201 | 1.8076 | (0.0833)* | 0.8531 | (0.0000)*** |
| 000538 | 1.9208 | (0.0225)** | 0.4081 | (0.0000)*** | 600252 | 2.7377 | (0.0397)** | 1.0903 | (0.0000)*** |
| 000540 | 2.5222 | (0.0936)* | 1.2434 | (0.0000)*** | 600256 | 2.0524 | (0.0807)* | 0.8669 | (0.0000)*** |
| 000550 | 1.7041 | (0.0772)* | 0.9931 | (0.0000)*** | 600276 | 2.3317 | (0.0116)** | 0.3501 | (0.0003)*** |
| 000566 | 2.0905 | (0.0959)* | 0.6591 | (0.0000)*** | 600312 | 2.0362 | (0.0782)* | 0.5685 | (0.0000)*** |
| 000568 | 1.4892 | (0.0945)* | 0.9219 | (0.0000)*** | 600335 | 2.3030 | (0.0833)* | 0.9792 | (0.0000)*** |
| 000596 | 2.9426 | (0.0539)* | 0.8868 | (0.0000)*** | 600340 | 3.9964 | (0.0086)*** | 0.8530 | (0.0000)*** |

(*continued*)

**Table 3.** (*continued*)

| Code | α | Prob. | β | P | Code | α | Prob. | β | P |
|---|---|---|---|---|---|---|---|---|---|
| 000598 | 1.9359 | (0.0800)* | 0.9810 | (0.0000)*** | 600373 | 2.2806 | (0.0671)* | 0.6524 | (0.0000)*** |
| 000623 | 1.6531 | (0.0997)* | 1.6981 | (0.0000)*** | 600388 | 2.1922 | (0.0512)* | 0.7227 | (0.0000)*** |
| 000651 | 2.1546 | (0.0099)*** | 0.8876 | (0.0000)*** | 600406 | 2.2481 | (0.0655)* | 0.5472 | (0.0000)*** |
| 000661 | 2.8474 | (0.0520)* | 0.8245 | (0.0000)*** | 600433 | 2.5813 | (0.0535)* | 0.6707 | (0.0000)*** |
| 000669 | 2.2398 | (0.0690)* | 0.7350 | (0.0000)*** | 600436 | 1.6787 | (0.0853)* | 0.4407 | (0.0000)*** |
| 000671 | 2.3115 | (0.0886)* | 0.8584 | (0.0000)*** | 600446 | 3.0846 | (0.0205)** | 0.6483 | (0.0000)*** |
| 000712 | 3.2486 | (0.0331)** | 0.8931 | (0.0000)*** | 600478 | 2.6267 | (0.0781)* | 0.8865 | (0.0000)*** |
| 000748 | 2.1799 | (0.0653)* | 1.1087 | (0.0000)*** | 600486 | 1.7549 | (0.0780)* | 0.7028 | (0.0000)*** |
| 000760 | 2.5334 | (0.0986)* | 0.8452 | (0.0000)*** | 600490 | 2.9228 | (0.0363)** | 0.7584 | (0.0000)*** |
| 000768 | 1.9174 | (0.0819)* | 1.0087 | (0.0000)*** | 600495 | 2.3037 | (0.0467)** | 0.6073 | (0.0000)*** |
| 000777 | 2.2659 | (0.0678)* | 1.1043 | (0.0000)*** | 600499 | 2.3096 | (0.0873)* | 1.0113 | (0.0000)*** |
| 000788 | 2.2920 | (0.0764)* | 0.6933 | (0.0000)*** | 600511 | 2.8032 | (0.0234)** | 0.4290 | (0.0009)*** |
| 000826 | 2.7041 | (0.0049)*** | 0.5628 | (0.0000)*** | 600517 | 2.7546 | (0.0375)** | 0.5730 | (0.0000)*** |
| 000848 | 2.4061 | (0.0364)** | 0.5939 | (0.0000)*** | 600518 | 2.4431 | (0.0187)** | 0.5152 | (0.0000)*** |
| 000887 | 2.8667 | (0.0144)** | 0.8166 | (0.0000)*** | 600519 | 1.8975 | (0.0600)* | 0.6285 | (0.0000)*** |
| 000915 | 1.8115 | (0.0918)* | 0.6846 | (0.0000)*** | 600522 | 1.5128 | (0.0984)* | 0.8334 | (0.0000)*** |

**Table 4.** The significance of abnormal return-2

| Code | α | Prob. | β | P | Code | α | Prob. | β | P |
|---|---|---|---|---|---|---|---|---|---|
| 000963 | 2.2179 | (0.0371)** | 0.4950 | (0.0000)*** | 600535 | 1.9516 | (0.0351)** | 0.4951 | (0.0000)*** |
| 000977 | 2.4827 | (0.0680)* | 0.7693 | (0.0000)*** | 600547 | 2.5091 | (0.0927)* | 0.9788 | (0.0000)*** |
| 000996 | 2.4827 | (0.0680)* | 0.7693 | (0.0000)*** | 600557 | 2.1365 | (0.0357)** | 0.4475 | (0.0000)*** |
| 002001 | 2.3286 | (0.0546)* | 0.7474 | (0.0000)*** | 600562 | 2.7889 | (0.0777)* | 0.9653 | (0.0000)*** |
| 002007 | 2.7431 | (0.0115)** | 0.4711 | (0.0000)*** | 600570 | 3.3656 | (0.0057)*** | 1.0041 | (0.0000)*** |
| 002008 | 2.0283 | (0.0782)* | 0.7702 | (0.0000)*** | 600572 | 1.9422 | (0.0587)* | 0.5818 | (0.0000)*** |
| 002013 | 2.7571 | (0.0471)** | 0.9373 | (0.0000)*** | 600587 | 2.8331 | (0.0116)** | 0.5088 | (0.0000)*** |
| 002022 | 2.2104 | (0.0264)** | 0.4774 | (0.0000)*** | 600588 | 2.3872 | (0.0362)** | 0.5669 | (0.0000)*** |
| 002030 | 2.2182 | (0.0422)** | 0.7832 | (0.0000)*** | 600594 | 2.2967 | (0.0727)* | 0.5710 | (0.0000)*** |
| 002038 | 2.8205 | (0.0125)** | 0.5027 | (0.0000)*** | 600612 | 2.0675 | (0.0673)* | 0.7841 | (0.0000)*** |
| 200028 | 2.0492 | (0.0520)* | 0.6623 | (0.0000)*** | 600645 | 2.6623 | (0.0449)** | 0.8025 | (0.0000)*** |
| 200418 | 1.4869 | (0.0772)* | 0.8047 | (0.0000)*** | 600674 | 2.3099 | (0.0603)* | 0.8430 | (0.0000)*** |
| 200550 | 1.9736 | (0.0237)** | 0.7797 | (0.0000)*** | 600685 | 1.9595 | (0.0851)* | 1.2676 | (0.0000)*** |
| 200553 | 1.5893 | (0.0981)* | 0.7628 | (0.0000)*** | 600690 | 1.4065 | (0.0951)* | 0.8333 | (0.0000)*** |
| 200596 | 2.9790 | (0.0434)** | 0.7809 | (0.0000)*** | 600697 | 1.2389 | (0.0861)* | 0.6120 | (0.0000)*** |
| 600000 | 1.2226 | (0.0975)* | 1.0240 | (0.0000)*** | 600763 | 2.5699 | (0.0871)* | 0.7720 | (0.0000)*** |
| 600016 | 1.3235 | (0.0664)* | 0.9391 | (0.0000)*** | 600783 | 2.4243 | (0.0840)* | 1.1417 | (0.0000)*** |
| 600030 | 2.0921 | (0.0469)** | 1.5898 | (0.0000)*** | 600794 | 2.1333 | (0.0653)* | 0.8035 | (0.0000)*** |
| 600031 | 2.0484 | (0.0463)** | 1.3520 | (0.0000)*** | 600804 | 2.8481 | (0.0532)* | 1.0628 | (0.0000)*** |
| 600056 | 1.6241 | (0.0896)* | 1.0316 | (0.0000)*** | 600867 | 2.3884 | (0.0404)** | 0.5197 | (0.0000)*** |
| 600066 | 1.7479 | (0.0190)** | 0.8423 | (0.0000)*** | 600887 | 1.7792 | (0.0734)* | 0.5655 | (0.0000)*** |
| 600079 | 2.0849 | (0.0518)* | 0.6569 | (0.0000)*** | 600967 | 2.3554 | (0.0489)** | 0.8213 | (0.0000)*** |
| 600089 | 2.0541 | (0.0787)* | 0.8734 | (0.0000)*** | 600990 | 2.5062 | (0.0658)* | 0.9113 | (0.0000)*** |
| 600109 | 2.8750 | (0.0980)* | 1.5365 | (0.0000)*** | 900904 | 2.1941 | (0.0409)** | 0.9388 | (0.0000)*** |
| | | | | | 900938 | 2.2162 | (0.0716)* | 0.8843 | (0.0000)*** |

**Table 5.** Statistical table for the significance of excess return.

| Significance level | 0.01 | 0.05 | 0.1 | No |
|---|---|---|---|---|
| Number | 4 | 34 | 65 | 1608 |

This paper discusses the risks of individual stocks, listing the risk significance of the 1171 companies in the Table 6. The risk return rate of 325 companies in the research sample is higher than that of the market risk return rate (accounting for 27.75%), while the risk return rate of 67.21% of companies is lower than that of the market risk return rate, and 5.04% of companies have the same risk conditions with the market.

**Table 6.** Table for risk degree of individual stock.

| Significance level | | 0.01 | 0.05 | 0.1 | Total | No |
|---|---|---|---|---|---|---|
| Number | + | 312 | 6 | 7 | 325 | 28 |
| | % | 26.64% | 0.51% | 0.60% | 27.75% | 2.39% |
| | − | 766 | 9 | 12 | 787 | 31 |
| | % | 65.41% | 0.77% | 1.02% | 67.21% | 2.65% |

The paper further analyzes the industry conditions as shown in Table 7. One company of scientific research and technological service as well as health and social work has excess return in the listed table. Apart from these 2 industries, the financial industry has highest ratio of excess return, which is up to 45.45%, followed by information transmission & software and manufacturing industry. The excess return proportion is respectively 18.52% and 10.33%.

**Table 7.** Table for the analysis on excess return in industry sectors.

| Industry sectors | Total | Number of significance | % |
|---|---|---|---|
| Agriculture, forestry, herding, fishing industry | 20 | | 0.00 |
| Mining industry | 38 | 3 | 7.89 |
| Manufacturing industry | 658 | 68 | 10.33 |
| Electricity, heat, gas and water | 65 | 3 | 4.62 |
| Agriculture | 22 | | 0.00 |
| Wholesale and retail industry | 109 | 9 | 8.26 |
| Transportation, storage & post services | 57 | 2 | 3.51 |
| Accommodation and food and beverage industry | 7 | | 0.00 |
| Information transmission & software | 27 | 5 | 18.52 |
| Financial industry | 11 | 5 | 45.45 |

(*continued*)

**Table 7.** (*continued*)

| Industry sectors | Total | Number of significance | % |
|---|---|---|---|
| Real estate | 102 | 3 | 2.94 |
| Leasing and business service industry | 10 | | 0.00 |
| Scientific research and technological service | 1 | 1 | 100.00 |
| Water conservancy, environment and public facilities | 15 | 1 | 6.67 |
| Education | 1 | | 0.00 |
| Health and social work | 1 | 1 | 100.00 |
| Culture, sport and entertainment industry | 9 | 1 | 11.11 |
| Comprehensive industry | 18 | 1 | 5.56 |

However, there is no excess return in companies of agriculture, forestry, herding, fishery, construction, leasing and business service industries have (and only 1 education industry).

The analysis of risks and industry sectors is listed in Table 8, which shows that the risk return rate is the highest in the financial industry (63.64%), followed by construction industry and real estate industry, accounting for over 40%.

**Table 8.** Table for the analysis on risk return in industry sectors.

| Industry sectors | B < 1 | | B > 1 | | $\beta = 1$ | | Total |
|---|---|---|---|---|---|---|---|
| | Number | % | Number | % | Number | % | |
| Agriculture, forestry, herding, fishing industry | 18 | 90.00 | 2 | 10.00 | 0 | 0.00 | 20 |
| Mining industry | 14 | 36.84 | 24 | 63.16 | 0 | 0.00 | 38 |
| Manufacturing industry | 449 | 68.24 | 178 | 27.05 | 31 | 4.71 | 658 |
| Electricity, heat, gas and water | 48 | 73.85 | 15 | 23.08 | 2 | 3.08 | 65 |
| Agriculture | 11 | 50.00 | 10 | 45.45 | 1 | 4.55 | 22 |
| Wholesale and retail industry | 79 | 72.48 | 23 | 21.10 | 7 | 6.42 | 109 |
| Transportation, storage & post services | 46 | 80.70 | 9 | 15.79 | 2 | 3.51 | 57 |
| Accommodation and food and beverage industry | 6 | 85.71 | | 0.00 | 1 | 14.29 | 7 |
| Information transmission &software | 23 | 85.19 | 2 | 7.41 | 2 | 7.41 | 27 |
| Financial industry | 4 | 36.36 | 7 | 63.64 | 0 | 0.00 | 11 |
| Real estate | 44 | 43.14 | 48 | 47.06 | 10 | 9.80 | 102 |
| Leasing and business service industry | 8 | 80.00 | 2 | 20.00 | 0 | 0.00 | 10 |
| Scientific research and technological service | 1 | 100.00 | | 0.00 | 0 | 0.00 | 1 |

(*continued*)

**Table 8.**  (*continued*)

| Industry sectors | B < 1 | | B > 1 | | β = 1 | | Total |
|---|---|---|---|---|---|---|---|
| | Number | % | Number | % | Number | % | |
| Water conservancy, environment and public facilities | 15 | 100.00 | | 0.00 | 0 | 0.00 | 15 |
| Education | 1 | 100.00 | | 0.00 | 0 | 0.00 | 1 |
| Health and social work | 1 | 100.00 | | 0.00 | 0 | 0.00 | 1 |
| Culture, sport and entertainment industry | 9 | 100.00 | | 0.00 | 0 | 0.00 | 9 |
| Comprehensive industry | 10 | 55.56 | 5 | 27.78 | 3 | 16.67 | 18 |
| **Total** | **787** | 67.21 | **325** | 27.75 | **59** | 5.04 | **1171** |

Some relevant size effects show that the return rate on investment for small companies is better than the large companies. Stock return rate and the size of the company are negatively related. The studies of Banz (1981), Reinganum (1981) and Basu (1983) on the U.S. stock market have the same result. This paper further analyzes whether the size of the company affects the excess return of individual stocks. The company scale in this research is measured by the number of employees. They are divided into 5 categories. Their excess return analysis is shown in Table 9, which shows that the excess return rate of companies with less than 1000 people is just 3.57%. The rest is all over 10%. The research results show that the excess return of small companies is lower than that of large companies.

**Table 9.**  Table for analysis of company scale and excess return.

| Scale | Total | Number of significance | % |
|---|---|---|---|
| Under 1000 | 252 | 9 | 3.57 |
| 1000 ∼ 2499 | 291 | 32 | 11.0 |
| 2500 ∼ 4999 | 252 | 22 | 8.33 |
| 5000 ∼ 9999 | 195 | 21 | 11.28 |
| Above 10000 | 181 | 19 | 10.05 |

The analysis on risk and company scale is listed in Table 10. As mentioned above, the risk return rate of most companies is lower than that of the market. As the company gets larger, the required risk return rate also increases (from around 20% to 43%).

**Table 10.**  Table for the analysis on company scale and risk.

| Scale | B < 1 | | B > 1 | | β = 1 | | Total |
|---|---|---|---|---|---|---|---|
| | No. | % | No. | .% | No. | No. | |
| Under 1000 | 172 | 68.25% | 67 | 26.59% | 31 | 12.30% | 252 |
| 1000 ∼ 2499 | 214 | 73.54% | 64 | 21.99% | 0 | 0.00% | 291 |
| 2500 ∼ 4999 | 186 | 73.81% | 55 | 21.83% | 2 | 0.79% | 252 |
| 5000 ∼ 9999 | 124 | 63.59% | 61 | 31.28% | 1 | 0.51% | 195 |
| Above 10000 | 91 | 50.28% | 78 | 43.09% | 0 | 0.00% | 181 |

# 4 Conclusion

This paper explored the excess return and the risk return of individual stock in Chinese listed companies, and analyzed the occurrence of January effect, combined with size effect and industry sectors.

The result showed that 103 China's listed companies have significant excess return. Up to 45.45% companies in financial industry has such condition. The risk of financial industry, however, is higher than that of the market. Investors must evaluate this situation while making investment decisions. However, no enterprises in agriculture, forestry, herding, fisheries, construction, leasing and business service industries have excess return. Their risk is lower than that of the market. From the point of size effect, excess return of small companies is lower than that of large companies, which seems inconsistent with the size effect proposed by Banz (1981) and Reinganum (1981).

**Acknowledgement.** The paper is a periodical achievement of the 2018 school-supported scientific research program A Study on Liability Theories about Insider Trading of Financial Derivatives of Beijing Institute of Technology, Zhuhai (XK-2018-19).

# References

Aggarwal, R., Rivoli, P.: Seasonal and day-of-the-week effects in hour emerging markets. Financ. Rev. **24**, 541–550 (1989)

Agrawal, A., Jaffe, J.F., Mandelker, G.N.: The post-merger performance of acquiring firms: a re-examination of an anomaly. J. Financ. **47**(4), 1605–1621 (1992)

Ariel, R.A.: High stock returns before holidays: existence and evidence on possible causes. J. Financ. **45**(5), 1611–1626 (1990)

Banz, R.W.: The relationship between return and market value of common stocks. J. Financ. Econ. **9**, 3–18 (1981)

Basu, S.: The relation between earnings yield, market value and return for NYSE common stock: further evidence. J. Financ. Econ. **12**, 129–156 (1983)

Berges, A., McConnell, J.J., Schlarbaum, G.G.: The turn-of-the-year in Canada. J. Financ. **3**, 185–192 (1984)

Brown, P., Keim, D.B., Kleidon, A.W., Marsh, T.A.: Stock return seasonalities and the tax-loss selling hypothesis: analysis of the arguments and Australian evidence. J. Financ. Econ. 12, 105–127 (1983)

Chan, M.W.L., Khanthavit, A., Thomas, H.: Seasonality and cultural influences on four Asian stock markets. Asia-Pac. J. Manag. **13**, 1–24 (1996)

Chen, Y.-F., Yang, S.-Y., Lin, F.-L.: Foreign instructional industrial Herding in Taiwan stock market. Manag. Financ. **38**(3), 325–340 (2012)

De Long, J., Bradford, A.S., Summers, L., Wldmnn, R.: Noise trade risk in financial market. J. Polit. Econ. **98**, 703–738 (1990)

Fame, E.F.: Efficient capital markets: a review of theory and empirical work. J. Financ. **25**, 383–417 (1970)

Fama, E.F., Fisher, L., Jensen, M.C., Roll, R.: The adjustment of stock price to new information. Int. Econ. Rev. **10**, 1–21 (1969)

Fama, E.F., French, K.R.: The cross-section of expected stock returns. J. Financ. **6**, 427–465 (1992)

French, K.R.: Stock returns and the weekend effect. J. Financ. Econ. **8**(1), 55–69 (1980)

Herrera, M.J., Lockwood, L.J.: The size effect in mexican stock market. J. Bank. Financ. **18**, 621–632 (1994)

Huang, Y.-S.: The size anomaly on Taiwan stock exchange. Appl. Econ. Lett. **4**, 7–12 (1997)

Daniel, K., Riepe, M.W.: Aspects of investor psychology. J. Portf. Manag. **24**(4), 52–65 (1998)

Keim, D.B.: Size-related anomalies and stock return seasonality: further empirical evidence. J. Financ. Econ. **6**, 13–32 (1983)

Lakonishok, J., Schmidt, S.: Are seasonal anomalies real? A ninety-year perspective. Rev. Financ. Stud. **1**(4), 403–425 (1988)

Liano, K., et al.: Business cycles and the pre-holiday effect in stock returns. Appl. Financ. Econ. **4**(3), 171–174 (1994)

Lintner, J.: The valuation of risk assets and selection of risky investments in stock portfolio and capital budgets. Rev. Econ. Stat. **47**(2), 13–47 (1965)

Mackinlay, A.C.: Event studies in economics and finance. J. Econ. Lit., 13–39 (1997)

Marrett, G.J., Worthington, A.C.: An empirical note on the holiday effect in the Australian stock market. Appl. Econ. Lett. **16**(17), 1769–1772 (2009)

Mossin, J.: Equilibrium in a capital asset market. Econometrica **34**, 768–783 (1966)

Mullainathan, S., Thaler, R.H.: Behavioral Economics. National Bureau of Economic Research. Working papers, 7948 (2000)

Nassir, A., Mohammad, S.: The January effect of stock traded on the Kuala Lumpur stock exchange: an empirical analysis. Hong Kong J. Bus. Manag. **5**, 33–50 (1987)

Pang, Q.K.L.: An analysis of Hong Kong stock return seasonality and firm size anomalies for the period 1977 to 1986. Hong Kong J. Bus. Manag. **6**, 69–90 (1988)

Reinganum, M.R.: Misspecification of capital asset pricing: empirical anomalies based on earnings' yields and market values. J. Financ. Econ. **9**(1), 19–46 (1981)

Rosenberg, B., Reid, K., Lanstein, R.: Persuasive evidence of market inefficiency. J. Portf. Manag. **11**, 9–17 (1985)

Rozeff, M.S., Kinney, W.R.: Capital market seasonality: the case of stock return. J. Financ. Econ. **13**(4), 379–402 (1976)

Sias, R.W.: Institutional herding. Rev. Financ. Stud. **17**(1), 165–206 (2004)

Sharpe, W.F.: Capital asset pricing theory of market equilibrium under conditions if risk. J. Financ. **19**, 425–442 (1964)

Shleifer, A., Vishny, R.W.: The limits of arbitrage. J. Financ. **52**(1), 35–55 (1997)

Watchel, S.B.: Certain obsernation on sesonal movements in stock price. J. Bisiness Univ. Chic. **15**(2), 184–193 (1942)

Tangjitprom, N.: Pre-holiday returns and volatility in Thai stock market. Asian J. Financ. Account. **2**(2), 41–54 (2010)

Tversky, A., Kanneman, D.: Rational choice. The framing of decisions. Science **211**, 453–458 (1979).

# Vehicular Ad Hoc Network

# A Load Statistics-Based Frequency-Hopping Multiple Access Protocol with QoS Guarantee

Yinuo Qin, Bo Li, Zhongjiang Yan$^{(\boxtimes)}$, Mao Yang, and Changtian Peng

Northwestern Polytechnical University, Xi'an Shaanxi, China
nuo@mail.nwpu.edu.cn,
{libo.npu,zhjyan,yangmao,flickert}@nwpu.edu.cn

**Abstract.** In order to satisfy the needs of flexible and invulnerability in aeronautical Ad hoc networks, statistic priority-based multiple access (SPMA) was applied to the tactical target network technology (TTNT) system, which is the latest generation of US military tactical data links. SPMA can provide different access rates and channel resources for different priority traffic. However, if the traffic is busy, low-priority traffic is likely to result in the problem of starvation. This paper proposes a load statistic-based frequency hopping multiple access protocol (LSMA) to solve the starvation problem of low-priority traffic in SPMA and also ensure the network throughput and packet loss rate. The protocol first schedules multiple priority queues. Then according to the statistical results of the physical layer network load, a rate adaption algorithm is designed to control the sending rate of each node in the network. Simulation results show that LSMA can not only solve the starvation problem of low-priority traffic in SPMA, but also provide weighted throughput for every priority traffic. And the network load under this protocol is more stable. When the throughput under high traffic volume in LSMA is same to that in SPMA, packet loss rate dropped from 27% to 10%.

**Keywords:** Multiple access · QoS · SPMA ·
Aeronautical ad hoc networks

## 1 Introduction

The Mobile Ad Hoc Network (MANET) [3,9] is a network in which nodes can communicate and relay with each other without the support of fixed facilities like base stations. Every node in the MANET has the same function. They can transmit, receive and even relay the wireless signal, so the networking mode is flexible. When the network topology has been destroyed, it can form a new network topology and recover communication quickly.

© ICST Institute for Computer Sciences, Social Informatics and Telecommunications Engineering 2019
Published by Springer Nature Switzerland AG 2019. All Rights Reserved
J.-L. Chen et al. (Eds.): WiCON 2018, LNICST 264, pp. 309–318, 2019.
https://doi.org/10.1007/978-3-030-06158-6_30

The MANET used in aeronautical communication is called Aeronautical Ad hoc Networks (AANET) [10]. In AANET, the network nodes are moving at a high speed, and the network topology changes continuously with an unstable channel, which greatly affects the quality of communication. As a plenty of new traffic has springing up, the quality of service (QoS) required by different services is various. Therefore, how to realize fast and efficient communication in AANET and ensure the QoS of the service, the design of multiple access control (MAC) protocol is very important.

In order to establish an efficient and reliable aerospace communication system with strong resistance to damage, the Collins company of the United States has proposed a patented technology statistic priority-based multiple access (SPMA) [4]. It is the multiple access protocol used by the US next generation Tactical Targeting Network Technology (TTNT) [5]. The TTNT data link uses frequency-hopping technology at physical layer to achieve virtual full-duplex communication [8,13]. Figure 1 shows a schematic of the SPMA protocol. In the SPMA protocol, each priority traffic occupies one queue for transmission independently, and Each priority queue sets a threshold in advance. And the physical layer counts the load status of the network and obtains a network load statistic. When there are data packets in the queue needing be sent, it will compare the current network load statistics and the threshold of this queue first. When the network load statistic is lower than the queues's threshold, the data packet is allowed to be transmit. Otherwise, backoff is required. After the backoff, the queue's threshold and the new network load statistics in the current period are compared again.

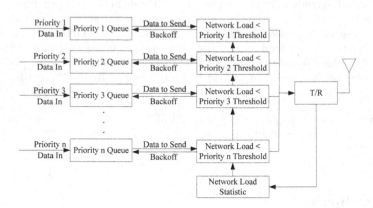

**Fig. 1.** SPMA protocol diagram

In [2,7], a multichannel Slotted-ALOHA protocol is proposed. The channel statistics are used to achieve feedback-free multiple access. The protocol flow is consistent with SPMA. The paper [11,12] propose a specific access control method based on the channel statistics of SPMA instead of the feedback mechanism. A channel collision model is established, and a method of setting a priority threshold is given. These articles all use SPMA's channel statistics instead of feedback mechanisms. The higher the service prioritiy is, the higher the threshold sets and the greater the possibility of access to the channel is. To ensure high timeliness of high priority traffic, if there are high-priority packets arriving while the low-priority queue is in a backoff state, canceling the backoff process. Then comparing the network load statistics with the threshold of the high-priority queue to decide if the high-priority packets can be transmit. This type of access guarantees high timeliness of high-priority traffic. And because of the higher threshold, high-priority traffic can occupy higher channel bandwidth. However, when the network load is high, the queues with threshold lower than the network load statistic cannot send packets. Because the backoff process of the low-priority queue can be interrupted the high-priority queue, if there are too many data packets in the high-priority queue (the high-priority queue can always send the data packet), the low-priority queue cannot send any data packet. Both of these conditions can cause the starvation problem in the low-priority queue (data packets cannot be sent).

Reference [6] proposed a priority weighted rate control algorithm in aeronautical Ad hoc networks. This article uses the classic weighted fair queue scheduling algorithm (WFQ) [1] to schedule multiple queues, and still sets a threshold for each priority queue based on SPMA. When the network load is higher than the threshold, it cannot send packets. This method solves the problem that the low-priority traffic cannot be sent if the low-priority traffic is saturated. However, when the network load is high, the low-priority traffic still cannot be sent. Then, this article will design a protocol (LSMA), which can solve the problems above.

This paper raises a load statistic-based frequency hopping multiple access protocol (LSMA) to ensure service QoS. The protocol allocates different bandwidths by scheduling multiple priority traffic first. Secondly, it calculates the load status of the network from the physical layer, and designs a load statistic-based rate control algorithm to control the network load and improve throughput.

The rest of this paper can be divided into the following sections: The Sect. 2 will introduce the system model of this article. The Sect. 3 will describe the protocol design and algorithm implementation of the LSMA specifically. It will also show how to schedule multiple priority traffic, calculate load statistic, and control the node's sending rate. In Sect. 4, the simulation scenario is designed. The simulation of LSMA and SPMA is compared using the OPNET simulation tool, and analyzing the system performance based on the simulation results. In the last Sect. 5, this paper will be summarized.

## 2   System Model

To ensure the QoS of different priority traffic and solve the starvation problem of low-priority traffic, the system model is given as follows:

In a fully connected network, $N$ nodes are distributed randomly and every node has the same functionality. Each node can generate $n$ different priority traffic. Each priority traffic is maintained by one queue, in which the data packets use first input first output (FIFO) system. The physical layer uses frequency hopping technology. The data packet is split into multiple pulses first, and sent according to the frequency-hopping pattern. And each node works in full-duplex mode, which can transmit data in 1 channel and receive data with 4 channels at the same time.

Network load statistics follow the method of SPMA. A packet is split into pulses before transmitting, and the corresponding frequency point is selected for each pulse according to the designed frequency hopping pattern. Therefore, different pulses can occupy different channels for sending or receiving simultaneously. Based on this, the SPMA protocol achieves 1 channel for transmission and 4 channels for reception. It can improve the throughput of the network effectively.

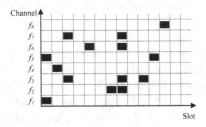

**Fig. 2.** System model

As shown in Fig. 2, when there are several nodes requiring to send packets in the network, each node will select one frequency for each pulse to transmit. Each frequency occupies one channel, and multiple channels are allowed to be occupied at the same time slot. When different nodes send the same frequency pulse in the same time slot, they will occupy the same channel, which causes collision. Setting the load statistics period is $T$, and counting the number of pulses sent by a node in the $T$ period, the pulse sending rate $\mu_s$ of the node can be obtained. In the same way, we can get the rate of pulse reception $\mu_r$.

## 3    Protocol Design and Algorithm Implementation

The core framework of the LSMA is shown in Fig. 3. This protocol includes multiple priority queues, service scheduler, rate control algorithm, network load statistic, and transmit and receive antennas. In order to solve the low-priority starvation problem, the data packets of multiple priority queues are scheduled first to ensure that every queue's packets have the opportunity to be scheduled. With the scheduling algorithm, every time the data packet is transmitted considering only one packet, instead of multiple queue packets. The priority threshold set by SPMA is not applicable. According to the network load statistic of physical layer, we can obtain the sending rate of the packet by the rate control algorithm to control the network load. After that backoff and send the data packet.

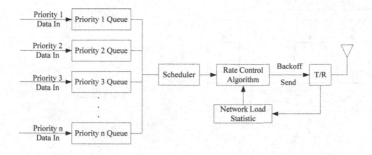

**Fig. 3.** LSMA protocol core framework

## 3.1  Multi-queue Scheduling Algorithm

The multi-queue scheduling algorithm is shown in Fig. 4. This algorithm schedules queues based on WFQ and considers non-saturated services. First, set a
sequence number $s$ for each packet in the queue, and the weight of queue $i$ is
$w_i$. Assuming that the sequence number of the header packet in queue $i$ is $s_i$,
then the sequence numbers of other packets in queue $i$ are increased $w_i$ in order,
which is $\{s_i + w_i, s_i + 2w_i, \cdots\}$.

When scheduling the packets, select the packet with the smallest sequence
number in the range of all the queues. This packet also has the smallest sequence
number in the header of all the queue. This sequence number is denoted as $S$,
and $S = \min_{i=0}^{n} s_i$. If there are several queues with the same sequence number,
they are sent according to the priority.

Assuming that the initial value of all queue serial numbers is 0. If there is
a new packet entering the non-empty queue $i$, the sequence number of the data
packet is added the weight $w_i$ on the base of the queue tail sequence number
$s_i^{tail}$. And it is $s_i^{tail} + w_i$. If there is a new data packet entering the empty queue
$i$, it is assumed that the sequence number of this packet is added weight $w_i$ based
on the sequence number of the last packet sent from the queue. We can get the
sequence number of this packet is $s_i' + w_i$. However, because the packet with the
sequence number $s_i'$ has been sent, $s_i' \leq S$, it is likely that $s_i' + w_i$ will be smaller
than the sequence number of packets that have higher priority than $i$ and have
not yet been sent. It will cause that the packets entered the queue with higher
priority earlier may be sent even later than the ones that have just entered the
lower priority queue. This is not fair.

In order to prevent that when non-saturated service packets enter the queue
the sequence number is too small, which will cause unfairness for existing packets
in the higher-priority queue. If there is a new packet entering the empty queue
$i$, the packet sequence number will be added the weight $w_i$ on the base of $S$,
which is, $S + w_i$. For example, the sequence number of new packet in queue 2 is
$s_2 = S + w_2$ in the Fig. 4.

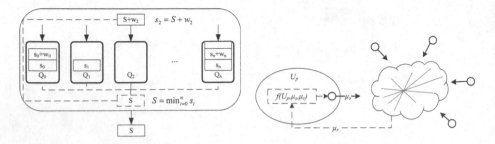

**Fig. 4.** Multi-queue scheduling algorithm

**Fig. 5.** Rate control algorithm

## 3.2 Rate Control Algorithm

The rate control algorithm is designed based on the node pulse sending rate $\mu_s$ and the receiving rate $\mu_r$ counted by physical layer. The sum of the pulse sending rate and the receiving rate $\mu_s + \mu_r$ constitutes the total network load. To control the packets loss rate and throughput in the network, we can limit the total load or the number of pulses.

First, let $U_p$ indicate the desired network load threshold. Secondly, physical layer calculates $\mu_s$ and $\mu_r$ once per rate update period T. Then, according to the rate update function $f(U_p, \mu_s, \mu_r)$, we can calculate the allowed rate $\mu_s'$ of the node as the next period sending rate. Update the sending rate every T periods. Finally, after the packets backoff time is calculated according to the sending rate $\mu_s'$, backoffing and sending it. The rate update formula is as follows:

$$
\mu_s' = \begin{cases} \mu_s + \Delta, & U_p - \mu_r - \mu_s > \Delta \\ \mu_s - \Delta, & \mu_r + \mu_s - U_p > \Delta \&\& \mu_s - \Delta > 0 \\ \mu_s, & other \end{cases} \tag{1}
$$

$$
\Delta = \begin{cases} \Delta_0, & |U_P - \mu_r - \mu_s| \leq B \\ 2\Delta, & U_p - \mu_r - \mu_s > \Delta or \begin{pmatrix} \mu_r + \mu_s - U_p > \Delta \\ \&\& \mu_s - \Delta > 0 \end{pmatrix} \\ \Delta/2, & other \end{cases} \tag{2}
$$

Equation (1) calculates the service sending rate $\mu_s'$ for the next period, where $\Delta$ is the rate change increment and $\Delta_0$ is the initial value of $\Delta$. $\Delta$ varies according to Eq. (2), where $B$ is the sending rate error tolerance.

For formula (1), when $U_p$ is greater than the total network load $\mu_s + \mu_r$ and the difference exceeds $\Delta$, the sending rate of the node need to be increased. Similarly, when $U_p$ is less than the total network load $\mu_s + \mu_r$, the sending rate needs to be reduced. Since the sending rate cannot be negative, $\mu_s - \Delta > 0$ must be guaranteed. In other cases keeping the sending rate unchanged.

For formula (2), when the difference of $\mu_s + \mu_r$ and $U_p$ are not more than the error tolerance B, it is considered that the network load at this time is in a stable state. Keeping the transmission rate unchanged while restoring $\Delta$ to the initial value $\Delta_0$. When the total network load and $U_p$ differ greatly and the sending rate needs to be adjusted, increasing $\Delta$ to double to enable the network load to be adjusted to $U_p$ quickly. In other cases, reducing $\Delta$ to half, including when the difference of $i\mu_s + \mu_r$ and $U_p$ are greater than the tolerance B but lower than $\Delta$, and when the total network load is too large but $\mu_s - \Delta > 0$. In the both cases, the transmission rate cannot be adjusted directly, we need reduce $\Delta$ to make sure the sending rate can be altered.

## 4    Performance Evaluation

To compare the performance of SPMA and the protocol designed in this paper, we need to simulate the two protocols. SPMA is simulated first. Building a network with size of 10 km × 10 km, and placing 6 identical nodes. Each node maintains 4 priority queues (priority order: Queue 1 > Queue 2 > Queue 3 > Queue 4). The service of each queue is Poisson's arrival service, and the size of the transmitted data packet is 1024 bits. Changing the size of the traffic and observing the changes of network throughput and packet loss rate.

The traffic rate for each queue is set to {100, 200, 500, 1000, 2000, 3000} packets per second. The parameter settings of SPMA protocol are shown in Table 1, including the thresholds of 4 priority queues and the load statistics period T.

Table 1. Simulation parameters of SPMA

| Paramter name | Values |
|---|---|
| T | 0.5s |
| The threshold of queue 1 | 80000(pulses/s) |
| The threshold of queue 2 | 60000(pulses/s) |
| The threshold of queue 3 | 40000(pulses/s) |
| The threshold of queue 4 | 20000(pulses/s) |

Figure 6 illustrates how the SPMA protocol network load changes with service traffic. It can be seen that as the increase of traffic, the total pulse sending rate in the network increases gradually, while the total pulse receiving rate increases first before stabilizing at about 68,000. Comparing the service delivery status of the 4 priority queues, the service is more saturation, the proportion of queue 1 in the sent packets becomes higher. And the queue with lower priority appears starvation problem earlier, until only the packets of queue 1 can be sent in the end.

In order to make the LSMA protocol compared with the SPMA protocol at the same throughput, we set the parameter $U_p$ according to the SPMA simulation result. When the SPMA throughput is maximum, the pulse receiving rate is approximately 68000 pulses per second. Considering that the network always

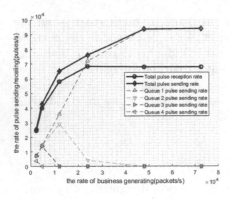

**Fig. 6.** Network load curve of SPMA

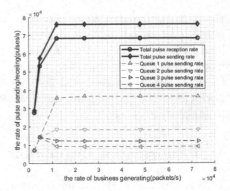

**Fig. 7.** Network load curve of LSMA

has packets loss, we set the value of $U_p$ to 72000 pulses per second [1]. Other parameter settings are shown in Table 2. The traffic rate setting for each queue is unchanged.

**Table 2.** Simulation parameters of LSMA

| Paramter name | Values |
|---|---|
| T | 0.5s |
| $U_p$ | 72000(pulses/s) |
| $\Delta$ | $0.25U_p/N$ |
| B | 60 |
| $w_1$ | 1 |
| $w_2$ | 2 |
| $w_3$ | 3 |
| $w_4$ | 4 |

Figure 7 show the changes of network load in LSMA. With the increase of traffic, the total pulse transmission rate and pulse reception rate in the network increase first, and then remain stable. It means that the LSMA's rate control algorithm can control the network load effectively, so that the network's total pulse sending rate is controlled in the vicinity of $U_p$. When the network load reaches the maximum, the service sending rate of the four queues becomes a certain ratio (12:6:4:3), which is inversely proportional to the weight (1:2:3:4). By setting the weight of the queue to allocate a different proportion of bandwidth for the queue, the resulting proportional throughput is called the weighted throughput.

---

[1] Testing several times, selecting the sending rate when the receiving rate is same to that in SPMA. We get the value is 72000. The test process is not given in this paper.

The changes of throughput and packet loss rate in SPMA and LSMA are illustrated in Figs. 8 and 9 respectively. Although the throughput of both increases first and then remains stable, the LSMA reaches its maximum value when the traffic is 12,000 packets per second. While the SPMA reaches its maximum value when the traffic is 24000 packets per second. And when the traffic is lower than this traffic, the throughput of SPMA is always lower than that of LSMA, but they packet loss rates are similar. It indicating that the sending rate of the SPMA protocol packet is lower, which causes a waste of network resources. When the traffic exceeds 24,000 packets per second, the packet loss rate of SPMA reaches about 27%, which is significantly higher than that of LSMA (only 10%).

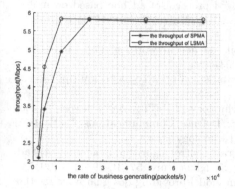

**Fig. 8.** Throughput comparison          **Fig. 9.** Loss rate comparison

Comparing SPMA and LSMA comprehensively, LSMA's multi-queue scheduling algorithm assigns weighted throughput to each priority queue. It satisfies the bandwidth requirements for different priority traffic. The network has a better performance in the LSMA protocol. Its packet loss rate is lower, when the throughput is the same.

## 5   Conclusion

In AANET, for the purpose of solving the low-priority starvation problem of SPMA and meet the QoS requirements of different priority traffic, this paper proposes a load statistic-based frequency hopping multiple access protocol LSMA.

LSMA allocates different bandwidths for different priority traffic by multi-queue scheduling algorithm, and obtains weighted throughput. Secondly, LSMA designs a rate adaptive adjustment algorithm in conjunction with the layer network load statistic to keep the network load steadily. Only using one parameter $U_p$ to control the sending of packets, and $U_p$ indicates the size of the network load approximately. Comparing LSMA with SPMA by simulation, LSMA not only solves starvation of low-priority queues in SPMA, but also can control network packet loss rate to a lower level and guarantee service QoS better.

318     Y. Qin et al.

**Acknowledgment.** This work was supported in part by the National Natural Science Foundations of CHINA (Grant No.61771392, 61771390, 61501373 and 61271279), the National Science and Technology Major Project (Grant No. 2016ZX03001018-004, and No. 2015ZX03002006-004), and the Fundamental Research Funds for the Central Universities (Grant No. 3102017ZY018).

# References

1. Bensaou, B., Wang, Y., Chi, C.K.: Fair medium access in 802.11 based wireless ad-hoc networks. In: 2000 First Workshop on Mobile and Ad Hoc Networking and Computing, Mobihoc 2000, pp. 99–106 (2000)
2. Bian, D., Zhang, H., Peng, S.: An improved protocol of ad hoc based on multichannel statistics on mac layer. J. Air Force Eng. Univ. (Natural Science Edition) **14**(1), 80–84 (2013)
3. Chlamtac, I., Conti, M., Liu, J.N.: Mobile ad hoc networking: imperatives and challenges. Ad Hoc Netw. **1**(1), 13–64 (2003)
4. Clark, S.M., Hoback, K.A., Zogg, S.J.F.: Statistical priority-based multiple access system and method (2010)
5. Collins, R.: Tactical targeting network technology (TT-NT) (2008). https://www.rockwellcollins.com/Products-and-Services/Defense/Communications/Tactical-Data-Links/Tactical-Targeting-Network-Technology.aspx
6. Gao, X., Yan, J., Lu, J.: Priority weighted rate control algorithm in aeronautical ad hoc networks. Qinghua Daxue Xuebao/J. Tsinghua Univ. **57**(3), 293–298 (2017)
7. Gao, X., Han, F., Yan, J., Lu, J.: Collision model providing qos guarantee for the feedback-free MAC in aeronautical ad hoc networks. J. Beijing Univ. Aeronaut. Astronaut. **42**(6), 1169–1175 (2016)
8. Guo, D., Zhang, L.: Virtual full-duplex wireless communication via rapid on-off-division duplex. In: Communication, Control, and Computing, pp. 412–419 (2010)
9. Haas, Z.J., Deng, J., Liang, B., Papadimitratos, P., Sajama, S.: Wireless ad hoc networks. IEEE J. Sel. Areas Commun. **17**(8), 1329–1332 (2007)
10. Sakhaee, E., Jamalipour, A., Kato, N.: Aeronautical ad hoc networks. In: 2006 Wireless Communications and Networking Conference, WCNC, pp. 246–251 (2006)
11. Wang, Y.Q., Yang, F., Huang, G.C., Zhang, H.Y., Guo, J.X.: Media access control protocol with differential service in aeronautical frequency-hopping ad hoc networks. J. Softw. **24**(8), 2214–2225 (2013)
12. Zhang, H., Peng, S., Zhao, Y., Bian, D.: An improved algorithm of slotted-aloha based on multichannel statistics. In: Fifth International Symposium on Computational Intelligence and Design, pp. 37–40 (2012)
13. Zhou, S.: On the MAC protocol of TTNT. Ph.D. thesis, Xidian University (2015)

# Developing a Context-Aware POI Network of Adaptive Vehicular Traffic Routing for Urban Logistics

Chih-Kun Ke[1(✉)], Szu-Cheng Lai[1], and Li-Te Huang[2]

[1] Department of Information Management, National Taichung University of Science and Technology, No.129, Sec.3, Sanmin Road, North Dist., Taichung 40401, Taiwan, R.O.C.
{ckk, s1810531013}@nutc.edu.tw
[2] Service Systems Technology Center, Industrial Technology Research Institute, 195, Sec. 4, Chung Hsing Rd., Chutung, Hsinchu 31057, Taiwan, R.O.C.
huanglite@itri.org.tw

**Abstract.** Advanced information and communication technology promote smart city development, especially in urban logistics. Vehicular traffic routing problem is the key factor to influence the logistics chauffeur's service quality. Different from traditional vehicular ad hoc networks, this study proposes a novel approach using data mining, skyline domination, and multi-criteria decision analysis to develop a context-aware point-of-interest network of vehicular traffic routing for urban logistics. The density-based clustering discovers the logistics destination, referred to as the "points-of-interest (POI)," nearby the logistics chauffeur. The candidate POI filtered by the skyline domination. The multi-criteria decision analysis produces a ranking of candidate POI based on the status of traffic criteria evaluation. We use open data from Google map and Foursquare to construct a context-aware POI network. An experimental system implementation to demonstrate the proposed approach effectiveness. The contribution is to optimize the adaptive vehicular traffic routing solution for the urban logistics in a smart city.

**Keywords:** Context-aware network · Points-of-interest · Density-based clustering · Skyline domination · Multi-criteria decision analysis
Urban logistics

## 1 Introduction

In order to satisfy the various needs of human life, people obtain product through different modes, such as shopping in a physical store or by phone. Due to the rapid development of information and communication technology, advanced data processing and information transmission have quickly promoted many emerging business models, such as e-commerce and m-commerce [1]. In order to make e-commerce working smoothly, the logistics industry supply chain ecosystem has been built. Logistics services have always played an important role in these models, collecting and delivering mechanisms to effectively deliver products to customers. Each participant can use the

© ICST Institute for Computer Sciences, Social Informatics and Telecommunications Engineering 2019
Published by Springer Nature Switzerland AG 2019. All Rights Reserved
J.-L. Chen et al. (Eds.): WiCON 2018, LNICST 264, pp. 319–328, 2019.
https://doi.org/10.1007/978-3-030-06158-6_31

convenient and friendly interface of the information system to add, modify, delete and query orders. It can also use the advantages of the Internet to prevent products from being limited by time and space. Accelerate and enhance the ability of traditional logistics service information flows through product status verification and tracking. Subscribers can obtain status in the delivery of products through web services, such as tracking of distribution centers and transfer stations. Mobile devices, including mobile phones, tablets, and personal portable assistants (PDA), bring greater convenience to users turning business models into action. In m-commerce, it is better than e-commerce to apply to the logistics industry supply chain ecosystem. The artificial intelligence technology is currently in full swing [2, 3]. It can be used for forecasting and recommending through massive data modeling and analysis, and will make the entire logistics industry supply chain ecosystem more intelligent. The application of communication technology will play an important role.

The restrictive conditions for the development of urban logistics involve the location, time, object and other facets. Logistics services must continuously deliver products to customers at the specified time and location throughout the delivery process, with the expectation of maximizing customer satisfaction. In the situation where urban traffic is congested during peak time periods, if trucks are used for logistics services, there is a risk of delivering the products on time. Due to a large number of large-scale freight transport products, once the traffic congestion is delayed, it will be out of control, which will affect the delivery of all products. This situation stimulates the question of how to improve mobility. The city has a special feature, which is a large number of small lanes. The locomotive quick service is constructed to solve the traffic congestion when trucks are transported. Unacceptable circumstances. Therefore, the promotion of locomotive quick service can help the domestic logistics industry to establish convenient and reliable delivery services. Through the flexibility of motor vehicles, it reduces the cost of urban logistics services.

The advancement of communication technology and the application of map mark sharing services have prompted the development of location-based social networks (LBSNs) such as Foursquare and Instagram application services on the Internet and communication platforms [4]. The points of Interest (POI) information on the network location quickly accumulates huge amounts of data over time. How to find the points of interest that meet the user's expectations will pose an important challenge. Therefore, in the huge amount of information covered by location-based social networks, recommending users with appropriate points of interest and paths becomes a research topic worth exploring [5–7]. Besides, mobile computing technology also promote smart city development, especially in urban logistics. Vehicular traffic routing problem is the key factor to influence the logistics chauffeur's service quality [8–10]. Different from traditional vehicular ad hoc networks, this study proposes a novel approach using data mining, skyline domination, and multi-criteria decision analysis to develop a context-aware POI network of adaptive vehicular traffic routing for urban logistics. The density-based clustering [11, 12] discovers the logistic destination, referred to as the "points-of-interest (POI)," nearby the logistics chauffeur. The candidate POI filtered by the skyline domination. The multi-criteria decision analysis [13] produces a ranking of candidate POI based on the status of traffic routing criteria evaluation. We use open data from Google map and Foursquare to construct a context-aware POI network. An experimental system implementation to demonstrate the proposed approach effectiveness. The contribution is to optimize the adaptive vehicular traffic routing solution for the urban logistics in a smart city.

The remainder of this paper is organized as follows. Section 2 introduces a novel approach using data mining, skyline domination, and multi-criteria decision analysis to develop a context-aware mobile network of adaptive vehicular traffic routing for urban logistics. The experiments are illustrated in Sect. 3. Finally, Sect. 4 presents our conclusions.

## 2   The Context-Aware POI Network of Adaptive Vehicular Traffic Routing for Urban Logistics

This section introduces a novel system framework using the density-based clustering, skyline domination and multi-criteria decision analysis to optimize the logistics destination (POI) recommendation mechanism. The proposed system includes the data extraction module, data preprocessing module, POI network construction module, multi-criteria decision analysis module, user configuration and recommendation module, and knowledge base. The system framework is shown in Fig. 1. Each module is illustrated as follows.

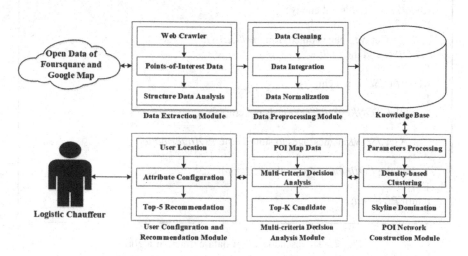

**Fig. 1.** The proposed system framework of adaptive vehicular traffic routing for urban logistics

- The data extraction module

The data extraction module collects the information of the logistics destination, as referred as points-of-interest (POI), required by the logistics chauffeur and analyze the relevant information through the proposed system. The information about the POI provided in the cloud server, i.e., Google map and Foursquare servers, is collected from the web pages. Then the collected contents, for example, the POI description and relevant attribute, are extracted through the JSON (JavaScript Object Notation, JSON) lightweight data-interchange format from the web pages to store in a knowledge base. The pseudocode of data extraction algorithm is shown in Fig. 2.

---

**Parameter Definition:**

| | |
|---|---|
| *OpenDataUrl* | The URL of open data website; |
| *FoursquareUrl* | The URL of Foursquare website; |
| *GoogleMapUrl* | The URL of Google map website; |
| *POI* | Data extraction from the cloud servers; |
| *urlSet* | A URL set of the open data websites; |
| *POISet* | A set of the POI; |
| *POIInformation* | Information of a POI; |
| *POIData* | A set of POI data; |
| *JSONKey* | The key of JSON; |
| *JSONKeySet* | A set of *JSONKey*; |

**Data extraction algorithm(pseudocode):**
**Input:** *OpenDataUrl, FoursquareUrl, GoogleMapUrl*
**Output:** *POIData*
**DataExtraction** (*OpenDataUrl, FoursquareUrl, GoogleMapUrl*)
{

    *urlSet*=Analysis of *OpenDataUrl, FoursquareUrl*, and *GoogleMapUrl*;
    while(*urlSet.Url* is not empty)
    {
      *POI*= Get web page content form *urlSet.Url*;
      *POISet* add the *POI*;
    }
    while(*POISet* is not empty)
    {
      while(*JSONKeySet.JSONKey* is not empty)
      {
        Get *JSONKey* messages to store in the *POIInformation*;
      }
      Add the *POIInformation* to the *POIData*;
    }
    return *POIData*;
}

---

**Fig. 2.** The pseudocode of data extraction algorithm

- The data pre-processing module

In the data pre-processing module, the proposed system analyzes the POI description and relevant attribute to remove the meaningless information. It includes data cleaning, data integration, and data normalization processes of the POI obtained by the data extraction module. Data preprocessing executes the non-symbol, stemming, and stop word removal tasks to prevent the interference in a POI network construction. The information of POI after data cleaning may contain duplicate attribute values in the dataset. The type of data will be difficult to analyze because of its inconsistency. Therefore, in the data integration process, the data will be merged. The information of POIs processed through data integration may include attribute values of different scopes and sizes, which will affect the subsequent analysis operations, so the data normalization process will be executed. For example, the Min-Max normalization method is used to normalize the data attributes, and the result will converge to [0, 1]. The pseudocode of data pre-processing algorithm is shown in Fig. 3.

---

**Parameter Definition:**

| | |
|---|---|
| *POIData* | A set of POI data; |
| *DCPOIDataSet* | A set of POI data after data cleaning; |
| *DCPOIData* | POI Data after data cleaning; |
| *FoursquareData* | Foursquare POI data after data cleaning; |
| *GoogleMapData* | Google map POI data after data cleaning; |
| *DIPOIDataSet* | A set of POI Data after data integration; |
| *DIPOIData* | A POI Data after data integration; |
| *MaxValue* | The maximum value of a POI attribute after data integration; |
| *MinValue* | The minimum value of a POI attribute after data integration; |
| *DNPOIDataSet* | A set of POI Data after data normalization; |

**Data pre-processing algorithm(pseudocode):**
**Input:** *POIData*
**Output:** *DNPOIDataSet*
**DataPreprocessing**(*POIData*)

```
{
   while(POIData is not empty)
   {
     if(POIData is duplicate)
     {
        DCPOIDataSet = POIData delete duplicate data;
     }
   }
   while(DCPOIDataSet.DCPOIData. GoogleMapData is not empty)
   {
     DIPOIDataSet = Combination of FoursquareData and GoogleMapData;
   }
   while(DIPOIDataSet.DIPOIData is not empty)
   {
     DNPOIDataSet = (DIPOIData minus MinValue) divided by
     (MaxValue minus MinValue);
   }
   return DNPOIDataSet;
}
```

**Fig. 3.** The pseudocode of data pre-processing algorithm

## 2.1    The point of interest (POI) network construction module

In the POI network construction module, a large number of POI information will be calculated using the Euclidean distance formula to calculate the mutual distance between all POI. The density-based clustering method in cluster analysis will be used to determine the optimal range. Filter out POI outside the range. The function mainly uses the concept of density-based clustering to exclude POI beyond the optimal radius, thereby reducing the number of POI for subsequent analysis. The cluster parameter processing algorithm is to take any POI as the starting point by the data pre-processing module. The module performs Euclidean distance calculation on the POI and other POI. Then, all the POI are density-based clustering [12] through the Euclidean distance set between the POIs, so as to filter out the edge POI in the density cluster to exclude by using DBSCAN [11] as the benchmark algorithm for density-based clustering. The k-nearest neighbor method (KNN) finds the best radius in the set of Euclidean distances between POI. Through this process, the edge POI existing on the map can be found and excluded. The pseudocode of density-based clustering algorithm is shown in Fig. 4.

```
Parameter Definition:
ProcessedPOIDataSet        A set of POI after data preprocessing;
ProcessedPOIData           POI data after data preprocessing;
EuclideanDistSet           A Euclidean distance set of POI;
EuclideanDist              The value of the Euclidean distance between POI;
BestRadius                 The best radius of density-based clustering;
DBScanPOIDataSet           A set of POI after density-based clustering;
Density-based clustering algorithm(pseudocode):
Input: ProcessedPOIDataSet
Output: DBScanPOIDataSet
DBSCAN(ProcessedPOIDataSet)
{
    BestRadius = KNN operation on EuclideanDistSet;
    while (EuclideanDistSet is not empty)
    {
        if(EuclideanDistSet.EuclideanDist less than or equal to BestRadius)
        {
            DBScanPOIDataSet = ProcessedPOIDataSet.ProcessedPOIData;
        }
    }
    return DBScanPOIDataSet;
}
```

**Fig. 4.** The pseudocode of density-based clustering algorithm

After excluding the divergence value in the POI, the skyline domination is used to find out the better solution. By the domination process, multiple attributes can be simultaneously compared and an optimal set is generated. The POI in the optimal set will not be worse than other POIs. The pseudocode of skyline domination algorithm is shown in Fig. 5.

```
Parameter Definition:
DBScanPOIDataSet       A set of POI after density-based clustering;
DBScanPOIData          POI data after density-based clustering;
Dominate               The domination of skyline method;
AValue                 Base POI for skyline domination;
BValue                 Comparable POI for skyline domination;
MapCreationPOIData     A set of POI after POI network construction;
Skyline Domination algorithm(pseudocode):
Input: MapCreationPOIData
Output: MapCreationPOIData
SkylineDomination(MapCreationPOIData)
{
    while (DBScanPOIDataSet is not empty)
    {
        if( AValue.x is better than BValue.x and AValue.y is not worse than
        BValue.y)
        {
            Dominate = DBScanPOIDataSet.DBScanPOIData;
        }
        else
        {
            Dominate = NA;
        }
    }
    MapCreationPOIData = Dominate;
    return MapCreationPOIData;
}
```

**Fig. 5.** The pseudocode of skyline domination algorithm

## 2.2 The Multi-criteria Decision Analysis Module

The multi-criteria decision analysis module is a core mechanism of the recommendation mechanism. After executing the density-based clustering, skyline domination, and multi-criteria decision analysis, the system recommends a reasonable logistics destination from among the candidate logistics destinations. The pseudocode of multi-criteria decision analysis algorithm is shown in Fig. 6.

---

**Parameter Definition:**

*CandidatePOISet*          A set of the candidate POI with feature values on
                                            issues for a user;

*RCandidatePOISet*         A set of candidate POI with normalized feature values;
*userWeightSet*             A criteria weight set by user configuration;
*RankingOrder*              The ranking order from a multi-criteria decision method;
*MCDACandidatePOISet* A set of the POIs with multi-criteria decision analysis;

**Multi-Criteria Decision Analysis algorithm(pseudocode):**
**Input:** *CandidatePOISet, userWeightSet;*
**Output:** *MCDACandidatePOISet;*
**MultiCriteriaDecisionAnalysis***(CandidatePOISet, userWeightSet)*
{
    switch
    {
      case *TOPSIS:*
        *RankingOrder* ≡ *TOPSIS(RCandidatePOISet, userWeightSet);*
      case *VIKOR:*
        *RankingOrder* ≡ *VIKOR(RCandidatePOISet, userWeightSet);*
      case *ELECTRE:*
        *RankingOrder* ≡ *ELECTRE(RCandidatePOISet, userWeightSet);*
      case *PROMETHEE:*
        *RankingOrder* ≡ *PROMETHEE(RCandidatePOISet, userWeightSet);*
      case *SAW:*
        *RankingOrder* ≡ *SAW(RCandidatePOISet, userWeightSet);*
    }
    return the *MCDACandidatePOISet* based on the *RankingOrder;*
}

---

**Fig. 6.** The pseudocode of multi-criteria decision analysis algorithm

### 2.3    The User Configuration and Recommendation Module

The user configuration module obtains the logistics chauffeur location, current traffic routing status. The logistics chauffeur can configure the preferences related to personal driving habit. Besides, he can receive the recommendation logistics destination from system for delivering the products and sends the feedback to help the system improvement for next recommendation.

## 3    Experiments

This section illustrates the proposed system platform and the experimental case. The development environment of proposed system is operated by Microsoft Windows 10 64-bit operating system, the core is Intel[R] Core[TM] i7-6700HQ CPU @ 2.60 GHz processor, the memory is 8 GB, and the programming language used is R language with version 3.3.3, and the web server is Apache 2.4.33 and the database system MySQL 5.7.22, and uses the shiny suite in the R language to implement the proposed system.

### 3.1   Experimental Case: Urban Logistics in Taichung City, R.O.C

Based on the data collection from open data of Taichung City Bus Station Information, Google map and Foursquare, we obtained a data set of which includes 19,192 POIs. After removing the duplicate data, the amount of data in the data set is reduced to 12,452 POIs. After Recursive Feature Elimination and Learning Vector Quantization processing, 7 attributes are selected from 70 attributes to execute the experiment. The POIs with 7 attributes are grouped by density-based clustering using radius value is 400 m and density value is 10. The logistics chauffeur selects an initial location, for example, National Taichung University of Science and Technology, and select the group of density-based POIs set for min-max normalization. The min-max normalized data set executes skyline domination to filter out bad POIs. Next, multi-criteria decision analysis are performed to get reasonable POI with vehicular traffic routing path. Finally, the experiment results of the POI and adaptive routing path selection by the proposed system for urban logistics are shown in Fig. 7.

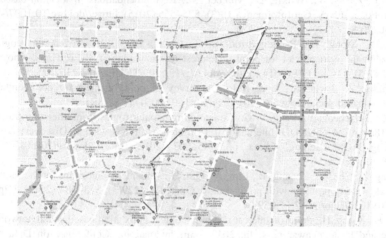

**Fig. 7.** The results present in Google Maps with the POIs and adaptive routing paths.

## 4   Conclusion

This study proposes a novel approach using data mining, skyline domination, and multi-criteria decision analysis to develop a context-aware mobile network of adaptive vehicular traffic routing for urban logistics. An experimental system implementation to demonstrate the proposed system effectiveness. The contribution is to get an optimal vehicular traffic routing solution for the urban logistics in a smart city. In future work, we will enforce collected data from several famous social media and searching platform to evaluate the proposed system framework effectiveness. Besides, this study proposes a novel intelligent POI recommendation system which provides a logistics chauffeur new operating model to provide better quality of service. The unified theory of acceptance & use of technology (UTAUT) can be used to test the novel system's acceptance.

328    C.-K. Ke et al.

**Acknowledgements.** This research was supported in part by the Ministry of Science and Technology, R.O.C. with a MOST grant 107-2221-E-025-005.

# References

1. Schafer, J.B., Konstan, J.A., Riedl, J.: E-commerce recommendation applications. Data Min. Knowl. Disc. **5**(1–2), 115–153 (2001). https://doi.org/10.1023/A:1009804230409
2. Mulvenna, M.D., Anand, S.S., Büchner, A.G.: Personalization on the net using web mining: introduction. Commun. ACM **43**(8), 122–125 (2000). https://doi.org/10.1145/345124.345165
3. Abbas, A., Zhang, l., Khan S.U.: A survey on context-aware recommender systems based on computational intelligence techniques. Computing **97**(7), 667–690 (2015). https://doi.org/10.1007/s00607-015-0448-7
4. Borris, J., Moreno, A., Valls, A.: Intelligent tourism recommender systems: a survey. Expert Syst. Appl. **41**(16), 7370–7389 (2014). https://doi.org/10.1016/j.eswa.2014.06.007
5. Bao, J., Zheng, Y., Wilkie, D., Mokbel, M.: Recommendations in location-based social networks: a survey. GeoInformatica **19**(3), 525–565 (2015). https://doi.org/10.1007/s10707-014-0220-8
6. Liu, B., Xiong, H., Papadimitriou, S., Fu, Y.J., Yao, Z.J.: A general geographical probabilistic factor model for point of interest recommendation. IEEE Trans. Knowl. Data Eng. **27**(5), 1167–1179 (2014). https://doi.org/10.1109/TKDE.2014.2362525
7. Shenglin, Z., Irwin, K., Lyu, M.R.: A survey of point-of-interest recommendation in location-based social network (2016). arXiv:1607.00647v1 [cs.IR]
8. Wei, L.Y., Zheng, Y., Peng, W.C.: Constructing popular routes from uncertain trajectories. In: 18th ACM SIGKDD International Conference on Knowledge Discovery and Data Mining, ACM, Beijing, China, pp. 195–203 (2012). https://doi.org/10.1145/2339530.2339562
9. Zhang, Z., Che, O., Cheang, B., Lim, A., Qin, H.: A memetic algorithm for the multiperiod vehicle routing problem with profit. Eur. J. Oper. Res. **229**(3), 573–584 (2013). https://doi.org/10.1016/j.ejor.2012.11.059
10. Liu, B., Xiong, H.: Point-of-Interest recommendation in location based social networks with topic and location awareness. In: 2013 Siam International Conference on Data Mining, pp. 396–404 (2013). https://doi.org/10.1137/1.9781611972832.44
11. Ankerst, M., Breunig, M.M., Kriegel, H.P., Sander, J.: OPTICS: ordering points to identify the clustering structure. In: 1999 ACM SIGMOD International Conference on Management of Data, vol. 28, no. 2, pp. 49–60 (1999). https://doi.org/10.1145/304181.304187
12. Ester, M., Kriegel, H.P., Sander, J., Xu, X.: A density-based algorithm for discovering in large spatial database with noise. In: Second International Conference on Knowledge Discovery and Data Mining, Portland, Oregon, pp. 226–231 (1996)
13. Nassereddine, M., Eskandari, H.: An integrated MCDM approach to evaluate public transportation systems in Tehran. Transp. Res. Part A Policy Pract. **106**, 427–439 (2017). https://doi.org/10.1016/j.tra.2017.10.013

# Efficient 3D Placement of Drone Base Stations with Frequency Planning

Le Xu and Yuliang Tang$^{(\boxtimes)}$ iD

School of Information Science and Engineering,
Xiamen University, Xiamen 361005, China
tyl@xmu.edu.cn

**Abstract.** It is anticipated that unmanned aerial vehicle base stations (UAV-BSs) will play a role in compensating network outages in case of temporary/unexpected events on account of flexibility. However, one of the key issues is how to deploy them efficiently. In this paper, the coverage, capacity and interference constraints are jointly considered, making the 3D placement more practical. Given available UAV-BS number, frequency band number and ground user distribution, the optimization objective is to maximize the number of serviced users and it is formulated into a mixed integer non-linear problem. Thereupon we develop a heuristic algorithm to find a suboptimal solution with polynomial time complexity. Numerical results show that available UAV-BS number is the critical factor of serviced user percent when user density is high, while the maximal allowable coverage radius is the critical factor when user density is low.

**Keywords:** UAV-BS · 3D placement · Frequency planning

## 1  Introduction

Deploying unmanned aerial vehicle base stations (UAV-BSs) is considered as a promising method to meet various communication requirements [1–3]. Compared with terrestrial infrastructures, on-demand UAV-BSs possess following advantages: (i) Flexibility—UAVs can be deployed without topography constraints, making them particularly applicable for temporary/unexpected situations. As a typical case, UAV-BSs constitute an emergency communication system after a natural disaster if ground base stations are damaged. Offloading traffic from congested ground base stations during big public events is another usage of UAV-BSs [1]; (ii) Maneuverability/Mobility—Dynamic deployment of UAV-BSs offers

This work was supported by National Natural Science Foundation of China (Grant number 61731012, 91638204, 61371081).

opportunities for performance enhancement; (iii) UAV-BSs have a high chance of line-of-sight (LoS) links to ground users owing to their high altitude, leading to significant performance improvement [2]. While the deployment of ground base stations are based on long-term traffic behavior, UAV-BSs require rapid and efficient placement [3]. 3D placement of UAV-BSs faces several challenges such as power consumption, altitude optimization, coverage planning, capacity constraint, and interference management [1].

The authors in [4] establish an air-to-ground channel model comprising free space pathloss and shadowing/scattering effects of obstacles, and they prove that there exists a unique altitude maximizing coverage radius and the optimum elevation angle only depends on the environment. Although the problem of altitude optimization has been addressed thoroughly, finding the best horizontal places of UAV-BSs is still challenging. The work in [5] aims to maximize the number of users covered by an UAV-BS and formulates the 3D placement problem into a quadratically-constrained mixed integer non-linear problem. In consideration of power saving, the authors in [6] take a further step and attempt to reduce the radius of the coverage region without decreasing the number of covered users by solving a smallest enclosing disc problem. It is pointed out in [7] that backhaul constraint is an important limitation since an UAV-BS has a wireless backhaul, and the authors try to maximize weighted user number so that spectrum, backhaul, and coverage constraints are satisfied for different rate requirements in a clustered user distribution. Some researchers have investigated multiple UAV-BSs deployment from different perspective. In [8], based on the downlink coverage probability and circle packing theory, the total coverage is maximum while the coverage areas of UAV-BSs do not overlap. Assuming all UAVs are flying at a fixed altitude, the authors in [9] propose a polynomial-time spiral algorithm to solve the geometric disk cover problem to cover a set of nodes in a region with the minimum number of disks of given radius. In [10], the authors using particle swarm optimization algorithm to find the minimum number of UAV-BSs and their 3D locations under coverage and capacity constraints.

In this paper, we study a novel 3D placement problem of multiple UAV-BSs. Given specific user distribution, UAV-BS number and frequency band number, we aim to maximize the total number of serviced users while the coverage regions of UAV-BSs using the same frequency band do not overlap. The main contributions of this paper are listed as follows

1. performs interference management in the deployment phase of UAV-BSs via frequency division multiplexing;
2. designs a heuristic algorithm to tackle the placement in the horizontal dimension[1] under constraints of coverage, capacity and interference.

The rest of this paper is organized as follows: In Sect. 2, we describe air-to-ground channel model and optimization problem. We detail the algorithm design

---

[1] The fundamental results presented in [4] enables that the placement can be decoupled in the horizontal dimension from the vertical dimension without loss of optimality.

in Sect. 3 and evaluate the algorithm via various test cases in Sect. 4. Finally, Sect. 5 concludes this work.

## 2 System Model

Consider $N$ stationary ground users randomly located in a rectangular $X \times Y$ geographical area, and $K$ available UAVs need to be deployed somewhere within the altitude range $[h_{\min}, h_{\max}]$. We assume that there is no ground base stations[2] and UAV-BSs are backhaul-connected via free space optical [11]. Assume there are $W$ different frequency band available in total ($W \geq 1$), each with bandwidth $B$. All ground user terminals have the same receiver sensitivity. Next, we briefly review the air-to-ground channel model proposed in [4] and use its conclusions directly as a prerequisite of our work.

### 2.1 Air to Ground Channel Model and Optimal Altitude

The ground users receive two main propagation components of a signal from an UAV-BS: one from LoS and another from non LoS (NLoS) with strong reflections and diffractions. The components exist with $P_{\text{LoS}}$ and $1 - P_{\text{LoS}}$ respectively. The probability of having a LoS connection is given by

$$P_{\text{LoS}} = \frac{1}{1 + a \cdot e^{-b(\theta - a)}} \tag{1}$$

where $\theta$ is the elevation angle, $a$ and $b$ are environment constants.

The average path losses for LoS and NLoS links in dB are

$$L_{\text{LoS}} = 20 \log\left(\frac{4\pi f_c d}{c}\right) + \eta_{\text{LoS}},$$

$$L_{\text{NLoS}} = 20 \log\left(\frac{4\pi f_c d}{c}\right) + \eta_{\text{NLoS}} \tag{2}$$

where $f_c$ is the carrier frequency, $d$ is the distance between the UAV and ground user, $\eta_{\text{LoS}}$ and $\eta_{\text{NLoS}}$ are the mean value of the excessive pathloss for LoS and NLoS, respectively. The pair ($\eta_{\text{LoS}}, \eta_{\text{NLoS}}$) take values (0.1, 21), (1.0, 20), (1.6, 23), (2.3, 34) corresponding to Suburban, Urban, Dense Urban, and Highrise Urban respectively. Therefore, the expectation of the pathloss can be expressed as

$$L = P_{\text{LoS}} \cdot L_{\text{LoS}} + (1 - P_{\text{LoS}}) \cdot L_{\text{NLoS}}. \tag{3}$$

Limited by receiver sensitivity $P_r$, the user is not covered if the total pathloss $L$ exceeds the threshold $L_{\max}$. Thus, the coverage of an UAV-BS in the ground

---

[2] In hotspot assistance scenarios, we can exclude the ground users served by ground base stations.

is a disc with radius $R$. Denote the UAV-BS altitude by $h$. Substituting (1) and (2) into (3) and noting that $\tan\theta = h/R$ yield

$$L_{max} = \frac{\eta_{LoS} - \eta_{NLoS}}{1 + a \cdot e^{-b(\arctan(h/R)-a)}} + 10\log(h^2 + R^2)$$
$$+ 20\log\left(\frac{4\pi f_c}{c}\right) + \eta_{NLoS}. \tag{4}$$

Given the transmitted power of the UAV-BS, i.e., as for a specific $L_{max}$, the optimal value of $h_{opt}$ that maximize $R$ satisfies the equation

$$\frac{\partial R}{\partial h} = 0. \tag{5}$$

The optimum elevation angle is then defined as $\theta_{opt} = \arctan(h_{opt}/R)$. By solving (5), we have

$$\frac{\pi}{9\ln 10}\tan\theta_{opt} + \frac{ab(\eta_{LoS} - \eta_{NLoS})e^{-b(\theta_{opt}-a)}}{(1 + a \cdot e^{-b(\theta_{opt}-a)})^2} = 0. \tag{6}$$

The solution of Eq. (6) is clearly independent of $L_{max}$ and only depends on the environment, which implies the ratio of $h_{opt}$ to $R$ is constant for any given transmitted power of the UAV-BS. Solving (6) numerically yields $\theta_{opt} = 20.34°, 42.44°, 54.62°, 75.52°$ for Suburban, Urban, Dense Urban, and Highrise Urban respectively [6].

## 2.2 Optimization Problem

Let $(u_i, v_i)$ be 2D coordinates of user $i$ and $(x_k, y_k, h_k)$ be 3D coordinates of UAV-BS $k$, $0 \le x_k \le X$, $0 \le y_k \le Y$, $h_{min} \le h_k \le h_{max}$ for all $k \in [1, K]$. In order to minimize transmitted power, an UAV-BS is optimally deployed if and only if equation $R = \xi h$ holds, where $\xi = 1/\tan\theta_{opt}$.

Let $c_{ik} \in \{0, 1\}$ be a binary decision variable such that $c_{ik} = 1$ if the user $i$ is inside the coverage of the UAV-BS $k$ and $c_{ik} = 0$ otherwise. By introducing a sufficiently large constant $M$, this coverage constraint can be written as

$$(u_i - x_k)^2 + (v_i - y_k)^2 \le R_k^2 + M(1 - c_{ik}) \tag{7}$$

where $R_k = \xi h_k$. When $c_{ik} = 0$, the right hand side of formula (7) is sufficiently large and any choice for $(x_k, y_k)$ within the rectangular area satisfies the inequality.

It is unrealistic to know the specific bandwidth requirement of each user in the deployment phase, so we assume all users have the same bandwidth requirement $b_r$. An UAV-BS is assigned one frequency band, thus an UAV-BS can serve $n_C = B/b_r$ users at most. When multiple UAV-BSs have overlapped coverage, a user in the overlapped region is served by one of the UAV-BSs. Let $s_{ik} \in \{0, 1\}$ be a binary decision variable such that $s_{ik} = 1$ if the user $i$ is served by UAV-BS

$k$ and $s_{ik} = 0$ otherwise. As a user cannot be served by UAV-BSs that do not cover it, $s_{ik} \leq c_{ik}$. Considering that a user can only be served by one UAV-BS, we have

$$\sum_{k=1}^{K} s_{ik} \leq 1, \quad i \in [1, N]. \tag{8}$$

Using $s_{ik}$, capacity constraint of UAV-BSs can be written as

$$\sum_{i=1}^{N} s_{ik} \leq n_C, \quad k \in [1, K]. \tag{9}$$

Apart from capacity constraint, we impose interference constraint on frequency band assignment. The coverage regions of UAV-BSs that operate on the same frequency band cannot overlap, which can be formulated as

$$(x_k - x_{k\prime})^2 + (y_k - y_{k\prime})^2 - (R_k + R_{k\prime})^2 \geq -M(w_k - w_{k\prime})^2 \tag{10}$$

where $k, k\prime \in [1, K]$, $k \neq k\prime$ and $w_k, w_{k\prime} \in [1, W]$. When the left side of inequality (10) equals to 0, it means that the coverage disks of UAV-BSs $k$ and $k\prime$ are externally tangent. Condition $w_k = w_{k\prime}$ requires that two coverage disks are disjoint. However, there is no specific constraint of two UAV-BSs when $w_k \neq w_{k\prime}$, as the right hand side of the inequality is sufficiently small. Note that when $W = 1$, there is no overlap among all UAV-BSs.

In summary, the optimization problem can be formulated as

$$\text{maximize} \sum_{k=1}^{K} \sum_{i=1}^{N} s_{ik} \tag{11}$$

subject to:

$$0 \leq x_k \leq X, \; 0 \leq y_k \leq Y, \; h_{\min} \leq h_k \leq h_{\max}, \; R_k = \xi h_k,$$
$$(u_i - x_k)^2 + (v_i - y_k)^2 \leq R_k^2 + M(1 - c_{ik}),$$
$$\xi = 1/\tan \theta_{\text{opt}}, \quad c_{ik} \in \{0, 1\}, \quad s_{ik} \in \{0, 1\}, \quad s_{ik} \leq c_{ik},$$
$$\sum_{k=1}^{K} s_{ik} \leq 1, \quad \sum_{i=1}^{N} s_{ik} \leq n_C,$$
$$(x_k - x_{k\prime})^2 + (y_k - y_{k\prime})^2 \geq (R_k + R_{k\prime})^2 - M(w_k - w_{k\prime})^2,$$
$$i \in [1, N], \quad k, k\prime \in [1, K], \quad k \neq k\prime, \quad w_k, w_{k\prime} \in [1, W].$$

## 3    Algorithm Design

The optimization problem is a mixed integer non-linear problem (MINLP), which is NP-hard. Therefore, we develop a heuristic algorithm, namely interference free drone base station placement (IFDBSP), to find a suboptimal solution with polynomial time complexity. We describe IFDBSP from macroscopic perspective to microscopic perspective and use some mathematical notations in the algorithm description for concision. All *deployed* UAVs are stored in list $\mathcal{U}$, i.e., $\mathcal{U}[k]$ refers to UAV $k$. Expression $\mathcal{U}[k] \cap \mathcal{U}[k\prime] = \emptyset$ holds if and only if the coverage areas of UAV $k$ and $k\prime$ do not overlap.

An overview of IFDBSP is presented in Algorithm 1. The main idea is to create a series of sample points $\mathcal{P}$ according to the granularity $g$, so that the whole rectangular area is divided into a number of $\lceil X/g \rceil \times \lceil Y/g \rceil$ uniform grids (using coordinates as the hash function, a user is mapped to a grid. This can greatly reduce the time of finding all users in a disc). The corners of these grids are sample points (excluding those corners on the border of the rectangular area), and we denote the number of them by $n_S$. Moreover, IFDBSP maintains a table $\mathcal{A}$ indicating if a sample point is allowed to deploy. Initially, all sample points are allowed to deploy. UAVs are sequentially deployed until none of them left. Each time when a new UAV (the radius of its coverage disc has been initialized) is to be deployed, all the sample points allowed to deploy are checked for the number of users that can be served if they are chosen for deployment. Note that the coverage radius is proportional to the height, whenever we set one of them, the other is set automatically. Since the user distribution is nonuniform and the deployment strategy is greedy, the coverage radius enlarges as users become sparse (we simply enlarge it linearly in line 7). The height $h_b$ used to set the first UAV should be set appropriately. Then, the covered users are sorted in ascending order by their distance to the UAV, and they are served sequentially until the capacity upper bound $n_C$ is reached. Afterwards, the coverage radius is minimized for energy purpose by solving a smallest enclosing disc problem similar to that in [6]. Note that the smallest enclosing disc for a set of $n$ points in the plane can be computed in $\mathcal{O}(n)$ expected time using worst-case linear storage [12]. Therefore, line 9 can be accomplished with $\mathcal{O}(n_C)$ since the number of serviced users is not greater than $n_C$. If this newly added UAV overlaps any deployed UAV, a procedure will be executed to adjust UAVs. The final step in the **for** loop is to update table $\mathcal{A}$. A sample point is allowed to deploy in next loop if the number of bands used by UAVs that cover it is less than $W$, which comes from interference constraint. This update operation costs $\mathcal{O}(n_S \cdot K)$ because all deployed UAVs are checked for each sample point. The time complexity of Algorithm 1 is summarized as $\mathcal{O}(K \cdot (n_S \cdot N + X + n_S \cdot K))$, where $X$ stands for the complexity of the adjustment procedure in line 12. Note that the actual running time can be much less than this worst-case complexity, since it is not necessarily the case that the adjustment procedure is revoked. The implementation of the adjustment procedure is not unique and it is a flexible part of IFDBSP, thus we do not detail it. The detailed description of IFDBSP as well as the code implementation can be found on the github [13].

## 4   Algorithm Evaluation

We use a large quantity of random cases to evaluate the performance of IFDBSP in this section.

**Algorithm 1. IFDBSP**

1: **Input:** $u_i, v_i, \quad i \in [1, N]$
2: **Output:** $x_k, y_k, h_k, w_k, \quad k \in [1, K]$
3: initialize coordinate table of sample points $\mathcal{P}$ according to the grid granularity $g$
4: set $h_b$ according to the average user density level
5: **for** $k = 1$ **to** $K$ **do**
6:    append newly added UAV $k$ to list $\mathcal{U}$
7:    $w_k \leftarrow 1, \quad h_k \leftarrow k/K \cdot (h_{\max} - h_b) + h_b$
8:    deploy UAV $k$ on the best sample point to maximize the number of unserviced users covered by it
9:    adjust UAV $k$ to minimize the radius of its coverage disc by solving a smallest enclosing disc problem
10:    **for** $j = 1$ **to** $k - 1$ **do**
11:     **if** $\mathcal{U}[j] \cap \mathcal{U}[k] \neq \emptyset$ **then**
12:      invoke an adjustment procedure
13:      **break**
14:     **end if**
15:    **end for**
16:    **for all** $p$ **in** $\mathcal{P}$ **do**
17:     decide if $p$ is allowed to deploy in the next loop
18:    **end for**
19: **end for**

## 4.1 Numeric Parameters

Some significant parameters and their default values are listed in Table 1. When studying the impact of a certain parameter, others are configured with their default values. Especially, parameter $h_b$ is determined by the average number of users per square kilometer and $h_{\min} \leq h_b \leq h_{\max}$.

**Table 1.** Parameters configuration

| Parm | $X$ | $Y$ | $N$ | $K$ | $W$ | $n_C$ | $f_c$ | $B$ | $\theta_{opt}$ |
|---|---|---|---|---|---|---|---|---|---|
| Value | 2000 m | 2000 m | 800 | 8 | 2 | 100 | 1950 MHz | 20 MHz | 42.44° |
| Parm | $h_{\min}$ | $h_{\max}$ | $g$ | $a$ | $b$ | $\eta_{LoS}$ | $\eta_{NLoS}$ | $P_r$ | |
| Value | 100 m | 400 m | 50 m | 9.612 | 0.158 | 1 dB | 20 dB | $-94$ dB | |

## 4.2 Impact of Ground User Density

All cases are grouped into 7 sets in accordance with uniformly spaced $N$ from 200 to 1400, and each set contains 100 cases corresponding to random seed 1–100 in the case generator. For each case, the number of available UAVs is given by $K = N/n_C$. Hence, the maximum number of users that can be served equals to $N$ theoretically[3]. The program runs on an Ubuntu laptop with a quad-core

---

[3] Owing to the randomness of user distribution, it is impossible to reach this upper bound in practice.

**Table 2.** Distinct user density

| $N$ | 200 | 400 | 600 | 800 | 1000 | 1200 | 1400 |
|---|---|---|---|---|---|---|---|
| $k = 1$ | 64.0 | 99.4 | 100.0 | 100.0 | 100.0 | 100.0 | 99.2 |
| $k = 2$ | 106.9 | 183.8 | 199.3 | 199.9 | 199.6 | 199.6 | 198.5 |
| $k = 3$ | / | 247.6 | 292.9 | 298.5 | 298.7 | 299.0 | 298.0 |
| $k = 4$ | / | 291.9 | 368.2 | 395.0 | 397.4 | 398.3 | 396.3 |
| $k = 5$ | / | / | 431.4 | 482.4 | 493.9 | 496.1 | 494.9 |
| $k = 6$ | / | / | 475.1 | 553.9 | 583.7 | 593.0 | 593.2 |
| $k = 7$ | / | / | / | 613.3 | 669.5 | 686.5 | 688.1 |
| $k = 8$ | / | / | / | 658.8 | 740.6 | 774.3 | 781.6 |
| $k = 9$ | / | / | / | / | 801.0 | 857.1 | 874.1 |
| $k = 10$ | / | / | / | / | 847.2 | 930.0 | 964.0 |
| $k = 11$ | / | / | / | / | / | 990.1 | 1046.7 |
| $k = 12$ | / | / | / | / | / | 1034.8 | 1119.4 |
| $k = 13$ | / | / | / | / | / | / | 1179.5 |
| $k = 14$ | / | / | / | / | / | / | 1226.2 |
| Percent (%) | 53.5 | 73.0 | 79.2 | 82.4 | 84.7 | 86.2 | 87.6 |
| Minimum | 84 | 246 | 409 | 590 | 774 | 933 | 1133 |
| Maximum | 128 | 329 | 523 | 697 | 908 | 1086 | 1285 |
| Time (ms) | 37.5 | 66.2 | 94.5 | 127.7 | 163.6 | 213.1 | 289.0 |

AMD A6-3420M APU (1.5 GHz). The average number of serviced users varying with the number of available UAVs[4] and the average execution time of each set are presented in Table 2. The *percent* row in the table reports the average percent of users that are served with all available UAVs being deployed, and the *minimum* row records the worst case of each set while the *maximum* row reflects the best. The increment of serviced users decreases as $k$ increases, in keeping with the greediness of IFDBSP. The average percent of serviced users increases as $N$ increases, because the possibility that an UAV reaches its capacity upper bound becomes larger when the ground user becomes denser. The difference between the percent of serviced users in the best case and that in the worse case decreases as $N$ increases, which is 22.0%, 20.8%, 19.0%, 13.4%, 13.4%, 12.8%, 10.8% corresponding to $N = 200, 400, \cdots, 1400$ respectively. This means the performance of IFDBSP is more stable in dense cases than sparse cases, since the impact of user distribution randomness is large when the average user density is small. In sparse cases, clustered distribution is more beneficial to coverage

---

[4] At the end of each loop from line 5 to 19 in Algorithm 1, the statistics with $k$ UAVs being deployed can be recorded.

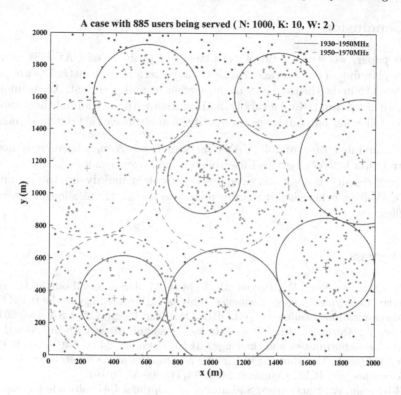

**Fig. 1.** An example from the fifth case set with 885 serviced users in total. Green points are serviced users while blue points are unserviced users. The coverage radii of UAV-BSs are inversely proportional to the user density.

than uniform distribution, and UAVs usually do not reach their capacity upper bound due to the maximal allowable coverage radius $R_{max}$. Figure 1 depicts a case example.

## 4.3   Impact of Frequency Band Number

The first four sets in previous subsection are executed with $W = 1$ and the last three sets are executed with $W = 3$ again. The average number of serviced users with all available UAVs being deployed are given in Table 3.

**Table 3.** Distinct band number

| $N$ | 200 | 400 | 600 | 800 | 1000 | 1200 | 1400 |
|---|---|---|---|---|---|---|---|
| $W = 1$ | 106.9 | 287.6 | 447.0 | 603.6 | / | / | / |
| $W = 2$ | 106.9 | 291.9 | 475.1 | 658.8 | 847.2 | 1034.8 | 1226.2 |
| $W = 3$ | / | / | / | / | 852.0 | 1042.5 | 1244.2 |

# 5    Conclusion

In this paper, we study a novel 3D placement problem of UAV-BSs with frequency planning. The coverage, capacity and interference constraints are jointly considered to make the deployment more efficient and practical. Accordingly, we design an algorithm to find a suboptimal solution with polynomial time complexity. The following outcomes are results of the analysis carried out in simulation:

- If the number of available UAVs satisfies $K = N/n_C$, there is a positive correlation between serviced user percent and user density;
- If user density is high, serviced user percent is mainly up to the number of UAV-BSs; otherwise, it mainly relates to the maximal allowable coverage radius.

# References

1. Mozaffari, M., Saad, W., Bennis, M., Debbah, M.: Drone small cells in the clouds: design, deployment and performance analysis. In: Proceedings of the IEEE Global Communications Conference (GLOBECOM), San Diego, CA, USA, Dec 2015
2. Zeng, Y., Zhang, R., Lim, T.J.: Wireless communications with unmanned aerial vehicles: opportunities and challenges. IEEE Commun. Mag. 54(5), 36–42 (2016)
3. Bor-Yaliniz, I., Yanikomeroglu, H.: The new frontier in RAN heterogeneity: multi-tier drone-cells. IEEE Commun. Mag. 54(11), 48–55 (2016)
4. Al-Hourani, A., Kandeepan, S., Lardner, S.: Optimal LAP altitude for maximum coverage. IEEE Wirel. Commun. Lett. 3(6), 569–572 (2014)
5. Bor-Yaliniz, R.I., El-Keyi, A., Yanikomeroglu, H.: Efficient 3-D placement of an aerial base station in next generation cellular networks. In: Proceedings of the IEEE International Conference Communications (ICC), Kuala Lumpur, Malaysia, May 2016
6. Alzenad, M., El-keyi, A., Lagum, F., Yanikomeroglu, H.: 3D placement of an unmanned aerial vehicle base station (UAV-BS) for energy-efficient maximal coverage. IEEE Wirel. Commun. Lett. 6(4), 434–437 (2017)
7. Kalantari, E., Shakir, M.Z., Yanikomeroglu, H., Yongacoglu, A.: Backhaul-aware robust 3D drone placement in 5G+ wireless networks. In: Proceedings of the IEEE International Conference Communications (ICC), Paris, France, May 2017
8. Mozaffari, M., Saad, W., Bennis, M., Debbah, M.: Efficient deployment of multiple unmanned aerial vehicles for optimal wireless coverage. IEEE Commun. Lett. 20(8), 1647–1650 (2016)
9. Lyu, J., Zeng, Y., Zhang, R., Lim, T.J.: Placement optimization of UAV-mounted mobile base stations. IEEE Commun. Lett. 21(3), 604–607 (2017)
10. Kalantari, E., Yanikomeroglu, H., Yongacoglu, A.: On the number and 3D placement of drone base stations in wireless cellular networks. In: Proceedings of the IEEE Vehicular Technology Conference (VTC Fall), Montreal, Canada, Sept 2016
11. Kaushal, H., Kaddoum, G.: Optical communication in space: challenges and mitigation techniques. IEEE Commun. Surv. Tuts. 19(1), 57–96 (2017)
12. Berg, M., Kreveld, M., Overmars, M., Schwarzkopf, O.: Computational Geometry: Algorithms and Applications, 2th edn. Springer, Berlin, GER (2000)
13. Github. https://github.com/Xu-Le/uav-bs. Accessed 27 Mar 2018

# GLCV: A Routing Scheme Based on Geographic Link Connectivity Management for Urban Vehicular Environments

Zhiping Lin, Wenting Zeng, Weihong Xu, and Yuliang Tang(✉)

School of Information Science and Engineering,
Xiamen University, Xiamen 361005, China
tyl@xmu.edu.cn

**Abstract.** Vehicular Ad Hoc Networks (VANETs) is an important part of Intelligent Transport System (ITS). As a special kind of mobile ad hoc networks (MANETs), VANETs supports dynamic inter-vehicle communications. However, the high mobility of vehicular nodes results in a highly dynamic network topology and the network fragmentations. All these bring a great challenge to routing in VANETs. In this paper, we propose a new VANETs routing scheme called GLCV (Geographic-based Link Connectivity for Vehicular Networks), based on Geographic Link Connectivity management, to overcome the frequent failures of links. Combined with a digital city map, GLCV manages the geographic location information of nodes and the connectivity of links. GLCV selects the shortest connected path to forward the packet by calculating the length and the connectivity of links. Simulation results have shown that GLCV offers stable end-to-end communications, and outperforms existing typical VANETs routing scheme in urban environment, especially in terms of packet delivery rate and average hops. Thus GLCV achieves a lower delay and jitter and a higher throughput.

**Keywords:** VANETs · Routing scheme · GLCV

## 1 Introduction

With the development of Intelligent Transportation System, Vehicular Ad Hoc Networks (VANETs) is proposed to build a safer transport system [1]. Obviously, VANETs will play a vital role in the future transportation network. Given the current limited spectrum resources, various governments have invested a lot

This work was supported by National Natural Science Foundation of China (Grant number 61731012,91638204,61371081).

of resources and technologies in car networking. In America, the U.S. Federal Communications Commission has allocated the specific spectrum for Dedicated Short Range Communication(DSRC) exclusively to realize reliable vehicle to vehicle (V2V) and vehicle to roadside infrastructure (V2I) communications [2,3]. Similarly, the European Conference of Postal and Telecommunications Administrations (CEPT) has allocated a 50 MHz bandwidth dedicated to VANETs communications.

VANETs special characteristics, such as high node mobility, network fragmentation, and diverse quality of service requirement of potential applications, result in significant challenges in the design of an efficient routing protocol. In urban environments, finding and maintaining routes is a much more challenging task. Its significant to select a stable link of high connectivity in V2V and V2I communications [6]. The Greedy Perimeter Stateless Routing (GPSR) [11] is one of the best known position-based routing protocols. In this protocol, each node in the network maintains a neighboring table to execute greedy forwarding. When greedy forwarding strategy fails, GPSR uses the right-hand rule to find a perimeter. Moreover, because direct communications between nodes may be blocked by obstacles, GPSR is often restricted at the intersections in a city scenario. The work [4] proposed a Software-Defined-Networking-based geographic routing protocol for VANETs. In this protocol, the controllers gathered basic information of vehicles and provided a global view to compute the optimal routing paths. While Jin et al. [5] have proposed a geographic routing protocol for cognitive radio mobile ad hoc networks, which provides three routing modes for this protocol. Oubbati [8] presented a new routing protocol, called Intelligent Routing protocol using real time Traffic Information in urban Vehicular environment (IRTIV). IRTIV aims to find the most connected and the shortest path by using its proposed calculation formula of connectivity and the Dijkstra Algorithm.

By analyzing the characteristics of VANETs, we propose a new routing algorithm, Geographic-based Link Connectivity for Vehicular Networks(GLCV). GLCV takes the length and the connectivity of links into account when determining a routing path. With the help of a digital map, vehicle nodes simplify the dynamic network topology as an undirected graph. Nodes dynamically maintain connected links and the connectivity of links in this graph. After path planning, GLCV uses an improved greedy forwarding strategy to pass the packet between adjacent intersections. The proposed scheme is applied to V2V scenarios or Vehicle to Infrastructure to Vehicle (V2I2V) scenarios. In terms of key indicators, such as routing success ratio, average number of hops, and transmission delay, GLCV has better performance than some other routing schemes. The rest of this paper is organized as follows: In Sect. 2, we discuss the system model, and we will detail the design process and the new routing algorithm in Sect. 3. In Sect. 4, we evaluate the simulations and performance of our proposed protocol. In Sect. 5, we present concluding remarks.

## 2   System Model

In this section, we present the system model of our proposed routing scheme for urban environments. Based on these prerequisites, we managed to propose a reasonable and efficient routing scheme based on link connectivity management. We defined the connectivity as the maximum interval between adjacent nodes is no more than $r$(radio range). In the proposed scheme, we assume that every node is equipped with a GPS device, and vehicle sensors can provide measurements of vehicle velocity and direction. Moreover, an open geographic information system is required, e.g. Google Map, which is used to locate junctions and obtain geographic location information (coordinate, road length, density, etc.).

The work [7] has proved that, the frame-success-ratio is greater than 0.9 when the maximum radio range of a vehicle node is 400 m on the One-dimensional road scenario. Commonly, the width of a lane is about 3.5 m, which is much far smaller than the maximum radio range. In this case, the road width has almost no influence on wireless transmission and routing strategy. Therefore, we regard the road as one-dimensional model. As we known, the Manhattan Grid Model, an urban road scenario, is a widely used urban road model in VANETs. We adopt this model to describe the urban road scene in our proposed routing scheme. Every road segment is a line segment according to the above one-dimensional model. We use an undirected graph $G < V, E >$ to depict the Manhattan Grid Model, where vertices $V$ are intersections of the grid and edges $E$ represent road segments.

Now we discuss one of road segments in the city map. Based on the assumption of ignoring the size of the vehicle, the probability of a node locating on any position of the road is the same, i.e. the position of vehicle nodes on the road segment follows even distribution. Assuming the road segment length is $L$, and the maximum radio range of each node is $R$. We normalize the road length as 1, radio range $r = \frac{R}{L}$. N nodes are distributed in the interval $(0, 1)$ of uniform distribution, and each node is independently in position. Supposing that the position of $N$ nodes are $X_i (i = 1, 2, \cdots, n)$ respectively, the above assumptions can be expressed as: $X_1, X_2, \ldots, X_n \sim U(0, 1)$.

## 3   Routing Scheme

### 3.1   Cost Function Based on Link Connectivity

Our proposed routing scheme takes the link connectivity into account with overall consideration of factors (path length, traffic density, etc.) affecting routing. The link connectivity affecting the path weight for route planning, and a higher connectivity will lead to a lower path weight. In this section, we managed to derive a more reasonable cost function of the path weight in accordance with the link connectivity. We sort the $N$ random variables $X_i (i = 1, 2, \ldots, n)$ of urban road model in order, and mark the ordered variables as $X_{(i)} (i = 1, 2, \ldots, n)$ satisfying $X_{(1)} \leq X_{(2)} \leq \cdots \leq X_{(n)}$. Defining random variables $Y_j (j = 1, 2, \ldots, n + 1)$, which $Y_1 = X_{(1)}, Y_2 = X_{(2)} - X_{(3)}, \cdots, Y_n = X_{(n)} - X_{(n-1)}, Y_{n+1} = 1 - X_{(n)}$.

$Y_j$ presents the distance of two neighboring nodes (Fig. 1). Notice that $Y_i \geq 0$, $\sum_{i=1}^{n+1} Y_j = 1$, according to the conclusion of [12], the joint probability density of $Y_j$ obeys the *Dirichlet* distribution with parameters $v_1 = \cdots = v_{n+1} = 1$. The probability density function of *Dirichlet* distribution is:

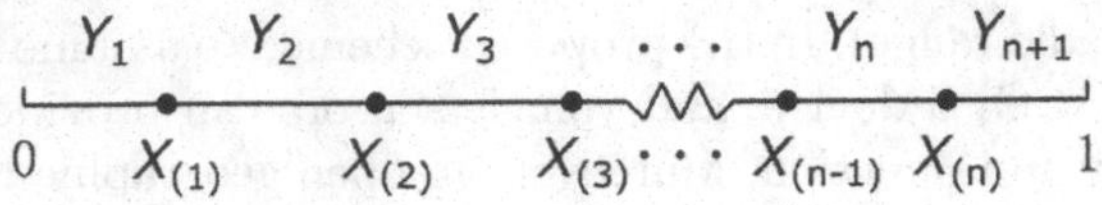

**Fig. 1.** The relationship between random variables $X_i$ and $Y_j$

$$f(x_1, \cdots, x_k) = \begin{cases} C(v_1, \cdots, v_k) \prod_{i=1}^{k} x_i^{v_i - 1}, x_1, \cdots, x_k \in S_x \\ 0, else. \end{cases} \tag{1}$$

where

$$C(v_1, \cdots, v_k) = \Gamma(v_1 + \cdots + v_k) \prod_{i=1}^{k} \frac{1}{\Gamma(v_i)} \tag{2}$$

$$S_x = (x_1, \cdots, x_n) : \sum_{i=1}^{n} x_i = 1, x_i \geq 0, i = 0, \ldots, n \tag{3}$$

$\Gamma()$ is Gamma function. Put $v_1 = \cdots = v_{n+1}$ into Eqs.(1) and (2), we have

$$f_{Y_1, \cdots, Y_{n+1}}(y_1, \cdots, y_{n+1}) = \begin{cases} n!, y_1, \cdots, y_{n+1} \in S_x \\ 0, else. \end{cases} \tag{4}$$

The link is connected if the distance of two neighboring nodes is less than $r$, then

$$P_c(n, r) = P\{Y_{n+1} \leq r\} \tag{5}$$

where $P_c$ denotes the connected probability. According to the conclusion of [12], the cumulative distribution function of $Y_{(n+1)}$ satisfies

$$F_{Y_{n+1}}(x) = \sum_{j=0}^{n+1} (-1)^j \binom{n+1}{j} (1 - jx)_+^n \tag{6}$$

where $(x)_+ = \begin{cases} x, & x > 0 \\ 0, & else \end{cases}$. Thus

$$P_c(n, r) = P_{Y_{n+1} \leq r} = F_{Y_{n+1}}(r) = \sum_{j=0}^{min(n+1, \frac{1}{r})} (-1)^j \binom{n+1}{j} (1 - jr)^n \tag{7}$$

Equation (7) is the $P_c$ after normalizing the road length. We put $r = \frac{R}{L}$ into Eq. (7). In addition, Google Map provides the road congestion information to estimate the traffic density. And a method of estimating traffic density by listening to radio beacon is introduced in literature [9]. We can obtain the real-time traffic density through these ways. After that, the number of vehicle nodes $N$, is calculated by formula: $n = \lambda L$. And we have:

$$P_c(\lambda, L, R) = \sum_{j=0}^{min(\lambda L+1, \frac{L}{R})} (-1)^j \binom{\lambda L+1}{j} (1 - j\frac{R}{L})^{\lambda L} \tag{8}$$

Figure 2 tells that when the link connectivity Pc versus traffic density $\lambda$ is greater than 90%, the contribution of increasing in cars number and traffic density becomes smaller and smaller to the link connectivity, until it reaches a saturation state. To solve these problems, we propose a cost function based on road length and link connectivity:

$$Weight = \frac{L}{P_c} \tag{9}$$

The main reasons why we use Eq. (9) as our cost function are described as follows: Firstly, the shorter distance usually means the fewer hops. However, if the density of the chosen path is too low, route is more likely to fail. In Eq. (9), the link connectivity probability is pulled-in as a compensation. In addition, Fig. 3 shows that the relations between the density of vehicles and Weight. Using Eq. (9) as the cost function, not only the influence of road length and traffic density on hops is considered, but also ensures the successful ratio of routing and avoids too frequently message forwarding.

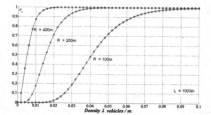

**Fig. 2.** Link connectivity

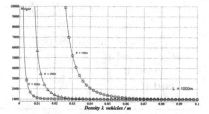

**Fig. 3.** Road Weight

## 3.2   GLCV in Different Scenarios

Based on the above analysis and conclusion, we propose a routing scheme named Geographic-based Link Connectivity for Vehicular Networks (GLCV). The implementation details of our scheme are different in the different scenarios, so the GLCV in a V2V scenario and in a V2I2V scenario are introduced respectively.

## A. GLCV in a V2V Scenario

We assume that communication only occurs between vehicles in this scenario. The undirected graph we mentioned in Sect. 2, $G < V, E >$, the vertices set $V$ represents a set of road intersection points, the edge set $E$ represents a set of roads. We use Google Map to locate junctions and obtain road length.

---

**Algorithm 1** GLCV forwarding algorithm

---

**Require:** $C$: the current vehicle node; $D$: the destination node
  $N$: the set of one hop neighbors of C; $V_i : V_i \in \{V_1, V_2, , V_k\}, 1 \leq i \leq k$
  $N_{next}$: the next hop; $N_{in}$: the set of internal road segment neighbors of C
  $N_{out}$: the set of external road segment neighbors of C
  **if** $C = D$ **then**
    **return**
  **else**
    **if** $D \in N$ **then**
      $N_{next} = D$
    **else**
      **if** $Positon(C) \in V_i$ areas$i < k$ **then**
        Delete $V_i$
        $\{V_{i+1}, \cdots, V_k\} \leftarrow Dijkstra(weight)$
        $Targetnode = V_{i+1}$
      **else if** $Positon(C) \in V_k$ areas **then** $DeleteV_k$
        $Targetnode = D$
      **else**
        **if** $\exists N \in N_{out}$ that $\| C - V \| - \| N - V \| > 0$ **then**
          $N_{next} = \underset{argmax}{N} (\| C - V \| - \| N - V \|)$
        **else if** $\exists N \in N_{in}$ that $\| C - V \| - \| N - V \| > 0$ **then**
          $N_{next} = \underset{argmax}{N} (\| C - V \| - \| N - V \|)$
        **else**
          C drops the packet
        **end if**
      **end if**
    **end if**
  **end if**

---

Like GPSR, each vehicle node in GLCV broadcasts "HELLO" massage to its one hop neighbors to maintain necessary location information. Differently, GLCV relies on a map to build routes. In order to predict the position of neighboring nodes, it needs to acquire the information of coordinate, road segment identifier and the movement speed of neighbors. The node will record the information on a table after receiving the "HELLO" message from a neighboring node. The table entry includes fields like ID, position coordinates, road segment identifier and update time. If a node does not receive a "HELLO" message from the same neighbor over a certain period, the node deletes the corresponding table entry of this neighbor. The current node divides its neighbors by the road segment identifier into internal road segment neighbors (neighbors are in the same road segment with the current node) and external road segment neighbors (neighbors are in the different road segment with the current node). The below forwarding Algorithm 1 takes different processing to the two kinds of neighbors. Because a time $\delta$ exists between updating the neighboring information table and looking up the table, the position of the neighboring node being looked up has changed comparing with the original information in neighboring information table. To eliminate the inconsistency, the position of the neighboring node will be recalculated according to the movement speed field in the table when looking up. GLCV uses the position-based greedy algorithm to forward packets. Therefore, when a node wants to communicate with another node, it needs to acquire the position and velocity of the target node (for predicting the movement of the target node). Finally, we introduce the routing and forwarding algorithm. Firstly, the weight of each road segment in the map has been calculated according to Eqs. (8) and (9). Node $S$ uses Dijkstra algorithm to compute a sequence of vertices with the minimum weight from itself to node $D$. The position coordinates of the passing $k$ vertices are marked as: $V_1, V_2, \ldots, V_k$. Node $S$ adds this sequence information into the header of GLCV packet, and broadcasts the packet to its neighbors. When a node $C$ receives a packet from its neighbor, node $C$ reads the header of the packet. If node $C$ is not the destination node of the packet, $C$ forwards the packet again. The process of forwarding obeys the following rules: Firstly, those passed vertices become invalid and will be deleted in the sequence. And secondly, middle nodes approximating to any one of vertices areas are responsible for updating the path. If the sequence of vertices has changed, the current node replaces the old vertices sequence with the new one. Thirdly, the other middle nodes regard the next vertex or the destination node as the target node to forward the packet by using an improved greedy forwarding strategy (they preferentially select their external road segment neighbors as the next hop). We use fountain code [10] to achieve more efficient and reliable data transmission. Different from Automatic Repeat-ReQuest (ARQ)protocol, packets loss is acceptable when using fountain code. Pseudo code of GLCV algorithm is illustrated in Algorithm 1.

## B. GLCV in a V2I2V Scenario

In a V2I2V scenario, communication not only occurs between vehicles, but also occurs between vehicles and RSUs. With the help of RSUs, vehicles in the V2I2V scenario are typically able to achieve better performance than in the V2V scenario. In this paragraph, we will introduce the function of RSUs. RSUs communicate each other by the wired network, which has higher reliability, wider bandwidth and less delay. The location of RSUs are fixed and they use wired network to communicate. Therefore the quality of the connection in RSUs is significantly better than the inter-vehicle network, we give high priority to RSUs when establishing a route. GLCV sets the weight between adjacent RSUs to 0 to increase the probability of using RSUs when building a route.

V2I2V communication process is similar to the V2V in our proposed scheme, so we extended the routing algorithm to fit V2I2V communications. The extended algorithm want to make full use of RSUs to optimize the quality of connection in a V2I2V scenario. Before communicating, source node $S$ calculates the minimum weight path from itself to destination node $D$. If the path does not contain a RSU vertex or contain only one RSU vertex (indicates that the RSU is the destination node, i.e., V2I communication), then it turns as same as the GLCV in a V2V scenario. If the path contains two RSUs or more, then the sequence of vertices will obey the following form: $V_{i_1}, \cdots, V_{i_m}, R_{in}, \cdots, R_{out}, V_{i_{m+1}}, \cdots, V_{in}$. The above sequence of vertices are divided into two segments: before the entry of RSUs, $V_{i_1}, \cdots, V_{i_m}, R_{in}$, and after leaving RSUs, $R_{out}, V_{i_{m+1}}, \cdots, V_{in}$. The two segments can be regarded as two segments of V2V communications: in the first half, from the source node $S$ to the vertex $R_{in}$; and in the second half, from the vertex $R_{out}$ to the destination node $D$. So each intermediate node needs to determine whether it is in the first or the second segment. Then, the above routing algorithm is implemented with the target is a RSU vertex or the destination node $D$.

**Table 1.** NS3 simulation parameters

| Parameter | Value |
|---|---|
| Number of grids | $5 \times 5$ |
| Map scale | $2000\,\text{m} \times 2000\,\text{m}$ |
| Road length | $500\,\text{m}$ |
| Number of OBU nodes | 100, 150, 200, 250, 300 |
| Number of RSU nodes | 0, 4 |
| Physical layer parameters | Bandwidth: $10\,\text{MHz}$, speed: $6\,\text{Mbps}$ |
| Wireless channel model | Log distance propagation loss model |
| Radio transmit power | $20\,\text{dBm}$ |
| Network protocol stack | IPv4 |
| Packet size | 1024 bytes |
| Data flow type | Constant bit rate (CBR), speed: $100\,\text{Kbps}$ |

## 4    Simulation Result and Evaluation

The main characteristics of VANETs in the urban environment have a great impact on the performance of wireless communication. In this part, we present the simulation experiment based on the urban simulation platform SUMO, and the network simulation platform NS3. We analyze performance of GLCV in the urban environment and compare it with GPSR. In this section, we present the simulation of GLCV scheme and evaluate the performance of our algorithm in the simulations. The simulation experiment parameters are indicated according to Table 1. We simulated the GPSR and the GLCV in V2V scenarios and V2I2V scenarios. The simulation of each group is repeated 100 times to take the mean value(the selected communication node pairs are different at each time). The simulation results are shown in Fig. 4. Figure 4(a) shows the relationship between packet loss rate and cars number. With the cars number increasing from 100 to 250, intermediate nodes number for multi-hop forwarding and the successful rate of multi-hop forwarding have increased, which leading to a lower packet loss rate. However, when nodes number increases to 300, the probability of congestion becomes greater because of the increasing node density. Those plenty of safety and non-safety messages produced by nodes will compete to access the limited channel resources. GLCV has lower packet loss rate than GPSR. This is because GLCV considers the link connectivity in path planning. In V2I2V scenarios, since GLCV uses RSUs proactively to assist in routing forwarding, GLCV performs much better than that in V2V scenarios. Figure 4(b) shows the relationship between the average delay and the cars number. When the node density is low, the probability of multi-hop communication is low. In this situation, there is less competition of network resources and end-to-end communication delay is smaller. With the increment of nodes density, multi-hop communication is more likely to happen, and the number of forwarding packets from end to end has increased. We can see the performance of GLCV is better than GPSR in terms of delay. GPSR turns to perimeter mode when the greedy forwarding fails, resulting in unnecessary forwarding and an increment in average number of hops and average delay. GLCV labels non-connected paths to guide nodes to following the shortest path to forward packets, which decreases the delay. The result of Fig. 4(c) shows the relationship between the delay jitter and the cars

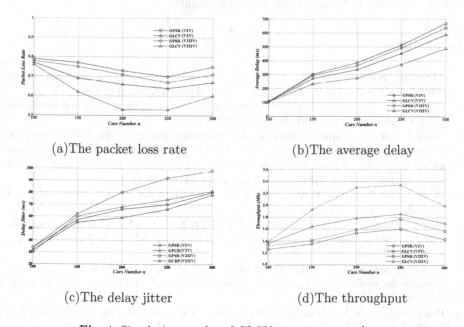

(a)The packet loss rate          (b)The average delay

(c)The delay jitter          (d)The throughput

**Fig. 4.** Simulation results of GLCV versus cars number n

number. The stability of multi-hop communication is worse than that of single-hop communication. So the increasing multi-hop communications bring a greater jitter. RSUs have a significant impact on the number of forwarding. Because of the changes of network topologies, the communication between nodes is switched on V2I2V and V2V, the delay jitter of GLCV and GPSR have increased when there are RSUs. GPSR uses RSUs to forwarding by random, so that the switch is more frequently, resulting in the increment of jitter delay.

The relationship between the throughput capacity and the cars number is shown in Fig. 4(d). With the cars number increasing from 100 to 250, the success rate and stability of multi-hop forwarding has increased, so the throughput has increased. But when the nodes number increases to 300, the competition in wireless resources is more fiercely, which result in the reducing of throughput. GLCV uses RSUs to assist in forwarding, so that the throughput is improved greatly in V2I2V scenarios.

## 5   Conclusion

Through our investigation and analysis of the existing VANETs routing scheme, this paper has presented a new VANETs routing scheme, based on geographical link connectivity management aimed at the shortages of those existing protocols in the urban environment. Simulation results have shown that our proposed scheme, namely GLCV, outperforms existing position-based routing protocols in terms of the packet delivery rate, the average hops, the packet loss rate, the average delay, the delay jitter and the throughput.

## References

1. Al-Sultan, S., Al-Doori, M., Al-Bayatti, M., et al.: A comprehensive survey on vehicular ad hoc network. J. Netw. Comput. Appl. **37**, 380–392 (2014)
2. Hartenstein, H., Laberteaux, L.P.: A tutorial survey on vehicular ad hoc networks. IEEE Commun. Mag. **46**(6), 164–171 (2008)
3. Astm, E.: Standard specification for telecommunications and information exchange between roadside and vehicle systems-5 GHz band dedicated short range communications (DSRC). Medium Access Control (MAC) and Physical Layer (PHY) Specifications. ASTM. DSRC. STD, pp. 2203–2213 (2003)
4. Ghafoor, H., Koo, I.: CR-SDVN: a cognitive routing protocol for software-defined vehicular networks. IEEE Sensors J. **18**, 1761–1772 (2018)
5. Jin, X., Zhang, R., Sun, J., Zhang, Y.: TIGHT: a geographic routing protocol for cognitive radio mobile ad hoc networks. IEEE Trans. Wireless Commun. **13**(8), 4670–4681 (2014)
6. Silva, C., Nogueira, M., Kim, D., et al.: Cognitive radio based connectivity management for resilient end-to-end communications in VANETs. Comput. Commun. **79**, 1–8 (2016)
7. Paier, A., Tresch, R., Alonso, A., et al.: Average downstream performance of measured IEEE 802.11 p infrastructure-to-vehicle links. In: IEEE International Conference on Communications Workshops, pp. 1–5, May 2010

8. Oubbati, O. S., Lagraa, N., et al.: Irtiv: intelligent routing protocol using real time traffic information in urban vehicular environment. In: IEEE 6th International Conference on New Technologies, Mobility and Security (NTMS), pp. 1–4, March 2014

9. Sanguesa, J.A., Fogue, M., Garrido, P., et al.: An infrastructureless approach to estimate vehicular density in urban environments. Sensors **13**(2), 2399–2418 (2013)

10. Rao, J.S., Sobel, M.: Incomplete Dirichlet integrals with applications to ordered uniform spacings. J. Multivar. Anal. **10**(4), 603–610 (1980)

11. Karp, B., Kung, H. T.: GPSR: greedy perimeter stateless routing for wireless networks. In: ACM 6th Proceedings of International Conference on Mobile Computing and Networking, pp. 243–254, August 2000

12. Wilks, S.S.: Mathematical Statistics. Wiley (1962)

# Services and Applications

# An Investigation of Alliance Portfolio Diversity Impact on Firm Performance

Chih-Ching Hung[1], Shang-En Yu[2], Nai-Chang Cheng[3]([⊠]),
Chun-Hsien Wang[4], Wen-Hsin Chiang[4], and Hong-Tsu Young[1]

[1] Department of Mechanical Engineering, National Taiwan University,
Taipei, Taiwan
{d96522004, hyoung}@ntu.edu.tw
[2] Department of Tourism, Ming Chuan University, Taipei, Taiwan
yushine@mail.mcu.edu.tw
[3] Tainan Human Resources Association, Taipei, Taiwan
chengnaichang@gmail.com
[4] Department of BioBusiness Management, National Chiayi University, Chiayi,
Taiwan
chwang@mail.ncyu.edu.tw, p259@nhsh.tp.edu.tw

**Abstract.** Looking for remotely accessible assets had been portrayed as a critical piece of the advancement procedure. To get outside learning sources, firms must associate their in-house imaginative based exercises with outer accomplice to get to outer assets and extend their agreeable district. This investigation look at the experimentally that the union accomplice decent variety and union geographic assorted variety influences the levels of item and imaginative curiosity. One of the key points of the investigation is to investigate how assorted variety vital influences item advancement accomplishment in the innovative setting. Expanding on the information based hypothesis perspective of the organizations, this examination suggests that how these assorted variety portfolio including accomplices decent variety and coalition geographic decent variety, impact firm item oddity since this element reflects whether the organizations are probably going to disguise outside assets to improve their development results. This examination tests speculations drawn from the Network Advancement Overview (CIS), review by the Taiwan Service of Science and Innovation. The observationally results finding that collusion accomplice assorted variety and coalition geographic decent variety demonstrates an upset U-molded impact on curiosity.

**Keywords:** Alliance partner diversity · Alliance geographic diversity · Product novelty · Openness · Portfolio

## 1 Introduction

Since the worldwide economy supports organized commerce, this pattern may prompt worldwide aggressiveness. To reflect focused weight in the worldwide economy period, firm are opening up their authoritative limits to catch important outside assets with outer accomplices (Chesbrough 2003). Given the significance of R&D forms, the

J.-L. Chen et al. (Eds.): WiCON 2018, LNICST 264, pp. 353–366, 2019.
https://doi.org/10.1007/978-3-030-06158-6_34

inside and outer assets incorporation is getting to be basic to catch the combination from such action.

Outside assets are especially critical for firms in quickly changing and aggressive situations in light of the fact that their inner assets might be lacking and even improper for accomplishing leap forward advancement, expecting them to secure outer assets and to consolidate wide assortment of assets and abilities in progressing development organizations. Consequently, cooperation with numerous accomplices give firms access to an extensive variety of important assets from various fields accomplices, help in overseeing danger and vulnerability, and empower firms to remarkably profit by the particular asset commitments of accomplices (Srivastava and Gnyawali 2011).

This examination in this manner tries to break down the components influencing open development action of the cutting edge industry in Taiwanese utilizing our proposed hypothetical and exact model. To begin with, this examination exhibit the union accomplices decent variety bring different outside mechanical information and watch the specifically impact of its learning acquisitions qualities on advancement results. Second, we exhibit the partnership geographic assorted variety of encouraging Taiwan cutting edge industry and solidifying its effect on development results by breaking down components influencing its advancement arrangement. Third, this examination breaks down the impacts of partnership portfolio decent variety to grow and to improve their insight and aptitudes in imaginative procedures. The theme of this examination is essentially vital to firm supervisors since it appears in which setting transparency key are advantageous for outside assets acquisitions.

Based on the research background and motivation, the purposes of the current study are listing as following.

1. To investigate the development and trends of openness strategic of the high-tech industries in Taiwan region,
2. To develop a theoretical and empirical model that examine the alliance partner diversity and alliance geographic diversity which may drive firms innovation performance,
3. To show the impact of the expansion in the receptiveness methodology of the cutting edge firms and thus investigate whether this broadening can upgrade the development results.

## 2   Literature Review

### 2.1   Open Innovation

Development show has happened colossal changes in which has moved from the idea of shut to open advancement (Chesbrough 2003; Lichtenthaler 2011). The scholarly world and practice have turned out to be progressively mindful of the significance of open development (Chesbrough 2003; Gassmann 2006; Lichtenthaler 2011). The spearheading work of the open development was proposed by Chesbrough (2003) in which firms depend on between firm union and joint effort for pooling reciprocal mechanical assets. Past research contends that organizations take part in open development key keeping in mind the end goal to get supplement and supplement their inward advancement endeavors (Chesbrough 2003; Hagedoorn 2002; Lichtenthaler 2008). Therefore, when a firm is opened to outside accomplices, they are probably going to seek after their own advantages for supplement or correlative in-house development sending. Firms that work together with different accomplices incorporate providers, clients, contenders, colleges, and labs that can improve the development ability they as of now have.

Two logical variables are proposed for examination as conceivable methodologies of the open development, in particular, inbound open advancement and outbound open advancement. The inbound open advancement allude to how firms to obtaining and getting to outer learning from outside performing artists. Conversely, outbound open development is to how firms to offering and uncovering thoughts or assets from and to outside associations (Chesbrough and Crowther 2006; Dahlander and Gann 2010).

## 2.2 External Sources and Alliance Partner Diversity

Tying down on the information based view (KBV) of the firm (Grant 1996), the essential commitments of the KBV is demonstrate how firms in giving proficient learning trade crosswise over various association limits. In the time of information economy, learning is perceived as a standout amongst the most vital and huge assets could help increment firms' advantages and make upper hand. As indicated by Grant (1996), a firm should utilize both outer and interior learning to build their esteem and make business openings. Indeed, the commitment of different accomplices to central firms' advancement procedure improvement is noteworthy (Laursen and Salter 2006; Noseleit and de Faria 2013). Cross outskirt open development instrument in cutting edge areas assume a critical part in connecting the outer assets of a firm to its inside advancement based. With the end goal of this investigation, cross outskirt open advancement is characterized as the coordinated effort between innovative firms from various fields, which may give advantage rich assets. Numerous organizations have begun to effectively gain outer information and innovation outside their limits in inward advancement base (Chesbrough 2003; Van de Vrande et al. 2006).

## 2.3 Alliance Portfolio Diversity and Performance

In the quick changing and aggressive market condition, it is broadly acknowledged that a company's capacity to team up is significantly depended upon the pool of various accomplices assets in supplementing their in-house development based. Researchers have analyzed the assets based view (RBV) of the organizations is the predominant hypothetical worldview in partnership portfolio decent variety (Wan et al. 2011). In like manner, discoveries on central firms taking part in working together with numerous union accomplices can give the manners by which they execute in-house advancement movement. Union accomplice assorted variety is of foremost significance for innovative firms. There firms more often than not do not have the full arrangement of cutting edge mechanical learning to viably create and deliver their R&D movement in developing business sector. In this examination we not just thought to be about coalition accomplice decent variety on the advancement results, yet in addition consider how partnership geographic assorted variety influences their organizations' development execution. Besides, existing examination has for the most part centered around the connection between coalition assorted variety and execution, and all the more particularly, the positive exertion on development results.

## 3   Methodologies

### 3.1   Theoretical Development and Hypotheses

An essential component in the transparency procedure of the firm is outside learning procurement by various accomplices and diverse topography. The hypothetical and experimental research propose that community oriented accomplice assorted variety is useful for the advancement execution yet just up to a bend point. We made some hypotheses as follows:

Hypothesis 1: Alliance partners diversity has an inverted U-shaped relationship with innovation performance.
Hypothesis 1a: Alliance partners diversity has an inverted U-shaped relationship with firm's novelty.
Hypothesis 1b: Alliance partners diversity has an inverted U-shaped relationship with market novelty.

Furthermore, the qualities of cutting edge firms vary along an extensive variety of measurements and their outer advancements and information bases are produced through various geographic joint effort accomplices. We also made some hypotheses in the following:

Hypothesis 2: Alliance geographic diversity has an inverted U-shaped relationship with innovation performance.
Hypothesis 2a: Alliance geographic diversity has an inverted U-shaped relationship with firm novelty.
Hypothesis 2b: Alliance geographic diversity has an inverted U-shaped relationship with market novelty.

The purpose of this study is to examine the impact of diversity on high tech innovation performance. The proposed research model is listing in Fig. 1.

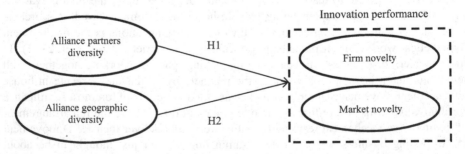

**Fig. 1.** Proposed research model

## 3.2    Data Collection

The database was utilized in this investigation embraced frame the third Network Advancement Review (CIS III) of National Science Board in Taiwan in 2012, together with a completely similar overview directed by the Establishment of Innovation, Development and Licensed innovation Administration, National Chengchi College. The example gathering relied upon Taiwan Standard Mechanical Arrangement (SIC) Framework and match OECD Standard Modern Characterization.

## 3.3    Estimation Methodology

### Collaborative partner diversity

To catch shared accomplice decent variety, the CIS overview that inquired as to whether the central firm had any participation game plans for mechanical development exercises in the past two years is utilized. Helpful assentions can be partitioned into eight classes accomplice composes in the CIS III review. The mechanical advancement cooperation and collusion accomplices are including (1) backups, (2) providers, (3) customers or clients, (4) contenders, (5) specialists and business labs or private research establishments, (6) the R&D foundations or lab of cross-industry, (7) colleges or other advanced education establishments, (8) government explore associations and other philanthropic research association. Along these lines, the assorted variety level of collusion accomplices utilized the Blau record which is broadly utilized in earlier examinations and is viewed as the most widely recognized proportion of decent variety (Blau 1977). The Blau diversity index is defined as

$$D = 1 - \sum_{i=0}^{n} P_i^2 = 1 - \sum_{i=0}^{n} \left(\frac{n_i}{n}\right)^2$$

Where i is a particular collaboration agreements and alliance partners which across eight categories, $n$ is the total number of possible collaboration agreements and alliance partners, $n_i$ is the particular collaboration agreements and alliance partners in particular category, and $P_i$ is the proportion of the potential particular collaboration agreements and alliance within the group.

### Alliance geographic diversity

An all around characterized of cross-outskirt of collective assentions and partnerships had been prove an extraordinarily affect on the inventive limit. This examination additionally utilized the Blau list to gauge cutting edge firms community oriented assentions and union geographic assorted variety. The assorted variety record depends on a typology of shared assentions and unions crosswise over geographic areas that including: (1) Taiwan, (2) China, (3) America, (4) Japan, (5) Korea, (6) India, (7) Europe, and (8) different nations. The Blau diversity index is defined as

$$D = 1 - \sum_{j=0}^{n} P_j^2 = 1 - \sum_{j=0}^{n} \left(\frac{n_j}{n}\right)^2$$

where i is a collaborative agreements and alliances in the particular category and j is a particular alliance region, $n_{ij}$ is the total number of possible collaborative agreements and alliances in particular category i across the j countries, and $P_j$ is the proportion of the potential alliance region within the group.

In this investigation, we lead our exact examination by methods for Probit relapse estimations. Such parallel Probit display detail ought to be extremely reasonable with respect to acknowledged double ward factors under the supposition that the organizations take part in development endeavors. Consequently, we address this issue by evaluating Probit show for testing our speculations. Moreover, to test our speculations of the hypothetical advancement, this investigation utilize various leveled relapse technique to evaluate our theory. We utilize the change expansion factors (VIFs) to decide the relationship of factors, the estimations of VIFs little than 10 cut-point are acknowledged in dataset and collinearity may not exist.

## Innovation performance

So as to test for the impact on development execution of a central firm, we operationalize the advancement results idea by utilizing two pointers as indicated by the CIS III review dataset. In accordance with earlier research (e.g., Köhler et al. 2012), the results of advancement endeavors was estimated utilizing a market oddity and firm oddity. From results of development endeavors, new procedures, new creates, and new administration can be spoken to the advancement achievement (Hagedoorn and Cloodt 2003).

To start with, the estimation of firm curiosity is utilized to catch the items and additionally benefits new to the firm in their advancement results. Thusly, firms offer new items or potentially benefit that are new to the firm, yet not new to the market. That is, we allude to an item and additionally administration to be another to-firm development results as it were. Second, the estimation of market curiosity was utilized to catch the development execution of a central firm through an item as well as administration as another to-showcase advancement. The study poll in CIS III got some information about whether the organizations' deliver or administration are new relative rivals in the market. The accomplishment of a development to a great extent relies upon advertise acknowledgment. Therefore, the new-to-advertise development speaks to the market oddity to catch the advancement execution in this investigation. Moreover, this investigation allude to an item as well as administration as another to-advertise development as the level of market oddity. Furthermore, this consider the item and additionally benefit new to the firm just to introduce the firm oddity.

## Control variables

There is a few variables may affect the advancement endeavors of the organizations. Along these lines, this examination controlled for firm qualities in our investigations including firm size, deals, R&D force, and backup. To start with, the quantities of aggregate representatives are estimated as the firm size which may influence firms' practices and their execution (Nadler and Tushman 1997) and the connection of advancement and execution (Caloghirou, Kastelli, and Tsakanikas 2004; Tsai 2009). That is, huge firms may have more chances to work together with outer accomplices for development assets acquisitions. Second, money related execution, for example, yearly deals (Garcia-Vega 2006), return on resources (Qian et al. 2010), return on deals, and profit for capital (Goerzen and Beamish 2005) may likewise affect on the innovative work action in upgrading imaginative results. Along these lines, we control the yearly deals that may impact the estimation consequences of development endeavors. Third, an association's R&D power speaks to development assets contribution to encouraging, recognizing, and abusing outside advancement learning and openings (Valvano and Vannoni 2003). Consequently, we incorporate the R&D force as control variable (Hitt et al. 1997). Thus, this investigation assessed R&D power as the proportion of the organizations' R&D imaginative use to yearly deal (de Leeuw et al. 2014; Quintana-García and Benavides-Velasco 2008). Furthermore, earlier research contend that backup as a remote parent organization which may bring an incredibly impact on new item advancement and development results (Belderbos et al. 2004). Subsequently, this investigation consider backup as the control variable on advancement execution.

In this examination, we lead our exact investigation by methods for Probit relapse estimations. Since our information depend on the CIS III overview, the needy factors in all model are yes or no, they are coned as 1 and zero, which implies in down to earth terms whether the firm has strived or not to new to market and new to firm advancement improvement. Such double Probit demonstrate detail ought to be exceptionally appropriate with respect to acknowledged twofold ward factors under the presumption that the organizations take part in advancement endeavors. Subsequently, we address this issue by assessing Probit show for testing our theories.

Moreover, to test our theories of the hypothetical improvement, this examination utilize progressive relapse methodology to evaluate our speculation. The progressive relapse was investigated the general clarification capacity, and how coalition accomplices decent variety and union geographic assorted variety influence the firm execution, or is it demonstrates the help of the hypothesis that our proposed. We ought to look at the autonomous factors whether have multicollinearity, that is, regardless of whether between factors have exceptionally connection. Along these lines, we utilize the difference swelling factors (VIFs) to decide the relationship of factors, the estimations of VIFs little than 10 cut-point are acknowledged in dataset and collinearity may not exist.

## 4 Empirical Results

### 4.1 Sample Analysis

In Table 1 introduces the depiction of collusion portfolio assorted variety on every industry structure, it demonstrates partnership portfolio decent variety are focuses on make of electronic parts and segments (106 firms) and make of PCs, electronic and optical items (103 firms).

Table 2 presents essential data and industry dispersion of our cutting edge test. The qualities of the examination including: the proportion of backup, firms' size, firms'

Table 1. Description of alliance portfolio diversity

| Industry | n | Alliance partner diversity | | Alliance geographic diversity | |
|---|---|---|---|---|---|
| | | Mean | S.D. | Mean | S.D |
| (1) Manufacturing of medicinal chemical products | 9 | 0.519 | 0.100 | 0.377 | 0.215 |
| (2) Manufacture of electronic parts and components | 106 | 0.363 | 0.308 | 0.385 | 0.312 |
| (3) Manufacture of computers, electronic and optical products | 103 | 0.379 | 0.328 | 0.304 | 0.289 |
| (4) Telecommunications | 10 | 0.063 | 0.198 | 0.063 | 0.198 |

Note: $N = 228$; Source: compiled by this study

deals, and their R&D force. As per the aftereffects of Table 2, we locate that most firms had not an auxiliary (75%) and just 25% had a backup in our investigation test. The mass of firm size is in 101-500 workers (115 firms), and right around 70.6% firms are under 500 representatives that mirror a vast sum test of innovative firms are little and middle endeavors (SMEs) in Taiwan producing industry of this example. The firm deals has focus on 1–5 million (82 firms), and have 26.3% firms over ten million even a large portion of firms are SMEs. Research and development force implies that association's aggregate consumption of R&D imaginative exercises on association's yearly deals. There are 61.0% cutting edge firms spend their yearly deals from 10% to 30% in inventive exercises.

## 4.2    Descriptive Statistics

Table 3 records the graphic insights of the investigation that incorporate mean, standard deviations, connection and difference swelling factors (VIF) of every single real factor by SPSS 20.0. The engaging measurements of factors including firm curiosity, advertise oddity, backup, firm size, firm deals, R&D power, collusion accomplices decent variety, and partnership geographic assorted variety.

Pearson correlations presents firm novelty and market novelty have positive correlation to each other. Firm novelty is negative correlated with collaboration diversity ($\beta = -0.08$), and market novelty is significant and negative correlated with collaboration diversity ($\beta = -0.195, p < 0.01$). The collaborator diversity is positively significant correlation with alliance geographic diversity ($\beta = 0.557, p < 0.01$). Firm sales is negative correlated with firm novelty ($\beta = -0.003$) and no statistical significant, but positive and significant correlated with market novelty ($\beta = 0.112, p < 0.1$). R&D intensity is the range of a firm to innovate, and also affect the product innovation. Furthermore, there are positive and significant correlation with firm novelty ($\beta = 0.219, p < 0.01$) and market novelty ($\beta = 0.113, p < 0.1$).

The VIF are deciding the impact of multicollinearity which this examination a scope of VIF is from 1.036 to 1.559 that inside as far as possible. Thusly, the multicollinear isn't an issue in our model setting.

**Table 2.** Description of data

| Item | Category | Frequency | % | Cumulative% |
|------|----------|-----------|---|-------------|
| Subsidiary | No | 171 | 75% | 75% |
| | Yes | 57 | 25% | 100% |
| Firm size | Less than 100 employees | 46 | 20.2% | 20.2% |
| | 101–500 | 115 | 50.4% | 70.6% |
| | 501–1000 | 30 | 13.2% | 83.8% |
| | 1001–5000 | 33 | 14.5% | 98.2% |
| | Above 5000 | 4 | 1.8% | 100.0% |
| Firm sales | Less than 50 ten thousand | 50 | 21.9% | 21.9% |
| | 51–100 | 36 | 15.8% | 37.7% |
| | 101–500 | 82 | 36.0% | 73.7% |
| | 501–1000 | 19 | 8.3% | 82.0% |
| | 1001–5000 | 26 | 11.4% | 93.4% |
| | 5001–10000 | 11 | 4.8% | 98.2% |
| | Above 10000 | 4 | 1.8% | 100.0% |
| R&D intensity | Less than 1% | 17 | 7.5% | 7.5% |
| | 1.01% ~ 5% | 47 | 20.6% | 28.1% |
| | 5.01% ~ 10% | 17 | 7.5% | 35.5% |
| | 10.01% ~ 20% | 72 | 31.6% | 67.1% |
| | 20.01% ~ 30% | 67 | 29.4% | 96.5% |
| | 30.01% ~ 40% | 3 | 1.3% | 97.8% |
| | Above 50% | 5 | 2.2% | 100% |

Note: $N = 228$; Source: compiled by this study.

## 4.3    Test of Hypotheses

Table 4 shows the aftereffects of Probit relapse for the blend of partner and collusion geographic decent variety as free factors influences the organizations' advancement execution. Model 1 and 5 shows the base model just incorporate the control factors including backup, firm size, firm deals, and Research and development power. The aftereffects of auxiliary and firm size don't effectsly affect firm oddity and market oddity. Firm sales has negative effects on firm novelty ($\beta = -0.03$), conversely, it has significant and positive effects on market novelty ($\beta = 0.09$, p < 0.1), which suggests that firm sales would confine the level of product innovation. In addition, R&D intensity has significant and positive effects ($\beta = 0.02, p < 0.01$ in Model 1; $\beta = 0.01$, $p < 0.1$ in Model 5) on firm novelty and market novelty, respectively. It is implies that firms invest large R&D resources can increase innovation activity in high tech context.

Model 2 and 6 in Table 4 test the inverted-U shaped relationship between the collaboration and alliance partners diversity and innovation performance. Model 2 and 6 in Table 3 shows that the collaboration alliance diversity is significantly positive ($\beta = 4.21$, $p < 0.01$ in Model 2; $\beta = 3.16$, $p < 0.05$ in Model 6) and the quadratic collaboration alliance diversity ($\beta = -6.09, p < 0.01$ in Model 2; $\beta = -5.33, p < 0.01$ in Model 6) is significantly negative, providing support for Hypothesis 1a and 1b,

**Table 3.** Descriptive statistics and Pearson correlation coefficients

| | (1) | (2) | (3) | (4) | (5) | (6) | (7) | (8) |
|---|---|---|---|---|---|---|---|---|
| (1) Firm novelty | 1 | | | | | | | |
| (2) Market novelty | $-0.248^{***}$ | 1 | | | | | | |
| (3) Subsidiary | 0.043 | 0.053 | 1 | | | | | |
| (4) Firm size | 0.030 | 0.036 | $-0.100$ | 1 | | | | |
| (5) Firm sales | $-0.003$ | $0.122^{*}$ | 0.064 | $0.424^{***}$ | 1 | | | |
| (6) R&D intensity | $0.219^{***}$ | $0.113^{*}$ | 0.000 | 0.035 | 0.067 | 1 | | |
| (7) Alliance partners diversity | $-0.080$ | $-0.195^{***}$ | 0.079 | $-0.006$ | $-0.113^{*}$ | $-0.178^{***}$ | 1 | |
| (8) Alliance geographic diversity | 0.058 | 0.037 | $-0.078$ | 0.057 | 0.032 | $-0.102$ | $0.557^{***}$ | 1 |
| Mean | 0.78 | 0.82 | 0.25 | 810.46 | 14.46 | 16.78 | 0.363 | 0.334 |
| S.D. | 0.418 | 0.381 | 0.434 | 2105.636 | 2.029 | 14.588 | 0.315 | 0.301 |
| VIF | | | 1.059 | 1.248 | 1.276 | 1.036 | 1.559 | 1.506 |

$^{*}p < 0.1$, $^{**}p < 0.05$, $^{***}p < 0.01$; $N = 228$;
Source: compiled by this study.

respectively. Moreover, the connection between district assorted variety and the advancement execution (firm curiosity and market oddity) additionally looked like transformed U-formed capacities in our hypothesis 2a and 2b. Model 3 and 7 in Table 3 demonstrates that the district assorted variety isn't fundamentally positive and the quadratic area decent variety is likewise not essentially negative, giving not support to Hypothesis 2a and 2b. However, while we incorporate the collaboration and alliance partners diversity and region diversity into the Model 4 and Model 8, we found an interesting phenomena that the region diversity is significantly positive ($\beta = 2.74$, $p < 0.1$ in Model 8) and the quadratic region diversity ($\beta = -2.63$, $p < 0.1$ in Model 8) is significantly negative, providing support for Hypothesis 2b.

**Table 4.** Results of Probit regression

| Variables | Firm novelty | | | | Market novelty | | | |
|---|---|---|---|---|---|---|---|---|
| | Model 1 | Model 2 | Model 3 | Model 4 | Model 5 | Model 6 | Model 7 | Model 8 |
| Constant | 0.84 (0.77) | 0.86 (0.84) | 0.85 (0.79) | 0.92 (0.84) | −0.59 (0.79) | −0.43 (0.88) | −0.68 (0.81) | −0.46 (0.87) |
| Subsidiary | 0.18 (0.23) | 0.24 (0.23) | 0.25 (0.23) | 0.29 (0.24) | 0.16 (0.24) | 0.25 (0.25) | 0.17 (.024) | 0.26 (0.25) |
| Firm size | 0.00 (0.00) | 0.00 (0.00) | 0.00 (0.00) | 0.00 (0.00) | −0.00 (0.00) | 0.00 (0.00) | −0.00 (0.00) | 0.00 (0.00) |
| Firm sales | −0.03 (0.05) | −0.04 (0.06) | −0.04 (0.06) | −0.05 (0.06) | 0.09 * (0.06) | 0.08 (0.06) | 0.09 * (0.06) | 0.08 (0.06) |
| R&D intensity | 0.02 *** (0.01) | 0.02 *** (0.01) | 0.02 *** (0.01) | 0.02 *** (0.01) | 0.01 * (0.01) | 0.02 * (0.01) | 0.01 * (0.01) | 0.02 * (0.01) |
| Alliance partners diversity | | 4.21 *** (1.28) | | 3.59 *** (1.39) | | 3.16 ** (1.33) | | 2.13 * (1.43) |
| Alliance partners diversity square | | −6.09 *** (1.68) | | −5.56 *** (1.74) | | −5.33 *** (1.72) | | −4.83 *** (1.78) |
| Alliance geographic diversity | | | −1.19 (1.33) | −0.40 (1.49) | | | 0.44 (1.35) | 2.74* (1.59) |
| Alliance geographic diversity square | | | 2.48 (2.02) | 1.41 (2.15) | | | −0.37 (1.99) | −2.63* (2.24) |
| Observations | 228 | 228 | 228 | 228 | 228 | 228 | 228 | 228 |
| Pseudo R-squared | 0.05 | 0.10 | 0.06 | 0.11 | 0.03 | 0.11 | 0.03 | 0.14 |

* $p < 0.1$, ** $p < 0.05$, *** $p < 0.01$. Source: compiled by this study.

## 5 Discussion and Conclusion

### 5.1 Discussion

The real discoveries are talked about as follows. In the first place, past research contended that organizations ought to continue cross fringe joint effort which can quicken advancement arrangement and require the common divulgence of logical important information (van Rijnsoever and Hessels 2011) that prompt encourage item contributions. As Escribano et al. (2009) contended outside information trade with various accomplices can give company's new and therefore to enhanced their items. Nonetheless, coalition accomplice assorted variety may bring information many-sided quality and increment administration troublesomely, and the attributes of various accomplices likely deter correspondence, learning exchange troublesome (Parkhe 1991), and worker oppose attributes (Østergaard et al. 2011) that would prompt decline advancement limit and diminish company's item improvement.

The outcomes in this examination additionally finding that the connection between union accomplices decent variety and development execution is as a reversed U-shape, which implies that the advantages of unreasonable accomplices assorted variety on cooperation may exceed its expenses and direct portfolio assorted variety can prompt noteworthy advancement execution. Collusion accomplices assorted variety has upgrade item development on firm curiosity which implies the items or administrations are just new to the firm and have other comparative or same substitute on advertise. In this way, regardless of whether there are other item substitutes in showcase, a trade of communitarian learning still reinforce the piece of the pie of item. Moreover, our experimental proof propose that for dodge negative impacts cutting edge firms should manufacture all around planned instrument of administration, including reconciliation component of the procurement of outside information, coordination administration a wide range of partners, and segregate workers' ability.

Second, earlier research demonstrated that organizations had an altered U-formed between partnership geographic decent variety and firm execution (Qian et al. 2010); and has an upset U-molded association with item development in China (Wu and Wu 2014). In view of the previously mentioned, locale decent variety has mix impacts to firm. This investigation found that locale assorted variety has diverse result on creative execution. Our observational confirmation recommends that firm still need to team up with cross-outskirt areas.

For market novelty, alliance geographic diversity has an inverted U-shaped statistical significant relationship that reflects collaborate with multiple regions would promote firms' innovative performance. This study argues that region diversity is a crucial factor on market expanded and its development, whether firm novelty is not significant impact in our dataset. Therefore, firms should build a well platform to integrated and managed each region's difference in order to increase collaborative successful and decrease collaborative conflict. The empirical results of hypotheses in portfolio diversity and innovation performance are listed as the following Table 5.

**Table 5.** Results of hypotheses

| Hypotheses | Results |
|---|---|
| Hypothesis 1: Alliance partners diversity has an inverted U-shaped relationship with innovation performance. | Support |
| Hypothesis 1a: Alliance partners diversity has an inverted U-shaped relationship with firm novelty. | Support |
| Hypothesis 1b: Alliance partners diversity has an inverted U-shaped relationship with market novelty. | Support |
| Hypothesis 2: Alliance geographic diversity has an inverted U-shaped relationship with innovation performance. | Partial support |
| Hypothesis 2a: Alliance geographic diversity has an inverted U-shaped relationship with firm novelty. | Not support |
| Hypothesis 2b: Alliance geographic diversity has an inverted U-shaped relationship with market novelty. | Support |

Source: compiled by this study

## 5.2    Conclusion

In outline, our investigation adds to the writing and cutting edge divisions in the accompanying ways. In the first place, firms face the quickly change worldwide condition and unhindered commerce understanding, Taiwanese cutting edge firms are getting to be to build their task weight and, in this way, they contribute expansive sum Research and development assets to encourage advancement improvement. Subsequently, this investigation additionally affirms the connection between different partners (e.g. providers, clients, college, explore foundations, et cetera) and advancement execution which demonstrate that can fortify and enhance their items as well as administration aggressiveness everywhere throughout the world. Second, this investigation offers a knowledge into partnership geographic assorted variety which estimated by Taiwan, China, America, Japan, Korea India, Europe, and different nations; it additionally has altogether constructive outcomes to dispatch new item and additionally benefit and to improve firm market advancement, however it likewise not has essentially connection on association's oddity. Indeed, even that, this examination likewise proposes firm joint effort crosswise over locales, it is prudent to take outside assets and increment advancement limit. Since Taiwan's cutting edge firms are for the most part of SMEs, subsequently, while transnational coordinated effort is prescribe that shape industry affiliations or business partnership (e.g. production network) to together face the deterrents in collaboration. What's more, experimental outcomes demonstrate a U-formed connection between locale decent variety and market oddity. In this manner, these demonstrated that the derivations were generally reliable over the distinctive market firms ought to grow well administration instrument in various locale and market coordination for reinforce their market oddity.

# References

Blau, P.M.: Inequality and Heterogeneity: A Primitive Theory of Social Structure, Vol. 7. Free Press, New York (1977)

Chesbrough, H.: Open Innovation: The New Imperative for Creating and Profiting From Technology. Harvard Business Review Press, Boston, MA (2003)

Chesbrough, H., Crowther, A.K.: Beyond high tech: early adopters of open innovation in other industries. R&D Manag. 36(3), 229–236 (2006)

Dahlander, L., Gann, D.M.: How open is innovation? Res. Policy 39(6), 699–709 (2010)

Escribano, A., Fosfuri, A., Tribó, J.A.: Managing external knowledge flows: the moderating role of absorptive capacity. Res. Policy 38(1), 96–105 (2009)

Gassmann, O.: Opening up the innovation process: towards an agenda. R&D Manag. 36(3), 223–228 (2006)

Grant, R.M.: Toward a knowledge-based theory of the firm. Strateg. Manag. J. 17, 109–122 (1996)

Hagedoorn, J.: Inter-firm R&D partnerships: an overview of major trends and patterns since 1960 (2002)

Laursen, K., Salter, A.: Open for innovation: the role of openness in explaining innovation performance among U.K. manufacturing firms. Strateg. Manag. J. 27(2), 131–150 (2006)

Lichtenthaler, U.: Open Innovation in practice: an analysis of strategic approaches to technology transactions. Eng. Manag. IEEE Trans. 55(1), 148–157 (2008)

Lichtenthaler, U.: Open Innovation: past research, current debates, and future directions. Acad. Manag. Perspect. **25**(1), 75–93 (2011)

Noseleit, F., de Faria, P.: Complementarities of internal R&D and alliances with different partner types. J. Bus. Res. **66**(10), 2000–2006 (2013)

Østergaard, C.R., Timmermans, B., Kristinsson, K.: Does a different view create something new? The effect of employee diversity on innovation. Res. Policy **40**(3), 500–509 (2011)

Parkhe, A.: Partner nationality and the structure-performance relationship in strategic alliances. Organ. Sci. **4**(2), 301–324 (1993)

Qian, G., Khoury, T.A., Peng, M.W., Qian, Z.: The performance implications of intra- and inter-regional geographic diversification. Strateg. Manag. J. **31**(9), 1018–1030 (2010)

Srivastava, M.K., Gnyawali, D.R.: When do relational resources matter? Leveraging portfolio technological resources for breakthrough innovation. Acad. Manag. J. **54**(4), 797–810 (2011)

Van de Vrande, V., Lemmens, C., Vanhaverbeke, W.: Choosing governance modes for external technology sourcing. R&D Manag. **36**(3), 347–363 (2006)

Van Rijnsoever, F.J., Hessels, L.K.: Factors associated with disciplinary and interdisciplinary research collaboration. Res. Policy **40**(3), 463–472 (2011)

Wu, J., Wu, Z.: ocal and international knowledge search and product innovation: The moderating role of technology boundary spanning. Int. Bus. Rev. **23**, 542–551 (2014)

# Research on the Related Issues About the Service of Mutual Legal Assistance Documents Through Electronic Delivery

Pei-Fen Tsai[✉]

Asia University, Taichung City 413, Taiwan (R.O.C.)
fen2006@gmail.com

**Abstract.** The service of mutual legal assistance documents through electronic delivery is prohibited by the formal diplomatic approach and not approved by many conventions and regulations in sending documents from one country to another over the past few years.

In the Internet of Things world, the service through electronic delivery is indispensible and convenience. Under the ideas, I want to research the related issues about the service of mutual legal assistance documents through electronic delivery to provide the legitimate and the feasibility.

Council Regulation (EC) No 1393/2007 of the European Parliament and of the Council of 13 November 2007 had amended and repealed the Council Regulation (EC) No 1348/2000 on the service in the Member States of judicial and extrajudicial documents in civil or commercial matters (service of documents). Expanding electronic service for delivery judicial or extra-judicial documents for every country will be popular in the future.

I boldly proposed in this article that the electronic delivery judicial or extra-judicial documents of mutual assistant in civil and commercial matters through the Blockchain method and take advantage of the Digital signature produced by Ethereum, or similar to this way, providing a digital signature as a reference to protect privacy and to be as the security protection.

Furthermore, this article introduces all of the defects of the electronic service will be improved if the delivery sends on the Blockchain.

**Keywords:** Mutual assistant · Electronic delivery · E-service

## 1 Preface and Research Scope

The service of mutual legal assistance documents through electronic delivery by network is used for a long time in investigation and information exchanging, that consistent with official cooperation and under the commitment and the sovereignty comity of those States but is different from what this article is about to discuss that the service direct delivery through electronic channels from judicial department to people.

The service of mutual legal assistance documents through electronic delivery is prohibited by the formal diplomatic approach and not approved by those convention and regulations (All of the service abroad of European conventions contain:

© ICST Institute for Computer Sciences, Social Informatics and Telecommunications Engineering 2019
Published by Springer Nature Switzerland AG 2019. All Rights Reserved
J.-L. Chen et al. (Eds.): WiCON 2018, LNICST 264, pp. 367–374, 2019.
https://doi.org/10.1007/978-3-030-06158-6_35

Convention On Civil Procedure, 1954 Convention On The Law Governing Transfer Of Title In International Sales Of Goods. 1958 Convention On Concerning The Recognition And Enforcement Of Decisions Relating To Maintenance Obligations Towards Children, 1958 Convention On Abolishing The Requirement Of Legalization For Foreign Public Documents, 1961 Convention On The Choice Of Court, 1965 Convention On The Service Abroad Of Judicial And Extrajudicial Documents In Civil Or Commercial Matters, 1965 Convention On The Recognition Of Divorces And Legal Separations, 1970 European Convention on State Immunity, 1972 Council Regulation (EC) No 1348/2000 Brussels Convention on Jurisdiction and the Enforcement of Judgments in Civil and Commercial Matters, 1968 Hague Convention on the Taking of Evidence Abroad in Civil or Commercial Matters, 1970 Convention On The Recognition And Enforcement Of Foreign Judgments In Civil And Commercial Matters, 1971 European Convention on State Immunity, 1972 Hague Convention the Recognition and Enforcement of Decisions Relating to Maintenance Obligations, 1973 Convention Concerning The International Administration Of The Estates Of Deceased Persons, 1973 Convention On The Law Applicable To Products Liability, 1973 Convention On The Law Applicable To Maintenance Obligations, 1973 Hague Convention on International Access to Justice, 1980.) in sending documents from one country to another.

But in the Internet of Things world, the service through electronic delivery is indispensible and convenience. Under the ideas, I want to research the related issues about the service of mutual legal assistance documents through electronic delivery to provide the legitimate and the feasibility.

Mutual legal assistance is very developed in Europe especially well develop in European Union, so the research scope of this article is restricted in the proceedings of the European countries and the documents covers not only judicial but also extrajudicial service of documents, because the service may arise in various out of the court proceeding such as documents seeking or informing the attendance of persons in the absence of any underlying judicial proceedings.

## 2    Legislation

Council Regulation (EC) No 1393/2007 of the European Parliament and of the Council of 13 November 2007 had amended and repealed the Council Regulation (EC) No 1348/2000 on the service in the Member States of judicial and extrajudicial documents in civil or commercial matters (service of documents), that not only prescribes the service in the Member States of judicial and extrajudicial documents in civil or commercial matters (service of documents) by electronic channel but also replace the direct delivery by post across borders to further bring people the greater convenience and more efficiencies.

According to article 23 of Council Regulation (EC) No 1393/2007, the electronic communication shall be available in particular through the European Judicial Network in Civil and Commercial Matters. Article 23 of Council Regulation (EC) No 1393/2007 regulates:" The Commission shall draw up and update regularly a manual containing the information referred to in paragraph 1, which shall be available electronically, in particular through the European Judicial Network in Civil and Commercial Matters."

According to the explanatory memorandum of Council Regulation (EC) No 1393/2007 On 31 May 2018 [1], the European Commission undertook a regulatory fitness evaluation by the Commission's Regulatory Fitness and Performance Programme(REFIT) [2], in line with the better regulation guidelines, to assess the operation of the instrument in relation to the five key mandatory evaluation criteria of effectiveness, efficiency, relevance, coherence and EU added value. The main conclusions of REFIT are set out below [3].

## 3 The Impact Assessment

The impact assessment concluded that benefits would result from using electronic communication for digitalisation of the judiciary, by simplifying and speeding up cross-border judicial procedures and judicial cooperation.

REFIT sets up a framework of judicial cooperation aligned with the digital single market strategy. It will help improve the speed and efficiency of cross-border proceedings by reducing the time spent on sending documents between agencies and by reducing reliance on paper-based communication. This would ensure the safe electronic communication and exchange of documents between the users of the decentralised IT system, and it would provide for automatic recording of all steps of the workflow. It would also have security features to ensure that only authorised participants with verified identities may use the system. [4] If only in half of the cases, where there are currently problems with the legal assessment of the returned acknowledgments of receipt, would postal service be successful in the future, 2.2 million EUR in each year could be saved, an amount currently wasted for letter post service not bringing any result [4].

## 4 Execution Method and Result

### 4.1 Electronic Service Methods and Subjects

Service is usually conducted through e-mail (e.g. Germany, Denmark, Portugal, Czech Republic and Estonia), Face book, Twitter, specified Platform [5], ICT (Information and Communications Technology) System, a special Mobil-ID or Fax.

The service via an e-mail by all of those countries always requires an e-signature for the confirmation on the receipt by the addressee and returns it to the executor. Generally, the method is only permitted as a possible mean of service and communication between the parties and with the court when the consent is given before the proceeding is instituted.

## 4.2   Overview of Priority 2 of REFIT Initiatives Taken by the Present Commission

**Overview of Priority 2 REFIT Initiatives taken by the present Commission:**

Initiatives proposed by the Commission and pending in legislative procedure:
1.   ENISA (European Union Agency for Network and Information Security)
2.   Revised Audiovisual Media Services Directive
3.   Satellite and Cable Directive 93/83/EEC
4.   Regulatory framework for electronic communications networks and services (Telecoms regulatory framework)
5.   Directive on Privacy and Electronic Communications Free Flow of Data
6.   Free Flow of Data – initiative on the free flow of non–personal data in the digital single market
7.   VAT for cross–border e–commerce (extension of the VAT Mini One Stop shop)

Initiatives planned by the Commission:
1.   .eu Domain Name Regulation
2.   Review of Public Sector Information

Areas being evaluated:
1.   Legal protection of databases

Resource: Andrus Ansip, Priority 2-Simplification And Burden Reduction In The Digital Single Market (European Commission, Regulatory Fitness And Performance Programme Refit Scoreboard Summary, p.13, 24. 10. 2017.)

### 4.3   Confirmation of Service

When the effectiveness of delivery is would be a matter of legislative policy decisions. Service is confirmed when the documents are opened to be read as a receipt is automatically returned to the sender in Estonia [6] and France [6], but reach rather than opened is in another country.

## 5   Problems Waiting to be Overcome

To support an e-service should solving many practical issues, such as the cost of establishing and maintaining the digital platform, time regulated to allow for instantaneous delivery, and the receipt by letting the system send a receipt when the document is received and read by the addressee. Those elements are easy to be solved, but the following problems are not easy.

### 5.1   Ambiguity Over Whom Actually Received the Documents

It may happen that the recipient overlooks the e-mail transmitted by the parties or with the court, but the e-mail has been opened by the others using the computer and the e-signature confirmation of the receipt automatically returned.

The addressee does not receive the e-mail due to the filtering software filters out the letter or the letter is isolated by antivirus software, and then a delivery notification automatically sends to the sender via the electronic platform or the special system.

## 5.2 Privacy

The judicial documents transmitted pursuant to this Regulation should be treated under suitable protection. Those matters fall within the scope of Directive 95/46/EC of the European Parliament and of the Council of 24 October 1995 on the protection of individuals with regard to the processing of personal data and on the free movement of such data, [7] and of Directive 2002/58/EC of the European Parliament and of the Council of 12 July 2002 concerning the processing of personal data and the protection of privacy in the electronic communications sector (Directive on privacy and electronic communications) [8].

## 5.3 Security

According to the proposal made of the Commission's Regulatory Fitness and Performance Programme(REFIT), the Safety checks need to be strengthened. [4] How to work? The proposal recommended strengthening the protection of privacy through an alignment with the General Data Protection Regulation, to ensure that exceptions to the 'consent' rule for cookies are possible provided that they do not create any privacy risk, to address national implementation problems and facilitate the exchange of best practice [9].

However, the letters of the text of the contract are usually very small and difficult to read. If you don't pay attention to read, you will ignore it, and agree all of the contents in the text of the contract. Moreover, the computer option is generally unknown, and it is easy to be misled.

## 5.4 No Unified Platform

Each Member State(s) of the European Union concerned seems to have developed its own IT system without paying attention to the possibility of making it inter-operable with the systems of other Member State(s) of the European Union. The discrepancies in the digital platform may result in the letter being unable to reach the recipient, or the receipt cannot be delivered to the sender.

## 5.5 Unable to Use Computer

The elder people or the persons with disabilities are not able to use computers will be excluded of access to justice for privacy and suitable safe because they have to ask someone to help for pre-registering and having a digital account to consent the way delivered through electronic service or the digital specified platform on the initiating proceeding.

## 5.6   Entailing the Risk of Failures

Using the ordinary method such as e-mail or the ICT (Information and Communications Technology) platform does not guarantee the transfer or the receipt by the addressee is always successful.

# 6   Overcome the Problems

## 6.1   Security and Privacy Protection

Under the principle, which would be the human common will, this article Boldly proposed the electronic delivery of mutual assistant in civil and commercial matters through the Blockchain method, taking advantage of the Digital signature produced by Ethereum, or similar to this way, to be as security and privacy protection, furthermore, in this way, the authenticity of the judicial or extra-judicial documents would be attested avoid fraud or verify for transnational litigation and service of Notice by Publication.

The basic theory of Blockchain is that each user has two keys, a public key and a private key. The public key can be known to others, the private key is known only to oneself and a one-time address to receive the letter or message. When A wants to send a message or trade to B, it needs to use B's public key to encrypt the transaction, and this encrypted message or transaction can only be unlocked by using B's private key [10]. Under the theory, A means the judicial institute and B is the addressee, lawyers or the parties of litigation. During the process, the privacy of the contents of documents and safeguard the security would be ensured.

Although everybody in the chain would know there is one delivery comes from the court or judicial institute to be served to someone, but no one knows who someone is because the addressee is composed of digital numbers and not to be specified to know who he/she is. Therefore, there is no scruple of privacy.

The news that the Exchange was hacked [11], for example, in January 2018, Virtual currency Coincheck $523 million New Dollar (NEM) was missing in Tokyo Headquarters, does not equal to the Blockchain is not safe, because the exchange is not built on the Blockchain.

## 6.2   Delivery Errors

The theory of Hash cash algorithm, Elliptic curve digital signing algorithm and various hash functions can solve the aforementioned problem of delivery errors, because the Hass cash algorithm and various hash functions ensure the data or documents not be falsified in electronic transmission [10].

## 6.3   Unified Platform Is Not Required

The unified platform is not required for the delivery through Blockchain. No need specified platform to execute there may achieve the same effect.

### 6.4  Specific Recipient

No one can open an e-letter without a private key, unless someone with a private key tells the other person the golden key code, or ask someone else to open the e-letter on behalf of the recipient; no one else can receive or open the e-letter, therefore the aforementioned problem of who received it can be specified.

## 7  Conclusion

Expanding electronic service for delivery judicial or extra-judicial documents for every country will be popular in the future. Messages containing confidential information must be encrypted or secured in some other manner. Security, safeguards, privacy and modifying the defect of the technology is connection with the authentic and human rights.

I boldly proposed in this article that the electronic delivery judicial or extra-judicial documents of mutual assistant in civil and commercial matters through the Blockchain method and take advantage of the Digital signature produced by Ethereum, or similar to this way, providing a digital signature as a reference to protect privacy and to be as the security protection. Furthermore, the delivery carried on the authorized key by the judicial institute would save time for service via parties without service carried on the court clerk or bailiff because the character of the decentralization and the Public Key Cryptosystem. All of the defects of the electronic service will be improved if the delivery sends on the Blockchain.

Until the development of Blockchain is used as the encryption method, for the identification of delivery in civil or commercial matters, a certificate complying with the requirements for a qualified certificate in the Act on Electronic Signatures or another secure and verifiable identification method shall be used.

## References

1. European Commission, COM (2018)397 final, 2018/0204 (COD), p. 2. Brussel, 31 May 2018
2. REFIT. https://ec.europa.eu/info/law/law-making-process/evaluating-and-improving-existing-laws/refit-making-eu-law-simpler-and-less-costly_en. Accessed 15 Sep 2018
3. According to the data on the website. https://ec.europa.eu/info/law/cross-border-cases/judicial-cooperation/types-judicial-cooperation/sending-documents-one-country-another_en. Accessed 15 Sep 2018
4. Explanatory memorandum of Regulation (EC) No 1393/2007, European Commission, COM (2018) 397 final, 2018/0204 (COD), p. 8. Brussel, 31 May 2018
5. Like Estonia, via E-toimik. http://www.e-toimik.ee. Accessed 15 Sep 2018
6. European Commission, Final Report-Study on the service of documents-Comparative legal analysis of the relevant laws and practices of the Member States, No JUST/2014/JCOO/PR/CIVI/0049, pp. 100–103, 5 Oct 2016
7. OJ(Official Journal) L 281, 23.11.1995, p. 31. Directive as amended by Regulation (EC) No 1882/2003 (OJ L 284, 31.10.2003, p. 1)

8. OJ(Official Journal) L 201, 31.7.2002, p. 37. Directive as amended by Directive 2006/24/EC (OJ L 105, 13.4.2006, p. 54)
9. Ansip, A.: Priority 2-Simplification And Burden Reduction In The Digital Single Market, European Commission, Regulatory Fitness And Performance Programme Refit Scoreboard Summary, p. 12, 24 Oct 2017
10. Yan, T.-Y.: Analysis of the operation principle of Blockchain: 5 key technologies, 23.4.2016. https://www.ithome.com.tw/news/105374. Accessed 15 Sep 2018
11. Gao, J.-Y.: Crack the Blockchain 8 common myths! The exchange is shackled, not equal to the Blockchain is not safe, 12.3.2018. https://www.bnext.com.tw/article/48454/13-common-blockchain-myths-explained. Accessed 15 Sep 2018

# Mathematical Demonstration of Astronomical and Geographical Knowledge

Wen-Chi Chen[1], Jin-De Chang[2], Wen-Hong Chiu[3],
Cheng-Lung Lee[4], Hui-Ru Chi[3], and Pei-Fen Tsai[5(✉)]

[1] Doctoral Program of Emerging Industry Strategies and Development,
Department of Business Administration, Asia University, Taichung City 413,
Taiwan (R.O.C.)
[2] Department of Accounting and Information Systems, Asia University,
Taichung City 413, Taiwan (R.O.C.)
[3] Department of Business Administration, Asia University, Taichung City 413,
Taiwan (R.O.C.)
[4] Taiwan Police College/Qatar Police College, Taichung City 413
Taiwan (R.O.C.)
[5] Department of Financial and Economic Law, Asia University, Arbitrator,
Taiwan (R.O.C.)
fen2006@gmail.com

**Abstract.** The theories about the eight diagrams and the five elements were first recorded in I Ching. In the ancient China, the enthronement of emperors faced southward, which is called "Becoming an Emperor Facing Southward". The directions and modern maps in the eight diagrams of The Book of Changes and in the theories on FengShui are the opposite to the aerial diagram, the cadastral diagram, the measurement diagram, the navigation diagram, the tourist diagram and architectural diagram of China. This is also one of the problems that scholars and users to solve. With the mathematical deduction method and according to the realities, this paper demonstrates the "heaven in the south and earth in the north" in The Book of Changes and explains the philosophical problems that have remained unsolved for years. In this way, it aims to allow researchers to analyze problems with appropriate principles and provide some help for researchers and users.

**Keywords:** Yi-Jing · Eight diagrams · Mystical diagram · Tortoise diagram
Heavenly south and earthly north

## 1 Introduction

At present, it is a fundamental commonplace that directions consist of north (up), south (down), west (left) and east (right), and this commonplace has taken root deep in people's mind. Nevertheless, the directions recorded in The Book of Changes and the books about FengShui are opposite to such commonplace. The reason for such an opposition has not been explained, so people are still confused about it. By far, few studies have been done to solve this problem. The mathematical deduction in this paper tries to uncover the myth of astronomical and geographical knowledge, and it is hoped

© ICST Institute for Computer Sciences, Social Informatics and Telecommunications Engineering 2019
Published by Springer Nature Switzerland AG 2019. All Rights Reserved
J.-L. Chen et al. (Eds.): WiCON 2018, LNICST 264, pp. 375–386, 2019.
https://doi.org/10.1007/978-3-030-06158-6_36

that this paper will clarify the confusion that the myth has brought to all Chinese and academic researchers around the world.

## 2   Literature Review

The former eight diagrams is called Fuxi Eight Diagrams, and the later one is called Wenwang Eight Diagrams. By observing nature, Fuxi established the former eight diagrams which includes Qian (heaven), Dui (river), Li (fire), Zhen (thunder), Xun (wind), Kan (water), Gen (mountain) and Kun (earth). Wenwang Eight Diagram is also called the later eight diagrams, and the directions of the eight diagrams are determined by four directions, namely, east, south, west and north. As such an array can be combined with directions, it is widely applied to FengShui (Fig. 1).

**Fig. 1.**  Later eight diagrams [1]

### Later Eight Diagrams

| 兌<br>Dui | 坤<br>Kun | 離<br>Li | 巽<br>Xun | 震<br>Zhen |
|---|---|---|---|---|
|  |  | 艮<br>Gen | 坎<br>Kan | 乾<br>Qian |

### Four orientations and central

| 北<br>North | 西<br>West | 中央<br>Central | 南<br>South | 東<br>East |
|---|---|---|---|---|

## Five Elements

| 水<br>Water | 金<br>Metal | 土<br>Earth | 火<br>Fire | 木<br>Wood |
|---|---|---|---|---|

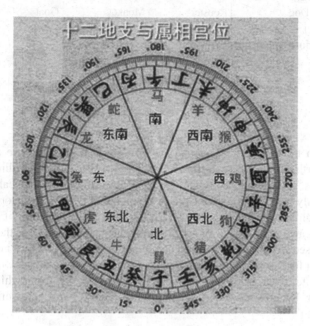

**Fig. 2.** The 12 terrestrial branches [1]

## Twenty-four mountains

| 寅<br>Yin | 艮<br>Gen | 丑<br>Chou | 癸<br>Gui | 子<br>Zi | 壬<br>Ren |
|---|---|---|---|---|---|
| 巳<br>Si | 巽<br>Xun | 辰<br>Chen | 乙<br>Yi | 卯<br>Mao | 甲<br>Jia |
| 申<br>Shen | 坤<br>Kun | 未<br>Wei | 丁<br>Ding | 午<br>Wu | 丙<br>Bing |
| 亥<br>Hai | 乾<br>Qian | 戌<br>Xu | 辛<br>Xin | 酉<br>You | 庚<br>Geng |

## Twelve earthly branches

| 巳<br>Si | 辰<br>Chen | 卯<br>Mao | 寅<br>Yin | 丑<br>Chou | 子<br>Zi |
|---|---|---|---|---|---|
| 亥<br>Hai | 戌<br>Xu | 酉<br>You | 申<br>Shen | 未<br>Wei | 午<br>Wu |

## Twelve zodiac

| 蛇 | 龍 | 兔 | 虎 | 牛 | 鼠 |
|---|---|---|---|---|---|
| Snake | Dragon | Rabbit | Tiger | Ox | Rat |
| 豬 | 狗 | 雞 | 猴 | 羊 | 馬 |
| Pig | Dog | Rooster | Monkey | Goat | Horse |

## Eight orientation

| 西南 | 南 | 東南 | 東 | 東北 | 北 |
|---|---|---|---|---|---|
| Southwest | South | Southeast | East | Northeast | North |
| | | | | 西北 | 西 |
| | | | | Northwest | West |

Aside from the 10 heavenly stems, the 12 terrestrial branches are also based on south (up), north (down), east (left) and west (right) (Fig. 2). According to the Fuxi Eight Diagrams, south is heaven (Qian) and north is earth (Kun), as is called "heavenly south and earthly north" among the Chinese people. In the Chinese history, emphasis is placed on "brightness-oriented governance". As south is the direction of brightness, all the maps are drawn on the basis of south. In the theory on FengShui, the 12 terrestrial branches are used for direction, with Zi standing for "north", Wu for "north", Mao for "east" and You for "west". There is a popular Chinese saying, "Black Dragon is on the left while White Tiger is on the right; Rosefinch is in the front while Xuanwu is behind." Black Dragon represents "east"; White Tiger, "west"; Rosefinch, "south"; Xuanwu, "north".

## 3   Research Contents and Methods

1. Apart from exploring the former and later eight diagrams in The Book of Changes, this paper will discuss Yin and Yang as well as the physical and chemical changes of the heavenly stems and terrestrial branches of the Five Elements. Despite that there were not such modern pronouns as "physics" or "chemistry" in the ancient times, the sages and men of virtue well applied them to the ethical meaning after changes, including the combination between "mean" and "integrity", "benevolence" and "righteousness", "authority" and "governance", "obscenity" and "anonymity", and "seniority" and "minority", and used them for astronomical observation.

(1)  The 10 heavenly stems: *Jia, Yi, Bing, Ding, Wu, Ji, Geng, Xin, Ren* and *Gui.*

(2)  The 12 terrestrial branches: *Zi, Chou, Yin, Mao, Wei, Chen, Si, Wu, Shen, You, Xu* and *Hai.*

(3)  Combination of the heavenly stems: the combination of *Jia* and *Ji* leads to "earth"; the combination of *Ji* and *Geng* leads to "metal"; the combination of *Bing* and *Xin* leads to "water"; the combination of *Ding* and *Ren* leads to "wood"; the combination of *Wu* and *Gui* leads to "fire".

(4) Combination of six terrestrial branches: the combination of *Zi* and *Chou* leads to "earth"; the combination of *Yin* and *Hai* leads to "wood"; the combination of *Mao* and *Xu* leads to "fire"; the combination of *Chen* and *You* leads to "metal"; the combination of *Wu* and *Wei* leads to "fire".

(5) Combination of three terrestrial branches: the combination of *Shen*, *Zi* and *Chen* leads to "water"; the combination of *Hai*, *Mao* and *Wei* leads to "wood"; the combination of *Yin*, *Wu* and *Xu* leads to "fire"; the combination of *Si*, *You* and *Chou* leads to "metal".

Combination of six terrestrial branches: the combination of *Zi* and *Chou* leads to "earth"; the combination of *Yin* and *Hai* leads to "wood"; the combination of *Mao* and *Xu* leads to "fire"; the combination of *Chen* and *You* leads to "metal"; the combination of *Si* and *Shen* leads to "water"; the combination of *Wu* and *Wei* leads to sun and moon (*Wu* is *Yang* and *Wei* is *Yin*).

(6) Contradiction of the terrestrial branches: There is contradiction between *Zi* and *Wu*, *Chou* and *Wei*, *Yin* and *Shen*, *Mao* and *You*, *Chen* and *Xu*, and *Si* and *Hai*.

(7) The direction created by the combination of three terrestrial branches: the combination of *Yin*, *Mao* and *Chen* leads to "wood" in the east; the combination of *Si*, *Wu* and *Wei* leads to "fire" in the south; the combination of *Shen*, *You* and *Xu* leads to "metal" in the west; the combination of *Hai*, *Zi* and *Chou* leads to "water" in the north [2].

2. According to the principles of the formation of the five elements, water starts at 0°. In the later eight diagrams, it evolves into wood, fire (earth), metal and finally water. There are four seasons, namely, spring, summer, autumn and winter, and each season has 90 days. The circle is divided at a right angle of 90°. Therefore, water is at 0° or 360°; wood, 90°; fire, 180° (fire and earth share the same destiny at 180°); metal, 270°; water, 360°. These are the numbers about the five elements as well as the positions of *Qian*, *Dui*, *Li*, *Zhen*, *Xun*, *Kan*, *Gen* and *Kun* in the later eight diagrams. According to *The Book of Pivot of God*, the five elements prosper at a different time, but only earth is unstable. It can be found in the four seasons and prospers for 18 days in each season. Hence, earth is in the position of Week and Day and changeable, without occupying any corner. The theories on this are as follows:

(1) The derivation of the formation of the five elements is as follows:

In this paper, wood is set as 90° and metal as 270° [3].

The formation of the five elements is based on the interaction between each other. Each degree between a "derivative" and a "generator" is 90°. (According to the setting, wood is 90°, fire is 180°; metal, 270°; water, 0° or 360°) (Fig. 3).

Water generates wood: $90° - 0° = 90°$.

Wood generates fire: $180° - 90° = 90°$ (Zi Ping Method: "fire" and "earth" share the same destiny, and they are in the same cycle in the 12 destinies).

Earth generates metal: $270° - 180° = 90°$.

Metal generates water: $360° - 270° = 90°$.

Fire generates earth: Earth follows the number of basis (As is described in the Zi Ping Method, "fire" and "earth" share the same destiny, and they are in the same cycle in the 12 destinies), so fire and earth generate each other without increment or decrement (Fig. 4).

| 金 Metal | 木 Wood | 水 Water | 火 Fire | 五行圖 Diagram of Five Elements |
|---|---|---|---|---|

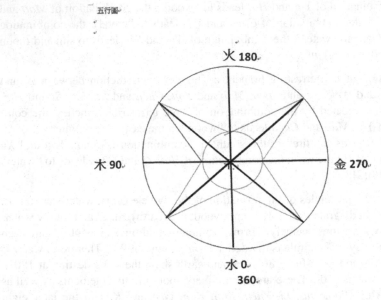

**Fig. 3.** Diagram of five elements in this paper

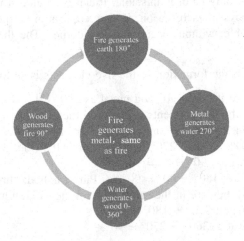

**Fig. 4.** Mutual generation of the five elements

(2)  Contradiction among the five elements refers to the gap between a "dominator" and "subordinate". (Water can be defined as 0° or 360°) (See Fig. 5).

Water dominates fire: 360° − 180° = 180°.
Metal dominates water: 270° − 90° = 180°.
Earth dominates water: 180° − 0° = 180°(Water can be either 0° or 360°).
Fire dominates metal: (180° + 360°) − 270° = 270°.
(As the subtraction between 180° and 270° would lead to a negative number and there was no negative number in the ancient times, the complete operation of the heaven and the earth is 360° for a circle, which is used as the number for increment.).
Wood dominates earth: (180° + 360°) − 270° = 270°.
(As the subtraction between 180° and 270° would lead to a negative number and there was no negative number in the ancient times, the complete operation of the

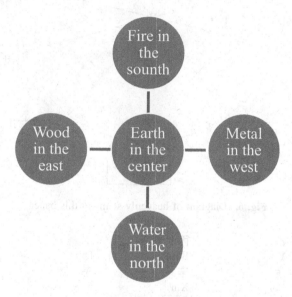

**Fig. 5.**  Contradiction among the five elements

heaven and the earth is 360° for a circle, which is used as the number for increment.)

(3)  Combination of the heavenly stems

According to the deduction of this paper, *Jia* is set as 36°; *Yi*, 72°; *Bing*, 108°; *Ding*, 144°; *Wu*, 180°; *Ji*, 216°; *Geng*, 252°; *Xin*, 288°; *Ren*, 324°; *Gui*, 360°)(Fig. 6).
Combination of *Jia* and *Ji*: *Ji*(216°) − *Jia*(36°) = 180°.
Combination of *Yi* and *Geng*: *Geng*(252°) − *Yi* (72°) = 180°.
Combination of *Bing* and *Xin*: *Xin*(288°) − *Bing* (108°) = 180°.
Combination of *Ding* and *Ren*: *Ren*(324°) − *Ding* (144°) = 180°.
Combination of *Wu* and *Gui*: *Gui*(360°) − *Xu*(180°) = 180°.

天干圖

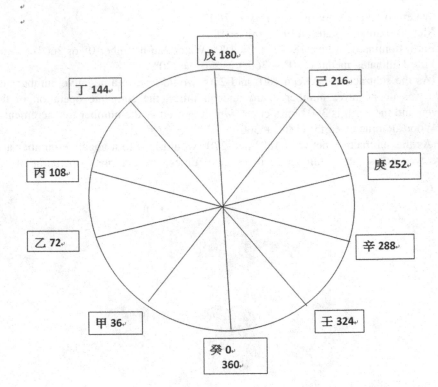

**Fig. 6.** Diagram of heavenly stems in this paper

| 甲 | 乙 | 丙 | 丁 | 戊 |
|------|------|------|------|------|
| Jia | Yi | Bing | Ding | Wu |
| 己 | 庚 | 辛 | 壬 | 癸 |
| Ji | Geng | Xin | Ren | Gui |

天干圖
Diagram of Heavenly Stems

(4)  Combination of the heavenly stems

According to the deduction in this paper: (as what has been mentioned above, water is defined as 0°(360°); wood, 90°; fire, 180°; metal, 270°. It runs clockwise.)

The combination of *Jia* and *Ji* leads to earth: *Jia*(90°) + *Ji*(180°)—One Square (90°) = 180°, which is the number of earth. Therefore, the combination leads to earth.

(Note: One Square (90°) comes from *Practical Numerology* by Shu-Hai Li and published by Taipei Life Type Society in September 1954: Page 52–58. The difference is that Li uses [+], while this paper uses [−].)

The combination of *Yi* and *Geng*leads to metal: *Yi* (90°) +*Geng*(270°)—One Square (90°) = 270°, which is the number of metal. Therefore, the combination leads to metal.

The combination of *Bing* and *Xin* leads to water: *Bing* (180°) + *Xin*(270°)—One Square (90°) = 360°, which is the number of water. Therefore, the combination leads to water.

The combination of *Ding* and *Ren*leads to wood: *Ding* (180°) + *Ren*(0°)—One Square (90°) = 90°, which is the number of wood. Therefore, the combination leads to wood.

The combination of *Wu* and *Gui*leads to fire: *Wu* (180°) + *Gui*(0°) = 180°, which is the number of fire. Therefore, the combination leads to fire. (Wu is in the middle, so (-One Square (90°)) is omitted).

(5)  Contradiction of the heavenly stems

According to the deduction in this paper:
*Jia* dominates *Wu*: *Wu* (180°) − *Jia* (36°) = 144°
*Yi* dominates *Ji*: *Ji*(216°) − *Yi* (72°) = 144°
*Bing* dominates *Geng*: *Geng*(252°) − *Bing* (108°) = 144°
*Ding* dominates *Xin*: *Xin*(288°) − *Ding* (144°) = 144°
*Wu* dominates *Ren*: *Ren*(324°) − *Wu* (180°) = 144°
*Ji*dominates *Gui*: *Gui*(360°) − *Ji*(216°) = 144°
*Geng*dominates *Jia*: *Jia*(36° + 360°) − *Geng*(252°) = 144°
(Note: As the subtraction between 36° and 252° would lead to a negative number and there was no negative number in the ancient times, the complete operation of the heaven and the earth is 360° for a circle, which is used as the number for increment.)
*Xin*dominates *Yi*: *Yi* (72° + 360°) − *Xin*(288°) = 144°
(Note: As the subtraction between 72° and 288° would lead to a negative number and there was no negative number in the ancient times, the complete operation of the heaven and the earth is 360° for a circle, which is used as the number for increment.)
*Ren*dominates *Bing*: *Bing* (108° + 360°) − 324° = 144°
(Note: As the subtraction between 108° and 324° would lead to a negative number and there was no negative number in the ancient times, the complete operation of the heaven and the earth is 360° for a circle, which is used as the number for increment.)
*Gui*dominates *Ding*: *Ding* (144° + 360°) − 360° = 144°
(Note: As the subtraction between 144° and 360° would lead to a negative number and there was no negative number in the ancient times, the complete operation of the heaven and the earth is 360° for a circle, which is used as the number for increment.)

(6)  Combination of six terrestrial branches

As is shown in Fig. 7, *Zi*, *Wu*, *Mao* and *You* are on the four axes respectively and in the four straight directions, with a circle of 360°. This circle is evenly divided into 12 branches, so each branch features 30°. The combination of any six portions is 30°.

The circle features 360°, so when a circle is subtracted from the combination of two, those featuring 30° will be concordance.

This is also applied to demonstrate that 30° is a natural concordance number.
The combination of *Zi* and *Chou*: *Zi* (0°) + *Chou* (30°) = 30°.
The combination of *Yin* and *Hai*: (*Yin* (60°) + *Hai*(360°)) − 360° = 30.

The combination of *Mao* and *Xu*: (*Mao* (90°) + *Xu*(300°)) − 360° = 30°.
The combination of *Chen* and *You*: ((*Chen* (120°) + *You* (270°)) − 360° = 30°.
The combination of *Si* and *Shen*: (*Si* (150°) + *Shen*(240°)) − 360° = 30°.
The combination of *Wu* and *Wei*: (*Wu* (180°) + *Wei* (210°)) − 360° = 30°.

(7)  Contradiction of six terrestrial branches

As is shown in Fig. 7, when two branches contradict with each other, the difference
between the subject and the object will be 180°.

Contradiction between *Zi* and *Wu*: *Wu* (180°) − *Zi* (0°) = 180°.
Contradiction between *Chou* and *Wei*: *Wei* (210°)−*Chou* (30°) = 180°.
Contradiction between *Yin* and *Shen*: *Shen*(240°) − *Yin* (60°) = 180°.
Contradiction between *Mao* and *You*: *You* (270°) − *Mao* (90°) = 180°.
Contradiction between *Chen* and *Xu*: *Xu*(300°) − *Chen* (120°) = 180°.
Contradiction between *Si* and *Hai*: *Hai*(330°) − *Si* (150°) = 180°.

地支圖

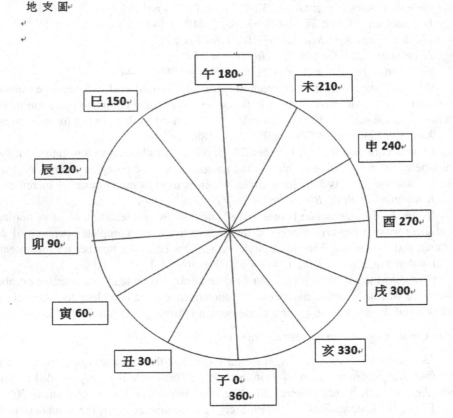

**Fig. 7.** Diagram of terrestrial branches in this paper

| 子<br>Zi | 丑<br>Chou | 寅<br>Yin | 卯<br>Mao |
|---|---|---|---|
| 未<br>Wei | 辰<br>Chen | 巳<br>Si | 午<br>Wu |
| 申<br>Shen | 酉<br>You | 戌<br>Xu | 亥<br>Hai |

地支圖
Diagram of Terrestrial Branches

(8) Combination of three terrestrial branches:

According to this paper, (this paper demonstrates that the combination of Hai, Mao and Wei leads to wood (90°) and that the combination of Si, You and Chou leads to metal (270°). It runs clockwise).

The combination of three terrestrial branches leads to the five elements: the combination of three terrestrial branches is subtracted from 360° or added to 360° (the difference lies in the order of the minuend and the subtractor).

The combination of *Shen, Zi* and *Chen* leads to water: $360° - (240° + 0° + 120°) - 360° = 0°$, which is the number of water.

The combination of *Hai, Mao* and *Wei* leads to wood: $720° - (330° + 90° + 210°) = 90°$, which is the number of wood.

The combination of *Yin, Wu* and *Xu* leads to fire: $720° - (60° + 180° + 300°) = 180°$, which is the number of fire.

The combination of *Si, You* and *Chou* leads to metal: $720° - (150° + 270° + 30°) = 270°$, which is the number of metal.

(9) The convergence of terrestrial branches

According to the deduction in this paper: (this paper demonstrates that the *Yin, Mao* and *Chen* converge in wood (90°) and that *Shen, You* and *Xu* converge in metal (270°). It runs clockwise).

*Hai, Zi* and *Chou* converge in water: $360° - (330° + 0° + 30°) = 0°$, which is the number of water.

*Yin, Mao* and *Chen* converge in wood: $360° - (60° + 90° + 120°) = 90°$, which is the number of wood.

*Si, Wu* and *Wei* converge in fire: $720° - (150° + 180° + 210°) = 180°$, which is the number of fire ($720° = 360° + 360°$).

*Shen, You* and *Xu* converge in metal: $1080 - (240 + 270 + 300) = 270$, which is the number of metal ($1080° = 720° + 360°$).

# 4  Conclusions

The popular Chinese saying, "heavenly south and earthly north", symbolizes the Chinese natural rules of the universe and underlines the status of all creatures in nature. The later eight diagrams depicts the orientation and combination rules of the earth and the real world and describes the laws of interactive formation and integration;

moreover, it elaborates on the influence of the celestial bodies on human being. The core contents are as follows: *Qian* is the heaven while *Kun* is the earth; *Yin* and *Yang* are mutually dependent; the five elements come into being and contradict with each other; there are rules of *Yin* and *Yang* as well as the changes to the eight diagrams. In this paper, scientific methods are applied to academic exploration according to realities, and the research is done to make contribution to society and allow researchers to analyze problems with appropriate principles.

# References

1. https://www.google.com.tw/search?hl = zh-TW&biw = 1280&bih = 629&tbm = isch&sa = 1&ei = NGiPW_aTB4qF8wX9-JaACg&q = 12%E5%9C%B0%E6%94% AF&oq = 12%E5%9C%B0%E6%94%AF&gs_l = img.12..35i39k1j0j0i24k1j0j0i24k1l6. 45800.46223.0.52123.3.3.0.0.0.0.109.300.1j2.3.0....0...1c.1.64.img..0.2.208....0.TBCAgu-F93k/1070905. Access 8 Sept 2018
2. Ming, Y.: Books, pp. 6–8, 11–12, 329–332, September 1984
3. Shuhuan, L.: Practical Numerology, Taipei Life Type Society, September 1954

# Practical Internet Usage for Cultural Appropriation Development

Ku-Yun Chen[✉]

Beijing Institute of Technology, Zhuhai 519000, Guangdong, China
kuyun1115@gmail.com

**Abstract.** This study provided three strategies for teachers to help students build up a sense of cultural appropriation: pictures, YouTube video clips, and group discussions. Each strategy aroused students' different degree of cultural stimulation. With an in-class experimental teaching method and action research in Beijing Institute of Technology, Zhuhai (BITZH) in Guangdong Province, China, the study has found effective teaching methods for creating a vivid classroom atmosphere, building bidirectional student-centered conversations, and developing students' cultural appropriation. The result from this study revealed the advantages of combining and interweaving internet usage while teaching students cultural appropriation.

**Keywords:** Cultural appropriation · Cultural empathy · Teaching methods

## 1 This Is My Culture, Not Yours!

In 2018, Keziah Daum, a 18-year-old white girl, wearing a red Chinese dress (qipao) to a prom night caused a huge debate on cultural appropriation and the pictures of her have been retweeted over 40,000 times (See the picture below). Suddenly, social media and online news went crazy for this incident. For example, South China Morning Post commented "This (news) is just another form of xenophobia[1]." According to Tam (2018), she believed that Daum probably never exposed herself in Chinese culture, so this was why she made this unintentional ignorance. Things usually come in pairs. Tam shared two examples of celebrities who encountered cultural appropriation. The first example was Jeremy Lin (Taiwanese American basketball player) converted his hair style into African-American style. The second example was Andy Warhol (Pope of pop art) painted Mao Zedong with pop art style. She stated: "Critics of cultural appropriation insist they are not opposed to cultural engagement, but merely wish to prevent inappropriate or disrespectful interpretation of a particular culture, or even messy interactions between cultures (see Footnote 1)". In spite of whether it is this girl's personal dressing choice, some people have lost their rationale and have called her a

---

[1] Tam, L. (2018, May 15). Those howling loudest about cultural appropriation over Utah schoolgirl wearing qipao do not own the culture they claim to be defending. This is just another form of xenophobia. *South China Morning Post*. Retrieved from: https://www.scmp.com/news/hong-kong/article/2146029/those-howling-loudest-about-cultural-appropriation-do-not-own-culture.

J.-L. Chen et al. (Eds.): WiCON 2018, LNICST 264, pp. 387–392, 2019.
https://doi.org/10.1007/978-3-030-06158-6_37

racist. After numerous debates, the researcher has wondered what the fine line between cultural appropriation and cultural appreciation is.

The picture is from http://omgnewsy.com/keziah-daum-wins-support-after-chinese-dress-at-prom-backlash/.

## 1.1 Definition of Cultural Appropriation

According to Cambridge Dictionary online, it defines cultural appropriation as "the act of taking or using things from a culture that is not your own, especially without showing that you understand or respect this culture[2]". In other words, the idea of borrowing someone's cultural traits without cultural awareness can cause a fight in our daily life. To a great extent, cultural appropriation is closely related to racism. Andrews (2018) commented that "with appropriation being such a huge conversation these days, it's easier than ever to educate yourself about cultural symbols. If you still choose to regard one as a disposable trend, it's because you simply don't respect the people behind it[3]". She argued that "when you can't see the humanity in people who are different from you, you find no fault in treating their sacred cultural symbols as something to be worn and discarded (see Footnote 3)". Rogers (2006) explained further that the word appropriation is "from the Latin *appropriare*, meaning 'to make one's own,' from the Latin root *proprius* meaning own, also the root of property". Under this implication, someone taking other's "culture's symbols, artifacts, genres, rituals, or technologies by members of another cultural" and make them as his or her own will be viewed as a cultural "theft" (pp. 474–475)[4].

## 1.2 Significance of Cultural Appropriation

Equipping students with cultural appropriation can reduce their culture shocks, help them respect different religions and politics, be open-minded foods, be aware of taboos and gestures, and use appropriate verbal and non-verbal communication in the different international scenarios. Young (2005) provided an offensive example of American Nazi Party parading via Skokie, Illinois, mainly a Jewish neighborhood in 1977. "Many Jews would find such a parade insulting, abusive, and derogatory." (p. 135)[5]. A similar incident occur in Taiwan in 2006. A home-room teacher from Kuang-Fu high school in HsinChu City had his students dress up like Nazi Party and expected the crowd to hail Adolf Hitler. The officials at the Israel Embassy and the German Embassy in Taiwan both condemned this ignorant behavior.

[2] Cultural Appropriation. (n.d.). In *Cambridge Dictionary*. Retrieve from: https://dictionarycambridge.org/zht/詞典/英語/cultural-appropriation.

[3] Andrews, J. (2018, April 13). How to avoid cultural appropriation at Coachella. *Teen Vogue*. Retrieved from: https://www.teenvogue.com/story/coachella-cultural-appropriation.

[4] Rogers, R. A. (2006). From cultural exchange to transculturation: A review and reconceptualization of cultural appropriation. *Communication Theory, 16*(4), 474–503. https://doi.org/10.1111/j.1468-2885.2006.00277.x.

[5] Young, J. O. (2005). Profound offense and cultural appropriation. *The Journal of Aesthetics and Art Criticism, 63*(2), 135–146. https://doi.org/10.1111/j.0021-8529.2005.00190.x.

Ipso facto, many colleges expect students to take cross-cultural communication courses because these cultural cultivating classes can benefit students' both common senses and future career. First, cross-cultural Communication is a required course for most English-major students in China. Students without being aware of cultural empathy can be ignorant, bad-mannered, and what is worst, judgmental. Second, when the Chinese students do business with international clients after graduating from colleges, they can identify what to do and what not to do to avoid culture appropriation or misinterpreting the messages. Therefore, students should be careful and culturally sensitive in the 21$^{st}$ century.

## 2   An in-Class Experimental Teaching Method

Since March, 2017, the researcher has been teaching the course of cross-cultural communication in Beijing Institute of Technology, Zhuhai (BITZH) in Guangdong Province, China. In order to arouse students' learning interests, the researcher has been searching for suitable teaching methods to meet students' academic needs. After the first semester's pilot study, the research chose participatory action research as the main investigation method.

### 2.1   Action Research

According to Hesse-Biber and Leavy (2011), action research as known as emancipatory research and two-way investigation. It can enhance pragmatic validity by including research participants, by brainstorming about data collection, and by analyzing and understanding the research findings (pp. 50–51)[6]. This is why many educators have labeled action research as "a collaborative research." The five fundamental steps are: (1) identify the problem, (2) set up an achievable goal, (3) make a plan to solve the problem, (4) implement the plan, and (5) evaluate the intervention. These five steps make an action research loop. If the problem can't be solved in the first loop, researchers are highly recommended to identify the problem again and repeat these five steps in the second loop, even third, fourth, and so on until the problem is solved. Blair (2010) mentioned that action research is an educational research method to find out two different ways of the truth: behaviorism and constructivism. He further explained as follows:

Behaviourism hopes to learn about participants through observing what they do; for many behaviourists it is folly for researchers to make assumptions about the thinking processes of the participant, as this is not scientific. Constructivists take a different view and postulate that, since humans are cognitive and can describe their thoughts and the reasons behind their actions, then we should make use of such information (p. 352)[7].

---

[6] Hesse-Biber, S. N. & Leavy, P. (2011). The practice of qualitative research (2nd). USA: SAGE.

[7] Blair, E. (2010). How does telling the truth help educational action research?. *Educational Action Research*, *18*(3), 349–358. https://doi.org/10.1080/09650792.2010.499810.

## 2.2    Three Teaching Aids

With five steps of action research and while teaching students' cross-cultural communication course, the research identified the students' cultural struggle and blind spot: ideology. According to Merriam-Webster Online Dictionary, ideology is "a manner of the content of thinking characteristic of an individual, group, or culture" and "the integrated assertions, theories and aims that constitute a sociopolitical program."[8] Gee (2008) argued that ideology also affect people's views, concepts, and definitions of every thing and term. For example, "a word like 'bachelor' means 'unmarried male.' (p. 6)"[9] After identifying ideology as the main problem of students' cross-cultural struggle, the researcher searched teaching aids to assist students in understanding different cultures and develop cultural empathy. However, few studies are related to this realm, not to mention, teaching aids. With personal in-class teaching experiences and interaction with students, the researcher has finally come up with three teaching aids to overcome students' existing ideology: pictures, video clips, and group discussion (GD). As Bhawuk and Brislin (2000) suggested that "trainers can use video films, slides, and other visual aids to show cultural differences[10]". Therefore, in this participatory action research, the research adopted these three common teaching tools: pictures, video clips, and group discussions.

First, pictures are very handy to access and it has been said that a picture is worth a thousand words. Students can observe the information of the target pictures and follow teachers' guide to make comparisons and contrasts. Most Asian students can distinguish similarities and differences of a thing. Nevertheless, some teachers seldom take advantages of analyzing similarities and differences. For example, a teacher can put two pictures side by side and ask students to compare and to contrast both. By doing picture comparison and contrast, students can observe and pick up the clues by themselves.

Second, video clips are more vivid and tangible, compared with pictures. Video clips stimulate students' feelings and make them be sensitive to others' feelings, meaning that students can relate themselves to the characters in pictures or put themselves in people's shoes. Video clips can assist students in appreciating foreign cultures. By watching contexts and scenarios from video clips, students can generate some new ideas and deeply perceive entire cultural atmosphere. This is why most people prefer animation to a single picture. While teaching this course, the researcher always received more feedback from students. The reason is obvious: video clips provide visual and audio help, while pictures can only deliver visual image. According to Tseng (2017), "audio input such as movies, movie-clips, video-clips were also regularly incorporated in class" (p. 27). She further explained video clips "were used for students to watch and to reflect upon issues such as diversity within a society, high and low context culture, different communication styles across culture, work ethics,

---

[8] Ideology. (n.d.). In *Merriam-Webster Dictionary*. Retrieve from: https://www.merriam-webster.com/dictionary/ideology.

[9] Gee, J. P. (2008). Social linguistics and literacies (3rd). New York, NY: Routledge.

[10] Bhawuk, D. P. S. & Brislin R. W. (2000). Cross-cultural training: A review. *Applied Psychology, 49* (1), 162–191. https://doi.org/10.1111/1464-0597.00009.

gender roles, interracial marriages, and etc." (p. 27). "Ted Talk" and "Voice Tubes" are two of the best examples for pro-video teaching[11].

Third, group discussions (GD) are very common in Western classrooms while they are rare to appear in Eastern classrooms. GD can let students exchange their own ideas and different opinions based on the interactions among them. Many new ideas or thoughts can be generated by just talking to people. GD is very similar as Socratic method in philosophy. Through teacher-and-student or student-and-student conversation, discussion, or even debate, teachers can inspire students' motivation to learn and guide them in walking on the path of cross-cultural communication.

# 3 Conclusion

With the three teaching aids (pictures, video clips, and group discussions), teachers can make their cross-cultural communication class more interesting and create a vivid learning atmosphere. Meanwhile, the information nowadays is updated swiftly. Adopting more on-line sources can benefit students' knowledge acquisition, can keep them catch up with current international topics or issues, and can alleviate their stereotypes and broaden their international worldview.

# References

Andrews, J.: How to avoid cultural appropriation at Coachella. Teen Vogue. Retrieved from https://www.teenvogue.com/story/coachella-cultural-appropriation

Bhawuk, D.P.S., Brislin, R.W.: Cross-cultural training: a review. Appl. Psychol. **49**(1), 162–191 (2000). https://doi.org/10.1111/1464-0597.00009

Blair, E.: How does telling the truth help educational action research? Educ. Action Res. **18**(3), 349–358 (2010). https://doi.org/10.1080/09650792.2010.499810

Cultural Appropriation (n.d.).: In Cambridge Dictionary. Retrieved from https://dictionary.cambridge.org/zht/詞典/英語/cultural-appropriation

Gee, J.P.: Social Linguistics and Literacies, vol. 3. Routledge, New York (2008)

Hesse-Biber, S.N., Leavy, P.: The Practice of Qualitative Research, vol. 2. SAGE, USA (2011)

Ideology (n.d.).: In Merriam-Webster Dictionary. Retrieved from https://www.merriam-webster.com/dictionary/ideology

Rogers, R.A.: From cultural exchange to transculturation: a review and reconceptualization of cultural appropriation. Commun. Theory **16**(4), 474–503 (2006). https://doi.org/10.1111/j.1468-2885.2006.00277.x

Tam, L.: Those howling loudest about cultural appropriation over Utah schoolgirl wearing Qipao do not own the culture they claim to be defending. This is just another form of xenophobia. South China Morning Post. Retrieved from https://www.scmp.com/news/hong-kong/article/2146029/those-howling-loudest-about-cultural-appropriation-do-not-own-culture (2018)

---

[11] Tseng, C. T. H. (2017). Teaching "Cross-cultural Communication" through content based instruction: Curriculum design and learning outcome from EFL learners' perspectives. English Language Teaching, 10(4), 22–34. https://doi.org/10.5539/elt.v10n4p22.

Tseng, C.T.H.: Teaching "Cross-cultural Communication" through content based instruction: curriculum design and learning outcome from EFL learners' perspectives. Engl. Lang. Teach. **10**(4), 22–34 (2017). https://doi.org/10.5539/elt.v10n4p22

Young, J.O.: Profound offense and cultural appropriation. J. Aesthet. Art Crit. **63**(2), 135–146 (2005). https://doi.org/10.1111/j.0021-8529.2005.00190.x

# Applying Information Quantity Analysis to the Ecological Conservation Development

Huan-Siang Luo[1] and Yee-Chaur Lee[2(✉)]

[1] Department of Civil Engineering, College of Architecture and Design,
Chung Hua University, 707, Sec.2, WuFu Rd., Hsinchu 30012, Taiwan
j2006ms660822@yahoo.com.tw
[2] Department of Landscape Architecture, College of Architecture and Design,
Chung Hua University, 707, Sec.2, WuFu Rd., Hsinchu 30012, Taiwan
joeychuc@yahoo.com.tw

**Abstract.** The ecological conservation development is fital to the natural surroundings and environmental progection. Due to the advantages of conference and confidentiality of traditional questionnaires, the purpose of this study aims to investigate and compare the various factors that influence the development of ecological conservation by means of Fuzzy Delphi Method. In addition, various professionals, including real estate marketers, university professors and relevant government officials, take part in the questionnaire for our analysis.

**Keywords:** Ecological conservation · Evaluation of development
Fuzzy delphi method

## 1 Introduction

This study aims to investigate and compare the various factors that influence the development of ecological conservation by means of Fuzzy Delphi Method. To build a strong foundation and a solid stepping stone for future research, we analyzed our data by insightful interviews with ecology and environment experts and professors, literature reviews, and the analysis of Fuzzy Delphi Method. The findings is significant in that it is critical for any legristrations or law making on the development of ecological and environmental development.

## 2 Literature Reviews

The locations of ecological and environmental development are usually targeted on higher mountains, which are more geologically fragil and steep. Most of them are reservation area for the aboriginal tribes. In addition, these areas of environmental protection include natural conservation zones, upstream river banks, ecological locations, water and soil conservation areas, water collecting area, fragil areas and restricted areas. Thus, it is important to take this matter seriously because a slight of careless and misevaluation will be detrimental to the land, the nature, the water and the animals that reside on these areas. The purpose is to investigate the optimal solution about how the

J.-L. Chen et al. (Eds.): WiCON 2018, LNICST 264, pp. 393–399, 2019.
https://doi.org/10.1007/978-3-030-06158-6_38

best interest and profits can be gained without harming the land and the nature. The findings will shed new lights on how environmental laws and relevant laws are made.

## 3  Methodology

### 3.1  Setting Up the Factors and Criteria

The objective of this study is to investigate and compare the various factors that affect the register of real estate sold price by means of Fuzzy Delphi Method. To maintain the authenticity of the current study and to keep its originality of the multi-criteria decision making, we invited real estate marketers, university professors, government officials, and experts to talk at interviews and to take part in our questionnaire. After collecting and analyzing these relevant factors, we used Fuzzy Delphi Method for quantification and description.

### 3.2  Fuzzy Delphi Method

Fuzzy Delphi Method was proposed by Ishikawa et al. and it was derived from the traditional Delphi technique and fuzzy set theory. Delphi method can direct measure perception of service, performance service quality measurement. Noorderhaben indicated that applying the Fuzzy Delphi Method to group decision can solve the fuzziness of common understanding of expert opinions. As for the selection of fuzzy membership functions, previous research was usually based on triangular fuzzy number, trapezoidal fuzzy number and Gaussian fuzzy number. This study applied the Two Triangle Fuzzy Numbers method and the Gray statistics method theory to solving the group decision. This research applied FDM for the screening of alternate factors. The fuzziness of common understanding of experts could be solved by using the fuzzy theory and could be evaluated on a more flexible scale. The efficiency and quality of questionnaires could be improved. Thus, more objective evaluation factors could be screened through the statistical results. The scores we got will fall on a continuum between the smallest value and the largest value. The latter is called the most optimistic value whereas the former is called the most conservative value.

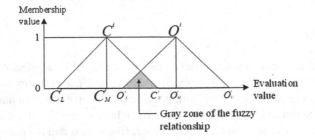

Two Triangle Fuzzy Numbers Method                    Source : Zheng Changbin, 2001

**Table 1.** Scores obtained by screen results of evaluation under the "Economic development" dimension

| Evaluation item | Conservative value | | Optimistic value | | Single value | | Geometric mean | | | | Verification value | | | Expert consensus |
|---|---|---|---|---|---|---|---|---|---|---|---|---|---|---|
| | Min | Max | Min | Max | Min | Max | $C^i$ | $O^i$ | $a^i$ | | $M^i$ | $Z^i$ | $M^i \cdot Z^i$ | $G^i$ |
| Industrial development | 6 | 9 | 9 | 10 | 5 | 10 | 7.94 | 9.32 | 8.03 | | 1.38 | 0.00 | 1.38 | 8.63 |
| Transportation | 6 | 9 | 8 | 10 | 6 | 10 | 7.70 | 9.38 | 7.59 | | 1.68 | 1.00 | 0.68 | 8.51 |
| Telecommunication equipment | 7 | 9 | 8 | 10 | 6 | 10 | 8.22 | 9.10 | 7.79 | | 0.88 | 1.00 | −0.12 | 8.59 |

**Table 2.** Scores obtained by screen results of evaluation under the "Land use" dimension

| Evaluation item | Conservative value | | Optimistic value | | Single value | | Geometric mean | | | Verification value | | | Expert consensus |
|---|---|---|---|---|---|---|---|---|---|---|---|---|---|
| | Min | Max | Min | Max | Min | Max | $C^i$ | $O^i$ | $a^i$ | $M^i$ | $Z^i$ | $M^i\text{-}Z^i$ | $G^i$ |
| Functions of land | 5 | 8 | 7 | 9 | 5 | 10 | 6.28 | 8.28 | 8.03 | 2.00 | 1.00 | 1.00 | 7.43 |
| Rules on land use | 3 | 8 | 9 | 9 | 6 | 10 | 5.95 | 9.00 | 7.59 | 3.05 | -1.00 | 4.05 | 7.48 |

**Table 3.** Scores obtained by screen results of evaluation under the "Environmental impact" dimension

| Evaluation item | Conservative value | | Optimistic value | | Single value | | Geometric mean | | | Verification value | | | Expert consensus |
|---|---|---|---|---|---|---|---|---|---|---|---|---|---|
| | Min | Max | Min | Max | Min | Max | $C^i$ | $O^i$ | $a^i$ | $M^i$ | $Z^i$ | $M^i$-$Z^i$ | $G^i$ |
| Rules on environment | 5 | 9 | 9 | 10 | 5 | 10 | 7.74 | 9.32 | 8.03 | 1.58 | 0.00 | 1.58 | 8.53 |
| Construction environment | 3 | 8 | 8 | 9 | 6 | 10 | 5.90 | 8.45 | 7.59 | 2.55 | 0.00 | 2.55 | 7.18 |
| Plants | 3 | 8 | 8 | 9 | 6 | 10 | 5.87 | 8.45 | 7.79 | 2.58 | 0.00 | 2.58 | 7.16 |
| Animals | 5 | 8 | 8 | 10 | 7 | 9 | 6.21 | 8.91 | 7.7 | 2.70 | 0.00 | 2.70 | 7.56 |

**Table 4.** Scores obtained by screen results of evaluation under the "Citizen participation" dimension

| Evaluation item | Conservative value | | Optimistic value | | Single value | | Geometric mean | | | Verification value | | | Expert consensus |
|---|---|---|---|---|---|---|---|---|---|---|---|---|---|
| | Min | Max | Min | Max | Min | Max | $C^i$ | $O^i$ | $a^i$ | $M^i$ | $Z^i$ | $M^i\text{-}Z^i$ | $G^i$ |
| Tribe meetings | 5 | 9 | 9 | 10 | 5 | 10 | 6.82 | 9.32 | 8.03 | 2.50 | 0.00 | 2.50 | 8.07 |
| County meetings | 5 | 8 | 9 | 9 | 6 | 10 | 6.94 | 9.00 | 7.65 | 2.06 | −1.00 | 3.06 | 7.97 |
| Representatives meetings | 3 | 7 | 7 | 9 | 6 | 10 | 5.64 | 7.94 | 7.79 | 2.30 | 0.00 | 2.30 | 6.79 |
| Leaders opinions | 5 | 8 | 6 | 9 | 7 | 9 | 6.21 | 7.63 | 7.7 | 1.42 | 2.00 | −0.58 | 6.95 |

Source: this study

### 3.3   Instrument

The purpose of this study is to examine the various factors that affect the development of ecological conservation by means of Fuzzy Delphi Method. Based on the previous studies related on the evaluation of the ecological conservation development, before the designing of our questionnaire, we also take into the consideration the evaluation criteria, the appropriateness, the feasibility and legislation of the environmental laws. We divided the questionnaire into four primary themes or categories. They include Economic Development, Land Use, Environmental Impact, and Citizen Participation.

### 3.4   Participants

The study proposed to investigate the various factors that influence the development of ecological conservation by means of Fuzzy Delphi Method. On the condition of its professionalism, various professionals, including ecology experts, conservation experts, environmentalists, university professors, local residents, and relevant government officials, take part in the questionnaire for our analysis.

## 4   Data Analysis and Results

Based on our questionnaire, the scores are obtained by the Fuzzy Delphi Method. Both geometric mean and verification value are calculated. The findings are as follows: Tables 1, 2, 3 and 4

## 5   Conclusion

The aim of this study is to investigate and compare the various factors that influence the development of ecological conservation by means of Fuzzy Delphi Method. The findings have revealed that among those which serve the most critical factors that influence the evaluation of ecological conservation development are industrial development, rules on land use, rules on environment, tribe meetings. The findings can shed new lights on the evaluation of the development and on the legristration of the environmental laws. Furthermore, effective developments will hing on long-term observation and various evaluations.

# Author Index

Printed in the United States
By Bookmasters